D1806679

# MONTROSE
## THE KING'S CHAMPION

*By the same author:*

AMERICA 1968: THE FIRE THIS TIME

ULSTER 1969: THE FIGHT FOR CIVIL RIGHTS IN NORTHERN
IRELAND

# MONTROSE

## THE KING'S CHAMPION

by

## MAX HASTINGS

---

"Those who dream by night in the dusty recesses of
their minds wake in the day to find that all was
vanity; but the dreamers of the day are dangerous
men, for they may act their dream with open eyes,
and make it possible."
—T. E. Lawrence, *Seven Pillars of Wisdom*

LONDON
VICTOR GOLLANCZ LTD
1977

© Max Hastings, 1977

ISBN 0 575 02226 4

The endpapers are from a seventeenth-century German woodcut showing Scottish soldiers during the Thirty Years War; it appears in *Tartans* (1961) by Christian Hesketh and is reproduced by permission of Weidenfeld and Nicolson.

Printed in Great Britain by
The Camelot Press Ltd, Southampton

*For Tricia*

*From*

# I'LL NEVER LOVE THEE MORE
## *by Montrose*

My dear and only love, I pray
This noble world of thee
Be governed by no other sway
But purest monarchie.
For if confusion have a part,
Which vertuous souls abhore,
And hold a synod in thy heart,
I'll never love thee more.

Like Alexander I will reign,
And I will reign alone,
My thoughts shall evermore disdain
A rival on my throne.
He either fears his fate too much,
Or his deserts are small,
That puts it not unto the touch
To win or lose it all.

But I must rule and govern still,
And always give the law,
And have each subject at my will,
And all to stand in awe.
But, gainst my battery if I find
Thou shun'st the prize so sore,
As that thou set'st me up a blind,
I'll never love thee more.

. . .

But if thou will be constant then,
And faithful of thy word,
I'll make thee glorious by my pen,
And famous by my sword.

I'll serve thee in such noble ways
Was never heard before;
I'll crown and deck thee all with
      bays,
And love thee evermore.

. . .

The misty mountains, smoking
      lakes,
The rocks' resounding echo,
The whistling wind that murmur
      makes,
Shall with me sing hey ho!
The tossing seas, the tumbling
      boats,
Tears dropping from each shore,
Shall tune with me their turtle
      notes,
I'll never love thee more.

. . .

And when that tracing goddess,
      Fame,
From east to west shall flee,
She shall record it, to thy shame,
How thou hast loved me;
And how in odds our love was such
As few have been before;
Thou loved too many, and I too
      much,
So I can love no more.

# Contents

# Illustrations

*Plates following pages 160 and 192*

Montrose by Honthorst (*by courtesy of the Earl of Dalhousie. Photo: Kenneth Hay*)

Montrose as a young man in 1629 by Jameson (*by courtesy of the Earl of Southesk. Photo: Tom Scott*)

Archibald, 1st Lord Napier, by Jameson (*by courtesy of Lord Napier and Ettrick. Photo: Peter Davey*)

The Marquis of Argyll in 1652 (*by courtesy of the Marquis of Lothian. Photo: Tom Scott*)

George, Lord Gordon (*by courtesy of the Duke of Hamilton. Photo: Tom Scott*)

George Gordon, 2nd Marquis of Huntly (*by courtesy of the Duke of Buccleuch and Queensberry VRD. Photo: Tom Scott*)

1st Earl of Airlie (*by courtesy of the Earl of Airlie. Photo: Spanphoto*)

Lord Ogilvy, later 2nd Earl of Airlie (*by courtesy of the Earl of Airlie. Photo: Spanphoto*)

## Maps

# INTRODUCTION

Most of the great cavaliers who rode for King Charles in the English Civil War fought and died amidst great armies, loving friends, admiring comrades. Yet in the last year of the struggle, while in England the royalists strove to save something from the wreck of their fortunes, one man alone in Scotland, execrated by his Scottish contemporaries, eclipsed the achievements of Prince Rupert and all his English captains. James Graham, Lord Marquis of Montrose, rode into the Highlands in August 1644, raised an army among the Gaelic clans, and won six of the most dazzling victories in the history of arms. He was outnumbered in all but one of his battles. He never commanded more than 5000 men—a fraction of Rupert's army at Marston Moor—yet the historian of the British Army Sir John Fortescue has called him "perhaps the most brilliant natural military genius disclosed by the Civil War".

Montrose was also a poet and a romantic. Through the centuries successive generations have been enchanted by the vision of this impossible dreamer, striding through the heather and the snows at the head of his wild army to try to save his King. The epic quality is all the greater because the King's enemies whom Montrose was fighting were among the ugliest exponents of religious bigotry ever to achieve power in Scotland. He knew this perfectly, because he himself had been an ardent adherent of the Covenant until he saw that the religious principles which it enshrined were corrupted by the Covenanters' political extremism.

Montrose's extraordinary, lonely crusade ended in failure. On the afternoon of May 21st, 1650, he walked to the scaffold with the courage and dignity that characterized his life. He had fought for tolerance, decency and moderation in religion and in government. Beyond these simple principles he was a political innocent and his downfall was assured. But his name and his story glitter down the centuries in contrast to the dour, grey tyranny of his executioners.

I have written about Montrose because I love royalists, romantics and the Highlands of Scotland. John Buchan wrote a splendid biography in 1928, and more recently Ronald

Williams has studied the Lord Marquis with a wealth of exacting detail which all future biographers must acknowledge. I hope that I can bring some of the virtues of a journalist to the story. I have tried to see the sights and hear the sounds of Scotland in the seventeenth century as contemporary observers saw them: to stand above Inverary with the Macdonalds before they swept down with the Royal Standard that great December day of 1644; to smell the dung in the streets of Edinburgh as the carters struggled up the Canongate; to curse the difficulties of keeping a musket match alight in a driving gale as the enemy prepared to charge. It may be worth something to know what it feels like to be in battle, for men's thrills and terrors were surely much the same in the seventeenth century as they are in the twentieth.

It has been delightful writing this book, because I have had an excuse to walk the hills and to read and write about heroes from a mould we have broken. I hope that I have not sentimentalized the hard, brutal world of the Highlands. Scottish friends are fond of reminding me that the English view their mountains rather more romantically than they do themselves. I owe a great many debts for help and hospitality far beyond the call of friendship. John Clare and my long-suffering labrador Stokeley shared my tent on the winter march from Blair Atholl to Inverary in December 1975. Patrick Murray, founder of the Museum of Childhood in Edinburgh and owner of one of the most marvellously eccentric libraries in Britain, was a mine of information. He surpassed himself by finding me a book entitled *The Small Horse in Warfare* when we were debating whether Montrose's cavalry rode full-size chargers or the shaggy little Highland garrons (surely it was ponies). Captain Ben Coutts, who helped me to fall in love with the Highlands fifteen years ago, entertained me in Montrose's own country of Perthshire. Neil Hughes-Onslow walked the field of Philiphaugh with his usual charming enthusiasm. My wife has sweetly forgiven me for all those evenings when the search for Montrose went on for so long after midnight.

The Forestry Commission have done their uttermost to destroy the beauty of the Scottish Highlands, but they have not yet wholly succeeded, even with the assistance of successive Labour governments. No one can walk those hills, especially with a dog or a rod or a gun, without becoming bewitched by their spells and their legends and their intense emotions. If today you stand above Inverlochy or climb the long pass from Tummel or look down on Blair Castle from Tulach Hill on a purple August afternoon, you too will find yourself in danger of starting to write a book about Montrose.

MAX HASTINGS

LONDON
APRIL 1976

# MONTROSE
## THE KING'S CHAMPION

# PROLOGUE

## Kilsyth, August 15th, 1645

IN THE STILL, warm early morning air of August 15th, 1645, the Lord Marquis of Montrose, King Charles I's Lieutenant-General in Scotland and the last hope of the royalist cause in the English Civil War, made his dispositions for battle. His army had not yet had breakfast. They had been surprised to find their enemy so anxious to fight immediately, without waiting for the reinforcements due to reach them in a few hours. But beyond the ridge in front of the royalists, at the head of the opposing army rode Argyll, Burleigh, Elcho, Lindsay—the great Covenanting Lords of Scotland. For twelve months past Montrose had been driving them flying from his battlefields. He had spoiled their lands. He threatened to ruin their power and pride. Now they outnumbered his army 7000 men to 5000. They stood upon the high ground while he lay upon the low. If they missed the chance to engage him today, he might begin another of his sword dances across the hills, attacking and slipping away at will, leaving every Covenanter in Scotland in fear of where he would strike tomorrow. General Baillie, nominally the commander of the Covenanting army, begged for caution, for delaying the battle. But Argyll and his colleagues were the rulers of Scotland, and they swept aside his protests. They had trapped Montrose, or so they believed. They must now destroy him.

As the sun rose and Montrose's regiments shook themselves out across the meadow in which they stood, they could see only the enemy's skirmishers. The main body of the Covenanters was hidden behind the crest of the ridge. Plainly it was to be a sweltering day, and the Highlanders would have to fight uphill. They were ordered to discard their plaids and strip to their long saffron shirts. The horsemen who wore cuirasses or heavily padded jerkins to blunt an enemy blade pulled their shirts over them so that every royalist was readily identifiable. With so many clans in the field, it was a necessary precaution.

Montrose himself took off his half-armour to sit his horse more
comfortably among his life-guard. Amidst the clatter of steel
as the army gathered their swords and targets, matchlocks and
axes and bows, he looked along the ranks of the greatest battle
line he had yet mustered for the King.

In front of the masses of Macleans and Macdonalds, Gordons
and Ogilvies, stood the legendary lieutenants with whom he had
shared so much: the blunt, gigantic Alasdair Macdonald at the
head of his Irish; dogged old Lord Airlie whose family had given
everything to the royalist cause and whose eldest son Lord
Ogilvy lay in the dungeons of the Covenant; young Aboyne,
wild like all the Huntly sons, a temperamental warrior who
had fought Montrose in the Bishops' Wars before becoming his
ally in this one. Only Lord Gordon, Aboyne's brother whom
Montrose had loved best of all, was missing. A musket ball had
snuffed out that bright flame in the very moment of victory at
Alford six weeks before.

Perhaps even now in the sunny meadow, the fairy washer-
women were appearing as Highland superstition would have
them, to wash the shirts of the men who were to die today. But
no one had voiced his fears aloud. At the Lord Marquis's
council that morning, every man among his officers had
voted for battle when he offered them the chance of retreat.
Now he rode along the ranks, graceful, unhurried, serene:
the slight figure who had charmed half the warriors in the
Highlands to lay their swords at his feet. In a year of campaigning, he had proved himself one of the greatest soldiers of his
age: a master of tactics, of timing, of leadership upon the
battlefield. Having set out with his Commission from the King's
court at Oxford as a forlorn hope, the wild card in the pack, he
had become the only remaining chance of salvation for the
royalist cause in the Two Kingdoms.

Montrose had wasted many months of the Civil War as a
spear carrier at the back of the stage, disdained by courtiers
and councillors, struggling to make himself heard among the
din of arguing generals around the King. But one by one
Charles's most cherished prospects had come to ruin. Naseby
had been fought and lost, then Langport. The King's fortunes
were everywhere in eclipse. And as the remaining pockets
of English royalism were pinched out one by one, every eye
turned desperately upon Montrose, the dazzling, astonishing

star in the north. From Scotland came news of his great victories
first at Tippermuir, then at Aberdeen, Inverlochy, Auldearn,
Alford. The King's Scottish enemies were broken and flying.
Wild hopes rose, of the Lord Marquis marching southwards
with his victorious forces, into England, against the armies of
Parliament.

On August 15th, when Montrose drew up his forces near the
little village of Kilsyth a day's ride from Glasgow, the King's
friends and enemies alike knew that a vital moment had come.
If he was defeated, if his progress southwards was arrested, then
there was no more to hope from Scotland, indeed no more for
the royalists to hope at all. If he was victorious against this,
the last and greatest Covenanting army standing against him
in Scotland, then nothing seemed impossible.

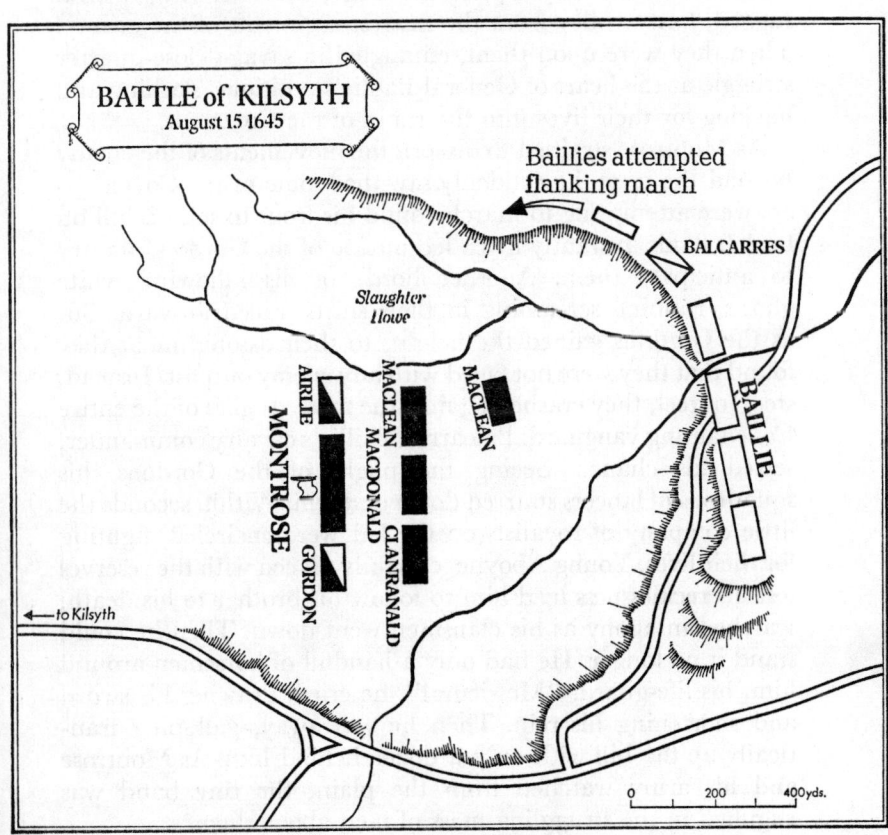

The battle began, like so many Scottish battles, with a skirmish undirected by either general. Montrose had put a hundred men into a cluster of cottages some distance in front of his position. A Covenanting officer also marked this as a key point of the battlefield, and rushed down the hill with a company of musketeers to seize it himself. The whole royalist line stood watching breathless as their men in the outpost first drove back the Covenanters and then, in utter defiance of their orders, threw themselves screaming triumphantly up the hill in pursuit of their retreating foe. It was too much for the Highlanders of Montrose's foremost division. It was impossible to watch others in action, and already victorious, while they stood by. Breaking ranks the Macleans and the Clanranalds poured forward, leaping up the rough hillside towards the Covenanters. As they topped the ridge, they were met with a ragged, hasty volley from the nearest regiments of the enemy. Then they were upon them, entangled in savage close-quarter struggle at the heart of General Baillie's positions, slashing and hacking for their lives into the ranks of the Covenant.

As Montrose strained to discern the movements of the enemy beyond the crest, he suddenly saw that some of the Covenanters were attempting to march round his front to seize a hill on his left flank. Instantly he called on 200 of the Gordon infantry to anticipate them. Another horde of his billowing white ghosts, running screaming in their shirts, raced forward. But as the Gordons gained the height, to their astonishment they found that they were not faced with any enemy outpost. Instead, steel to steel, they crashed against the massed pikes of the entire Covenanting vanguard. Balcarres, Baillie's cavalry commander, seized his chance. Seeing the plight of the Gordons, his squadrons of lancers spurred down on them. Within seconds the little company of royalists on the left were encircled, fighting for their lives. Young Aboyne, carefully placed with the reserves lest his recklessness lead him to follow his brother to his death, watched in agony as his clansmen went down. Then he could stand it no longer. He had only a handful of horsemen around him, his life-guard. "Messieurs!", he cried, drawing his sword and shortening his rein. Then he was away, galloping frantically up the hill with only a dozen behind him. As Montrose and his army watched from the plain, the tiny band was engulfed in the struggling mass of men above them.

But the Lord Marquis now grasped perfectly what was taking place before him. The Covenanting army had attempted an extraordinary and reckless manœuvre. Despite Baillie's protests, Argyll and his colleagues had sought to trap the royalists by marching their whole army across and around Montrose's front, to seize the ground to the north. They had tried to conceal the movement by remaining beyond the skyline, but their own confusion and the attacks of the High-landers had exposed them. The Covenanters were not deployed to face a frontal attack, as they should have been against the greatest general in Scotland. They were spread straggling in a long column of march along the high ground. The Gordons had engaged their forward regiments. Alasdair Macdonald and the Highland vanguard's attack had slashed into the heart of the Covenanting column, cutting the whole force in two. The decisive moment of the battle had come.

Montrose's most urgent concern was to support the struggling Gordons on the left. He called his cavalry to action. There was a terrible pause. The royalist horse hesitated before the chaos in their path. They were scratch levies recruited by Aboyne only a few weeks before, and they were appalled by the prospect of riding cold-blooded into the butcher's shop on the hill. But now, as always, there was Airlie. Montrose cried to the old Ogilvy at the head of his clan horsemen to save the Gordons from their plight. Airlie and his men wheeled to the charge, eighty strong, courage unbending. Then behind them, fired by their example, the rest of the cavalry sprang forward at last.

Now it was time to strike in the centre, to burst open the great wound in the Covenanting line opened by the first wave of Highlanders who were still fighting for their lives on the crest of the ridge. Montrose's infantry surged forward up the hill, smashing into Baillie's regiments. They faltered and fell back under the shock. The levies in the rear of the Covenanting army were beginning to melt away now, to slip shaking from the field as they saw the wounded and the panic-stricken men emerging from the cauldron of blood, yells, smoke and struggling swordsmen at the heart of the battle.

On the left, Airlie and the Gordons and Ogilvies broke through the pikemen and lancers of the Covenanting vanguard. Balcarres fled from the field. Regiments of infantry were crumbling—some, like Cassilis's and Lindsay's, veterans who had held the line at Marston Moor. Men were begging for quarter and being cut down by blood-maddened Highlanders as they ran. Montrose himself accepted honourable surrender from such few Covenanting gentlemen as could reach him to offer their swords, but his men were hunting the flying enemy across the hill, hacking any that checked, lingering only to tear off the purses of the dead. Clusters of dogged and desperate pikemen and musketeers were broken one by one. Baillie was gone now, and Argyll and Lindsay who acknowledged the huge consequences of their defeat by fleeing on, past Edinburgh and the Lowlands to the border, to seek sanctuary with the Covenanting garrison at Berwick. Colours and baggage, arms —including a cannon named "Prince Rupert" lost by the royalists at York—all fell to the victors. One by one, Montrose's officers gathered around him to report their portion of triumph. As his army trickled back from the thrill of pursuit, the Lord Marquis ordered them to camp upon the battlefield. The wounded must be tended, the prisoners mustered, the booty gathered before they marched on to reap the harvest of their victory. Glasgow and Edinburgh lay defenceless before them now. The lives of all the royalist prisoners held by the Covenant could be saved. The first of the flock of Lowland lairds and nobles who had held back from the King's cause for so long would be coming in to offer their submission and support.

There were dispatches to be written to the King. The doubters could not doubt now. "All this work of Montrose is beyond what can be attributed to mankind," wrote the marvelling Digby from Charles's side. The Covenanting ministers who had excommunicated "James Graham, that viperous brood of Satan", might tremble in their pulpits, for no corner of Scotland was safe from his sword. Inexplicably, the hand of the Lord had turned most monstrously against those so certain that they were his chosen instruments. On the field of Kilsyth that evening of August 15th, 1645, the Lord Marquis of Montrose knew that at last he was the master of Scotland for his King.

# CHAPTER ONE

## *Jamie Graham*

---

IT IS A wild tumble down the sheer hill from Kincardine castle wall to the Ruthven burn a hundred yards below. Jamie Graham in his childhood must often have made it, because no small boy can ever resist such a race. He will have leapt down the bank, clutching branches to check his fall, slipping and rolling and sliding to the stream, splashing across the water, then panting up the long climb of Eastbow hill on the other side.

When he was very young, the farm boys or some urchin from the stables might have run with him. But as he grew up, consciousness grew with him that the distance between them was immeasurable. He was the Lord Graham, the Earl's son, the future master of Kincardine, of Old Montrose, of Mugdock in Stirlingshire, of Garscube in Dumbartonshire, of all the trappings of a great magnate born to great possessions. As usual in these situations, even if he himself chose to forget all this, those around him would not. He could play with his sisters (which isn't the same thing at all), or hang around the great shaggy deerhounds in the kennels, or ride out across the Ochill hills with a hawk and a groom, or hit a golf ball in the fields. It was an age when children were quickly hastened towards adulthood and marriage. He was the son of one of the greatest families in Scotland, heir to ancestors who had fallen in the steel ring at Flodden and in the bloody shambles of Pinkie. Much was expected of him accordingly.

He was born into that Scottish elite to whom not even a crown seemed completely impossible for a man with the iron in his soul to reach for it, and a clean neck for the block if he failed. While English history was the story of kings, the history of Scotland was that of great nobles and their ruthless struggles for power. It was an exhilarating birthright for the sons of a few dozen great houses, if also a very perilous one.

The Grahams had to give precedence to a handful of families greater than themselves in the peerage of Scotland: Argyll, Hamilton, Huntly, Angus. But they held an old and honoured place along with the Ogilvies, Mars, and Eglintons as wardens of that vulnerable hinterland between the Lowlands and the Highlands of Scotland. They were also traditional servants of the King. James Graham's grandfather, the third Earl of Montrose, was Treasurer, Chancellor, and finally Viceroy of Scotland for James VI. His father John, the fourth Earl, was unusual in the family. He had no appetite for high intrigue and power-mongering. He struck a spark of youthful fame when he fought a duel in Edinburgh with Sir James Sandilands in 1595 to avenge some family injury. In 1616, he represented the King at the Aberdeen Convention of the Kirk. For a brief spell before his death he held the largely ceremonial office of Chancellor. But he was happiest spending his days pottering contentedly around his broad acres, enjoying his game of golf and his pipe of tobacco. He left it to others to struggle for place and influence in Edinburgh and London. The only other evidence of his tastes that he left behind him at his death was an illegitimate son named Harry who grew up as a member of the family.

Young Lord James was the only son among six legitimate children, and he was probably spoilt accordingly. His childhood was spent in procession around the family homes with his father. There were weeks at Old Montrose, the house where he had been born on the flat, windy coast of Angus, where the South Esk river flows into the sea. There were long stays at Kincardine, the old Earl's principal castle just south of Auchterarder in Perthshire. There were expeditions to Mugdock, and to Garscube, and later to the estates of his brothers-in-law.

It must have been a tiresome business, moving house along the atrocious boggy, ill-marked roads, young Lord James on his hack, the women riding pillion, the tapestries and silver on pack animals or sledges—even carts made hard work of a journey across the hills, and of any journey at all in winter. Heavy baggage went by sea whenever it was possible. The noble families of the seventeenth century were constantly in the saddle. They were much, much poorer than their English counterparts. Even the greatest never had enough furniture to equip all their houses in the manner to which they were accustomed. Dutch linen, English chairs and beds, Scottish silverware were wildly expensive, and had to be prized accordingly.

Young James Graham was fortunate to be born into Scottish life at a moment of unprecedented peace, after the unending turbulence of the sixteenth century and before. The Border raiders had at last been suppressed after their leaders had been hanged in scores. Some of the terrible family feuds and seiges had abated. But it was still a world in which violence and physical danger were very close to the surface. "Scotland is a quagmire," wrote the despairing Cecil fifty years earlier, "no one seems to stand still."[1] Every great house had to be capable of defending itself, every gentleman was bred to arms. Even in 1621, Campbell of Glenorchy was still collecting an annual four croscats of iron from every tenant on his Perthshire estates for the suppression of wolves. Three-quarters of Scotland's million or so inhabitants were peasants, eking out miserable lives in their low drystone-walled huts, roofed with turf, heated by the warmth of the animals with whom they shared them.

On his long rides between the family estates, young James Graham must have seen the great herds of cattle being driven south from the highlands to market by the clansmen who provoked such horror and disgust among Edinburgh merchants and their wives. The Highlands were an alien region, peopled as it seemed by a race of thieves and plunderers who fought for booty and pleasure.

"As for the Highlands," wrote King James himself, "I shortly comprehend them all into two sorts of people: the one, that dwelleth in our mainland, that are barbarous for the most part yet mixed with some show of civility; the other that dwelleth in the isles and are all utterly barbarous. . . ."

"He was a very active man," wrote a respectful contemporary of the chief of the Mackenzies of Kintail, "he burnt and harried Sleat for his pleasure. . . ."

A Campbell chieftain excused his tenants all rent if they hunted mercilessly any man of the Macgregors. The distant hills seemed to Scottish Lowlanders places of infinite gloom and terror, perhaps above all because so many of the people who sheltered in them were still avowed papists.

It was a cruel society, full of religion yet starved of Christianity, talking much of justice, yet doubtful about the merits of mercy. The English viewed Scotland with unalloyed horror: "A bankrupt dependency on the periphery of civilization," as a modern historian writing of the period has dismissed it.[2] James Graham, at Kincardine, grew up between the Lowland Scottish civilization centred upon Glasgow and Edinburgh, and the hills reaching northwards to the wild horizon. It was probably here, in his youth, that he learnt to speak some Gaelic, for he could never have commanded a Highland army without it. Perhaps he picked up a little from the men who came down to the house bringing the grouse and ptarmigan and blackgame that the family consumed in such numbers. He might have talked to salmon fishers from the north, or to falconers who brought new hawks to the mews. There is no evidence that he travelled deep into the Highlands as a child, but growing up as he did among the tame oats and barley of southern Perthshire, perhaps he learnt that yearning for the promise and romance of the hills in the north that is so common among twentieth century sportsmen with warm firesides to come home to, yet was so rare among his own contemporaries, for whom life was brutal enough on the flatlands without seeking out the ghastly mysteries above the treeline.

When so much is uncertain about times and places, September 29th, 1620 is a pleasantly substantial date[3] in the life of young Lord Graham. Perhaps it was one of those wonderfully warm, purple autumn days that make Scotland seem so innocent, or perhaps it was one of those sulking, damp, drizzling days when the rain dripped off the trees beside Kincardine and down into the river below. In the forge at Aberuthven, a few miles up the valley, Thomas Smythe was shoeing the family horses "before his Lordship rode to Rossdhu". "The Lord James's two nags" were among them. All the family were at Kincardine, the old Earl and his son preparing to set out for a visit to his married daughter Lilias, at her new home on the western shore of Loch Lomond.

That September 1620, Lord James was almost eight. The evidence is overwhelming that he was born in 1612, and there are indications that it was late in that year. The unreliable and malicious old gossip, Scot of Scotstarvit, records that his mother consulted with witches at his birth, and that as a small boy, he

ate a toad. Scotstarvit was twisting the knife in a family wound:
Lady Montrose, the former Lady Margaret Ruthven, was
sister to the murdered Earl of Gowrie, of whom there had been
dark rumours that he was a necromancer. In those days when
superstition and the black arts flourished, nothing seemed
impossible. In Rosshire a few years before, Lady Foulis had
quarrelled with her stepson and his wife, and sent for a local
wizard named Lasky Loncart to dispatch them. He failed in his
efforts throwing magic arrows at images of butter, but
triumphed in the end with rat poison. If Lady Montrose sent
for the local soothsayer before her son's birth, it was no less a
sensible precaution in the seventeenth century than insuring
against twins in the twentieth.

James Graham was only five when his mother died, in April
1618. Of his five sisters, the first to marry was Margaret. A
year after her mother's death, she celebrated her wedding to Sir
Archibald Napier of Merchiston, later to become Lord Napier,
and already one of the most respected statesmen in Scotland.
He was to be almost a father-figure to James Graham. His
father had been celebrated across Europe as the inventor of
logarithms. He himself was already forty, a thin-faced man of
sharp, piercing eyes, with the slim moustaches and trim beard
fashionable at the period. He was a Privy Councillor, a man of
the world who held a succession of important public offices
including those of Treasurer-Depute for Scotland and Lord
Justice-Clerk. He was just the adviser that the old Earl of
Montrose, with his distaste for public life, could never be to his
son. Although Lady Margaret died in 1626, Archie Napier and
Jamie Graham were to remain devoted to each other until
death.

The sister whom the Earl and Lord James rode to visit in
September 1620, Lady Lilias, had just attached herself to Sir
John Colquhoun of Luss, a magnate with large estates around
Loch Lomond, who was to entertain his young brother-in-law
many times in his boyhood giving him the freedom of the hills
around Rossdhu. There were also three other girls—Dorothea,
Katherine, and "the bairn Beatrix" as she was always referred
to in letters. These were all still living at home—Beatrix was
only four. They were kept busy learning tapestry and needle-
work and all the other suitable womanly skills, perhaps from
Margaret Stirling, the Kincardine housekeeper.

The castle must have been a bustling, crowded place, with its little army of domestic servants and their families, of farm labourers and grooms and hangers-on. The old Earl thought nothing of sitting down to dine with twelve or twenty-four at his table. Rural Scottish hospitality was generous and easy-going for it was impossible to give warning of everyone's coming, and it was the right of any gentleman to look for a place at an equal's board. Although the Earl of Montrose lived quietly, like the rest of the Scottish nobility he was probably perpetually short of ready cash. None of them thought of risking their capital or investing their income like the merchants of Edinburgh and Glasgow. All they knew was a life of conspicuous consumption and consequent debt.

Young Lord James spent much of his time at Kincardine in the saddle or at his foils or his targets. Harry Blackwood, the family's Master of Horse, probably taught him to ride. James Myln made his bows, and often appears in the family accounts charging a few shillings for mending them. Perhaps he also taught his young lordship how to use them. If so, he did it well, for the boy grew into a deadly marksman. He also learnt to use a gun. There were the family gamekeepers to teach him. "Powder and lead for my lord's gunner" is another charge on the household bills.

James Graham probably grew up much as he chose, in a household with his mother dead and his father a retiring soul who would do anything for peace and quiet. In his later years at least, the Earl sounds a little of an old woman. One of his letters gives the flavour of his domestic round:

"Laurence Graham," he wrote to his factor at Kincardine one day,* "I doubt not but you have been careful in causing haste the making of my daughter Beatrix her gown, as I directed you. I have sent this bearer, Harry Blackwood, to bring her to me, as he will show you. It is my will also, that the tapestry in my upper chamber in Kincardine be taken down, and packed well, to come to me at Mugdock. I have sent Margaret Stirling and Robert Taylor word to be careful of it, which you shall see well done; and send a good carriage horse with it, with all expedition; and send Robert Taylor to convoy

---

* Throughout the text, when quoting contemporary sources I have modernized the spelling, except in a few cases where the original lines convey an especially vivid impression.

it. Further, it is my will that you deliver to Harry Blackwood eight bolls of meal, and four stones of cheese. From Mugdock, the 28th July 1625 MONTROSE.

"I have directed, as I told you that I would do, my two grey hackneys to be put to the grass at Kincardine; and have directed Robert Mailer to wait on them."

One day in 1624, the beggars at the gates of Glasgow sprang forward to greet a stately little procession advancing into the city. James, Lord Graham, on his white horse—no doubt sitting his saddle with all the self-conscious dignity of a twelve-year-old—was on his way to begin his formal education. His father shared the view of many seventeenth-century Scottish peers that learning was best done away from home—indeed one of the remedies the Scottish Privy Council had been attempting against the turbulence of the Highlands was to have the great clan chiefs' sons sent south, to the "in country" of the Lowlands, to be educated at a distance from their brutish native environment. There was no such compulsion for young James Graham, but his father sent him to lodge at the home of Sir George Elphinstone of Blythwood, the Lord Justice-Clerk of Scotland, to get himself a little learning.

If until now Lord James had been allowed to splash in the burns of Perthshire and the mud of his father's farmyards with whoever he chose, those days were gone for ever. He had become, for every eye to see, one of the gilded youth of Scotland. He wore the sword presented to him by Napier, on the silk and silver-mounted scarf given to him by his father. He tossed gold to the beggars at the gates of Glasgow with all the condescension that was expected of him—from now on the family accounts are full of casual largesse. Behind him rode his namesake James Graham, who was something between his valet and aide-de-camp, and his two pages Willy and Mungo Graham in their scarlet suits and cloaks. And there also in the little cavalcade was his lordship's newly-acquired tutor, Master William Forrett.

It must have been a testing business to tutor the wilful and high-spirited son—and only son at that—of a great family like the Grahams. If the boy sickened and died or got himself run through in a brawl (as was by no means unlikely), matters would go hard for the wretched pedagogue responsible for him. There were few sanctions a master could use against such a

pupil to make him learn anything. But Master William
Forrett and young Lord James established a very happy
relationship, a mutual affection that lasted all their lives. The
boy's future taste for Latin quotation and romantic verse
suggest that his teacher had not laboured entirely in vain.

Lord James and his entourage had their own set of rooms at
Sir George Elphinstone's house, with yellow curtains and
arras-work cushions, his own silver spoons and napkins and
tablecloths, his crossbow mounted with mother-of-pearl and
his "brazen hagbut" for sport and the trunk full of his most
valuable possessions to which Forrett kept the key.

Glasgow at this time ranked with Dundee and Aberdeen,
the three great cities of Scotland after Edinburgh. It had a population of perhaps 10,000 people, packed in tall, crowded tene-
ments, as squalid and plague-ridden as any seventeenth-century
community. The city boasted a busy foreign trade with France,
Norway, and Ireland. It was one of the familiar sights of
Glasgow to see Hebrideans from the Western Isles sailing up
the Clyde to the city to beach their little boats and sell plaids,
hides, marten and deerskins. James Graham must already have
seen something of Scottish citics, for Edinburgh was only a day
or two's journey from Kincardine. He would have learnt
already to notice the stocks and the gallows no more than the
steaming horse manure in the streets. Now he lived alongside
the merchants whose access to ready money made them the
envy of even the greatest noble landowners in Scotland. In
1639 Sir William Dick, the Edinburgh man who farmed the
Scottish customs, was able to raise half a million pounds for
the Covenanting war chest from his own treasury. Scotland
might be poor, but a few Scots were already demonstrating a
remarkable talent for making themselves rich.

In Glasgow every Sunday, young Lord James walked to
Kirk with one of his pages trotting in front of him carrying his
brown velvet prayer cushion. The ministers ruled every
corner of Scottish life with an iron hand. Homosexuals were
burnt. Adultery, fornication, and sabbath breaking were
statutory offences. "Searchers" prowled the streets on Sunday,
hunting out the ungodly. Detected adulterers were summoned
to do penance in sackcloth at the church door. James Graham
himself seems to have been risking the displeasure of the
Elders in 1625 by wearing his "stand of mixed grey English

cloth clothes, and a cloak with pasments". Pasments were a form of embroidery condemned by the Assembly of the Kirk. Such frivolities, they said sourly, "declare the lightness of the mind".

A few of the books that he studied in Glasgow are on record, because William Forrett compiled a list of them when he was later called on to give an account of his stewardship of Lord James's property. There was Sabellicus's *Universal History*, an Italian fifteenth-century work; Camerarius's natural history; *A Treatise of the Orders of Knighthood*; *The Life and Death of Queen Mary*—a new book, this one, published in London in 1624; Godfrye De Bulloigne's history, a Latin Xenophon; and Seneca with Lipsius's commentary. One can no more pretend to judge Jamie Graham's personal tastes from such a list as those of a modern schoolboy from studying the 'A' Level syllabus. But there is one clue to his own enthusiasm—the fact that while he left all these books with Forrett when he went to St Andrews, he took with him Sir Walter Raleigh's *History of the World*. Ever since its publication in 1614, the first volume of Raleigh's massive work, describing classical history to the end of the Macedonian Empire, had been popular reading especially among English puritans. It was one of young Oliver Cromwell's favourite books. It is enchanting to imagine that in some low-beamed chamber in Glasgow, the light streaming dimly through the leaded windows, young James Graham pored over the tale of Alexander and kindled the romantic spark which was to burst into the great flame of Montrose.

On or about November 10th, 1626, James Graham's education in Glasgow came to an end. Word reached him that his father, at Kincardine, was seriously ill. He rode hastily home with his little entourage, and arrived on November 12th, in time to see the old Earl on his deathbed. On November 14th, he died. Jamie Graham became the fifth and most illustrious Earl of Montrose. Henceforth, it will be inappropriate for any but his closest friends to refer to him as anything else.*

The whole tribe of Grahams descended on Kincardine for the three-week wake that followed the old Earl's death. There was Lord Wigton, Montrose's first cousin, Lord Napier, Sir

* There is little doubt that he and his contemporaries pronounced his name "Montross", as they so often spelt it. But it seems pointless now to try to undo modern custom.

B

John Colquhoun, Sir William Graham of Braco, Robert
Graham of Morphie, William Graham of Claverhouse, Patrick
Graham of Inchbrakie, David Graham of Fintry, and a host
of others besides. It gives some impression of the size of the old
castle at Kincardine that it could accommodate so many of
them. The household accounts testify that they feasted
enormously. It was lucky that most guests had the good grace to
bring an offering for the larder with them, either a great hind
from Glenorchy, or a few brace of grouse or blackgame. The
Kincardine stewards must have been thankful that it was the
season when the great flocks of wild geese swarm onto the fields
of southern Perthshire.

For a boy of fourteen, to sit at the head of the family table
under such circumstances must have been a great strain. He
will have been glad of Archie Napier's support, and of the
company of some of his younger cousins like Pat Graham of
Inchbrakie. His tenants and his servants were offering their
sympathy with weary persistence. His factors and the local
merchants demanded their instructions. They had hastily
submitted all the bills due from the late Earl. The last business
concerned with the funeral was not completed until January 7th,
1627. A council of nine guardians had been appointed among
the Grahams to keep an eye upon the new Earl. It was agreed
that Kincardine was no place for his sisters. Katherine and
Beatrix rode away to Rossdhu with their elder sister Margaret
and her husband Sir John Colquhoun. Dorothea went down to
Edinburgh with Lady Napier, her other sister. The servants
and factors kept their places, but the family circle was breaking
up. Had his father lived, young Montrose might have gone to
university a little later, but under the circumstances the decision
was made at once. Old William Forrett was paid off with
400 merks, and on January 23rd the new Earl rode out of
Kincardine for St Andrews accompanied by Inchbrakie, his
uncle Sir William Graham of Braco, and a little escort of
friends. On January 26th, "Jacobus Gramus, comes Montrouse"
was entered in the rolls of Scotland's leading university, "the
principall fountayne of religione and good letters in the
kingdom".

It was an English conceit of the seventeenth century as much
as later, to imagine Scotland as a savage land of small parts and
scanty civilization. In reality, from the Middle Ages onwards,

there was much greater concern about public education north
of the Border than there was south of it. St Andrews had been
famous for many years as a haven for European Protestants,
and already boasted a tradition two centuries old.

Then as now, the university stood in the midst of one of the
most graceful little burghs in Scotland. From his rooms in St
Salvator's College, Montrose could look out at the North Sea
in all its moods, taste the breezes in summer and curse the
winter gales that blew smoke down the chimneys. It would be
fanciful to imagine that a young Earl was just a member of the
University, treated like any other. In reality, like Argyll and
Lauderdale before him and like his contemporaries Lord
Lindsay and Lord Kinghorn, he ranked as a "Primar" in the
language of St Andrews. Lairds' sons were "seconders",
yeomen's and craftsmen's sons "tertiars".

A modern historian of the university suggests that the 1620's
were among its less happy academic periods, when "instruction
in the arts at least had sunk to a routine of dictated lectures
and formal disputations that might discipline the intellect, but
did little to inspire it".[4] Some of the entries in the Montrose
family accounts, by now being maintained by the Earl's new
secretary John Lambie, make it clear that he did not approach
his lectures with much dedication: "Item: to ane scholar who
wrote my lord's notes in the school, 29 shillings."

He was a young blade who could do as he chose, coming and
going at his pleasure. In the spring of 1627, he was down in
Edinburgh to be served heir to his father and to sign the papers
concerned with the family estates. It was all arranged for him
by the family lawyer, Thomas Hope, the finest legal mind in
Scotland. Hope looked after the affairs of most of the Scottish
nobility, and a few years later he was to become well known as
Lord Advocate of Scotland under the Covenanters. His young
client stayed with Lord Napier at his home outside Edinburgh,
and Napier no doubt helped to steer him through the
formalities.

The following spring, he was in Edinburgh again when his
sister Dorothea, who had been living with the Napiers, was
married to Sir James Rollo. He stayed from April 22nd to
29th, running up the usual sizeable bills for spurs and bow-
strings, getting his hunting cap mended, paying the Beadle of
the West Kirk "for the testimonial of that church before the

marriage of my Lord's sister", and tipping the staff of Lord Napier's house before he left. He then rode on to Carnock, in Fife, for more celebrations with the wedding party that continued until May 2nd. He returned to St Andrews on May 7th, after stopping off for a short visit at Kincardine.

Perhaps as a result of some infection he picked up on his travels, he fell seriously ill on May 24th. At times in the following few weeks, his life was despaired of. John Lambie had to ride to Dundee to fetch Doctor Maal on the 28th. This learned gentleman, together with his colleague Doctor Arnot, the leech, between them ran up bills of more than a hundred pounds in the weeks that followed, mercifully failing to kill off their patient with the usual ruthlessness of seventeenth-century G.P.s. Montrose lay bedridden in his chamber, playing cards and occasionally chess—Lambie paid out six shillings for a chessboard to be sent post from Edinburgh for him. Well into June he was living off chicken broth, jelly made of "capons and veels feet", and liquorice and whey. The long locks that he cared for so carefully had been cut off in his fever. The summer was well advanced before he was once again fit to go back to his horses and his golf clubs.

He spent much of the year progressing pleasantly around the houses of friends and relations, hunting and hawking and banqueting from Cumbernauld to Kinnaird and Gleneagles to Inchbrakie. His friends were his equals: Lord Wigton, Lord Lindsay, Kinghorn, Sinclair, Sutherland, Colville. He dressed fastidiously—the accounts are full of such items as "ane pair of fyne weill favourit ryding gloves", "to the gardener, giving my lord ane flower on Sunday, 12 shillings".[5] He tipped the servants generously at the houses in which he stayed. He always carried his purse for the poor outside kirk on Sunday, and for the beggars at his stirrups as he rode out of the city gates. He heard much of the music of pipers and fiddlers and drummers sent to amuse him wherever he was staying, and he seems to have enjoyed mummery and masques among the house parties he frequented, although a friend noted later that he never seemed to like dancing.[6] Sometimes, perhaps, they sang the great ballads of the period, "Sir Patrick Spens", "The Queen's Marie", "Kinmont Willie". Because the peerage was the great and only fount of patronage for any form of art or culture, every hopeful composer and author and painter had to solicit his own protector, and Montrose was not immune from their sycophantic attentions. "Given, at my lords' direction, to ane Hungarian poet who made some verses to my lord, fifty-eight shillings", runs an entry in the accounts. That rather fanciful travel writer Mr William Lithgow seems to have hung around Montrose a good deal, and to have presented to him in 1629 a copy of his *Adventures and Painful Peregrinations of Long Nineteen Years Travel in Scotland to the Most Famous Kingdoms in Europe, Asia, and Africa.*

And it was not only impoverished writers who looked for favours from young lords. Great issues in Scotland turned on the moods of the great peers, and the causes they could be seduced into supporting. Although Montrose was still in his 'teens, there was never any harm in making an early impression. At St Andrews, he often visited Darsay, the seat of Archbishop Spottiswoode, whose son was to be his close friend. In Edinburgh, he went to dine with the Lord Chancellor and the Lord Justice-General. By birth and possessions, Montrose would be among the most influential men in Scotland, if he chose to exert his powers as his father had not.

Apart from much entertaining and being entertained, Montrose spent much of his time at St Andrews riding or shooting. He kept a stable, and hunted whenever he could: "Item, to my lord's horse after his hunting, a pint of ale and a loaf, two shillings and eightpence." He was one of those lucky people who could ride hell for leather all day, then toss their reins to a groom and go home to dinner as soon as they chose to dismount. When he played a round of golf, there was always a caddy. Whenever he went to the butts, he took a boy to carry his bow. "To John Pett, James Pett's son, for to bring arrows from London to my lord", runs an entry in the accounts, near another "for ane pair of butt arrows made in Dundee".

Probably the sweetest triumph of his years at the university came the day he won the Silver Arrow for archery in 1628. Argyll, that squinting, secret man with whom he was to try so many bouts in the years to come, had won the same prize when he was up some time earlier. Among his own contemporaries, Montrose seems to have been the chief patron of archery. He paid the drummer of St Andrews twelve shillings for "proclaiming the Silver Arrow to be shot for". He paid five pounds eight shillings one evening for supper for the archers, and then after his victory, "my Lord having dined in the fields, and supped in William Geddes's with the archers, his loss that day, three pounds four shillings".

It was a delightfully pampered, leisured existence, and it only seems remarkable that their young lordships learnt anything at all in between Cupar races, and tennis, and their endless great dinners for each other. Montrose obviously enjoyed being open-handed, perhaps to the point of rashness, because he was later in debt. In October 1628, he held a great house party at Kincardine. Now it must have been enormous fun to sit at the head of his own table, to be able to call for more money from his own estates at an age when most of his friends were still in thrall to their parents. After centuries of upheaval, his generation was enjoying the extraordinary luxury of passing their youth with-out the shadow of war, relaxing for a brief idyll between Scotland's endless tragedies. These were Montrose's salad days, and he filled them to the full.

The Earl's formal education came to an end on November 10th, 1629. At the age of seventeen, he was married. His bride was Magdalen Carnegie, the youngest daughter of Lord Kinnaird, the future Lord Southesk, who was a near neighbour of the Grahams at Old Montrose. Kinnaird was among dozens of great houses that young Montrose regularly visited on his seasonal social round of Scotland, and had his father been alive he would have agreed that it was a perfectly suitable match. All the Carnegie girls married peers. Napier records the legend that Magdalen had been pursued by the Master of Ogilvy, Montrose's future close friend. The tale goes that Ogilvy was on his way to Kinnaird to propose when his horse slipped in a stream and ducked him in the water, cooling his passion for ever. Magdalen was consoled for the loss by marrying the even more eligible Montrose.

His marriage month of November 1629 was a hectic one. On the 3rd, he was in Aberdeen to have his portrait painted by Jameson, the most notable artist in Scotland. Portraits were coming into fashion in Scotland, and the finished picture was delivered to Magdalen Carnegie on December 2nd, as a wedding present from Graham of Morphie. It shows a gentle, humorous, almost impish-looking young man, still unsullied, untempered by treachery, deceit, misfortune, doubt. He was also made a burgess of Aberdeen during his visit to the city. It was an honour which cost Aberdeen's Fathers nothing, and might one day, they reckoned, be worth something in patronage. Montrose was indeed to see a great deal of Aberdeen in his life. But the city's hopes turned bitterly sour. He invariably rode upon it at the head of horse, foot and guns.

On November 5th, the bridegroom began a four-day progress southwards, staying with friends and relations on the road until he came to Montrose. A family party had assembled for the wedding, and he played golf on the 9th with Sir John Colquhoun, his brother-in-law. Later that day, he rode over to Kinnaird, paying a boy at the gate six shillings to hold his horse while he went in to see his future in-laws and his bride. That night he stayed with Graham of Morphie, and it was from his house that he rode out the following day to be married in the castle kirk of Kinnaird.

It was arranged in the marriage contract that he and his bride, still very young to set up their own household, would live with Lord Carnegie for the first few years of their married life. Montrose's accounts notice twenty-four shillings "given to the minister, Mr George Wishart, his servants, who had kept and transported the furniture and trunks" from St Andrews to Kinnaird. Wishart was Minister of St Andrews, and delighted to do a favour for a young noble like Montrose. This was the first flowering of the relationship between the Earl and his future chaplain and biographer that was to last all his life.

The story of Montrose is one of the supremely romantic tales of Scottish history. It is sad to admit that having reported Montrose's marriage, there will be very little more to say about his relations with women. He must have loved Magdalen Carnegie when he married her, for there is no suggestion that this was a politically-directed marriage such as that organised by James VI, for instance, to reconcile Campbells and Gordons by marrying an Argyll daughter to a Huntly son. The Countess of Montrose gave birth to the first two of their four sons while they were living together at Kinnaird. Hardly anything is ever said of her again by any of her contemporaries. It is dangerous to draw conclusions from mere lack of evidence. But it seems fair to surmise that Montrose and his Countess drifted apart after their first few years together. Had they been close, there was a host of chroniclers and ballad-writers to exploit any opportunity to enrich the romantic legend of Montrose. Several writers have suggested that the death of Montrose's eldest son while campaigning with his father alienated his wife. It seems more significant to notice that her father, Southesk, all his life remained dedicated to the preservation of his estates, to riding comfortably with the largest party in Scotland to save his own interest. Southesk became a Covenanter after Montrose and his friends had laid all they possessed at the feet of Charles I. Montrose was a rebel, a troublemaker who sowed destruction in his path across Scotland and whose principles brought ruin upon his own homes and estates. All these considerations may have embittered his wife. Influenced by her father's sensible trimming, Montrose's nobility and sacrifice may have seemed to her merely obstinacy and foolishness. Many of Montrose's Scottish contemporaries regarded him as a vain, impetuous brigand who brought discord upon his own society. If Magdalen Carnegie, like many wives, wanted only to live a gracious and prosperous life as Countess of Montrose and hostess at Kincardine, then her husband was a tragic disappointment to her.

But it is also interesting that Montrose's name was never to be coupled with that of another woman while his wife was alive, even by his enemies who would have libelled him in any way they could. In 1641, when the Covenanters sent Lord Sinclair to rifle Montrose's papers for evidence to use against him, he found only "some letters from ladies to him, in his younger days, flowered with Arcadian compliments". Much later, in his exile, Montrose fascinated Elizabeth of Bohemia, Charles I's sister the Winter Queen. There was some suggestion that with his wife dead, he might marry one of her daughters. But for all his passion for honour, his romantic poetry and his lifelong pursuit of dreams, Montrose was a man more at ease with his comrades in arms beside the camp fire than among great ladies at court or in castle. In the manner of the great Greek heroes, he seems to have saved his deepest affections for the happy few, the band of brothers around him on the battlefield. If his marriage had been important to him, we would know more about it than the number of his children and the fact that he rode from his headquarters to attend his wife's funeral.

Montrose enjoyed almost two quiet years with his father-in-law amidst the spacious beauty of Kinnaird. Then some time in September 1631, a thunderbolt struck which destroyed any hope of domestic peace for months to come: his brother-in-law,

Sir John Colquhoun, vanished from Rossdhu with his German valet Carlippis, carrying off with them Montrose's young sister Katherine. The abandoned and distraught Lady Lilias had to send word to Kinnaird of the scandal. Katherine and little Beatrix had been living at Rossdhu since the old Earl of Montrose's death in 1626. In the indictment prepared against the fugitive Colquhoun by the Lord Advocate, Sir Thomas Hope, it was alleged that he had begun his seduction as far back as 1629. The age being what it was, it seemed to make the role of the wretched Lady Katherine less disgraceful if her seducer had worked his evil ways by means of necromancy, witchcraft, and sorcery. "Certain philtra, or poisons of love" had been used, it was said, "a jewell of gold, set with divers precious diamonds or rubies, which was poisoned and intoxicat by the said necromancer".

It is not unlikely that Hope intimated to Montrose, in his capacity as family legal adviser, that the necromancy allegations would lessen the unpleasantness of what was obviously a straightforward, almost certainly willing elopement. But the horror of incest provided a scandal that set the great houses of Scotland buzzing for months. Poor Montrose and his family must have spent endless days riding grimly to and fro between the Edinburgh lawyers and Rossdhu giving evidence and making inquiries, bitterly conscious of the wagging tongues and ill-concealed public laughter. Nothing more was ever heard of poor Lady Katherine, and it can only be assumed that she disappeared or died abroad. Colquhoun eventually slunk back into Scotland in 1647, and found the Kirk perfectly willing to accept his pleas of penitence. By then, no man who had done the House of Graham a bad turn could be harshly judged in Edinburgh.

It is generally agreed that it was the Colquhoun scandal that persuaded Montrose to leave Scotland to travel abroad some time early in 1633, thus missing the greatest event in Scottish life for many years, the Coronation in Edinburgh of Charles I. William Lithgow, ever eager to please, had already written flattering lines about Montrose in his new epic poem "Scotland's Welcome to her native son and Sovereign Lord, King Charles". It is clear that everyone had taken the Grahams' presence for granted at the glittering ceremonies. The Coronation should have been the moment at which the young Earl stepped forward in a blaze of glory and finery to make his bow before his King, and perhaps to begin a career at Court. But after an affair such as that of Colquhoun, with all the petitions and indictments that were still flying wearily to and fro between Edinburgh and London, it was completely in character that the proud young man turned aside. He bridled furiously at the notion of having every eye upon him for all the worst possible reasons. He imagined himself making his debut among the sniggerers of Scotland. With his wounded family pride, with an urge to escape to new places and new faces, perhaps even to search for his poor sister, he saddled his horses. He gathered around him a little retinue of friends and servants; Graham of Morphie, Thomas Saintserf, son of the Bishop of Galloway, Basil Fielding, son of Lord Denbigh, John Lambie his secretary, and his usual pages and grooms. Then he rode away from his young family and his troubles. He did not see Scotland again for three years.

For even the best educated and best informed of young gentlemen, the journey to France—whether by land through England or direct by sea to the French Channel ports—was a revelation. Scotland was a poor country by the standards of seventeenth-century Europe, although it produced some fine scholars and skilful soldiers. Montrose saw before him the prosperity of England and the great cities and cathedrals of France. All his life he had been a big fish in a small pool. Now, on the continent, he became another of the innumerable haughty but gauche young men who travelled every year to marvel at its wonders. Scottish gentlemen had been taking the Grand Tour to complete their education for many years, and they had become a familiar sight, especially in France. The great Richelieu himself had been known to entertain them kindly, and down at Saumur on the Loire there had always been a well-established colony of young expatriate Scots hungry for culture.

Montrose had arranged to draw money through the Paris agents of the ubiquitous Sir William Dick, and he must have spent some time in the city. There was a thriving Scottish community, and he may well have called upon the Earl of Enzie, who was commanding King Louis XIII's famous Scots Guard, and had set up house in Paris with all his family. Enzie was soon to return home to succeed as Marquis of Huntly and the ruler of north-east Scotland, and in the years to come his family's relationship with Montrose would be a critical factor in Scottish politics. His sons never forgot their upbringing among the nobility of France. Years later, Lord Gordon still had a French servant, and when Lord Aboyne called his escort to charge at Kilsyth, it was as "Messieurs" that he addressed them.

Montrose arrived in Paris when the Thirty Years War, the Protestant crusade which obsessed Europe, was at its height. The whole continent was an armed camp and every boast was of prowess in arms. Men talked of their service with the legendary Gustavus Adolphus of Sweden as another generation had stripped their sleeves to tell of Crispin's Day. Germany lay ruined by years of counter-marching armies, famine and slaughter. In Paris, on the other hand, there was the martial pomp and glitter with none of the bitter consequences. Montrose would have been less than a man to be unimpressed by it all.

He was already very much attracted by the profession of arms. When William Lithgow wrote lines in his Coronation welcome to Charles I with which he hoped to please the Earl, he flattered him as the latest in a long line of Graham soldiers.

> James Earl of Montarouse, whose warlike name
> Sprung from redoubted worth, made manhood try
> Their matchless deeds in unmatched chivalry. . . .

In France, Montrose had come to the temple of Mars. There were no wars in Scotland, nor did there seem likely to be. Perhaps he then contemplated, as he certainly did a few years later, the possibility of taking a commission with one of the European monarchs. There were thousands of Scots serving in Germany. It was widely accepted that to become a soldier was the finest means by which a man without other prospects might advance and enrich himself, if he lived. Montrose hardly needed social advancement, but he was searching earnestly for a destiny.

Late in 1633, he set out for Angers, the beautiful city above the Loire where in the seventeenth century stood the most famous military school in Europe. The Duke of Buckingham had been a pupil there (and a hundred and fifty years later so was Wellington). In 1633, Angers was a rendezvous for the keenest blades on the continent. The school's original home had become too small for its new reputation, and since 1629 it had been quartered at the Hotel De Cazenove which Joachim Martin, its principal, had bought from the Prince of Guemene.

In this class of 1633–34, Montrose and a gentleman named William Fleming (perhaps his cousin) were the only "Ecossois".[7] There were also an Englishman named Henry Parquer, Danes like Ovidius Lunge and Nicolaus Wind, and countless Swedes, Germans, Bohemians and Frenchmen. The two Scots must have marvelled at the great fortress that dominated the city, greater than anything in Scotland, more massive even than the castle of Edinburgh or Stirling. The intricately decorated timber-fronted houses were very different from the steep, tall houses of Edinburgh's wynds. In one of them, Montrose and his little party set up their quarters for the winter, and began making the acquaintance of their fellow pupils.

The principal points of the syllabus at Angers were mathematics, the use of arms, dancing and horsemanship. Montrose was among those who also studied Greek with a local lawyer named Bruneau de Tartifume, who recorded his name among the many students he met over the years. It must have been a cooling experience for the young Earl to have become only the unknown Scot "Montros" instead of the celebrated gallant of Edinburgh and St Andrews. France in 1633 was just entering an era of sparkling military greatness, and her schools of arms had become the nurseries of her heroes. At Bernardi's Academy, soon to open as the Paris counterpart of Martin's college in Angers, every summer the pupils practised attacking and defending a fortress specially constructed for them in the Luxemburg Gardens. Montrose must have heard the passionate arguments about the merits of deploying cavalry three or six deep, learnt the impossibility (in those days before the bayonet) of musketeers resisting cavalry without pikemen in support, studied the art of arraying cavalry and musketeers chequer-pattern for mutual support. No gentleman could have spent a year in France at that period without hearing every battle of the great war in Germany fought out over a hundred dinner tables.

"He made it his work to pick up the best of their qualities (of France and Italy) necessary for a person of honour," wrote Thomas Saintserf[8] almost thirty years later. "Having rendered himself perfect in the Academies, his next delight was to

improve his intellectuals; which he did by allotting a pro-
portionable time to reading, and conversing with learned men;
yet still so, that he used his exercise as he might not forget it.
He studied as much of the mathematics as is required for a
soldier. But his great study was to read men, and the actions of
great men. . . ."

Most of this, of course, is just the flummery of an admirer. But
it says something for Montrose's determination to make a mark
in the world that he chose to study as seriously as he did at
Angers, rather than to progress carelessly around the courts of
Europe.

He left the college to ride southwards, through the incom-
parable beauties of the Loire valley, having met men of many
nationalities and a smattering of many things. He must have
learnt a good deal of French. He had seen some of the greatest
architecture in Europe. He passed on into Italy, probably
through Padua and Florence, to Rome. He seems to have
travelled for a time with some like-minded Scottish gentlemen
whom he met upon the road. At the English College in Rome,
he dined with Lord Angus, the future Marquis of Douglas, and
some of his friends. Together they must have walked the Forum
and climbed the Coliseum. He saw paintings that would
afterwards make him smile when his own countrymen talked of
Jameson with reverence. He dined at palazzos that made his
own halls at Old Montrose and Kincardine seem bare caverns.
Probably he wintered in Italy in 1635, luxuriating in a climate
so much more generous than his own. "Thus he spent three
years in France and Italy," wrote Saintserf, "and would have
surveyed the rarities of the East if his domestic affairs had not
obliged his return home."

At the age of twenty-three, Montrose was a mature man
ready to play his part in the great drama that was about to
unfold. He had grown into a slight figure, something less than
six feet tall, his chestnut locks flowing to his shoulders in the
fashion of the period, his piercing grey eyes staring boldly at the
world. Bishop Burnet, who was no friend of Montrose, none
the less made an interesting criticism of him as "a young man
well learned, who had travelled, but had taken upon him the
part of a hero too much, and lived as in a romance; for his
whole manner was stately to affectation".

While he rode across Europe for those three years, he seems

to have nursed romantic dreams, proud hopes for the future that none of his company dared to tease with reality. He seems to have been forging in his mind a determination to seek some high purpose, some great cause into which to throw himself. Even in his 'teens, he had scribbled verses that betrayed his romantic ambitions. "Though Caesar's paragon I cannot be," he wrote on a leaf of his Commentaries, "yet shall I soar in thoughts as high as he." He was always fascinated by Alexander the Great, and in his copy of Lucan he scribbled:

> As Macedo his Homer, I'll thee still,
> Lucan, esteem as my most precious gem;
> And though my fortune second not my will,
> That I may witness to the world the same,
> Yet, if she would but smile even so on me,
> My mind desires as his, and soars as high.

In the same vein he wrote in his copy of Quintus Curtius:

> As Philip's noble son did still disdain,
> All but the dear applause of merited fame,
> And nothing harboured in that lofty brain
> But how to conquer an eternal name;
> So, great attempts, heroic ventures, shall
> Advance my fortune, or renown my fall.

Montrose's delight in writing verse, his passion for honour and honourable things, were not just the whim of a schoolboy. In France, he bought a pocket Bible and carried it with him around Europe, using it to note mottoes that pleased him such as "Honor mihi vita potior". Montrose craved an honourable cause that could be more to him than life. His most celebrated quatrain was to be the key to his career:

> He either fears his fate too much,
> Or his Deserts are small,
> That dares not put it to the touch,
> To win or lose it all.

Montrose sought a destiny, a course for energy and passion, a challenge upon which to risk everything, a Holy Grail worthy of a great knight. Politicians quake when they see such men approaching, for they care nothing for "realities", nor for compromises, nor for ordinary rewards, because they are searching for higher things. They become random factors, the wild cards in the pack. Montrose rode back across Europe full of youthful conceit and high ambition. One day early in 1636, he crossed the Channel back into the Twin Kingdoms. He was on his way to take his rightful place among the peers of Scotland.

# CHAPTER TWO

## The Apostle of Rebellion

SCOTTISH SOCIETY, TO which Montrose returned in 1636, was a cauldron at boiling point.[1] Religious tensions that had been growing since the Reformation, political grievances—all the pressures of a dynamic age—burst upon Charles I, creating a major constitutional crisis. A man who was one of the poorest arguments in British history for an hereditary monarchy found himself confronted by problems and personalities with which he was wholly unequipped to contend. The tortuous development of the struggle between the King and the Scots is a dry diet for those who hanker for the battlefield, but it is impossible to understand the career of Montrose, his triumph and his tragedy, without examining the rise of the Covenanting movement.

When Charles's father, James VI, rode southwards from Edinburgh in 1603 to become King James I of England, he promised his Scottish subjects that he would return north every three years to visit them. In the event, only once in the ensuing twenty-three years did he see Holyrood Palace again. The Scots had lost their King, and were never really to find one again. But whatever his shortcomings as King of England, at least James retained a very good understanding of his fellow-countrymen in the years he ruled them from London. He played his nobles skilfully against each other, never allowing Gordons or Campbells or Hamiltons to indulge their dangerous jealousies. He had a considerable measure of success in reducing the fearful level of domestic warfare in Scotland, making use of the new power base that his English throne had created for him, together with the support of the merchants and lawyers— the infant urban middle class—who thoroughly disliked feudal violence because it threatened their trade and prosperity. James doggedly resisted the Presbyterian extremists of the Kirk, while never pushing them too far. Bishops had been abolished in Scotland in the late sixteenth century, in the heat of post-

Reformation fervour. By 1600, James had won them back their
seats in the Scottish parliament. They had little ecclesiastical
power over the Kirk, but they provided a check against the
fanatics who burned so angrily in their pulpits for an egalitarian
church in which they would have great power and the King
none.

In 1606, James at last forced the exile of Andrew Melville, the
extremist minister who had pressed the Reformation in Scotland to its uttermost limits, and been for so long a spear in the
King's side. In 1618, the celebrated Five Articles of Perth came
into force. They gave James and moderate Protestantism as
much as they could possibly hope for in Scotland: kneeling at
communion, the right to the sacrament and to baptism in
private, confirmation by bishops and the continuation of the
great Christian festivals. "Diabolical inventions", Knox himself
had called the rituals now legitimized once more. His successors
of the 1618 Kirk waxed particularly warm against the celebra-
tion of Christmas, and it was a gratifying indication of the
King's success against them that by 1620 the Archbishop of
St Andrews was able to imprison a local tailor who failed to
observe the holiday. Old Spottiswoode gained great satisfaction from the rage he caused the ministers by playing a regular
round of golf on the sabbath after service.

But it was always a matter of restraining a torrent of religious
passion. Cold climates have often inspired dour, melancholy,
non-conformist religions. The brooding hills and grey winters,
the granite and slate and drizzle of Scotland gave birth to
one of the most joyless, bitter, merciless forms of low church
worship the Christian church has ever conceived. For those who
wish to see it preserved alive today, it is only necessary to
travel to Ulster, where the Knoxian Reformation is still a living
thing; so too is the bloodshed, hatred and intolerance that
always went with it.

The Reformation in Scotland imbued its ministers with
extraordinary missionary zeal, almost messianic fervour, in the
years after 1560. Before the church revolution, there had been
far too few clergy in Scotland, now there were many spread
among the nation's thousand parishes. Where the old breed
had been notorious for their drunkenness and corruption and
womanizing, the ministers of the seventeenth-century Kirk,
with their ferocious certainty of predestination, heaped hellfire

upon papists, adulterers, sabbath-breakers and those so weak in the Lord as to advocate tolerance of belief. Scottish public education suddenly flourished in the late sixteenth century chiefly because the ministers denied the existence of childish innocence. They believed, that children were merely born "ignorant of all godliness" and must be dealt with accordingly.

Even those who have sought to defend the ministers can find little to say for their obsession with witchcraft. Between 1560 and 1707, one historian has calculated, between 3000 and 4500 people were executed for witchcraft in Scotland,[2] as against only 1000 in England, with five times the population. During the periodic orgies of persecution—a notable one took place in the late 1620's—the sabbath pulpits echoed across Scotland with terrible denunciations. Under torture, the poor accused wretches babbled charge after desperate charge against friends and acquaintances. Witches were believed to work their will in covens of thirteen, and the Kirk needed twelve more names before their first victim could be sent to burn in peace. Again and again during the Covenanting wars, it was to be the ministers who urged their generals to slaughter prisoners, who damned those who talked of mercy as faint-hearted in the Lord. These were men to whom the six days of the Creation were certain, literal reality; to whom Man was ordained by God as the centre of the Universe; to whom papists were mere outriders of Satan. Whatever pleas have been entered in mitigation for them in the court of history, the Scottish ministers of the seventeenth century must have been dreadful men. The emphasis their creed placed upon sermons and their place at the centre of their communities, often as the only sources of news and directors of opinion, gave them huge power. Their barbarities in the name of God echo down the years in the same terrible tradition as those of the Spanish Inquisition. They mercilessly compounded the miseries of seventeenth-century Scotland, and infused a spirit of personal hatred and unyielding vengeance into political life that was not matched in England until the King's execution in 1649.

But throughout his reign, James VI had played a canny part to keep the lid on this Pandora's Box. His son Charles, at his accession, burst it open. With the obstinacy and stupidity, the lack of judgement and rash Christianity that characterized his tragic life, he unleashed forces in his northern kingdom that were to provoke his ruin in his southern one also.

Charles was a deeply religious man in a sense that his father —too much of a scholarly haggler—never was. It was his cherished ambition to bring the church in Scotland into tidy uniformity with that in England. In 1626 he began a long struggle to work his will upon the Kirk with the announcement of the Act of Revocation. In the widespread looting of church rents and properties that had accompanied the Reformation in Scotland, tithes had become merely a tax in kind levied by landlords upon their peasants. Charles now proposed that the money should be diverted to provide a living for the ministers of the Kirk. He announced the creation of a commission to investigate the prospects of recovering some church lands from those who had seized them.

The Act of Revocation was one of the few wise and just religious measures of Charles's reign. Unfortunately, half the nobility of Scotland stood to lose by it. Their reaction was predictably forceful. The Earl of Rothes, Lord Loudon, and Lord Linlithgow arrived in London to petition the King on behalf of the tithe-holders, and representatives of the aristocracy of Scotland. Charles was still in the full conceit of his kingly power. He received the prickly trio in a style that must have enraged them, so much on their mettle at the alien English court. He said that they had been treated like so many young does, whom the old ones, finding themselves hotly pursued and in hazard of being taken, cunningly expose to the hunter's fury to save their own carcases. He told them, in short, that they were silly young fools sent to London because wiser men stayed at home. Then, content that he had won their hearts by showing them mercy rather than anger, he dismissed them to retail their grievances to his politically impotent secretary, Sir William Alexander.

When Charles arrived in Edinburgh in 1633 on his first visit to his Scottish kingdom since his accession, he introduced the full English Laudian high church ritual to his chapel at Holyrood. There was a row before the Coronation ceremony when Sir George Hay the Chancellor, a difficult old man at the best of times, was abruptly informed that he must give precedence to Archbishop Spottiswoode of St Andrews. Hay told the King furiously that he would resign rather than do so—"never a stoled priest should set a foot before him, so long as his blood was hot"—and Charles grudgingly gave way. A few days later, Rothes once again angered his monarch by attempting to present a petition against the bishops. It was a distressingly acrimonious visit, all in all, and it established a loveless relationship between Charles and the nobility of Scotland. They remembered the old relaxed, intimately vulgar relationship between a Scottish king and his peers, in the days when he was regarded simply as *primus inter pares*, a man who ate, drank, fornicated and defecated just as they did. Now here came Charles demanding to be received as their awful, distant ruler by Divine Right, standing betwixt God and men, and nearer the first than the last. It was a very dangerous mood for the King to have created. There was no great engine of government, no army of royal servants whom he could employ to govern Scotland as he wished. In the seventeenth century, he could implement his commands only with the goodwill of the nobility, acting through the Privy Council of which the most significant of them were members. To be a successful tyrant requires the machinery of tyranny.

The lords of Scotland did not like what they saw, and no more did Charles. Characteristically, he decided that it was time to call the dogs to heel, to flick the lash in the face of all this peevish opposition. A gentleman named Hay of Naughton, allegedly to satisfy a personal grudge, tipped off Archbishop Spottiswoode that Lord Balmerino was in possession of yet another petition against the bishops. Charles had the dissident peer put on trial for his life before the Scots Privy Council on a charge of high treason. By the casting vote of Lord Traquair he was found guilty and sentenced to death. All Scotland was appalled. Charles decided that the salutary lesson had been administered, his point made. Balmerino was reprieved.

But there was no gratitude in Scotland for Charles's mercy, only anger that the whole farce had taken place, and perhaps a secret contempt for the King's weakness. Once again Charles was trying to maintain the powers of an absolute monarch while flinching from the ruthlessness of method that is inseparably associated with them. Had Balmerino, had Rothes and Hampden and Pym gone instantly to the block, Charles might have avoided his own journey there for the price of a few slings and arrows from future generations of liberal historians.

But neither the dissensions visible during his Coronation visit to Scotland, nor the Balmerino affair persuaded the King to modify his purpose. With the encouragement of Laud far away in England, organs and altars and even surplices began to appear in some Scottish churches. In 1634, a Court of High Commission had been established by royal warrant, giving the Scottish bishops wide disciplinary powers over their flock. A new book of Canons, replacing Knox's Book of Discipline and setting aside the long Genevan tradition in Kirk practice, was sent to Scotland. In 1635 Kinnoul died, and was replaced as Lord Chancellor by Archbishop Spottiswoode, the first churchman to hold the office since the Reformation. The post had been largely honorific in the hands of men like Kinnoul and the late Earl of Montrose, but since even Charles was well aware by now of Scottish hostility towards the bishops, Spottiswoode's appointment was a contemptuous thrust at public opinion. The King seemed determined to use the episcopate as the instrument of his rule in Scotland, displacing the power of the lay nobility and trampling upon all the prejudices of the Kirk.

As early as 1629, Bishop Laud had proposed to Charles that his new English prayer book should be sent north for use by the Scottish church. Charles delayed a decision for some time, and consulted the Scottish bishops, making some minor changes at their request. But in November 1636 he wrote to Scotland confirming the horrifying rumour that had been circulating the shocked nation for months: the new Laudian Liturgy was to become compulsory in every church in the country the following year, and every minister must provide himself with copies of it by Easter, failing to do so at his peril. It was a blunder of awesome dimensions. "The Puritans, that year, who afterward we called the Covenanters, had some quiet meetings," recorded a Scottish Chronicler.[3] The meetings were not to remain quiet for very much longer.

The King had achieved the miracle of uniting almost every element in Scottish society against him. He could never look for much love from the burgesses and merchants who were weary of his taxes and interference with trade. Any wisp of gratitude the Kirk might have felt for the royal generosity in the matter of the tithes was blown away by the gale of their anger on every other issue. Finally, with the notable exceptions of the Huntly, Lennox and Hamilton families, the chief nobles of Scotland were united in their hostility to all that the King was seeking to do to them. Some of the members of the Scottish Privy Council might continue for a time in their public loyalty to the throne, but their private dismay was as great as that expressed openly by the peers who were not embarrassed by office.

In his single-minded concern with religious reform in Scotland, Charles I made a grievous error. He failed to see that his nobles' protests about altars and surplices masked a real grievance that was highly political. In the years since 1603, the Scottish nobility had slowly come to realize that the removal of the seat of monarchy to London had taken away the fount of power and patronage, and destroyed their long tradition of local government. Their influence on events in their own country had declined steadily. Their resentment against the English usurpers had grown. Relations between gentlemen of the two nations had always been delicate, and most Scottish lords hated the Court in London, where their poverty and their accents provoked endless jokes. Clarendon claimed that Charles I was "always an immoderate lover of the Scottish nation". But to the Scots themselves, there seemed to be precious little evidence of it. It appeared in Edinburgh that the destinies of Scotland were being wantonly perverted from London by the whims of a handful of self-seeking, unfriendly, foppish, haughty courtiers around the King. The only Scots who had influence over him appeared to be those who had renounced their Scottishness in order to serve him. With each generation, the Stuarts became more anglicized. When the young Prince of Wales's household was established, it was composed entirely of Englishmen. It was yet another insult that did not go unnoticed in Edinburgh.

Half a century before, Elizabeth had armed herself against the tensions of a dynamic age by choosing the most dynamic men of all to be her own servants.* Charles I, however, confronted the upheavals of the seventeenth century under the guidance of counsellors who embraced all that was worst in the traditions of hereditary monarchy. Holland, Hamilton,

---

* Although even she was dismayed by the difficulties of dealing with the Scots: "I am in a labyrinth about Scottish affairs," she wrote gloomily in 1564, and she continued so for much of her reign.

Cottington, Vane, Windebanke and that endlessly meddling Scottish Gentleman of the Bedchamber Will Murray, were self-seeking men with no more cogent political purpose than the maintenance of the system which was enriching them. They were chronic intriguers, loving deception for its own sake, yet hopelessly incompetent at it. Their plans were invariably uncovered, their ruses collapsed, their enemies anticipated them. Charles has been too harshly criticized for his lifetime of broken faith and deceit and false witness. All these things are essential to the business of ruling, as Elizabeth would have been the first to testify. In Charles's case, the fault was not the plotting but the fact that it was always found out. He and his courtiers to the end of their days embraced endless machiavellian schemes and deceptions, each more futile and self-defeating than the last.

Charles's weakness of character caused him to be led by others all his life. And because of his deeply-held religious and political convictions, his guide always had to be a man who shared or professed to share them. It was thus hardly surprising that the counsel he received was usually disastrous. In spiritual matters Laud, first as Bishop of London and then as Archbishop of Canterbury, was the dominant influence. Arrogant and testy, clever but politically insensitive, he shared all Charles's high church love of outward beauty in church architecture and in ritual. He was detested by the ministers of the Scottish Kirk.

In politics, and especially in Scottish politics, James Marquis of Hamilton exercised an influence over the King which was only to be matched by that of the Queen and of Digby during the Civil War. Charles consulted his English Privy Council as seldom as possible about Scotland, often deliberately concealing from them intelligence about his second kingdom. His Scottish, increasingly alien Privy Council in Edinburgh was six days away for a post rider. At the King's court in the years before the Civil War, Hamilton was chief of men saving only the King himself. Neither Wentworth nor Rupert, the outstanding servants of Charles I, ever had any command over their sovereign's mind to approach that of his best loved courtier. "The Marquis's ways were so ambiguous that no man understood him," wrote Baillie[4] the Covenanter, "only his absolute power with the King was oft there clearly to be seen."

"His natural darkness and reservation of discourse made him thought to be a wise man," said Clarendon,[5] "and his having been in command under the King of Sweden and his continual discourse of battles and fortifications, made him thought to be a soldier, and both these mistakes were the cause that made him be looked upon as a worse and more dangerous man than in truth he deserved to be."

Hamilton was a plausible ass. Even his enemies allowed him his good temper and uncommon courtesy to servants. But his attitude towards his native land and its leading lords was anything but temperate. "This miserable country", as he called it in one letter to Charles. He hated it "next to hell". He was a failed soldier—his experience in Europe had been brief and absurd—and a royal favourite who had been playing petticoat politics since his childhood as one of Charles's pages. In 1636, he was thirty years old, handsome despite a weak face and posturing manner, and full of quite unfounded confidence in his own powers. "His mind had a purposeless subtlety," writes C. V. Wedgwood.[6] "He concealed from his left hand what his right hand was doing, though there was usually no reason why he should. . . . Opportunity made him a fool and accident made a villain of him, as little by little in the next eleven years, he became, in popular opinion, the arch-traitor."

Thus in 1636 the Scottish nobility heard a tale from London that aroused their deepest anger and jealousy. Their King was living in a serene dream world inhabited by his favourite painters and architects and courtiers, while the business of governing Scotland was in the hands of Englishmen such as Laud or of expatriates such as Hamilton. The Queen heard mass in her chapel every day with her friends and boasted about it, while a Londoner rash enough to suggest that the King attended with her had been fined £5000 for his prattle, a sure sign of guilty embarrassment somewhere. Despite the penal law against Catholics, Scots travellers reported that priests were walking openly in the streets of London. Puritans who attempted to pursue the Lord's will and to speak out against popery, on the other hand, were visited with the most savage penalties. The King seemed oblivious to Scotland's imprecations. He noticed his native land only when he sent some peremptory instruction to its church, insulting Scotland's religion by seeking to impose English idolatry upon it. The bishops grew constantly more obtrusive as agents of the King's will, and they had greater and greater temporal powers thrust upon them. By the year 1636, nationalism, religion and outraged self-interest had combined to put the nobility of Scotland in the mood for a showdown with their high-handed monarch.

In this climate, the young Earl of Montrose returned after his years of travelling the continent. In happier times, he would have reached home to find his friends eager to gather around his hearth and hear endless tales of Rome and of Paris, of the war in Europe and of his studies at Angers. Instead, however, he came back to a society deep in its own troubles. His fellow peers were brimming with bitterness about recent injustices, bubbling with anger about the coming of the new Liturgy. All his life Montrose was a proud Scottish gentleman. There is no evidence that he ever enjoyed very happy or intimate relations with the English. Now, he heard of Balmerino's trial and of the new Book of Canons, of the injuries done to Scottish peers at the Coronation, of his old and dearly-loved friend Lord Napier's deep misgivings about the bishops. The King was even on the point of commanding the use of a new translation of the psalter because part of it was the work of his royal father. The dignity of the Scottish peerage was being despised, and Montrose was as incensed as any of his fellow lords.

He himself had also returned northwards with his own tale of the King and of the odious gaggle of courtiers who seemed to command him. He had a personal grievance to add to the national anger against Charles. Having missed the Coronation in Scotland because of his absence abroad, he visited London on his way home. He made himself known at court, to Hamilton, who was not only a fellow Scot but had the ear of the King. Montrose was the latest of a long line of Grahams, each of whom had in turn held the highest offices in the kingdom. Returning from the continent bent on some high fulfilment for his talents and his energies, Montrose may have expected much from a meeting with the King.

But the writer Heylin in his *Life of Laud* reports that Hamilton at once detected an unwelcome potential rival in this highly bred, gracefully-mannered young man who was offering so much to his King if he would take it. Hamilton told Montrose that Scots were less than popular with Charles, who nowadays

preferred to see Englishmen around himself. He then primed
the King about Montrose's arrival, with a warning that he was
a young man of great power and influence and ambition, who
would endanger the King's interests in Scotland if his conceits
were in any way to be flattered. He must be cut down to size.
When Montrose was brought before Charles, Heylin says that
he was abruptly and coldly received. The King held out a hand
to be kissed and then turned brusquely aside. It was the sort of
decisive snub that would set the Court buzzing with malicious
gossip, and send the proud young man home to Scotland
nursing a sad store of humiliation and disappointment.

Heylin is by no means a reliable witness, as is proved by the
fact that in this account he confused Montrose with Enzie,
asserting that he had been commanding the Scots Guard in
Paris. But he used Lord Napier as one of his authorities, and
the circumstantial evidence seems in favour of the story;
Montrose was overdue for presentation at court, and it would
be natural for him to turn to Hamilton to arrange it. The
enthusiasm with which he later plunged himself into the
Covenanting struggle becomes more readily comprehensible if
he had been deeply wounded by the same King and the same
Hamilton whom he was to have the opportunity to set at
defiance. It would be to debase Montrose's sincere calvinism
and political principles to suggest that the encounter in London
alone drove him among the King's enemies. It would also
ignore the pause of a year between his return to Scotland and
his first recorded appearance on the political scene. But it
seems reasonable to suppose that he had become very wary of
his King and of the Court.

On Sunday July 23rd, 1637, the new prayer book was read
in Scotland for the first time. The King's Council, who marched
in procession to St Giles's Cathedral in Edinburgh for the
occasion, found that they had arrived without either Lord
Traquair or Lord Lorne, son and heir of the Earl of Argyll and
the richest and most powerful man in Scotland. All those
concerned had a fair idea of what was about to happen. As
Dr Hannah, the Dean of St Giles, began to read the service,
he was met by a hail of Bibles and prayer stools hurled from the
congregation. Guards struggled to push out the dissidents,
almost all of them women whose cries and torrents of abuse
rained down on Dr Hannah as they were driven through the

doors. A riot developed which continued outside the Cathedral all through the service. All over Scotland, similar scenes took place.

It was a deliberate, carefully-planned, well-orchestrated protest. It had been organized by the leading ministers and dissident nobles, but it reflected the heart-felt fury of many Scots. The women of Edinburgh led the riot because they had been instructed to do so, perhaps because the authorities would find it more difficult to punish them. When the Scottish Privy Council assembled the following week, they condemned the rioters as traitors, but they suspended the use of the Service Book. Surrounded as they were by the outraged population of Edinburgh, they understood how near they stood to some uncontrollable upheaval. Most of the lay nobles of the Council were as disgusted by the introduction of the Service Book— "naught but the mass in English"—as a minister of the Kirk had damned it—as the rest of Scotland. In their report to the King, they described the protests as "that barbarous tumult, occasioned solely, for anything we can learn as yet, by a number of base and rascally people".

But if this were really so, as Charles angrily demanded when he received their report at Oatlands a few days later, why had they been so cowardly as to withdraw the Service Book? With his usual contempt for reality, he sent word back to Scotland post-haste that the Book was to be used, and that those who rioted against it were to be tried and punished. He continued either unaware or unmoved by the fact that the few ministers who persevered with the Book found themselves in peril of their lives. A Glasgow clergyman named William Annan was almost torn apart by his own congregation. In Dunblane, Ross and Brechin intrepid souls braved the mob, but the respect shown to the Bishop of Brechin by his congregation may have owed something to the pair of loaded pistols he laid on the satin cushion before him when he began. The mob tried to seize him when he left afterwards.

That autumn, once the harvest was in, public meetings and petitions against the Prayer Book sprang up and multiplied in every major town in Scotland. Only Aberdeen, where the Huntly and Catholic influence was still strong, remained quiet. It happened that in September the Duke of Lennox's mother died, and the young Duke himself had to leave his usual haunts at Court in London to come north and settle her affairs. Both sides in the struggle saw an opportunity to explore each other's positions. Lennox was not a very bright young man, but he was honest enough, and he was also a royal favourite. Only a few weeks before, he had married the only daughter of Charles's late loved Duke of Buckingham, amidst much Court goodwill. When Lennox arrived in Edinburgh, the Privy Council invited him to attend their meeting on September 20th. As the King's cousin, he represented their best hope of making Charles perceive the chasm yawning before him. The Councillors showed him the great heap of petitions and denunciations of the Liturgy that had come to them from every corner of Scotland. Lennox returned to London to pass on their earnest pleas to exercise moderation. Charles, however, replied only with instructions to disperse the petitioners still lingering clamouring around Edinburgh. He might as well have ordered them to attack a wasps' nest with a shrimping net.

The prime mover in the new campaign against the Liturgy and thus against the King was his old antagonist John Leslie, Earl of Rothes. Rothes was a handsome, dashing, earthy politician of wide experience, very well-liked in Scotland and no fanatic in matters of religion. In his late thirties, he lacked the power of the great landowners such as Lorne and Huntly. But since all the Scottish nobles of the first rank were still disqualified from the struggle by caution, by royalism, or by membership of the Privy Council, Rothes was able to seize the leadership of the dissidents. A strong faction of the other Lowland lords mustered openly to support him: Balmerino, Lothian, Lindsay, Loudon, Cassilis. By October 1637, they also counted among their number James Graham, Earl of Montrose.

Montrose first became identifiable among the dissidents when he signed one of the innumerable protests against the King's church policy on October 18th, entitled "Scotland's supplication and complaint against the Book of Common Prayer, the Book of Canons, and the Prelates". Baillie[7] says that Montrose was brought into the opposition party "by the canniness of Rothes". A few years later Montrose himself said that Robert Murray, the minister of Methven who was sent by the dissenting lords and ministers into Perthshire and Stirlingshire to gather support, had been "an instrument of bringing me to this cause". Murray probably called upon Montrose at home at Kincardine. Rothes must have turned all his great charm on the young man, touching on their common experiences of insult from the King and his courtiers, playing his cynical wit across the dinner table. Rothes seems sincerely to have liked Montrose, and the affection was returned by his protégé. They were soon commonly talked of in tandem, boon companions in arms. Montrose was a great capture for the party. He was brave, lively and popular. Lord Lorne and Sir Thomas Hope and other members of the Privy Council had intimated a certain tacit sympathy with the cause. But to confront the King's intractable obstinacy, they needed open and daring adherents, and Montrose was among the most useful. He was never one of the strategists and planners among the opposition— more cautious men brooded and talked for hours behind locked doors. But Montrose yearned to ride in the van of a crusade. The King's enemies in Scotland were very willing to accord him the honour.

On November 15th, with Hope's assurance that their proceedings were not treasonable, the dissidents met to organize themselves. It was decided that at their future gatherings, all the nobles involved, together with two lairds from each shire, two burgesses from each burgh and one minister from each presbytery were to become the arbiters of the movement. In the event these provisions were seldom carried out exactly, because the ministers swarming around Edinburgh like so many cackling crows often overran the meetings. At the November gathering, commissioners were chosen to represent each of the four estates. They became known as the Tables, and they were the beginning of the revolution that was soon to wrest power from the King in Scotland. The Earl of Montrose was one of those elected to the Tables of the lords. To all this, the Privy Council that still nominally ruled the country was unable or unwilling to offer serious opposition.

It was the wretched Traquair, as Lord Treasurer, who had to go to London to face Charles in the wake of these events. The Treasurer had always been a small-minded creature who enjoyed the petty pomp of his office, and loved dropping indiscreet (and usually inaccurate) hints at Edinburgh dinner tables to emphasize his intimacy with royal thinking in London. He possessed no obvious principles, only an urge for self-preservation, which had persuaded him to go to a relation's wedding far from Edinburgh on the day the new Liturgy was first read. That had been a betrayal for which Charles never forgave him. He was now enmeshed in matters much too deep for him. He understood all too clearly that he could expect only the anger and mistrust of both sides. He tried to escape by betraying his countrymen and his King impartially to each other. It was not a happy time for him. "I am in all these things left alone," he wrote miserably to Hamilton that autumn, "and God is my witness, never so perplexed what to do. Shall I give way to this people's fury which, without force and the strong hand, cannot be opposed?"

On his arrival in London, he found that he had briefly escaped from the fury of the dissident Scottish nobles only to face that of the King. Charles addressed himself to the situation as if he was contending with some turbulent band of Border cattle thieves, rather than one of his kingdoms arrayed against him. "We do in no way approve the same," he wrote to his Council, reprimanding their negligence, "because your course hath been more derogatory to our authority than conducive to the true quiet of the country, for we can never conceive that the country is truly quiet when regal authority is infringed."

Traquair squelched miserably back up the winter roads to Edinburgh in his coach, arriving home in February 1638 with Charles's letter and a royal proclamation condemning all the nobles who had protested against the Service Book. He was empowered to pardon them if they now immediately conformed to the King's pleasure. On February 20th, the proclamation was issued at a council meeting in Stirling from which Lord Lorne was once against absent, and which most of the bishops dared not attend for fear of their lives. The mob began their terrible baying as soon as the King's herald read the proclamation, and the despairing Council could think of nothing better to do than send for Rothes and Montrose and beg them to quell their supporters to avoid a riot. Two days later when the proclamation was read in Edinburgh, Rothes and Montrose were in the capital with their followers to hold another noisy demonstration. Young Montrose leapt on a barrel to address the crowd, and Rothes made his celebrated jest: "Jamie, ye will never be at rest till ye be lifted up there above the rest in three fathom of rope."

Historians have searched Montrose's soul to examine his

motives and his actions as one of the leaders of the great
national movement that was shortly to become an armed
rebellion. In 1638 Montrose was a young man still green in
politics, more than a little intoxicated by the great events in
which he suddenly found himself taking so great a part. Rothes
and Montrose, swords on their hips and their cluster of armed
bravos behind them, addressed the Edinburgh mob with
exuberant relish. Both had been ill-used, or thought they had,
by Charles. Montrose was full of eagerness and ambition to do
great deeds, to prove himself. The King had not made him a
member of the Scottish Privy Council, as he probably felt that
his great name demanded. Above all, looking back down the
centuries, the dissident Scots' initial grievances against their
King, and thus the stand of Montrose, seem perfectly justified.

It is hard to believe that the Graham was happy amidst
the dour cackling of the ministers, or at ease at meetings such
as that in Balmerino's lodgings late in 1637, when one of the
Kirk suddenly began to harangue the peers present about "the
reformation of their persons, and using the exercise of piety in
their families; which all took well; and promised fair".[8] But he
bore with it all, because he believed that he had found a great
cause, preserving Scotland's religion and her nobles' dignity.
Perhaps also, it is not too unkind to suggest that to an exuberant
young man of twenty-six, it was immensely satisfying to singe
the King of England's beard.

Less than a week after the Edinburgh proclamation was read,
on February 28th, 1638, the leaders of the dissident forces in
Scotland—lords, ministers, burgesses and gentlemen assembled
at Greyfriars Kirk and heard a sermon preached by Alexander
Henderson, leader of the Table of the clergy and by common
consent the wisest and most distinguished minister in the
country. They were then addressed by Loudon, from among the
lords. Finally, the whole assembly stood while Archibald
Johnston of Warriston read for the first time the National
Covenant. It was to be the manifesto and rallying cry of
Scottish presbyterianism for generations to come, and they all
raised their hands and swore to abide by it with ringing
fervour. Among the lords, Montrose was one of the first to
scratch his name on the great parchment document along with
Sutherland, Rothes, and Loudon. After the ministers and the
lairds and the burgesses had signed, for days afterwards score

upon score of the people of Scotland followed them, filing solemnly into the kirkyard to add their names or their marks. Copies circulated all over the country. In the general tumult, it became the mark of a coward or a bishops' man or a papist to refuse to sign. The Covenant's enemies sneered at the children who made their marks, and at the crude threats used to drive the doubters to add their names. But the Covenant had a vast and very real appeal for a majority of the people of Scotland. It was their only opportunity to act—to transfer the unhappiness and anger and uncertainty of many months into a personal deed, however modest. In many places, there were scenes of wild emotion as people queued to add their names. However justly the fanatics may be condemned for rousing fantastic fears and frenzies, there was a sincerity and purpose about the Covenant that cannot be denied.

The document itself seems to have been conceived by that extraordinary, haunted, driven young man Archibald Johnston of Warriston. Warriston, an advocate of twenty-seven at this time, tottered uneasily all his life between brilliance and religious mania, as his diaries frighteningly reveal. He was sometimes on his knees at prayer for twelve or fourteen hours at a stretch. His feverish brain could keep him awake for twenty-one hours out of the twenty-four. A delight in fishing was his only visibly human frailty, and even his own family found him a hard man with whom to share a roof. He seemed to respect only God, and later the Earl of Argyll, after whom he named a son. Examining the all-consuming devotion, the passion that a man like Warriston brought to the cause of the Covenant, the pale temporal ambitions and petty intrigues of men like Hamilton, who were attempting to defeat it, shrink into insignificance.

Warriston, together with Alexander Henderson and another minister named David Dickson, had searched for weeks for a formula that would enable them to focus opposition to the bishops, the prayer book and the royal reforms of the Kirk under a single heading that would win wide support. They conceived the idea of reviving a Confession of Faith that had been signed by young James VI in 1580, embracing Calvinism for Scotland. Although James had signed under duress, the document had never been formally withdrawn, and thus could not easily be labelled treasonable by his son. The National

Covenant of 1638, embodying the 1580 Confession, claimed only to demand a return to Scotland's traditional form of worship, and the end of attempts to modify it. The Covenanters, as they so quickly became known, were at pains to declare their unswerving allegiance to King Charles I.

"From the knowledge and conscience of our duty to God, to our King and country without any worldly respect or inducement," ran the last paragraph of the Covenant, "we promise and swear by the great name of the Lord our God to continue in the profession and obedience of the aforesaid religion; that we shall defend the same and resist all those contrary errors and corruptions according to our vocation, and to the utmost of that power that God hath put into our hands, all the days of our life."

Warriston celebrated the signing of the Covenant as "the great marriage day of this nation with God". For years to come, the Covenanters continued to insist that their creed in no way threatened their loyalty to the King. But in their hearts the cleverer men among them understood perfectly well that to attack the King's religious policy was to attack the King. It was an extraordinary public fiction that they sought to preserve. Even as late as 1643 when the Covenanting army entered England to support Parliament in the Civil War, its leaders proclaimed that they came to rescue "His Majesty's person and honour so unhappily entangled in the counsels of those whose actions speak their ends to be little better than popery or tyranny". Montrose was to give his life in his attempt to be both an honest Covenanter and an honest servant of his King. On the scaffold itself he reaffirmed his support for the paper he had signed that frosty February morning in Greyfriars kirkyard.

All that spring of 1638, copies of the Covenant travelled the length of Scotland, save only the western Highlands where the incorrigible clansmen cared for nothing but their cattle and their deer and their raiding. John Livingston rode to London with one copy, which he gave to the Covenanters' agent in the capital, Ebenezer Borthwick. Borthwick, who was in secret contact with many English dissident groups, circulated it among sympathetic puritans and members of parliament. It became the wonder of the hour.

The Scots understood that they were on a course that must lead to a collision with the King. Old Alexander Leslie, the

C

same who had held Stralsund against Wallenstein, was back
from the German wars with a fine reputation as a soldier, and a
nose for opportunities in his own country. It was said that he had
originally come home to test the mercenary market in London,
hearing of the possibility of a command under the King to
support the Elector Palatine in Europe. But this came to
nothing, and he rode north to see the Covenanters. From
small beginnings, he had built up fame and fortune for himself,
and he was not averse to more of either. He had several long
talks with Rothes, and then returned to the continent with copies
of the Covenant for the thousands of Scottish soldiers serving with
the Protestant armies. Leslie was a great exponent of Sir James
Turner's[9] celebrated dictum about seventeenth-century professional soldiers, believing that it did not much matter which
master a man served, so long as he served him well. Once
Leslie had taken the Covenanters' salt, he was to serve them
with all the canniness and diligence at his command.

In Edinburgh, the Committee of the Tables was beginning
to raise money for a war chest, and the lords gave generously.
Montrose contributed twenty-five dollars, and he and his
colleagues began to consider introducing compulsory taxation
to finance the rebellion. There was constant unrest, especially
in south-western Scotland. A rumour spread in Galloway that
Bishop Saintserf, father of Montrose's friend Thomas,[10] wore a
golden crucifix hidden under his gown. He was set upon and
stoned by a mob when he ventured out of doors. An Edinburgh
minister who had declined the Covenant, David Mitchel,
complained fearfully that he was followed everywhere by groups
of armed gentlemen muttering curses and threats. Most of the
bishops simply fled the country, poor old Spottiswoode among
them. He was allowed to surrender his seals and pensioned off.
A broken man overwhelmed by events so much greater than
his own spirit, he died in London the following year.

There was a stream of coaches creaking and rattling down the
London road from Edinburgh that spring. Before the snow was
off the hills, Lorne, Traquair and Roxburgh were summoned
south to explain in person to the King the actions of his
Scottish Privy Council. It seems that Lorne minced no words.
He tried to explain to Charles that this was not a matter of some
bawdy riot in the Canongate, but of a nation on the brink of
rebellion. He failed in his attempt to make Charles face the

facts, but it must have become obvious even to the King that Lorne was no ally. It has been suggested that Charles sent for him from Edinburgh because as the most powerful noble in Scotland, he was the obvious choice to become King's Commissioner to suppress the rebels. After their meeting, it was clear that Lorne was out of sympathy with Charles's entire religious policy. It was only remarkable that he had not already declared openly for the Covenanters. Self-interest may have played a part in this. Lorne's father, the Earl of Argyll, had been disinherited in favour of his son when he became a Roman Catholic and retired to live in London in 1617. But theoretically at least, the King could still reverse Lorne's inheritance in favour of his father at any time. Not until that autumn of 1638 when the old man died and Lorne succeeded at last to the Earldom, was he secure from the threat to his great possessions.

When Lorne returned to Scotland from the Court one May day that year, he was still an unknown quantity, an enigma both to King and Covenanters. He went home in the same coach as Traquair and Bishop Saintserf, with whom he had previously quarrelled violently about religion, and at a moment when most Scots lords would sooner break bread with the devil than with a bishop. All his life Lorne kept his own counsel, and he hated to show a hand unless it was called. Charles now knew Lorne was no friend, but the Campbell heir may well have allowed the King to harbour hopes that he would prove no enemy.

The visit of his Scottish councillors at least served to make Charles see at last that there was no King's party in the north on whom he might rely for a political solution to the crisis. A stronger or a weaker man would have concluded that the only recourse was to make generous concessions with the best possible grace, to attempt to salvage something from a hopeless situation. A more realistic man, still bent on having his own way, would critically have examined the means at his disposal to accomplish it. But Charles drove relentlessly onwards along his intended course without thought of compromise or regard for difficulties. Privately, he resolved that war was the only means of breaking the Covenanters to his lawful authority. He proposed to use one of his kingdoms—and much the greater, at that—to bend the other to his will. He did not trouble

himself about the unrest in England concerning Ship Money,
concerning the puritans, concerning the further shores of royal
authority and the pressing demands for a parliament. As King,
he proposed to command the raising of an army. Because he
was King, he assumed that it would be done.

But he needed time, and he wanted the intractability of the
Scottish rebels thoroughly to be understood throughout his
kingdoms. Negotiations must be seen to continue until every
possibility had been exhausted. It was known that the Scots
were making preparations of their own for war. It would also
be very helpful if they could somehow be lulled into abandoning
them.

Charles's chosen instrument for this delicate task was James,
Marquis of Hamilton. Even Laud, who had scarcely been
cautious about Scottish affairs, baulked when he heard of the
appointment. But early in May 1638, it was announced that
Hamilton was to be the King's Commissioner in the north,
charged publicly with the pursuit of a compromise settlement,
and privately with restraining the rebels until the cannon were
ready for them. "I give you leave to flatter them with what
hopes you please," Charles told him, ". . . till I be ready to
suppress them. . . . I will rather die than yield to these imperti-
nent and damnable demands."

Hamilton displayed astonishing modesty in the face of
Charles's summons to take his Commission. He begged the
King for a promise that whatever happened would not be held
against him. Much more than Charles, he saw the strength of
the forces arrayed against him, and knew the worm in the
shaft of the spear which the King proposed to hurl upon the
Scots. But he was the King's man, and he did as he was told.
He had the widest latitude. Promises cost nothing when Charles
had no intention of keeping them. The Prayer Book was to
remain withdrawn. Hamilton could do anything he liked to
change the make-up of the Privy Council. He could bribe
whoever he wanted, use force against rioters, and—this with
most sincerity—threaten dire consequences if agreement was
not reached: "You shall declare that if there be not sufficient
strength within the Kingdom to force the refractory to
obedience, power shall come from England, and that myself
will come in person with them, being resolved to hazard my
life rather than to suffer authority to be contemned," declared

the King solemnly. Only one point was Hamilton required to gain from the enemy: that the National Covenant be utterly repudiated.

If there was no King's party in Scotland upon which to found a restoration of royal authority, then one must be created. As Hamilton prepared to journey north, delayed by the death of his not-much-regretted wife, he rounded up every Scottish lord who could be found skulking in the royal palaces. Morton, Linlithgow, Kellie, Mar, Kinnoul, Haddington and Almond (most of them to be found faithless) were dispatched unwillingly northwards to rouse their tenants and friends and to form the core of a royal faction. Hamilton proposed to arrive in Scotland in suitable style, and ordered all his friends and vassals and those thought to be of the King's party to meet him at Haddington and ride with him to Dalkeith. It was a fine prospect. But Warriston circulated his own note to the gentlemen in question, decreeing flatly that "such noblemen as are not joined in Covenant with us, whether they favour our cause or not, are not to be attending at this time". He was obeyed. It was the Covenanters who received Hamilton with intimidating ceremony. On June 6th, he arrived at Dalkeith, a town notorious as "a veritable nest of warlocks and witches", and presented his Commission. He then rode on to Edinburgh. A vast crowd of 20,000 people awaited him, six hundred clergy among them in their black cloaks, "the gentry standing all in ranks along the seaside till very near the end of the sands". It was, as its organizers intended, a formidable demonstration of the forces arrayed against the King.

Hamilton came to Scotland armed with two alternative drafts of a royal proclamation. One of these demanded the surrender of all copies of the Covenant, the other, more vaguely, called for a testimony of obedience from the dissidents. Common to each was the King's instruction that anyone who raised his voice in protest against it should be arrested. Hamilton had scarcely unpacked his trunks in Holyrood before it became clear that there was going to be trouble, whichever version was published. And if he tried to arrest the protesters, he would precipitate some sort of immediate uprising. There was no longer a vestige of hope of avoiding war if Charles was to get his way. Hamilton's only function was to keep the ball in play until the King was ready. Charles urged him to try to secure

Edinburgh and Stirling castles, but the Covenanters were
watching the royalists closely to prevent just such a coup.
Pointless, tortuous negotiations dragged on until the beginning
of July, when Hamilton announced that he was going to London
for consultations with the King. It was the customary politician's
device for gaining time. But he was hardly on the road before
new orders from Charles arrived by messenger to halt him.
He was instructed immediately to issue a new proclamation.

The King's latest wishes were proclaimed to the people on
July 4th. He avowed his willingness to summon a General
Assembly of the Kirk and a Scottish Parliament. He announced
that he would continue the suspension of the Book of Canons
and of the Service Book. But on June 30th, instructions had
already gone out to muster the trained bands of the six northern
English counties. On July 1st, Charles had for the first time
formally addressed his English Privy Council about his
intention to suppress the Scottish rebellion by force. To those
in Edinburgh who had already heard the rumours of all these
things, his new proclamation hardly sounded convincing. It
was met by an immediate, wildly applauded public protest
read by Warriston. The Scottish Privy Council, who with the
notable exceptions of Lorne and Southesk had grudgingly
approved the Proclamation before it was delivered, now
insisted on withdrawing their assent after an angry row with
Hamilton. And after the formal, harsh exchanges between the
King's Commissioner and his Council, Hamilton further
confused the situation by taking some of the Covenanting
leaders privately aside to assure them "as a kindly Scotsman,
if you go on with courage and resolution you will carry what
you please; but if you faint or give ground in the least you are
undone. A word is enough to wise men."

It was an extraordinary, clumsy intervention, which did no
more than deepen the Scots' mistrust of Hamilton. It was yet
another of his machiavellian strokes which miscarried. The
advantage of using small men as royal servants was that they
owed everything to the King. Hamilton, however, was periodi-
cally racked by consciousness that he was a Scottish landowner
with huge interests to protect. Like many weak men, he
imagined that it was possible to be liked by most of the people
most of the time if he exerted his charm upon them all
impartially. Throughout the next decade, he was to work

half-heartedly for the King while struggling whole-heartedly to save his own affairs. He could never admit, perhaps not even to himself, that this created an irreconcilable conflict of interests. His discreet flirtation with the opposition at Holyrood that July merely caused men to look at each other in puzzlement and shrug wearily at the Marquis's latest extravagance.

That summer, as Hamilton skipped to and fro between London and Edinburgh with an increasingly irrelevant stream of proposals and counter-proposals, it seemed to most men wiser to assess the situation by what was being done rather than by what was being said. While the talking continued, both sides were arming, the Covenanters with evidently greater skill and success. They could draw upon the countless Scots officers who had served in the Protestant armies in Europe, the veterans of Lumsden's and Ramsey's and Reay's regiments, men who had fought at Breitenfeld and learnt the new ways of waging great wars for years on end under the greatest captains alive. Lists were being drawn up of those "that has been abroad and is able to do any service in wars". Warning beacons were built to signal a royal invasion, and shiploads of arms were landed despite all that Charles's beloved navy could do to stop them.

The King and his Court lived in a fairytale world, untroubled by any inkling that the troubles that beset them might prove fatal. Almost to the last day of the Civil War Charles and his advisers flew on wings of insane optimism. That summer of 1638, it was a fashionable supper table game around the Court to plan the master strategy for crushing the Scots rebels. Huntly and the Gordons in the north would form one prong of the assault. The navy would blockade the coasts. The King's army would march up from the south. And after all the earnest pleas and promises of the irresistibly amusing Lord Antrim, his Irishmen could descend upon the west. Antrim was a stage Irishman, reared at Charles's court with no money, no brains, and a limitless supply of charm and vain promises. He had married the blowsy, ageing widow of the Duke of Buckingham. As chief of the Macdonalds of Antrim, the Catholic clan closely linked to the Macdonalds of northwest Scotland, he liked to count his swordsmen as if he was Lord Lorne himself. His Macdonalds had some claim to the Scottish west coast lands of Kintyre and Islay, but early in the century the Campbells had dispossessed them. Charles now seems to have made some suggestion to Antrim (who of course rushed all over London talking about it) that his Macdonalds could look to own Kintyre again if they helped in the war against the Scots rebels.

That brutal realist Wentworth was exasperated by the whole scheme. He had enough trouble keeping the peace in Ireland without giving the wild Macdonalds a warrant for making war on any pretext. Anyway, Antrim had no means of raising a real army: "He is as well able to do it as I to take upon me the Cross with so many for the Holy Land." Wentworth's fears were confirmed in every respect. Antrim's schemes struck frightening sparks on the tinder of civil war in Ireland, while his forces for the Scots war never materialized. Lord Lorne, however, was not unreasonably infuriated by the threat to his possessions. That summer, his men were arming and drilling as keenly as any in Scotland. Covenanter or no Covenanter, he would tolerate no invasion of Campbell lands by the King or the Macdonalds.

The King's schemes flickered feebly between tragedy and farce. Despising firearms, Arundel, the creaking old Earl Marshal, was recommending arming the Borderers with bows and spears. The Northern levies were mustering reluctantly, a rabble without officers to train them or gentlemen to lead them who felt any enthusiasm for the war. Only the Catholics were proving diligent in the King's service, by doing so damning the King's cause in the eyes of many Protestant Englishmen. The Court rang with fantastical suggestions. Sir William Monson recommended fortifying a line from Glasgow to Stirling, incorporating everything south of it in England, and abandoning everything northwards as "not fit for civil men to live". Charles proposed to spend £200,000 on the war, but his exchequer was empty. It is much more dangerous for a King to be laughed at than to be hated, and that summer there was much laughter among Charles's enemies in London, as his expedition into Scotland appeared more and more akin to one of the wilder jousts of Don Quixote.

In the north, meanwhile, the Covenanters had much cause for satisfaction. The greater part of Scotland was under their uncontested control. Their army was mustering rapidly. The Scottish people's enthusiasm and unity contrasted marvellously with the sullen indifference of the King's followers in England.

The Tables were disturbed by only one irritating, potentially serious threat: the intractability of the Gordon country, and the city of Aberdeen. The chief of Clan Gordon, the Marquis of Huntly, remained an unbending royalist and a doubtful Protestant, for all his moodiness and melancholy and bankruptcy. Colonel Robert Monro, a distinguished professional soldier high in the confidence of the Tables, arrived at the Marquis's door one morning bearing a copy of the Covenant for his signature. Huntly bore down on him with the massive dignity and haughty contempt of all his line: "My house has risen by the Kings of Scotland," he declared solemnly. "It has ever stood for them, and with them shall fall. Nor will I quit the path of my predecessors. And if the event be the ruin of my Sovereign, then shall the rubbish of his house bury beneath it all that belong to mine."

The doctors of Aberdeen's famous colleges remained obstinate in their support of the bishops and of the Articles of Perth. The town seemed embarrassed and disturbed by the rebellious doings in the Lowlands, and wanted no part of them. But Aberdeen was too important to be allowed to remain hostile or even neutral. Late in July, a small but influential delegation of Covenanting leaders was dispatched northwards in a new effort to make the Aberdonians repent of their ways. It was led by Montrose.

All through this long and complicated period of religious and political struggle, before the lines were at last drawn and the Civil War began, Montrose was one among many actors upon the Scottish stage. It is important for a biographer to keep this perspective, not to paint too boldly minor episodes merely because they provide a stage for Montrose. It is not yet his moment to step forth from the crowd, to tower over the fortunes of his country as he is later to do. The delegation to Aberdeen in July 1638 was not a central episode in the developing revolution. It is simply interesting to see Montrose used by the Covenanting party as a popular spokesman, to sing their song. His charm and his eloquence were already well-known. When the Tables wanted to impress Aberdeen, Montrose's warm wit and transparent honesty were an ideal leavening for the ministers' sermonizing.

He had probably attended the meeting of the nobles and gentlemen of his district to discuss preparations for war, held at Perth on July 17th. On the 20th accompanied by Lord Coupar and three of the most distinguished of the ministers—Henderson, Andrew Cant and David Dickson—he rode into Aberdeen.

The capital of the North-East was a fine town of high, stone houses, the usual forestairs reaching up from the cobbled streets to the upper stories, wooden galleries rising above them. Behind the larger mansions stood the generous gardens and orchards that made the city look so green and gentle to a traveller first seeing it from a distance. Aberdeen had a fine reputation for learning, and even boasted a language school offering French lessons. The city had strong links with France, and a flourishing salmon export trade.

Rothes had given Montrose a letter to his cousin the Provost, Patrick Leslie: "Do ye all the good ye can in that town, and in the country about—ye will not repent it—and attend my lord Montrose, who is a noble and true-hearted cavalier."

The Council of Aberdeen were perfectly willing to be civil to the young lord whom they had made a burgess nine years before. They had prepared a banquet for Montrose and his party. But when the Covenanting delegation arrived and brusquely spurned their hospitality, demanding only that their ministers should be granted access to the pulpits the following day, Sunday, the atmosphere chilled rapidly. All the food laid out for the banquet was swept angrily away to the poor of the city, who fell upon it with bewildered delight. And the ministers were denied their pulpits.

Unabashed, the party moved into the home of the Earl Marischal in the new town, where his sister Lady Pitsligo was living. The Marischal family, who were always to be good Covenanters, had been broken to the will of the Kirk a generation back. The splendid sinner who then held the title for years defied the ministers with dazzling impudence. Charged with fornication in 1609, he replied cheerfully that if he had known of the accusation, he would have asked for fifty other offences to be taken into account. For years Marischal jeered at and abused the ministers, emptying his pistol into the Kirk door during service and hounding them mercilessly. But in the end, like so many others, he bowed to them. He did public repentance for his sins, and now his family provided the Covenant's headquarters in Aberdeen.

After morning service that Sunday, Henderson stepped out onto the gallery of the Marischal house, and used it as his pulpit to address the people of Aberdeen now streaming out of their kirks. After he had preached his sermon, Dickson and Cant followed him in turn. They were heard in apathetic silence broken by an occasional jeer. Still, by managing to speak at all they had saved some face in an embarrassing situation.

They came away from Aberdeen after touring the surrounding villages. They had gained a few dozen signatures to the Covenant only after adding qualifying clauses to appease Aberdonian scruples: "That we neither have nor had any intention but of loyalty to his Majesty, as the Covenant bears," and a note to concede that the Articles of Perth and the episcopacy were not unlawful. The fact that Henderson and Dickson were willing to allow signatures to be collected on such terms is an indication of the straits to which they were reduced. The Aberdeen expedition was a failure, and the resistance of north-east Scotland to the Covenant continued to be a powerful irritant to the Tables.

On September 22nd, 1638, a new royal proclamation was read at the Mercat Cross in Edinburgh, embodying Charles's latest thrust at the Covenant. The long-demanded General Assembly of the Kirk was to be held in Glasgow two months thence, on November 21st, and a Scottish Parliament was to meet the following May. Apparently on advice from Hamilton, Traquair, Roxburgh and Southesk, the King had also devised a scheme for a royal Covenant all of his own. A document was to be circulated in his name, embodying the 1580 "Negative Confession" on which the Covenant was based, together with a new anti-Catholic clause of the King's making. The Negative Confession—or Anti-Covenant as the Covenanters were quick to dub it—was a royal attempt to seize the ground on which his enemies had entrenched themselves, to convince the people of Scotland that their cause was also his. The Anti-Covenant deeply distressed Charles, who of course believed no part of it, but Hamilton and the others convinced him that there was now no prospect of going to war until the following year, and that something must be done to gain time.

The document was in fact an embarrassing failure. 12,000 of the 28,000 signatures collected came from the Gordon country.

Lord Huntly rode into Aberdeen one day with his sons and his retinue behind him to call on the city to show its loyalty, and to undo the effects of the mischief-making Montrose's visit. But some ardent royalists refused to sign because they believed that the Negative Confession compromised royalism, and the Convenanters themselves gleefully interpreted the Anti-Covenant as a sign of royal assent to the abolition of the episcopate. Rothes, Warriston and the others had initially been disconcerted by the apparent generosity of the new terms the King was offering. But royal credit by now stood so low that no proclamation could redeem it. The excitement about the Negative Confession died away, and men focused their attention on the coming great Assembly in Glasgow.

James VI had successfully used General Assemblies as a means of working his will upon Scotland, packing them with his own chosen representatives. Charles for a brief moment entertained hopes that he might be able to do likewise. At first it seemed that the bishops would be able to take their seats in Glasgow, that they might even be able to dominate the Assembly. But the Covenanters had little difficulty in preventing this. A letter to Warriston "from your own whom you knowe G" reveals the ruthlessness of their tactics. It had been suggested that old Spottiswoode might be dragged northwards again to sit in the Assembly, and "G" discussed the preparations being made to deal with him—"how he might be entertained in such places as he should come unto". It was "altogether inconvenient that he, or any of that kind, should show themselves in public". Similar plans were afoot for the Bishop of Brechin, and Warriston was recommended to see that "in a private way, some course may be taken for his terror and disgrace if he offer to show himself publicly".

Yet to the Scots and the English alike, the outcome of the Assembly as a trial of strength with the King was by no means pre-ordained as it later came to appear. Glasgow had been chosen as the rendezvous because it lay in the heart of Hamilton country, and the King hoped that his Commissioner's local influence could be powerfully brought to bear. Many key figures in Scottish politics including Lorne—who now succeeded to his father's title and became Earl of Argyll—were as yet undeclared, and had not signed the Covenant. It was generally agreed that the Assembly would be a critical test of the King's power. Many feared that it would prove the undoing of the Covenant.

But as the leaders of Scotland assembled in Glasgow, the Covenanters' overwhelming dominance became apparent. They jammed every inn in the city, defying royal commands by surrounding themselves with "great bands and troops of men . . . with guns and pistols". The Covenanting nobles took their seats in the Cathedral, where the Assembly met, as elders of their respective presbyteries. Montrose sat for Auchterarder, his home parish. There were 98 laymen and 142 ministers in all, in addition to the Privy Council (less Sir Thomas Hope who had been forbidden by Hamilton to attend), and the Marquis himself. Alexander Henderson was elected Moderator and Warriston Clerk, despite Hamilton's protests and his demands for procedures more congenial to the royal cause. He must already have begun bitterly to regret that this fearsome body, the power of Scotland apparently united against the King's wishes, should ever have been permitted to assemble under one roof. The opposition had clenched the bit firmly between their teeth. Now they bent to gallop far and hard from the path of loyal subjects of King Charles.

The first session of the Assembly provided a sharp insight into the temper of Montrose at this time. Hamilton questioned the commissions of many of the lay elders present, including that of Erskine of Dun, who sat for Brechin. Montrose's own brother-in-law, Lord Carnegie, had originally been nominated by Brechin presbytery. It now emerged that he had been displaced by special command of the Tables, apparently on Montrose's personal orders. It was an act of astonishing bitterness against his wife's family, yet in the Assembly he defended it hotly against his father-in-law Southesk, and even against David Dickson, who expressed his own misgivings about what Montrose had done. "The contest betwixt Montrose and Southesk grew so hot that it terrified the whole Assembly," wrote Gordon of Rothiemay, "so that the Commissioner took upon him the Moderator's place, and commanded them all to peace."

It was an impetuous, intemperate performance by Montrose, and the Assembly seems to have found it tiresome. Some of the calmer spirits in Scotland, men who were still agonizing deeply about the justice of their revolt and how far it might be carried, found Montrose's youthful certainty and brashness very trying. He wanted to stand in the stirrups on his white horse and raise his lance against the powers of darkness, whoever he conceived these to be. He was popular for his gaiety and wit and charm. But in November 1638, he was still dancing very lightly upon the devil's table. There was "none more vainly foolish than Montrose", wrote Hamilton crossly to the King as he described the antics of the Assembly. It was the verdict of a man pretty vainly foolish himself, but it was not unfair.

On November 28th, 1638, seeing that the Assembly was bent only on the destruction of episcopacy and was wholly out of his control, Hamilton declared it discharged "under pain of treason", improperly elected and unconstitutional. Then followed one of the decisive moments in the reign of Charles I, to rank with the King's attempt in England to seize the Five Members. The Earl of Argyll rose to his feet. He was not a member of the Assembly, indeed he had not signed the Covenant. But he was the greatest man in Scotland. "I have not striven to blow the bellows," he said, "but studied to keep matters in as soft a temper as I could. And I now desire to make it known to you that I take you all for members of a lawful Assembly and my honest countrymen."

Hamilton ordered Henderson to dissolve the gathering, but the members bawled at him to do no such thing. Hamilton rose to his feet and stalked angrily to the door, seeking by his departure to remove the King's authority from the Assembly. To his fury he found the entrances locked, and he had to stand fuming while his men smashed them open. Then he escaped, with the thunder of the Covenanting preachers' appeals to the Lord echoing down the nave behind him. The Assembly was left thrilling with that exhilaration, partly made of fear, that comes to men who know that a turning point has been passed.

Hamilton retired to Glasgow Castle, and as his men began to pack his trunks, he called the Privy Council to him. Contemptibly, he asked them for a testimonial certifying that he had done all that was possible for the King's service. Argyll and Hope did not attend the meeting, nor did they endorse the proclamation ordering the Assembly to disperse. Instead, Argyll sat on with that gathering for the three heady weeks that followed. They abolished bishops and the Five Articles. They established a commission to examine abuses and excommunication. They disposed of all the hated ceremonies and rituals. Only a handful of members obeyed Hamilton's order to go home. None of them heeded his later Proclamation annulling every act of the Assembly. He was impotent, and Scotland understood it well.

He reported gloomily and self-pityingly to Charles: "So unfortunate have I been in this unlucky world," he wrote, "that though I did prefer your service before all worldly considerations, nay, even strained my conscience in some points, by subscribing the Negative Confession; yet all hath been to small purpose; for I have missed my end in not being able to make Your Majesty so considerable a party as will be able to curb the insolency of this rebellious nation, without assistance from England, and greater charge to your Majesty, than this miserable country is worth."

Before he left Glasgow, Hamilton spoke privately and apparently amicably with the Earl of Argyll: it was yet another of his grotesque little parleys aimed at preserving his personal position, whatever ruin befell his King or his country. It was the characteristic act of a weak man to seek private conciliation with a powerful man with whom he had been unable to avoid differing publicly. Hamilton had endured months of personal loneliness as the King's Commissioner in Scotland, bitterly conscious that almost every man who came to sit at his table was an enemy of his purpose. It was now evident that the King's dispute with his Scottish subjects must advance at push of pike or not at all. As soon as Christmas was over, Hamilton packed up the King's tapestries and plate in Holyrood and dispatched them southwards. He himself followed quickly behind. He left Traquair to rule Scotland in the King's name. In reality, as the whole country and Hamilton himself perfectly understood, the kingdom was now entirely in the hands of the Tables, the Covenanters, and the Earl of Argyll.

# CHAPTER THREE

## *Apprentice in Arms*

NOW THAT IT was to be war, the wilder spirits of the Covenant yearned for the struggle to start in earnest. While Charles's lumbering army gathered in England amidst scenes of unrivalled muddle and incompetence, in the north the first brushes and scrambles began, and with them the career of Montrose in arms.

February 1st, 1639, found him at Forfar in Angus "stenting" or assessing the landlords of the shire for taxes on the orders of the Tables, and demanding signatures to the latest version of the Covenant that unequivocally abolished the episcopate. He had ridden into the town along with Lord Kinghorn, Lyon of Auldbar and a group of others to set up his tribunal in the Tolbooth. But he quickly discovered opposition to his presumption.

Montrose's father-in-law Lord Southesk marched in on the proceedings with the Master of Ogilvy, the Constable of Dundee, the Master of Spynie and other royalists at his back. "By what authority," he demanded angrily, "were they thus stenting the King's lieges? Montrose . . . answered that their warrant was from the Tables, requiring him also, and the rest that were there, to number their men, and have them well armed, and in readiness to concur and assist the Table. Southesk answered, they were all the King's men, subject to his service, but to no Table nor subject sitting thereat, and that their lands were not subject to be stented, nor their men numbered, but at the King's command in his service. And so they took their departure, leaving Montrose and the rest sitting still in the tollbooth of Forfar at their committee."[1]

Several north-eastern magnates who were doubtful about the justice of the King's cause, or for that matter of the Covenant's, were enraged to be ridden roughshod over within their own marches by young hotheads who were seeking to stir up the country. Montrose and a group of Covenanting lords including the Master of Forbes, Lord Fraser and Crichton of Frendraught had arranged to meet again at Turriff to discuss plans on February 14th. The royalists decided that they had had enough. Sir George Ogilvy of Banff, the most active of them, persuaded the Marquis of Huntly, whose castle of Strathbogie lay only a few miles from the Turriff rendezvous, that these incursions were an intolerable insult to his dignity in the midst of his own country. As the greatest lord in northern Scotland, Huntly summoned all the men at his command to ride to Turriff on February 14th.

But Montrose was before him. Hearing of Huntly's plan, he gathered every man he could raise, and rode hell for leather through the Grampian passes with 200 horse. At Turriff, 600 more came in to meet him. At dawn on February 14th "eight hundred well horsed, well armed gentlemen, and foot, together with buff coats, swords, corselets, jacks, pistols, carbines, hagbuts, and other weapons—they took into the town of Turriff, and busked very advantageously their muskets round about the dykes of the kirkyard, and sat within the kirk thereof, such as were of the committee, viz Montrose, Kinghorn, Cooper, Frazer and Forbes".[2]

Montrose's men were hardly deployed when Huntly, with 2500 men at his back, rode up to Turriff. His sons Lord Gordon and Lord Aboyne, together with most of his lairds, at once urged him to join battle and crush the rebels where they stood in the churchyard. Instead, with his usual hesitancy, Huntly sent Lord Finlater in to parley. Finlater emerged to report that Montrose was graciously offering the Marquis and his men liberty to go wherever they liked in Turriff as long as they did not interfere with the Covenanting Committee. To the disgust of most of his force, Huntly announced that his instructions from Hamilton specified that he was not to fight. Wheeling their horses, the column rode smarting away under the guns of Montrose's men, leaving the Covenanters holding the field. Montrose had won his first, bloodless victory.

George Gordon, Marquis of Huntly, was destined all his life to be a broken reed in the King's service. In the years to come it was Montrose who would have most cause to regret it. Huntly's strong sense of royalism was utterly set at naught by his lack of the will and the intelligence to pursue it. Moody, melancholic, he was hopelessly bankrupt and heavily mortgaged to Argyll, whose sister he had married on the wishes of James VI. Much of his life had been spent abroad as Captain of Louis XIII's Scots Guard in France, yet he was no soldier, and had no notion of how to command loyalty. "Old servants for whom there was no use must be brushed or rubbed off as spots from clothes," wrote Gordon of Ruthven,[3] a friendly witness who nevertheless could not ignore the Marquis's glaring failings. "He seemed desirous to keep a distance with his inferiors, without distinction of quality. For friends and followers were equalled with domestics and common observance unless his affairs required it, and then he could be both familiar and obsequious. He never spoke a wrong word, nor intended an action that succeeded right."

He was no coward, or else he would never have sent such defiant answers to the Covenanters and such loyal ones to his King. Yet he was certainly no hero, or he would not later have skulked for so long in Strathnaver when the King's fortunes hung in the balance. He was an honourable, stupid man of obsessive pride. He suffered from the common failing of disliking to have cleverer or more popular men around him, and he shunned them when they approached him. The best thing about him was his progeny. His eldest sons Lord Gordon and Lord Aboyne had the flair, courage, and warmth that their father lacked, even if they suffered from the ancestral Gordon wildness. Much will be seen of all their qualities later in this tale. Unfortunately, they did not have command of the clan and its claymores. They lacked the absolute powers of their father as clan chief. If the King's affairs were to flourish in the north, Huntly could at least have delegated his authority to his sons or to men of sense, even if he had none himself. But this he would never do. As a result he was the worst possible representative of the King at the crisis of his affairs.

After the encounter at Turriff, Huntly spent the following month at Aberdeen with the force of more than 2000 men that he had gathered around himself. Initially, he expected men and arms to arrive from the King, to support his army as the northern prong of the royal assault upon the Covenanters. But Hamilton seems to have instructed Huntly to do nothing until the King himself marched up to the Border, and to expect no reinforcements for some time to come. He was at his old

game of interposing himself between the King and any possible
rival for the royal ear. He seems to have dealt very coolly with
Huntly, a sensitive plant at the best of times. Characteristically
at the end of it all the King's Lieutenant in the North threw up
his elegant hands in cross bewilderment, and ignoring the
protests of his sons and many of his followers, he withdrew to his
castle of Strathbogie to sit passive while the Covenanters made
their moves.

They were quick enough to do so. Alexander Leslie, back
from Germany once more with his experience at the disposal of
the Covenant, rushed Edinburgh Castle with a force of picked
musketeers. Dumbarton in the west was seized, and on March
21st Traquair was summoned to yield Dalkeith, where he sat
upon a huge arsenal and the Scottish crown jewels. He refused
to hand over the keys, but made no serious resistance when the
Covenanters forced an entry. He fled south to the royal army,
and was at once put under arrest by the furious Charles for his
negligence and treachery. Meanwhile in the west again,
Argyll's men had been busy. With Cameron help they laid
waste the Huntly lands in Badenoch, and strongly garrisoned
Kintyre, where Antrim's vaunted Irish invasion was supposed
to take place. With Dumbarton and Kintyre held for the
Covenant, the western arm of the King's strategic fantasy had
ceased to exist before it ever came to be. It only remained to
sever the eastern one at Aberdeen.

Montrose probably had to plead for command of the
expeditionary force against the Huntly country. He had
never ridden with a sizeable army. He knew nothing of war
beyond what he had read and learnt at Angers. But he had the
habit of commanding a great semi-feudal household, which
instilled the qualities of command in any seventeenth-century
nobleman if he had the right instincts. His ride to Turriff had
shown that he had the reflexes of a general, and his strong
connections in the north-east and knowledge of the area
would stand him in good stead. The Tables made him General,
but they sent Alexander Leslie to ride with him.

Montrose must have deferred to Leslie as the veteran
organizer of armies and teacher of their ways, a little as a
modern subaltern takes many of his cues from his platoon
sergeant. It must have been Leslie who ordered the camps
when they halted at nightfall, who proposed the order of

regiments and dictated the pace as they marched up Deeside more than three thousand strong. The old man never showed a feather of that genius for ordering a battle which was to mark Montrose as one of the great captains of the age, but he understood perfectly the habits and necessities of war, and he was exceptionally tactful in steering mettlesome young peers away from rash disaster: "We were feared," wrote Baillie[4] a few weeks later, "that emulation among our nobles might have done harm when they should be met in the field. But such was the wisdom of that old, little crooked soldier that all, with an incredible submission to the end, gave over themselves to be guided by him, as if he had been great Solomon . . . that was the man's understanding of our Scots humours that gave out, not only to the nobles, but to very mean gentlemen, his directions in a very homely way and simple form, as if they had been but the advices of their neighbours and companions."

With fourteen guns being dragged in the Covenanting train, Aberdeen had little chance of resisting. The royalists abandoned the trenches they had been digging, and made for the harbour or the hills. On March 28th, the doctors from the colleges, and such royalist lairds as had not retired to Strathbogie with Huntly, put to sea to join the King. Messengers from Huntly to Montrose made a feeble attempt to arrange an agreement, as between nobleman and nobleman, that neither would enter the other's territory. But that sort of arrangement, so convenient in feudal war, hardly answered in a national rebellion. On March 30th, Montrose and Leslie entered the Over-Kirkgateport of Aberdeen in the easy humour of men who have gained a bloodless triumph. A troop of Covenanting nobles rode with them—Kinghorn, Elcho, Frazer, the Master of Forbes—even Carnegie, Montrose's brother-in-law whom he had sought so hard to embarrass at the Glasgow Assembly. Almost every man in the army was wearing a blue ribbon or scarf that Montrose had gaily ordered them to adopt in defiance of the red Huntly favour: "This was Montrose's whimsy. To these ribbons, ordinarily, the cavalry did append their spanners for their firelocks, and the foot had them stuck up in bunches in their blue caps; which device seemed so plausible that when the army marched towards the Border some short time afterwards, many of the gentry threw away their hats, and would carry nothing but bonnets, and bunches of blue ribbons, or pannashes, therein, despite the English who disdainfully called them blue caps and jockies".[5]

The army marched through the city and then "muster being made, all men were commanded by sound of trumpet, in General Montrose's name, to go to breakfast, either in the links or in the town. The general himself, the nobles, captains and commanders, for the most part, sat down on the links; and, of their own provision, with a servit on their knee, took breakfast".[6]

It seems certain that before the northern expedition set out, it had been decided that the force could only be spared for a few weeks to deal with Huntly, and that thereafter Leslie and most of the men must march south against the King. The day that the Covenanters marched into Aberdeen, Charles rode into York to review his gathering army. Before the King came upon them, the Scots knew that they must remove the threat of Huntly by one means or another. As soon as they had picnicked on the golf course at Aberdeen, Montrose and his staff inspected their troops. Then the young general sent for the city magistrates and ordered them to dismantle such fortifications as had been set up. He also warned them to deal kindly with his men—there was soon to be trouble with defiant royalists who provoked them by turning their dogs loose in the streets wearing the blue ribbon. After the formalities, Montrose lingered only to appoint Kinghorn Governor and tell off 1500 men to remain behind as a garrison. Then he set off with the remainder of his forces to look for Huntly. That night, they camped at Inverury, ten miles north of the city.

Montrose and Leslie's difficulty in dealing with the moody Marquis was that while he had dissolved his clan army before their arrival, and thus could not be brought to any immediate trial of strength, he could equally rapidly summon it to muster again after they had departed. The only guarantee of the Covenanters' northern rear remaining secure was for Huntly himself to be in their hands.

The Marquis seems to have been anxious enough to reach some agreement with Montrose. Having now shut himself up in his castle at Bog of Gight, he was faced with the spectacle of the large Covenanting army living at free quarter around Inverury, laying waste such little as was left of his substance.

Gordon of Straloch was sent to Montrose to discover whether he was willing to negotiate. A parley was arranged to take place a few days later at a safe distance from the Covenanting camp. At the appointed hour, Montrose rode up with Elcho, Couper and nine of their men, while Huntly was flanked by his son Aboyne, Lord Oliphant, and his own escort of nine. It was a tense, guarded encounter. After they had dismounted, a gentleman from each party searched his opponents for hidden arms. Then, while the others watched uncertainly, Montrose and Huntly drew apart alone and held a long conversation. It ended, to the amazement of the spectators, with the Marquis and his men falling in beside Montrose to ride to Inverury. There, Huntly signed a heavily qualified and vaguely-worded version of the Covenant, binding him "to maintain the King's authority, together with the liberties both of Church and State, Religion and Laws". It was also agreed that the many Catholics among the Gordons should be exempted from signing, if they respected the laws and liberties of the country. Huntly and his party rode away tolerably content, while Montrose must have believed that he had gained a diplomatic triumph of the first importance. He anyway regarded the agreement as significant enough to break camp at Inverury and return to Aberdeen.

On April 9th, Murray, Seaforth, the Master of Lovat and a large party of Covenanting nobles arrived in Aberdeen. There was a long discussion among all the leaders of the party in the city about what to do next. Time was pressing for Leslie and the army to march south. Charles was readying himself to move on the Border, and Leslie had his Commission as Commander-in-chief to take up, much to Montrose's jealousy, according to his enemies. Huntly was a difficult, changeable creature, widely disliked for personal as well as for political reasons in north-east Scotland. To tough, cynical men with their lives and lands at stake, Montrose's assurance that he had Huntly's word as a gentleman to remain neutral seemed very frail. Even the Marquis himself was obviously conscious of the likelihood of further trouble. He heard how many of his personal enemies were in camp with the Covenanters. He sent Gordon of Straloch to warn Montrose before he even left Inverury that to take him prisoner would provoke an immediate rising of the Gordons. Montrose, embarrassed, answered that "there is this difficulty, that business here is all transacted by vote and a committee, nor can I get anything done of myself".

It remains a lasting slur upon Montrose that when his colleagues brought pressure upon him, he sent word to Huntly to come to the camp under safe conduct. When the Marquis arrived, he was at once asked to accept new terms, and even to contribute to the Covenant war chest. Not unexpectedly, he declined. He was then invited to ride south with the Covenanting army. As a prisoner or as a free man? he asked. He was told that he had the choice. He declared that he would go voluntarily. He only requested that his son Aboyne might be allowed to go home to fetch him some clothes and money. Permission was given, and the young man left his father and elder brother in Aberdeen while he rode away to Strathbogie.

Back in his own Gordon country, he found consternation at the news of his father's seizure. Ogilvy of Banff, who often seems to have taken the initiative in spurring the Huntly family into action, insisted that Aboyne must on no account return to the Covenanting camp. He was the only adult son still at liberty—Lord Lewis was scarcely thirteen and the others even younger. After some deliberation, they decided that Banff himself would do what he could to mend the royalist fortunes around Aberdeen, while Aboyne went south, to the King's camp at Newcastle. With Charles's help, the Gordons might find the means to answer the Covenanters who had betrayed their chief, in the only way they would understand—down the muzzle of a cannon.

Around April 19th, Montrose and his army marched away southwards with Huntly and his eldest son Lord Gordon. The Marquis was locked up in Edinburgh Castle as soon as they reached the capital, proclaiming with his usual irrelevant courage that "they could take my head from my shoulders, but not my heart from my Sovereign". The great historian, Gardiner, has denounced the Huntly episode as "the only mean action" in Montrose's life, and indeed it is difficult to regard it honourably. If he knew that he lacked the power to guarantee Huntly's safe conduct, he should never have put his hand to it. But it must be said that this is to judge Montrose by the very high standards that he set himself, rather than by those of his age. The muddy episode of Huntly glares only because it was extraordinary in a life otherwise so utterly honourable.

Montrose was exceptional in a society which paid very little heed to loyalty or principle. Treachery or enlightened self-interest was a way of life to most Scottish lords. Many of them were to change sides two or three times during the Civil Wars. Absolute commitment to a cause, whether that of King or of Covenant, was always unusual. Montrose with his strong loyalties and passions was much less typical of his period than Traquair or Southesk with their equivocations. Most Scottish peers thought much less of their country and of allegiance to the King than of duty to their families, to preserve their lands and if possible to despoil those of their neighbours.

Lord Gordon and Lord Aboyne both later forgave Montrose, and indeed became his brothers-in-arms, so his treachery to their father cannot have seemed impossibly heinous. It was Huntly himself who forever afterwards disdained and hated Montrose, probably more for humiliating him in his own country than for betraying him. "He could never be gained to join cordially with him, nor swallow that indignity . . .", wrote Gordon of Rothiemay.[7] Montrose in his youth showed no tact, and was reluctant to waste his great charm on those he did not think worth it—"he was too apt to condemn those he did not love", in the words of Clarendon.[8] Huntly may have lacked parts, but he commanded great power. The fact that he would never raise it effectively in conjunction with Montrose was to be a fatal blow to the royalist cause in Scotland.

Young Aboyne seems to have made a very kindly impression upon the King when he arrived at Newcastle with the unfortunate news from the north. Charles had little time for his father, "feeble and false", as he called Huntly, but he recognized Aboyne's passionate eagerness to strike a blow for the cause. As the royal army lumbered northwards towards the border, Hamilton was sailing up and down the Forth with a squadron of nineteen ships and 5000 men. The Covenanters were waiting for him if he attempted a landing, among them his own fire-breathing mother, who sat seething with holsters on her saddle, promising to shoot her son with her own pistols if he put his head within her range. It was obvious even at court that Hamilton was wasting precious resources and accomplishing nothing. Charles sent Aboyne to him with a letter urging that he be given any force that could be spared: "I shall be glad of it, if you find it may do good; if, with the countenance and assistance of what force you have, you may uphold my party in the north, and the rest of these noblemen I have sent you, I shall esteem it a very great service." In the event, of course, Hamilton was as reluctant to assist this young man as any other upon whom the King seemed to smile. But he felt obliged to give him something. Late in May, Aboyne set sail for Aberdeen with a handful of men, two sixteen-gun ships and a small collier. The Gordons might yet have a day in the north-east.

Montrose was in Edinburgh preparing to march with Leslie, and Aboyne was only newly arrived with Hamilton, when on May 18th the Tables learnt that Ogilvy of Banff with the Urquharts and the Setons and other royalists had fallen to the Master of Forbes's Covenanting garrison at Turriff, and driven them headlong out of the town. The Trot of Turriff, as the little skirmish became known, was the first battle of the Civil Wars. The Earl Marischal at once hastened north to rally the Covenanting forces around Aberdeen. Montrose gathered all the men he could raise. Then leaving Leslie with the bulk of the army, he marched to Aberdeen 4000 strong, mostly levies. He reached the city on May 25th. The royalists had evacuated it five days earlier, after occupying it for less than a week. The young Earl Marischal had been able to secure it without difficulty for the Covenant. But it was evident that the Gordon threat must be summarily crushed while the force to do so was available. On May 30th, after resisting some of his colleagues' demands that the city be burned to the ground, Montrose moved on with his army to Sir George Gordon's castle of Gight, which he began to bombard as the first step towards crushing the royalist barons. But Gight's defences were organized by Lieutenant-Colonel Johnston, an able professional who had been in the forefront of the Turriff raid. Montrose's light artillery made little impact on its defences. The army had been fruitlessly engaged for two days when word came that Aboyne and his ships were at hand. Montrose hastily broke off the action and retired to Aberdeen.

The Covenanters assumed—and no doubt the Gordons had been boasting of it—that Aboyne's return meant that he had brought Hamilton or at least a large proportion of his forces with him. On June 4th, Montrose gathered his army and moved away southwards, leaving Aberdeen open behind him. The

following day, young Aboyne landed triumphantly with Lord
Tullibardine, Lord Glencairn, Ogilvy of Banff and a professional
officer named Colonel Gun, whom Hamilton had wished upon
the expedition. It was a splendid moment for the Gordons.
Thirteen-year-old Lord Lewis "had broken away from his
grandmother at the Bog of Gight, and had foresaken the school
and his tutor, leaping over the walls so hazardously that he
went near to break one of his arms. He, I say, in Highland
habits, being as yet a young boy, had the name of leader to
those Highlanders".[9] Lord Lewis was to earn a fearsome
reputation for recklessness—he once stole the family jewels and
ran away to Holland. Now, he started his own campaign. He
hastily "raised his father's ground, friends and followers, men,
tenants and servants, who most gladly and willingly came with
him, and upon Friday June 7th, marched in brave order, about
a thousand men on horse and foot, well armed brave men . . .
and to Aberdeen came they, to meet the Lord Aboyne . . .".[10]

But Montrose was now able to judge the weight of his
opponents more accurately, and he was not impressed. After
leaving Aberdeen, he had fallen back on Stonehaven,
Marischal's territory around his castle of Dunnottar. Aboyne
advanced towards the Covenanters on June 14th, but a few
rounds from Montrose's light artillery drove back his highland
levies so precipitately that the young Viscount had great
difficulty in rallying them again around Aberdeen. Highland
armies detested and feared "the musket's mother" above all
things. It was now Montrose's turn to seek an engagement. He
advanced on the city, his cavalry outposts skirmishing with those
of Aboyne, which included both Colonel Johnston and
Nathaniel Gordon, that superb royalist officer of whom much
more will be heard. Aboyne was able to gather only a scratch
force of Aberdeen citizens, together with some 600 of his own
clan cavalry, a few little brass cannon from Strathbogie, and
those of the clan levies who had not drifted home. Colonel Gun,
his professional adviser, was clearly a fool, if not a traitor as
Napier believes that he was. It was an unenviable and depressing
situation for the eighteen-year-old Aboyne.

It was apparent both to himself and to Montrose that the
key to Aberdeen was the bridge that crossed the swollen river
Dee two miles outside the city. Colonel Johnston led the defence
of the bridge as Montrose's men made their first charge on the

morning of June 18th. It quickly became clear that the royalist position, strengthened by trenches and earthworks, could not be rushed. Both sides settled down to shoot it out. It was a long, hot fighting day. "In a short time," wrote the Gordon historian, "the very servant girls got such courage that nobly they brought meat, drink and other necessaries to their masters and relations upon the bridge, not regarding the cannon or musket balls that were continually flying among them."[11]

Successful command in battle calls for a set of vital instincts: a general must know what men can do, how they will behave at a critical moment; he must see dead ground at a glance, know when infantry are fit to charge, have that sixth sense for the hinge of fortune. Montrose had now spent six months almost continually among armies, in the company of professional soldiers and of Leslie himself. He had been taught to judge the range of a demi-culverin and a falcon, he had learnt how difficult it is to rally cavalry after a charge, and how an army that loses heart melts like butter in the sun. He understood that timing is all, that the law of rising returns which operates in warfare gives everything to the commander who can make a breakthrough at a critical moment. Now he had felt the exhilaration of surviving under fire, of defeating death while other men were falling around him. He had experienced that vivid extra dimension, that needle-sharpness of the senses that comes to almost every man in action.

There is a wonderful moment that comes to some men when they play tennis, to others when they paint pictures, to others again when they stand upon a battlefield: they know, suddenly, with perfect certainty, that they can play the game, use the paint brush, fight the battle better than anyone else. They have the instincts and impulses and confidence and genius. Perhaps it was here at the Bridge of Dee, as musket balls ricocheted off the parapets and cannon fire hurled chunks of masonry into the river, and men shouted as they always do in action and the horse raised great dust clouds as they charged, that Montrose sat in his saddle with his staff around him and understood that it was for this that he had been born.

That night of June 18th, the two little armies rested where they stood. The citizens of Aberdeen had resisted every attack upon them at the bridge. The following morning, Montrose played a stroke that hinted at the great tactician to come: the river could not be forded, but by sending his cavalry noisily upstream across the royalist front, he frightened the wretched Colonel Gun into believing that it could be. Gun turned the Gordon cavalry frantically after them, racing away along their own bank of the river. Montrose had moved up his guns during the night, and under covering fire from the artillery commanded by Colonel Henderson, Major Middleton led the Covenanting vanguard against the royalists on the bridge. The gallant Colonel Johnston, who had held out so well, was crushed by falling masonry at a critical moment. He had to be helped into a saddle and led painfully away, one leg dangling uselessly, to the temporary safety of Aberdeen. The royalists broke, and poor Aboyne found himself fleeing for his life with his Gordon horse. Aberdeen was lost. It had not been much of a battle by any standards—perhaps twenty killed on either side. But it had established Montrose as a commander of men, blooded him in action.

As Montrose and Marischal lay in Aberdeen that night, a ship put into harbour bearing news that peace had been proclaimed at Berwick between King and Covenant. The truce had officially been already in force as Aboyne and Montrose fought across the bridge. Theirs had been the only real encounter of the war. Charles's hopelessly ineffectual army with its fumbling commanders and demoralized men, wracked by internal wrangling and treachery, was so obviously incapable of facing Leslie's forces across the Tweed that even the King had felt compelled to recognize realities. The Pacification of Berwick provided for the summoning of a new Scots Assembly and Scots Parliament. To the King, it was a means of postponing settlement with his enemies until he was better prepared. Many Covenanters, somewhat naïvely, believed it was the triumph of their cause.

On hearing the news, Montrose released his prisoners and disbanded his army. Once again he had disappointed his men by declining them leave to pillage Aberdeen as they considered their right, and as the ministers had urged him to do. He contented himself with imposing another large fine on the city. Then he rode fast for the south with Marischal, towards the Scottish camp upon the Tweed, "to have their part in the joy as well they did deserve, in the common peace; where they were made most welcome both to their comrades and their King".[12]

# CHAPTER FOUR

## *Icarus*

---

ROTHES, HENDERSON AND Warriston had led the Covenanting delegation in the peace talks with the King at Berwick. Argyll had a long audience with Charles, but remained aloof and deeply suspicious of the Pacification. The day after it was signed, many of the English peers were entertained to dinner in the Scottish camp, where they were warmly received with cries of "God Bless His Majesty and The Devil Confound the Bishops!". It was obvious that one side or the other was under a complete misapprehension about the terms of the treaty, or at least about the spirit of them. Montrose had scarcely reached the Scottish camp to celebrate his little victory and the coming of peace before men were talking freely about the next campaign. The Covenanters believed that Charles had agreed not to fortify any of the fortresses surrendered back to him, yet as soon as Hamilton received the keys of Edinburgh Castle, supplies and ammunition were trundling up the hill to its gates. The mob in the capital was rumbling, and the Tables suffered deep misgivings that too much had been surrendered on too vague terms. On July 1st, their worst fears were confirmed. The royal proclamation was read for the summoning of the new Assembly of the Kirk. It called for the attendance of the bishops. To the Covenanters, this was the deepest royal treachery. Two days later riots broke out in the capital. Leading royalists including Traquair, Kinnoul and Aboyne (now reunited with his father and brother who had been freed from their imprisonment) were set upon and manhandled by the mob.

Charles, at Berwick, affected to regard the disorders in Edinburgh as a breach of faith by the rebels. He sent word for fourteen of the most prominent leaders of the Covenant to call on him at once, allegedly to discuss plans for his forthcoming visit to Edinburgh for the Assembly and the Parliament. The Tables were deeply, perhaps justly, suspicious that this was no more than "a trap to catch some of the prime Covenanters". At a meeting in Edinburgh on July 13th, they discussed their fears. Argyll flatly refused to go to Berwick, and several others were less than enthusiastic. A division in their ranks had been apparent since the negotiations at Berwick, between those who were still prepared to believe the King a man of his word, and those who were not—Argyll and Warriston prominent amongst them. It was finally agreed that a delegation of only six would wait on Charles—Loudon, Lothian, Dunfermline, Rothes, Montrose and Henderson. On July 17th, they reached Berwick, and settled down for the next three days at the King's Court. They achieved nothing. Charles was furious that Argyll and the others had failed to attend as he had demanded. When the party returned to Edinburgh, they were ordered to send their colleagues immediately to Berwick. The King also sent a note to the Tables citing eighteen alleged breaches of the Pacification by their supporters.

But Loudon and Lindsay were the only lords who came back from Edinburgh, bringing with them the Tables' own paper citing six alleged breaches of the Pacification by the King, and empty regrets from all the others who still declined to appear before him. Charles had had enough. He sent word that he would no longer be coming north to attend the Scottish Parliament, and broke up his court at Berwick in royal rage. He returned to London on August 3rd. One of his first acts on reaching the capital was to order the burning by the public hangman of the Covenanters' pamphlet giving their version of what had taken place in the north. He was no closer to overpowering his rebellious Scottish subjects than he had been at the beginning of the summer, and he had now effectively abandoned the field to them. He had never intended to keep his part of the Pacification of Berwick, but he flattered himself that his opponents would not perceive this. Instead their leaders had understood him only too well.

But in the months following the King's reception of the Covenanting leaders at Berwick, it became increasingly apparent that Charles had made a deep mark upon one of them at least: Montrose. In that impulsive, romantic soul, his second meeting with the King created a wholly different impression from the first. All his life, Charles appeared to greatest advantage in adversity. His dignity and serenity

at their meeting pierced Montrose to the heart, in contrast to
the cynicism of Warriston and the jovial disrespect of Rothes.
There was so much that was crude and ugly and distasteful
about the Tables and the ministers and the Edinburgh mob and
the endless backstairs intrigue and treachery. Montrose was
never politically sophisticated. At the time of the negotiations
in Berwick and afterwards, he believed that the King was
telling the truth, that his promises were sincere. Then, too,
there was the extraordinary personal appeal of Charles Stuart.
He had a magnetism that transcended charm, some certainty of
divine kingly purpose and family loyalty and love that inspired
all who saw it.

"The worthiest gentleman, the best master, the best friend,
the best husband, the best father, and the best Christian,"
wrote Clarendon.[1] "I do wonder at the admirable temper of
the King," wrote Sir Henry Slingsby, one of his officers, in
the grimmest hour of the Civil War a few years later, "whose
constancy was such that no perils never so unavoidable could
move him to astonishment, but that still he set the same face,
and settled countenance, upon whatsoever adverse fortune
befell him, and neither was he exalted by prosperity nor
dejected in adversity. Which was the more admirable in him
seeing he had no other to have recourse unto, but must bear the
whole burden upon his own shoulders." Baillie[2] admitted that
"his Majesty was ever the longer the better loved of all that
heard him, as one of the most just, reasonable, sweet persons
they had ever seen".

It would be wrong to imagine Montrose enjoying, at Berwick,
some instant conversion on the road to Damascus. There were
still to be diversions and blind alleys before he set out on the
path on which he was to die. Those who have imagined him
the King's man from the summer of 1639 onwards make too
light of his place in the invading Covenanting army that fought
the King at Newburn a year later. But henceforth Montrose was
to be regarded by the rest of the Covenanting leadership as a
moderate, then as a waverer in their councils. His evident
tolerance and propensity for mercy and for compromise
seemed more and more incongruous in that gloomy company
bent on institutionalizing "the religion of the Old Testament
run amok". Privately at least, most of the leading men of the
Tables had long ago understood that they could not fight

the King's religious policy without fighting the King himself.
While Montrose remained totally committed to the Covenant,
to the abolition of the episcopate, to Scottish Calvinism, he
cherished the belief that these things could be compatible with
his loyalty to his King. From now on he was to assert his
royalism more and more strongly. The Covenanters had
preserved a few phrases in the Covenant about loyalty.
Montrose was one of the few to whom they were much more
than a gesture. As the Tables's thoughts began to turn more
emphatically from religious reform to political revolution, he
was increasingly at odds with them. He was deeply distressed
by their apparent breach of faith with the King. They, in their
turn, were increasingly impatient with an idealistic, ambitious
young man who wore his heart upon his sleeve and was so
eager to draw his sword and set out after the Holy Grail.

On August 12th, 1639, the new General Assembly of the Kirk
met in Edinburgh with Traquair as the Royal Commissioner
in place of Hamilton, and David Dickson—Montrose's
companion on the ride to Aberdeen a year before—as Moderator. Charles instructed Traquair that he might accept almost
anything from the rebels—even the abolition of episcopacy—
but it was vital that the bishops were not declared "unlawful".
This was a denunciation so absolute that it would raise all
manner of ecclesiastical spectres in England as well as in
Scotland. Charles had no more intention of accepting the
validity of the Edinburgh Assembly's deliberations than those
of the Glasgow one, but he clung to every possible legalistic
justification. "Perhaps we may give way for the present," he
told the Archbishop of St Andrews, "to that which will be
prejudicial both to the Church and our own Government, yet
we shall not leave thinking in time, how to remedy both."

The courts and wynds of Edinburgh were crowded with
ministers and peers and their entourages that summer, filling
all the lodgings and spilling over into the surrounding villages,
the nobles' coaches making hard work of the steep climb up
the Canongate from Holyrood, tempers strained by confinement in the hot, stinking city in August. The King's dignity
was not enhanced by the presence of Huntly alongside Traquair
at the first session of the Assembly. Everybody present knew
that he was only able to set foot in Edinburgh because of a
special dispensation protecting him from his creditors. The

same day the Bishop of Orkney, a brother of Inchbrakie and kinsman of Montrose, further embarrassed the royal cause by publicly renouncing his own office and his mistaken belief in the virtue of episcopacy. Then the King's troubles began in earnest.

The Assembly ran rapidly through each of the points that had been debated a few months earlier in Glasgow, and ratified them all once again. Montrose was among the members of a committee that demanded the signing of the Covenant by every Scot, adding only the qualification about loyalty to the King which he had devised for Huntly earlier in the year. Worst of all, episcopacy was declared "unlawful to this Kirk" and "contrary to the Word of God". The Assembly voted to meet again a year thence in Aberdeen. Traquair feebly assented to almost everything in the interests of peace, and the members parted in a euphoric mood of triumph. Charles was furious, not least with Traquair. "I cannot omit to tell you," wrote Hamilton from his master's side, "that the word 'unlawful' has infinitely distressed his Majesty . . . and you will do well to think how to relieve it." But it was too late for any of that.

On August 31st, the Scottish Parliament assembled in the unfinished parliament building in Edinburgh in which the Tables had been holding their deliberations for some months past. Traquair was once again upon his bed of nails as King's Commissioner, and around him sat the fifty bishops, forty-eight barons of the shire, fifty-two burgesses and three officers of state who made up the gathering. The critical dispute began immediately. It concerned the make-up of the body known as the Lords of the Articles, the committee drawn from members of Parliament that traditionally exercised all real power on their behalf. Traditionally also, the King had been able to pack the committee by using the votes of his faithful bishops, who sat representing the estate of the clergy. But now there were no longer any bishops, and no longer any clerical estate. After "a great contest amongst them, for the space of four or five hours", the Covenanting nobles succeeded in nominating a majority of their own men to represent all three Estates, nobles, shire barons and burgesses, as Lords of the Articles. The newly-chosen Lords at once ratified all the acts of the Assembly of the Kirk and transferred control of the Mint to themselves. They then debated a proposal originating with the Earl of Argyll, that

D

in future the Lords of the Articles should always be chosen by the Estates themselves. By this means, Argyll could effectively wrest permanent control of the Committee away from the King and into the hands of the Covenanters. The shire barons and burgesses were overwhelmingly Covenanters, despite the division among the nobles between Covenanters and royalists.

Argyll's admirers over the last three centuries have seized on this initiative as an example of his far-sighted constitutional thinking. He has been described as the founder of Cabinet government in Scotland. But to his contemporaries, it was simply a ruthless piece of personal power-mongering. As the Scottish rebellion against the King unfolded, so far it had been a matter of consensus protests, of manœuvring among men of various talents and importance. Some of them had gained greatly from their part in the upheavals, others had burnt their fingers and faded quickly into obscurity. But now, at this Parliament of 1639 came the rising voice and power of Archibald Campbell, 8th Earl of Argyll. It was as if some great pike had at last stirred from the mud at the bottom of the lake, and come twisting slowly towards the surface, sending minnows and roach and perch and even the smaller jack flying for the weeds. For the next two decades, Argyll towers bleakly over the politics of Scotland.

The Marquis of Hamilton was not notable as a shrewd judge either of events or of character, but during the Glasgow Assembly a year before he wrote to Charles, drawing his attention to the growing menace of the Campbell. "The Earl of Argyll," he reported, "is the only man now called up as a true patriot, a loyal subject, a faithful counsellor, and above all, right set for the preservation of the purity of religion. He must be well looked to; for it fears me he will prove the dangerousest man in this state. He is so far from favouring episcopal government that with all his soul he wishes it totally abolished. What course to advise you to take with him, the part I cannot say, but remit it to your Majesty's severe consideration."

Argyll's role and character[3] were in classical contrast to those of Montrose. He was Priam to Montrose's Achilles, a gloomy Cerberus who stands as grey and gaunt in the pages of history as Montrose glitters gold. It is impossible to learn to love Argyll, he of the red hair and squinting eye. "Cam is thy name, cam ar thyne eyies and wayes",[4] went a contemporary saying of infinite malice, for cam meant only crooked. Yet it would have seemed to him an intolerable injustice that history has made so much of the gay Montrose and his army of plunderers and outlaws, and so little of Archibald Campbell, the devout helmsman of Scotland through the stormy seas that were approaching.

He was born in 1607, five years before Montrose, the only son among six children, destined to be the MacCailein Mhor, hereditary clan chief of the Campbells with five thousand claymores and countless acres at his command. He had a thoroughly unhappy childhood. After his mother died, his father remarried a woman young Archibald detested, and became a Catholic to the embarrassment of his son and many of his clan. His estates were burdened with debt, and it took years of prudent management by the young heir to put them on a sound footing again. The boy was brought up by his cousin, the Earl of Morton, and the best-known tale of the relationship between old Argyll and young Lorne is the Earl's sombre warning to Charles I that his son would do the King a mischief if ever he had the chance. The boy grew up lonely, complex, brooding. At St Andrews he won the Silver Arrow like Montrose a few years later, but in every other way he was a sombre contrast to his brother Earl. It would be surprising if Argyll had not cherished some personal resentments towards Montrose long before he developed political ones. The Graham was handsome, extrovert, gallant, graceful. The Campbell's face was distorted by his severe squint and his long, hooked nose. He lacked elegance or presence however carefully he chose his tailor, however majestically he arranged his court of young gentlemen around himself. In his youth, King Charles wanted to marry him to Elizabeth Stuart, sister of his favourite the Duke of Lennox. But the match collapsed under circumstances as humiliating as possible for Argyll. Lady Elizabeth fell in love and married Lord Maltravers. Not for the first or last time in his life, Argyll heard cruel laughter at his expense. In 1626 he married Margaret Douglas, his guardian Morton's second daughter. But he can never have had much affection for courtiers and gallants after the Stuart episode.

His enemies were always to taunt his incompetence as a soldier, which was real enough, and his physical cowardice, which was not. Montrose himself was quick enough to fly from a stricken field. It was a matter of common prudence for Argyll to escape from Kilsyth and Inverlochy when all was lost. In the end he went to the scaffold with dignity. It was simply not in his star to play the hero. Clarendon noted Montrose's intense personal dislike of him, and as a royalist he must have shared some of it himself, but he says of Argyll that he "wanted nothing but honesty and courage to be a very extraordinary man, having all other good talents in a great degree". His exceptional ability and intellect were unquestioned. He was simply thoroughly unloved.*

The Campbell was always a lonely and introverted man. He never had the good fortune to be teased, to confide in others, to trust a company sufficiently to relax in it. Like most people of this sort, he was deeply serious, apparently humourless. Montrose's frivolities and impetuousness irked him very much, all the more so when he noticed the popularity that went with them. Argyll never stopped weighing opportunities and responsibilities. He was a very religious man. He often preached the sermon himself at home in Inverary, and he devoted hours to prayer. As Buchan[5] has said: "No mortal, however consummate an actor, could simulate such enthusiasm as Argyll revealed during the remainder of his troubled life."

He was a very shrewd, subtle, vengeful politician. He had been born to wield great powers, and the Scots' falling out with their King gave him opportunities to wield even greater ones. He developed a vision in his mind of a calvinistic Scotland with himself as its actual—conceivably even its crowned—head. He pursued it ruthlessly. Those who opposed him were cut down without mercy. He never forgot his position as chief of Clan Campbell when an opportunity arose to harry traditional clan enemies and to seize their lands and wealth. He was widely feared and sometimes pitied for his loneliness and tortured ambition, even by his contemporaries. Gordon of Ruthven, no Covenanter, said that "to speak truly of this nobleman the Marquis of Argyll, he had many good and laudable parts if the iniquity of the time had not carried him away with the main

* Those seeking to suggest that Argyll was quite human have drawn attention to his keen sportsmanship. In *Instructions to a Son*, he urged his boy to work hard at "that excellent recreation of golf-ball, than which I do not know a better". Golfers no doubt find this an endearing facet of this gloomy man. To the unconverted it may seem entirely in character.

current. . . . He suffered his best qualities to be much overruled by Machiavelli's Prince, which by his practices in the most part of his following actions, he seemed perfectly to have studied. . . . He proved the deepest statesman, the most crafty, subtle and overreaching politician that this age could produce."[6]

Argyll's initiative at the Scottish Parliament of 1639 was his decisive step towards assuming the leadership of the Covenanting cause, and it struck alarm and anger into many hearts. The Campbells already wielded great influence, and Argyll himself was the very pattern of the "over-mighty subject". The Marquis of Huntly demanded that the King be given the right to confirm the appointment of the Lords of the Articles. He must have been startled to discover himself supported by no less a zealot of the Covenant than his late captor, Montrose.

It was Montrose's first clash with Argyll, and he lost it. By fourteen votes to twelve, Huntly's proposal to refer appointments to the King was defeated. But the Covenanters, and Argyll himself, had been annoyed and embarrassed by Montrose's apparent weakening. He was regarded with growing suspicion by many of his colleagues. It was one morning at about this time that he discovered pinned to his door a paper on which was scrawled "Invictus Armis, verbis vincitur". His enemies whispered across Edinburgh that the man who had won the Bridge of Dee had been seduced by the gracious posturings of Charles Stuart. All that autumn, it is clear, Montrose was advancing the argument for the King's rights when the opportunity occurred. His kinsman Lord Airth, who was trying to ingratiate himself with Charles after a long period of disgrace, wrote winsomely to His Majesty on September 20th informing him that "my cousin Montrose hath carried himself both faithfully, and is more willing to contribute to his uttermost in anything for your Majesty's service, than any of these Lords Covenanters". Even Baillie seemed conscious that the extremists were rapidly driving their moderate brethren into troubled water: "I fear we press more than he [the King] can grant; and when we are fully satisfied, it is likely England will begin where we have left off."[7]

It was obvious that it must once again be war. On November 14th, Traquair prorogued parliament on the King's instructions, having declined to ratify its acts. The members considered ignoring the royal dismissal and continuing in session. But they decided instead merely to maintain the Lords of the Articles in session, to represent the interests of the Estates. As Traquair followed Hamilton's weary footsteps down the road to London to report his failure, the committee was left free to govern Scotland as it chose.

It was the beginning of a bleak winter. The fortifications of Edinburgh Castle were being strengthened on the King's orders—not before time since part of the walls fell down on November 19th under the shock of the firing of the Royal Birthday Salute. A steady trickle of deserters slunk away from the garrison each night. Traquair arrived in London to find himself in disgrace as usual, the King blaming him for the farcical failures of the Assembly and the Parliament. Charles appears at this time to have made an attempt to bring Montrose openly into his camp, for he sent word to Scotland summoning him to London. But the Graham was already under suspicion. He had no wish to break with his Covenanting colleagues so decisively. He sent his elaborate regrets to the King, explaining that certain parties in Edinburgh "being still filled with their usual and unwonted jealousies", would draw the worst conclusions from his journeying south. "Hoping that your Majesty will do me the honour to think that this is no shift—for all of that kind is too much contrary to my humour", he would go home to Kincardine. Warriston applauded his discretion.

Four Commissioners from the Estates waited upon the King on February 20th, 1640. They negotiated cursorily at intervals in March. But both sides knew it was to be war, and Charles was angered by their lack of ceremony towards him: "The Scottish are more for realities in expressions of kindness than of words and gestures", the Commissioners explained sourly. They would have liked to pack up and go home after pursuing the futile meetings until the end of March, but Charles made them remain. He wanted them at hand when he made his next move, which was not long delayed.

On April 11th, he had all four of them arrested. Two days later, the English Parliament that he had at last summoned to vote money for the Scots war met for the first time. He played his hidden ace, only to watch it fall limp upon the table without taking a trick. Charles had got possession of a letter signed by the Covenanting leaders and sent to Louis XIII of France, pleading for his intercession in support of their grievances. It was a bizarre request from Calvinists to a Catholic monarch. Charles tried to argue that his Scottish subjects were dealing treasonably with foreign powers. But the Short Parliament was wholly unimpressed. They rudely brushed aside the King's talk of his Scottish war and demanded to discuss their own, English grievances. After a series of bitter, factious debates on such matters as Ship Money, breach of privilege and religion, it became apparent that the King would get nothing from Pym and his friends. On May 5th, he dissolved Parliament. It was now vital that he show himself able to suppress the dissension and opposition that was threatening him upon every side. It had become essential that his war against the Scots should end in victory. The credibility of the throne was at stake.

Yet the forces of the Covenant had never seemed more determined or more united. On June 2nd, the prorogued Parliament met again in Edinburgh despite a royal proclamation forbidding them. Unabashed by the absence of a King's Commissioner to legitimize their doings, they chose Lord Burleigh as their President, and set about voting through a massive body of carefully prepared legislation. They passed a triennial act for their own meetings, ratified all the acts of the Edinburgh Kirk Assembly, decreed their preparations for raising an army for war, and instituted a Committee of Estates to replace the Articles. All these were quite unconstitutional acts, which the Long Parliament in England were soon to take as their example. Montrose was almost alone in publicly opposing them to the uttermost. Many of the leading royalists such as Huntly and Airlie had already fled from Edinburgh, some to join the King's Court. Their enemies were once again left in possession of the field. "Montrose did dispute against Argyll, Rothes, Balmerino and myself," wrote Warriston later, "because some urged that as long as we had a King, we could not sit without him."

The Committee of Estates that now assumed the government of Scotland was simply the Tables in new robes. In war, it was agreed, the Committee would divide itself in half, one part remaining in Edinburgh while the other rode with the army, each empowered to act independently. A few years hence, this provision was to give Montrose some fine days watching his enemies' agonized debates upon the battlefield. Now, in June of 1640, he was appointed one of the Committee's forty members. But in reality, he was rapidly losing effective power in the councils of the Covenant.

The first evidence of his eclipse came swiftly. As in the previous year's campaign the first concern of the members of the Committee of Estates was to secure their rear, the north-east of Scotland, before facing the King in the south. The Stewarts of Atholl and the Ogilvies nearby in Angus were still staunchly hostile to the Covenant, and now they were reported to be stirring for the King. Montrose held his commission from the shire committees of Forfar and Perth to command their forces in war. Atholl lay within his acknowledged sphere of influence. Yet it was the Earl of Argyll who was nominated by the Committee of Estates to lead an army into Perthshire and harry the rebels. Colonel Robert Monro and the Earl Marischal were likewise sent north to bring fire and the sword down on the unfortunate Ogilvy of Banff, who had spurred the Gordons to action the previous summer, and now paid the penalty. Aberdeen and the Gordon country were harried by Monro with none of the ungodly mercifulness so absurdly displayed by Montrose in the last campaign.

On June 18th, 1640, Argyll marched with 4000 of his own Clan Campbell soldiers against Atholl. "I should be very glad that the Atholl men would draw to a head and make a stand, for then I should know where to find them," he wrote. This was Argyll at his most ruthless. With a characteristic eye for family profit as well as political expediency, he used the expedition to seize possession of estates in Badenoch and Lochaber, Huntly property which had been mortgaged to him by his brother-in-law, which he now claimed had fallen due. He met little opposition on his march and collected much booty. "We are King Campbell's men and no more King Stuart's," sang his triumphant clansmen as they strode along behind him. These were the men whom the English had met with such amazement the previous summer when the Scots army was encamped at Duns Law, Argyll's personal Highland division which made him such a force to be reckoned with: "all, or most part of them, well timbered men, tall and active," wrote one of the English officers,[8] describing these classic clan soldiers of the seventeenth century, "apparelled in the woollen waist-coats and blue bonnets, a pair of bans of plaid and stockings of the same, and a pair of pumps on their feet, a mantle of plaid cast over the left shoulder and under the right arm, a pocket before the knapsack, and a pair of dirks on either side the pocket. They are left to their own election for their weapons. Some carry only a sword and targe, others muskets, and the greater part bow and arrow, with a quiver to hold six shafts, made of the mane of a goat or colt, with the hair hanging on, and fastened by some belt or suchlike, so as it appears almost a tail to them. They had bagpipes, for the most part, for their warlike instrument . . . their ensigns had strange devices and strange words. . . ."

Argyll dealt economically with the Stewarts by inviting their leaders to his tent under safe conduct and then placing them under arrest. He turned to the Ogilvies. The head of the family, the Earl of Airlie, was in England with the King, but his son, Lord Ogilvy, was holding Airlie Castle. A few days before the Campbells arrived, Montrose reached the fortress, perhaps partly to do his neighbours and friends a good turn, and even more plausibly, to score off Argyll. He persuaded Ogilvy to surrender the castle to him, and placed Colonel Sibbald, one of his officers, in command of a token garrison. Then he wrote to Argyll assuring him that his journey into Angus was no longer necessary, that the matter of the Ogilvies had been settled.

Argyll ignored him. He marched to Airlie, sent Montrose's handful of men packing, turned loose his men to sack the castle, and finally put it to the torch. He then proceeded to Forfar, another Ogilvy residence, where young Lady Ogilvy was waiting for the birth of her baby. She was driven out and the house sacked, on Argyll's personal orders, although he later attempted to hide his responsibility. It was a campaign in the great tradition of Campbell blackguardry through the centuries, and the ballad writers wrote it into legend:

> Lady Ogilvy looks o'er her bower window,
> And O but she looks warely!
> And there she spied the great Argyll,
> Come to plunder the bonnie house of Airlie.

Argyll vented his anger on Montrose for his leniency towards the Ogilvies, and especially for allowing Lord Ogilvy to escape two days before the Campbells reached Airlie, allegedly taking with him some of his most valuable possessions. Montrose, in his turn, made his way southwards with the regiments under his command, deeply angered and disturbed by the feudal arrogance of Argyll. He was appalled to hear a rumour that Argyll might be given a commission to govern the entire north of Scotland, including his own territory around Strathearn. The Campbells' song about their "King" Argyll sounded less and less amusing. Montrose left his men with the army, and rode to Edinburgh where he talked to his friends, most importantly Lord Lindsay who seemed to confirm all his fears that Argyll was planning to create a dictatorship. That summer, it seemed that the Campbell had the personal power, the private army, the respect of the Kirk, the political influence to be able to lead Scotland where he chose. There had been much muttering about the possibility of creating a republic. Scotland had already become one in all but name, went the dangerous argument, and Charles Stuart could never be trusted to keep his word, even if he could ever be brought to be King of Scotland again on reasonable terms.

Against this background, at the instigation of Montrose, some time early in August 1640 a group of nobles met at Lord Wigton's house near Glasgow, Cumbernauld. There they signed a secret compact that became known as the Cumbernauld Band.

"Whereas we under-subscribers," it began, "out of our duty to Religion, King, and Country, were forced to join ourselves in a Covenant for the maintenance and defence of eithers, and everyone of other, in that behalf; now finding how that, by the particular and indirect practising of a few, the country, and cause now depending, does so much suffer, do heartily hereby bind and oblige ourselves, out of our duty to all these respects above-mentioned, but chiefly and namely that Covenant already signed, to wed and study all public ends which may tend to the safety both of Religion, Laws, and Liberties of this poor kingdom. . . ."

The critical phrase in all these tortured sentences concerned resisting "the particular and indirect practising of a few". This was the thrust aimed straight at Argyll, at the black rumours of a plan to make "a particular man" absolute ruler, tyrant over Scotland. Each of the signatories bound himself to act in concert with the others, and for the protection of each other if necessary. The Band was signed by Montrose, Wigton, Marischal, Home, Atholl, Kinghorn, Mar, Perth, Galloway, Seaforth, Almond and nine others. Some of the signatories were not present at Cumbernauld, but added their names later.

It is hard to judge exactly what Montrose hoped from his Band, since it was not to be published and thus could not become a public rallying point. The nobles who signed it did not constitute a strong enough party to stand in the same ring as Argyll and the Covenanting extremists. Although several of the Banders later fought against the King in the Civil War, it may have been opposition to republicanism that brought them together. When a killer whale such as Argyll was at sea, a conjunction of smaller fry may have seemed comforting and attractive. But there is no escaping the conclusion that the Band was a sad failure as a political initiative by Montrose. The group never managed to stand publicly together on any issue. They were soon, indeed, to be bitter foes.

By late August, Montrose was back with his regiments at the Scottish camp at Duns. When the Scots marched for the Border, supposedly to petition their King to ratify the doings of their Assembly and Parliament, his biographer Wishart has him leading 2000 foot and 500 horse in their midst. On August 20th, 1640, the day Charles left London to join his own army at York, the Scots were fording the Tweed at Coldstream. Whatever Montrose's private political agonies, with an army he was in his element.

"The lot gave the van that day to Montrose," recounts Baillie,[9] "to whom I think it was very welcome. He went on foot himself first through, and returned to encourage his men; yet one of his soldiers, and he only of all the army, did drown."

It was characteristic that Montrose should have tossed his reins to a groom and waded waist-deep through the ford. He was to prove one of the great natural leaders of men in the history of arms, and it is by such acts that generals come to be loved. Wishart would have it that Montrose and some of his friends were already scheming to take their men over to the King, and that he pushed himself to the fore as the army advanced so as to lull the Covenanters' suspicions of him. But he was never that kind of plotter—indeed he was always too transparent in his political doings. Riding with that army he may have allowed himself momentarily to forget his deep misgivings.

A squadron or two of Leslie's horse were ordered forward to stand in the river and slow the current while the infantry crossed, and as Baillie says, the man of Montrose's brigade who was swept away was the army's only casualty. Without other loss or check, the Scots moved stolidly southwards to the Tyne, while at Newcastle the King's meagre army pondered desperately how to meet them. Charles had had the utmost difficulty in mustering his sullen and semi-mutinous levies, who would sooner have joined a lynch mob to hang Laud or Strafford than march against the Scots. The only officers who had come forward willingly were the Catholic gentry, who were thus as usual more of an embarrassment than a blessing to the King's cause. In many counties, the muster had been attended by rioting. The arms and equipment available for the men were very poor stuff by comparison with those of the Covenant. Deep resentments were stirring all over England against the King's religious policy and his taxation and his long flirtation with the hated Spaniards. Some of the most prominent men in his Court were in constant secret communication with the Covenanters, who were thus thoroughly informed of his plans. Lord Conway, his commander at Newcastle, was an ineffectual fumbler struggling in vain to assert his authority over his forces. As Leslie and the Scots approached the Tweed, Conway hastened clumsily forward to dig in at the Newburn crossing of the Tyne, the most vulnerable point on the enemy line of advance. But soldiers who do not believe that they can win— even worse, those who do not want to fight—are already three parts beaten. The Scots had achieved complete psychological dominance of the campaign since the confrontation the previous year. Leslie reached Newburn while the English were still throwing up their breastworks, and made no delay in attempting the crossing.

Conway had proclaimed importantly that the Tyne must be held at all costs. But he had added apologetically that "there goes more to it than to bid it to be done". Only 2000 foot and 1000 horse supported by four guns held the English position. Leslie's gunners laid down a heavy bombardment to cover their crossing, on the afternoon of August 28th. One piece had been swung up into the tower of Newburn church to bring plunging fire down on the English lines across the river. One of Lord Advocate Hope's sons was first into the water with a company of volunteers from Edinburgh College of Justice. After a stiff skirmish, reinforcements came up to support them and they overran the English positions. Most of the defenders fled. The English cavalry under Harry Wilmot, a brash young cavalier who had fought in Europe, attempted a counter-attack and even claimed to have killed Montrose. In reality, the Scots beat them off with cool musket volleys. They fled away down the road in disorder. Only an hour and a half after the crossing began, the rising tide made the river impassable for the rest of the night. But the Scots in their bridgehead on the south side were not attacked again. They lingered by the Tyne all the next day completing their crossing, then on Sunday, August 30th, they marched the four miles to Newcastle. To their amazement, they found that the city, one of the greatest in England, had been utterly abandoned. Conway had no notion how to defend it once his line at Newburn had been broken. He had sent away his ammunition by sea, and then marched for Durham.

The King's castle of dreams crumbled rapidly now. A few days earlier, he had still cherished absurd illusions that his forces would be invading Scotland that summer. Instead, while the Scots had been preparing to take the Tyne crossing, Dumbarton Castle surrendered to Argyll. Even as Charles sat at York trying to regroup his forces and rally support for his cause, on September 15th the royal garrison of Edinburgh Castle yielded on terms. The castle guns had been shelling the city intermittently for weeks, killing 200 people. But sickness and desertion and the shortage of water had eroded the garrison's strength, and it had become obvious that there was no hope of relief from the King. The north-east, the Gordon country, was considered sufficiently secure for the Covenanters to order Monro and his men south for service on the Borders. The Committee of Estates were well content. They were aware of the bitter opposition to the King in London, and they sat back to wait for English political pressure to work its will. They had no wish to advance any further. To do so would be to expose their lines of communication, and to risk antagonizing the people of England who for the present bore

them no ill-will. With Newcastle as a powerful bargaining
counter in their hands, they had only to keep their patience and
their nerve.

The King's Great Council met at York on September 24th,
and pressure from Charles's opponents made it inevitable that
he would have to call a Parliament. The sixteen peers nominated to treat with the Scots were almost all hostile to him.
Negotiations began at Ripon on October 2nd, and subsequently
continued in London. It was quickly conceded that the English
would pay £860 a day to support the Scots army in Newcastle,
and the Scots' seizure of the six northern counties was accepted
until a permanent settlement was reached. Henderson,
Warriston, Loudon and Dunfermline were among the eight
Scottish Commissioners who conducted the long negotiations
for peace. During their stay in the south there was a long
and unprecedented exchange of views and ideas with the chief
puritans and political opponents of the King. The Scottish
rebels and the English dissidents filled each other with new
confidence. The King had not only failed in his desperate
attempt to make an example of his Scots subjects, he had
allowed the Scots to inspire the English with a perilous
example. The Covenanters were everywhere victorious, and
the King's personal position had become alarmingly exposed.

In the Scottish camp at Newcastle, Montrose was bitter and
full of doubts. He loved the profession of arms, but he found
himself baffled and unhappy in the struggle of political loyalties.
"The Earl of Montrose told me he was desirous to follow the
wars abroad," said Colonel Cochrane, one of his fellow officers,
"and wished the business were settled at home, that he might
employ his talents that way." It seems very plausible that he
thought of having an end of all the backstairs intrigue, dis-
simulation and treachery, and going to ride with one of the
Protestant armies in Europe, where his title would quickly
give him the opportunity to prove his talents. But he was too
deeply entangled in the politics of Scotland now. There comes a
moment when, however much a man dislikes what he is doing,
the magnet of events is too strong to allow him to detach
himself. He knows all the actors, he has played in so many of
the scenes, he cannot resist remaining for the curtain fall.

Caught as he thus was, with his usual compulsive frankness
Montrose embarked on an impossibly dangerous path. From

Newcastle, he wrote to the King affirming his loyalty. One of the innumerable spies around Charles reported the letter to the Estates, and Montrose was at once under deep suspicion. He was faced with his accusers and charged with corresponding treasonably with the enemy. "Montrose, whose pride long ago was intolerable . . . was accused publicly by the General, in the face of the Committee," reported Baillie.[10] "His bedfellow Drummond, his cousin Fleming, his ally Boyd, and too many others were thought to be of his humour. The coolness of the good old General, and the diligence of the preachers, did shortly cast water on this spunk beginning untimeously to smoke." Montrose turned boldly on the Committee. Rather than deny his correspondence, he declared that it could be no treason to correspond with his lawful Sovereign. The Estates felt unable to punish him, perhaps not least because he and his friends still commanded several brigades of the Scots army. But his position was precarious.

The next blow was the exposure of the Cumbernauld Band. This can hardly have been unexpected when so many men were involved, several of lukewarm sympathy to Montrose's purpose. But coming so soon after the inquiry into his letter to the King, this new revelation was deeply embarrassing. It was Argyll, inevitably, whose long nose had scented a plot against himself. Young Lord Boyd, one of the signatories to the Band, fell seriously ill of fever, and rambled about Cumbernauld in his delirium, shortly before he died on November 19th. Argyll made inquiries, and paid a personal call on Lord Almond at Callendar. Almond revealed all. Argyll laid his cards before the Committee of Estates. Before November was out Montrose was summoned to appear in front of them to explain this latest of his meddlesome schemes.

Once again, it was very difficult to bring any formal indictment against him when his fellow conspirators included men of unimpeachable loyalty to the cause, and when their avowed purpose was to defend the Covenant. The Estates "consulted to pack up the business upon a declaration under their hands that they intended nothing against the public, together with a surrendering of the Band, which the Committee having gotten caused it to be burnt".

But Montrose's defiance was only encouraged by successive warnings and reprimands and attempts to silence him. It is obvious that he now identified Argyll as the chief enemy of the King and of the moderate policies to which he himself had become devoted. Personal antipathy towards Argyll and his ruthlessly wielded power loomed all the larger in Montrose's mind that winter of 1640–41, because he was so uncertain about so much else in the politics of Scotland and of the King. He concealed nothing of his feelings. Riding with General Leslie and Colonel Cochrane one day in January, he began to explain his reasons for organizing the Cumbernauld Band, and said "he could prove there were some of the prime leaders of the business in the country, guilty of high treason in the highest manner, and that they had entered into motions for deposing the King". But even if old Leslie had once dallied before deciding to whom to sell his loyalties, after he had received his commission, he never wavered. Montrose can hardly have been surprised to find this conversation recorded later on the charge sheet against him. He was not behaving wisely. He had failed to create a significant moderate party in Scotland. Even some of those most bitterly opposed to Argyll and the extremists hesitated to ally themselves with so fiery and unpredictable a comet as The Graham. Argyll had no need to do anything but watch his opponent thrash himself deep and deeper into a tangle of intrigue and indiscretion.

Montrose always leant heavily upon his old counsellor Lord Napier for political advice, and Napier* almost certainly played a large part in drafting the long letter which at about this time Montrose dispatched to the King, setting out his

---

* Mark Napier, Montrose's major nineteenth-century biographer, attached great importance to another document, a "Letter on Sovereign Power" which he uncovered in the course of researches on this period of his life, and which he believed to be the work of Montrose, although he acknowledged Lord Napier's probable influence upon it. Today it seems more likely that the "Letter", a long tract on the nature of monarchy and government addressed to an anonymous "Noble Sir", was written by Napier himself. Its sentiments are pedestrian, if honourable. They reflect Napier's devotion to the cause of moderate government, which can only be achieved by the temperance of both the Prince and his subjects. "The perpetual cause of the controversies, between the prince and his subjects, is the ambitious design of rule in great men," says the letter in an obvious thrust at Argyll, "veiled under the specious pretext of religion and the subject's liberties, seconded with the arguments and false positions of seditious preachers." I shall not follow Montrose's earlier biographers in quoting the text in full.

views on the situation in Scotland and suggesting Charles's best course to contend with it. "Your ancient and native kingdom of Scotland is in a mighty distemper," he began. "It is incumbent upon your Majesty to find out the disease, remove the cause, and apply convenient remedies. . . . The disease is in my opinion contagious and may infect the rest of your Majesty's dominions. . . . The remedy of this dangerous disease consisteth only in your Majesty's presence for a space in that Kingdom. It is easy to you in person to settle their troubles, and to disperse these mists of apprehension and mistaking—impossible to any other. If you send down a Commission[er], whatever he be, he shall neither give nor get contentment, but shall render the disease incurable. . . . Practise, sir, the temperate government. It fittest the humour and disposition of the nation best. . . . Let your last act there be the settling of offices of State upon men of known integrity and sufficiency. . . . Let them not be such as are obliged to others than yourself for their preferment; not factious nor popular; neither such as are much hated . . . they who are preferred and obliged to your Majesty will study to behave them well and dutifully in their places, if it were for no other reason yet for this, that they make not your Majesty ashamed of your choice. . . ."

It has been suggested by some historians that the phrases commending the King to find himself new counsellors "of known integrity and sufficiency" are no more nor less than a personal bid for office by Montrose and his friends. This seems perfectly plausible, and by no means unworthy. It also shows Montrose's blissful indifference to the political realities. He and his party were far too small a minority to govern Scotland with any semblance of consent. They had made too many powerful enemies, and had revealed that very ignorance of the art of the possible which had already brought the King's affairs into such straits. The letter puts great emphasis on the importance of satisfying the King's subjects "in point of religion and liberties". It confirms, if more evidence is needed, Montrose's happy unawareness of Charles's implacable resolution on the matter of religion. The suggestion that a royal visit to Scotland might have softened the hearts of his subjects to obedience is absurd. The advice to "temperate government" came tragically too late. Charles had practised intemperance, and as a result had lost the governance of Scotland altogether. There was no longer any reason for his enemies to be moderate in their demands or to accept compromise. They were already victorious. Montrose's letter is valuable because it displays so gracefully the decency, fairness, moderation and kindliness of his own political creed. There is not a line in it that any man of good heart and liberal conviction could be ashamed of in any century. But as political advice, it was sadly naïve.

Argyll's spies in Scotland and in London had informed him about Montrose's correspondence with the King, and constant complaints against himself. He was beginning to find the nuisance intolerable. John Graham, minister in Montrose's own parish of Auchterarder, addressed his congregation one Sunday about an alleged conspiracy by Argyll to overthrow the King. He was asked on what information he had thus slandered the Earl. He said he had heard it from Robert Murray, minister of Methven, the man who had played a part in persuading Montrose first to join the Covenant. Murray, when called to account in his turn, cited the word of Montrose himself.

So Montrose was summoned to explain himself before the Committee, with Argyll's anger to spur them to judgement. He said that while visiting Lord Stormont at Scone, he had heard from Atholl, Stewart of Ladywell and Stewart of Grandtully that when Argyll was on his expedition against the Ogilvies the previous summer, he had spoken of wishing to depose the King. Lindsay, Cassilis, Mar and Stewart of Ladywell would witness the truth of his allegations. Lindsay was called, and said he remembered a conversation, but not an exact charge against Argyll. Ladywell, on the other hand, signed a statement confirming all that Montrose had claimed. On May 31st, 1641, he was committed to Edinburgh Castle while the matter was investigated with all the seriousness it merited.

In reality, it was very improbable that Argyll, a man of obsessive secrecy, would have been so rash as to commit himself publicly to a specific denunciation of the King, whatever discourtesies he might have uttered about monarchs in general. Montrose had almost certainly hastened to believe the worst because it suited him to do so. It is also only fair to Argyll to notice that men had been sent to the block on far flimsier evidence. Politics in the seventeenth century were a matter of private enterprise in its purest form: for an ambitious man playing the power game, the rewards of success were enormous and the penalties of failure were absolute. A man who won and held the King's ear could look for a fortune and a dukedom; he who lost it, for a short walk at dawn. Montrose had become a menace, all the more seriously so when Ladywell revealed under interrogation that an account of Argyll's alleged treasonable conversation at the Ford of Lyon had already been sent to the King by the hand of Montrose's usual messenger, a certain Colonel Stewart. Poor Ladywell, who was only Commissary of Dunkeld, had blundered into matters much too deep for him. Balmerino and Lord Durie visited him in his cell, and by a forceful blast of bribes, threats and promises supported by Argyll, induced him to confess that he had fabricated his charges. He now claimed, devastatingly, to have been one of a group of plotters, chief amongst whom were Montrose, Napier, Sir George Stirling of Keir, and Keir's brother-in-law Stewart of Blackhall.

The Committee's agents watched the London road until on the evening of June 4th, Stewart came riding by on his way back from the King's Court. He was taken into the city, straight to Balmerino's lodgings. Young Sir Thomas Hope, the Lord Advocate's son, was present at his interrogation: "After many shifts, he was brought to promise plain dealings. . . . After he had denied he had any more papers than were in his cloth bag, there was a leather bag found in the pannel of his saddle. . . ." It contained a letter from the King to Montrose, innocent enough, dealing with his intention of coming to Edinburgh. There was also a strange note referring to "elephants" and "dromedaries" and other members of some mysterious menagerie. It was never satisfactorily interpreted, but seemed to be a communication in code. "I believe this business shall prove deeper than yet is found," wrote Hope darkly.

Montrose now stood in extreme peril. Argyll was strongly placed to take the offensive after the flood of unproven slanders and libels against him, and he wrote to the King to demand some explanations. It was suggested that Montrose and his friends had contrived some avaricious conspiracy to take over the government of Scotland. Stewart had babbled as much in his efforts to satisfy his inquisitors. Charles wrote back on June 12th, assuring Argyll that he "never made any particular promise for the disposing of any places in that kingdom, but mean to dispose them for the best advantage of my service . . . and as for my letter to Montrose, I do avow it, as fit for me to write, both for the matter, and for the person to whom it is written; who, for anything I yet know, is no ways unworthy of such a favour."

But by the time Charles's letter reached Edinburgh, Montrose, Napier, Stewart of Blackhall and Sir George Stirling of Keir had all been sent to Edinburgh Castle to join Ladywell. Men were sent to Kincardine to examine Montrose's personal papers, although they found only a note about the Cumbernauld Band and some old love letters. On June 22nd, his old friend of St Andrews days, the Earl of Sutherland, came to fetch him from his cell to appear before the Committee of Estates. He refused to leave the Castle, on the grounds that there were no legitimate charges for him to answer. The following day, 400 men were marched into the courtyard to collect him. He went resignedly with them, but stood mute when he was brought in front of his accusers. Back he was sent to the Castle, to live in solitary confinement—the Captain of the Guard was cashiered when it was learnt that he had allowed the Plotters to speak to each other.

At this time began the long process of ruin that was eventually to destroy all Montrose's estates during his struggle against the Covenanters. His house at Mugdock in Stirlingshire was burnt. His secretary John Lambie—the man who had served him since his St Andrews days—was hauled out of the family mansion at Old Montrose to be taken to Edinburgh for interrogation. The doors and gates of the house were torn down and every room ransacked. The same was done at Kincardine. Montrose cannot have been surprised. It was always part of the price of strife in Scotland that the party in the ascendant ruthlessly harried the estates of the party in eclipse. He was to have his own turn at this game, against his enemies, before he was many years older. His only vital concern now was to keep his head on his shoulders, and this was by no means assured.

On July 27th, he was brought before Parliament, still insisting that there was no charge against him. He was once again returned to the Castle. The following day, the wretched Stewart of Ladywell, with neither title nor interest to recommend him, went to the block. Montrose was twice again

brought before Parliament, on August 6th and 14th, on each
occasion pleading that he be granted a fair hearing. His trial
was set for August 25th, and he was returned hastily to his cell,
to be out of sight and out of earshot by the evening of the 14th.
That night, with Lennox, Hamilton, and all the panoply of
State, King Charles arrived at Holyrood to preside over the
Parliament of Scotland, and to restore the Scots to lawful
subjection. The King had heeded the urgings of Montrose and
his other advisers. He came to attempt a personal stroke in the
north.

It was to be Charles's last political throw in his Scottish
kingdom, and a very poor one. Only a summer before, he had
been dreaming of using his power in England to reduce the
rebels of Scotland. Instead, the strain his Scottish adventures
had placed upon the groaning political seams of England had
caused them to crack wide open. A torrent of grievances had
come pouring forth, swamping King, and Court, and councillors. The great Strafford was dead. Laud lay in the Tower. On
August 10th the King had been compelled to ratify a treaty of
peace with the Scots which utterly humiliated him. All the
acts of the 1640 parliament passed into law, £300,000 cash
was to be paid to the Scots army, and the Scots gained the right
Charles had so bitterly contested to try "Incendiaries" who had
been responsible for the Troubles, or more precisely those who
had been loyal to his own cause. Some of the King's closest
English advisers had been forced to flee London to escape the
fate of Laud and Strafford. In nine months the Long Parliament
had laid the foundations of a revolution.

Charles came north now in the fantastic hope that he might
be able to employ his Scottish subjects and their excellent army
against the English rebels. Instead, the Covenanters contemptuously humiliated him. Lennox, Hamilton, Roxburgh and
Morton had to sign the Covenant. Hamilton, desperately
aware of his precarious position and shortage of friends,
attempted in vain to bring off a hasty marriage of one of his
daughters to Argyll's son. Charles was forced to acquiesce in
the act guaranteeing triennial parliaments. Loudon became
Chancellor. The post of Treasurer was left vacant because none
of the King's nominees was acceptable to the Estates. The
provision whereby Parliament chose its own executive was
formally accepted by the King. The wreck of his power in

Scotland was almost complete. The strange events that took place in Edinburgh that autumn finished the matter.

Throughout the King's stay in his northern kingdom, the air had been heavy with suspicion and recrimination about alleged plots and treachery, with Montrose and his friends a convenient focus for the Covenanters' righteous anger. The Graham himself pleaded in vain for a hearing: "What I have done is known to a great many and what I have done amiss is unknown to myself. As truth does not seek corners, it needeth no favours. . . ." But on August 28th, he was left locked in his cell when Napier and the others were brought before Parliament. Charles nodded amiably to Napier, but otherwise sat silent, impotent while the case was postponed and the prisoners were led away back to the Castle. Argyll delivered various vague threats concerning the enemies of the Covenant, begging the King's care in steering the Ship of State "since that for her safety he had given way to cast out some of the naughtiest baggage to lighten her". Montrose must have been near to desperation, understanding with appalling clarity how near he stood to the gallows and how little power the King possessed on his own throne. It was said that Charles secretly promised Montrose that he would not leave Scotland without ensuring his safety "for, if he leave him, all the world will not save his life", as a courtier noted grimly. From the Castle Montrose wrote to the King begging for an interview. He may have written several times, but the most notable letter was sent on October 11th, when he promised that he could prove a clear case of treachery if he was given the opportunity. He was not. He was still in his cell when his case was overtaken by a more immediate and mysterious scandal that became known as The Incident.

The chief Covenanters had for months past ridden everywhere with armed escorts. That autumn, some defiant royalists, Lord Ker most prominent among them, caused great alarm by bringing their own armed bands into Edinburgh. The situation became more serious when rumours spread of a plan to suborn some of the Covenanting officers and stage some coup against the persons of Argyll and Hamilton. Colonel John Hurry, a veteran of the European wars now serving with the Covenanters, shocked the Estates by revealing that mysterious approaches had been made to him and to other officers. At every turn, the

name of Will Murray, Charles's endlessly scheming Scottish
Gentleman of the Bedchamber, cropped up. On October 11th,
Hamilton and Argyll suddenly bolted from Edinburgh to
Kinneil, 20 miles away, alleging that their lives were at risk.
Argyll made it clear that he believed the King was a party to a
plot against them. In the panicky inquiries that followed,
Montrose's letter to the King became public knowledge, and
even more extraordinary tales spread of a conspiracy master-
minded by the prisoners in the Castle against the government
of Scotland. The King denied everything. But far too many
people had vested interests in stirring mud and blood for him to
be believed. The Incident destroyed the last remote possibility
of accord between the King and the Covenanting leadership.

The most likely explanation of the autumn's events in Edinburgh is that there was a group of ardent royalist officers and
courtiers who were fumbling their way towards some stroke
that never came close to execution. Will Murray was probably
involved—it was the sort of affair in which he was all too often
inclined to meddle. It is almost impossible to believe that
Charles was implicated. At that stage, he was still earnestly
wooing the Covenanters. His confidence in Hamilton was
shaken, but it is unthinkable that he designed his death.
Montrose, in Edinburgh Castle, could not have had any part,
and anyway an assassination plot of any sort would have been
abhorrent to him. The Incident was an absurd trifle which was
blown up into a major public scandal only because it suited the
Covenanters to undermine the King's credibility. They
succeeded triumphantly.

Charles was playing golf on Leith Links on October 27th
when news was brought to him of the great rising in Ireland.
The chaos of his dominions was complete. His affairs in Scotland
had to be left to their ruin while he went south to contend with
the new crisis across the water. Pathetically, before he left he
loaded honours upon each of his enemies. Henderson became
Dean of the Chapel Royal at Holyrood. Warriston was
knighted. Loudon became an Earl. Leslie chose the title Earl
of Leven, promising never again to ride against the King.
Argyll, even Argyll was dignified with a Marquisate. For the
King's friends, the Scottish royalists, there was nothing. Charles
never understood how to reward loyalty, and in this case he
probably believed that he dared not. On November 18th, he

departed for London leaving Scotland entirely in the hands of
his enemies, although as usual he clung to pathetic shreds of
optimism that he had won them to be his friends.

He had extorted only one concession in return for his vast
humiliating surrender: Montrose was released from Edinburgh
Castle on bail just before the King rode south. His thrust
against Argyll had been contemptuously parried. He had been
humbled and disarmed. The case against him was no longer
important. It was finally dropped in March 1642. He had
been driven defeated from the stage of events in Scotland.
He was pushed rudely away into the shadows just as the great
drama of civil war began to unfold around the King.

# CHAPTER FIVE

## Cavalier in Waiting

---

MONTROSE RETIRED TO his estates that winter of 1641 lucky that he still had his head on his shoulders. He had been a glittering young man full of promise who had now become an embarrassing failure. He came into the life of Scotland bearing passion, ambition, energy, indiscretion and intemperance. He meddled rather clumsily with high politics, and fell like Icarus. Now he had committed himself to the King's cause, joining a small clique of Scottish royalists despised either for their personal weaknesses like Huntly and Hamilton, or for their political impotence like Napier and the Ogilvies. The royalists had been successfully driven out of the mainstream of politics, of power-broking. The Covenanters ruled Scotland, and faced no serious difficulties in crushing opposition. Some of their enemies fled south to the King. There was a move to try several of the most prominent "Incendiaries" for their role in past events, but only Traquair was called to account, and even his hearing eventually petered out. Montrose and his friends settled uneasily to the routine of life on their estates, exiled from the affairs of their own country. There could be no more Cumbernauld Bands, no more impassioned speeches if they wished to keep their lives and lands. The Covenanting leadership had a grudging respect for Montrose's personal popularity and powers of leadership on the battlefield, and various offers were made to him to serve them once more as a commander. But it was always to be upon their terms. His surrender would be welcome. There was no question of his influencing their political intentions. When he declined their advances, he was left to seek his own damnation. It was a deeply frustrating phase of his life. He lived at Kincardine as a country gentleman with his wife and children, while down the length of England and Scotland the greatest events of the century were unfolding.

The King had gone home from Scotland in November 1641

to face Parliament's Grand Remonstrance. Through that winter the march to tragedy quickened pace. England advanced towards civil war. On January 4th, Charles made his attempt on the Five Members. By the beginning of March, the confrontation between parliamentarians and royalists in the capital had become intolerable. The Queen had already been sent away to Holland. Charles now rode north to begin gathering his forces. On August 22nd, 1642, the Royal Standard was raised at Nottingham. The Civil War formally opened.

Ever since the previous autumn, both King and Parliament had been nervously and incessantly wooing the Scottish Covenanters. The Scots possessed the only demonstrably effective military machine in the two Kingdoms, and thoroughly experienced officers to direct it. When the Irish rebellion broke out, the Scots had been quickly requested to send an army against the Catholic rebels, partly because so many of their own Protestant colonists were under attack in Ulster, but chiefly because they commanded the only immediately available forces. For all Parliament's suspicions of the King and of the movement of troops by his order on any pretext, Pym and his friends could only endorse the dispatch of the Scottish expeditionary force to Ireland. The first regiments reached the battlefield in February 1642.

The Scottish Covenanters were not modest about their pivotal role in the struggle between the King and Parliament in England. Henderson had given assurances that he never believed that presbyterianism should be introduced in England against the will of the English people. But ever since their victory in 1641 gave them such unexpected political power, the Covenanting leadership had been debating how best to export the joys of the Kirk. They were inspired by immaculate conceit, an unshakeable conviction that they had discovered the perfect form of worship and that it was their duty to ensure that the English shared the hope of salvation from it. From the beginning of 1642 until the signing of the Solemn League and Covenant with the English Parliament in August 1643, a desperate auction was taking place, with King and Parliament bidding more and more drastic changes in the English Church against each other, as they fought for the support of the Scots. It was difficult to negotiate compromises and concessions with a party so certain of its own course upon the path of righteousness.

Even Pym and his colleagues found the Covenanters exasperating, and their creed appalling. But both sides in England
understood the critical ability of the Scots to tilt the balance
of power. Each was in the mood to agree to anything in return
for the sight of Scottish regiments fording the Tweed to join its
banners. The Scots coldly weighed the promises of each side.
While Parliament's sincerity might be in doubt, the Covenanters knew with absolute certainty that the King loathed and
despised presbyterianism from the depths of his soul. Whatever
the royalists agreed on paper, it was certain that Charles in his
heart would abjure it.

The Covenanters had become the prisoners of their own
revolution. They had considerable residual political loyalty to
the King—all but the fanatics among them, anyway. But they
knew Charles well enough to be sure that he would never allow
their regime in Scotland to continue for a day once it was in his
power to undo it. All their past victories, religious and political,
were secure only as long as the King was occupied in suppressing
his English rebellion. The only guarantee of the Covenant's
survival was the success of the English puritans, of Pym and
Parliament. From the beginning of the English Civil War, this
logic made the Solemn League and Covenant eventually
inevitable.

It is doubtful whether there was ever a chance of creating an
effective King's party in Scotland after Charles's visit in the
autumn of 1641. A number of nobles such as Dunfermline and
Montgomery were won over by Charles's concessions, and
alarmed by the despotic rule of Argyll and his cohorts. But the
Covenanters maintained a remarkably solid front. The alliance
of Argyll and the ministers and the burgesses held, whatever
wavering took place among the nobility. There were quarrels
about how vehemently to press for the establishment of
presbyterianism in England, but surprisingly few about the
government of Scotland. These were men fired and sustained
by their religion, while Hamilton and his friends of the Court
party chased only the next trick in the game, their own selfish
ambitions. Even after The Incident, after all his blunderings
over a decade, Hamilton—the dissembling, equivocating,
foolish Hamilton—was still whispering fantastic nonsenses into
his royal master's ear and getting a hearing, while continuing
his bewildering flirtation with Argyll. At one moment Hamilton

suggested to Charles that the Queen—the Catholic Queen—might be sent into Scotland to act as mediator between King and Covenant.

The King's desire to woo the Covenanters in 1642 persuaded him that he must avoid associating with their enemies. Montrose, Airlie and others seem to have been deliberately dissuaded from joining the Court at York when the King established himself there to begin the war. Charles's coolness to the Scottish royalists must have bewildered and distressed them. He wrote several times to Montrose, assuring him of his private regard and affection, perhaps because the Graham had been expressing his dismay at the King's public posture.

"As I think fit, in respect of your sufferings for me, by these lines to acknowledge it to you—so I think it unfit to mention, by writ, any particulars, but to refer you to the faithful relation of this honest bearer, Mungo Murray," wrote Charles from Windsor in January 1642. Murray was probably sent to explain to Montrose and other Scottish royalists the need for public discretion, even coldness towards them. The King told Lanark, Hamilton's brother, that it was his "positive pleasure that the first breach should not come from his party; but they should draw things out as long as was possible before they hazarded on a rupture" with the Covenanters. In May 1642, Charles was once again soothing Montrose in a letter from York: "I will have you to believe of me, that I would not invite you to share of my hard fortune, if I intended you not to be a plentiful partaker of my good. The bearer will acquaint you of my designs . . . I will say no more but that I am your assured friend CHARLES R."

Nothing is more difficult in war or in politics than to persuade a distant subordinate, especially one of such impatient spirit as Montrose, that those directing the battle have good reasons for inaction. It was especially difficult for any servant of Charles I to think well of the ideas of the Court and of royal headquarters, which so often proved disastrous. But the King was certainly right in dealing warily with the Covenanters throughout 1642 and 1643, and Montrose was wrong to urge an immediate revolt against them.

From the moment that the English Civil War became inevitable, Charles's only chance of victory lay in speed. He had a great initial advantage: the gentlemen who flocked to his Standard were bred to the use of arms and horses, every man accustomed to command at least his own household. The longer the war continued, the more heavily the balance would tilt against the King as Parliament's hold on the arsenals, the fleet and the City of London began to tell. In the summer of 1642, every month that the Scots could be kept out of the war was a month gained for the King.

Montrose had a reputation as a hot spirit whose political judgement had proved poor. He had gained little credit at Court for the intellectual honesty of his conversion from Covenanter to royalist, or the soul-searching that he had undertaken before making it. Instead, men of the stamp of Hamilton and Digby saw only an arrogant young man who had rushed misguidedly onto the wrong side, and then run even more hastily back again. His military reputation rested upon the little skirmish at the Bridge of Dee and his few months as a brigade commander under Leven. He had not fought in a major action. The King had done a good deal of tedious private negotiating to save Montrose's neck the previous autumn, at the young man's earnest imprecation. Having been saved from his own indiscretions once, he was now yet again urging the King to drastic action in Scotland. His credentials for being taken seriously were not impressive.

A revolt in Scotland would probably have to be engineered from the Gordon country, and the last venture of that sort had foundered without escaping from its own borders. The Highland clans were a doubtful quantity. In the Lowlands, most of the professional soldiers were committed to the Covenant. Even the estates of great royalists such as Hamilton were being watched by local Covenanters who were strong enough even to prevent him from mustering his own tenants. The prospects of a successful rising were negligible. The only certain outcome of such a venture was that the Covenanters would throw in their lot decisively with the English Parliament. Charles was foolish to nourish hopes, as he continued to do throughout 1642, that he could bring in a Covenanting army on his own side against the English rebels. But he was perfectly right to seek at all costs to keep the Scots neutral for as long as possible. An unsuccessful rising in Scotland would have brought a Scots army to join the Parliamentary forces in England by late 1642 or early 1643. In the event, Leven and his men did not cross the

border until January 1644. The King had his chance to make
war unimpeded upon his English enemies for eighteen months.
It was time for him to open hostilities against the Scots only
when they committed themselves to doing so against him.

But to Montrose and his little party in Scotland, it was
intolerable to hear of Hamilton in Edinburgh dining affably
with the King's enemies and sending word to Charles that there
was no danger of their intervening in England. In July 1642,
Argyll had stage-managed the proceedings of the annual
General Assembly of the Kirk in St Andrews, although
Dunfermline had sat as King's Commissioner. In November,
the English Parliament had formally appealed for assistance
from the Scots. The frail remains of royal authority in Scotland
had suffered a further blow when Charles's own proclamation
in defence of his cause was published only on condition that
Parliament's was issued alongside it. The tide of opinion in
Edinburgh was running strongly for Parliament, all the more
so after the King's military successes in the Midlands and the
West country. The longer the Covenanters contemplated the
prospect of Parliament's defeat, the less agreeable it seemed. At
the beginning of 1643, they sent a delegation that included
Loudon, Lindsay and Alexander Henderson to meet the King
at his headquarters at Oxford to ask him to summon a Scottish
Parliament, and to test the temperature at Court. Montrose and
his friends were convinced that Charles remained blind to the
urgent danger facing him from Scotland. Soon after the
Covenanting party had taken the Oxford road, Montrose,
together with Ogilvy and Aboyne, were in the saddle after them.

"Our heart burnings increase, and with them our dangers,"
wrote Baillie[1] warily, "so much the more as Montrose, Ogilvy
and Aboyne who this long while have been very quiet, are on a
sudden to the King, for what we cannot tell. . . ."

But when the little band of royalists reached Newcastle,
they learnt that the Queen, Henrietta Maria, had just landed
at Bridlington Bay on her return from Holland. It was a godsent
opportunity to solicit her support and explain the urgency with
which they viewed the situation. Montrose turned aside for
Bridlington, leaving the others to ride on to Oxford. Henrietta
had been raising money and arms for the royal cause, and pawn-
ing the crown jewels. The Dutch navy had obligingly convoyed
her back to England through the Parliamentary blockade. But

although the blockaders could not prevent her landing, they bombarded Bridlington harbour while she lay resting after her queasy crossing, sending shot crashing through her bedroom and driving her skurrying into a ditch outside for safety. At the best of times, she was a silly, fecklessly optimistic, dangerous woman. She had wheedled her husband into some of the worst blunders of his reign, had wormed some of the most foolish favourites of the Court into positions of power, and to the last remained obstinately incapable of understanding the nature of the disaster facing the throne. Even if Montrose's knowledge of the Queen was based only on hearsay, he should have known better how to tackle such a woman than to burst upon her at Bridlington full of earnest plans for his Scottish rising. "But being fatigued and ill after a very stormy passage," says Wishart,[2] "she told him that she would advise with him more fully when they came to York." It is easy to picture the scene at Bridlington, with the Queen chattering compulsively about the debris that had so recently been falling about her ears, the stink aboard the ship, the dreariness of the Dutch and the difficulties of negotiating in Europe. Montrose's attempts to get a sympathetic hearing would have seemed to her tiresome beyond endurance. Their relations were never to be cordial, although the courtesies were maintained. She was essentially frivolous. Montrose, in this of all things, was utterly earnest.

He rode behind her to York, where she installed herself in a splendid house close to the Minster which belonged to Sir Arthur Ingram. From his headquarters in the city, the Earl of Newcastle conducted the affairs of the King in the North with the utmost pomp and circumstance, and the Queen was able to bask in the loyalty and luxury of York surrounded by the most delightful crowd of officers and gallants. Sir Marmaduke Langdale and Lord George Goring were leading cavalry flying columns with sparkling success. Henrietta had brought with her from Holland General James King, a veteran of the European wars who now became Newcastle's chief-of-staff. There was a constant clamour of officers and peers arguing for advances and marches, sieges and raids that might bring advantage to the royal cause. Amidst it all, the Queen had to contend with Montrose, urging his wild Scottish projects. When Hamilton appeared at York, she was thankful to be able to refer the whole matter to him.

"He did not, indeed, deny but that there was some danger from the Covenanters," says Wishart,[3] "but he endeavoured to extenuate it, and condemned Montrose's advice as rash, imprudent, and unseasonable. That stout and warlike nation, he said, was not to be reduced by force of arms, but by gentleness and good treatment; war, a civil war especially ought to be the last remedy. . . ." Stripping Hamilton's comments of their irksome selfrighteousness, it is hard to disagree with him.

The Queen accepted his advice to do nothing, and must have been thankful to be able to dismiss Montrose. His stay at York was obviously tense and fractious, with Hamilton's bile to discomfit him. There was an incident in the Queen's garden that suggested the rude, bullying streak in the royal favourite. He saw two dogs fighting, and promptly drew his sword and ran one of them through. Typically, Montrose made a verse of it, and wrote the poor brute's epitaph:

> Here lies a dog whom quality did plead
> such fatal end from a renowned blade;
> And blame him not that he succumbed now
> E'en Hercules could not combat against two;
> for while he on his foe revenge did take,
> He manfully was killed behind his back.
> Then say, to eternize the cur that's gone,
> He fleshed the maiden sword of Hamilton.

But it was Hamilton who easily defeated Montrose at York, and soon afterwards was made a Duke by the King in token of his unshaken faith in his old favourite. Montrose, chastened, rode home nursing his frustration. The political news grew rapidly worse. The Covenanting delegation came back to Edinburgh thoroughly frustrated by their visit to the King. At Argyll's prompting, it was agreed that a Convention of Estates should be called to debate the state of the nation, since Charles would sanction no parliament. When Charles heard, he at once took steps to forbid it, but Hamilton dissuaded him for the simple reason that he would only be defied if he did so. According to Wishart, Hamilton then wrote to every royalist in Scotland urging them to attend the Convention and bring their influence to bear upon it. Montrose sent back word that he would come only on certain conditions: he wanted Hamilton's word that if no satisfactory settlement emerged from the Convention, then it would be the signal for war. He demanded, in other words, that the King's men should seek a showdown with the Covenanters. Hamilton not unexpectedly declined this ultimatum. Montrose and his little party determined to boycott the Convention.

The Graham's sour relations with Hamilton and his rebuff by the Queen at York seem to have provoked the Covenanters to try once more to persuade him to accept a military command under their orders. They promised that all his debts would be paid—apparently he had become seriously embarrassed about money during his imprisonment in Edinburgh Castle. At this late hour, it is hard to believe that he seriously entertained the idea. But the rumour of it reached the Queen, alarming her sufficiently to write to Montrose:

Cousin—I have received your letter, and learn therefrom that you consider affairs in Scotland to be in a very bad state, as regards the interests of the King; and this owing to my own neglect of certain propositions submitted to me when I first arrived. In that I have followed the commands of the King. But still I am of the opinion that, if his Majesty's faithful servants would only agree among themselves, and not lose time, all the evil to be dreaded from that quarter may be prevented ... I ... have been given to understand that you have struck up an alliance with certain persons that might well create apprehension in my mind. But my trust in you, and the esteem with which I regard you, are not built upon so slippery a foundation as mere rumour; nor is it to be shaken by an event, which, if it be as reported, could only have been occasioned by your zeal for his Majesty's service.

Early in June, Montrose was in the Gordon country once again, in futile pursuit of an alliance between Huntly, Airlie and the Earl Marischal to rise for the King. His efforts came to nothing. He was soon to understand that Huntly would never join any band that included the upstart Graham who had humiliated himself and his family three years earlier. To complicate matters further, the Covenanting leadership in Edinburgh had just been apprised of yet another mad plot by

E

Lord Antrim to land Irish troops in western Scotland. Antrim
had been captured by the Scots army in Ulster, had escaped,
but had now been taken again, carrying letters from Nithsdale
and Aboyne which referred to military plans involving the
Queen, Huntly and Montrose. Montrose seems to have been
only peripherally concerned, but at a moment when the
political situation in Scotland was already delicate, the
Antrim revelations gave Argyll still more ammunition in his
struggle to drag his country into the Civil War against the King.
Scotland was becoming a warm place for any royalist, and
Montrose's personal position had become intolerable.

There was one more peaceful, even picturesque encounter
between the Covenanting leadership and the man who was to
humiliate them. On June 22nd, 1643, as the Convention
assembled in Edinburgh, Alexander Henderson met Montrose
on the banks of the Forth, at Stirling bridge, to make a final
attempt to bring him back under the bough of the Covenant.
Napier, Ogilvy, and Stirling of Keir—Montrose's closest allies
and friends—rode to the rendezvous beside him. Sir James
Rollo, Montrose's brother-in-law and now an ardent Covenanter, accompanied Henderson. That summer day as they stood
in a field beside the river, their horses and grooms and escorts
idling curiously at a distance behind them, Henderson told
Montrose plainly "that they were resolved to send as powerful
an army as possible to the assistance of their brethren in
England against the King's forces; and that all the Covenanters
in both Kingdoms were unanimously agreed either to die or
force the King to order; that nothing was more earnestly
desired than that he should join in favour and friendship with
his peers and the other estates of the realm, it would bring joy
to all, and not only profit, but also honour to himself. His
example would at once bring over the few, if there were any,
who respected the empty shadow of royalty."[4]

Montrose temporized. He asked Rollo if Henderson spoke
for the Convention, and when Rollo replied that he had not
been explicitly authorized by them, seized the excuse to make
no immediate reply. After two hours together, the little party
broke up to go their separate ways, and Henderson and
Montrose said farewell for the last time. On June 26th,
Hamilton and Lanark lost a critical battle in the Convention
when they were refused leave for the reading of a letter addressed

to its members by the King. Although a majority of nobles supported Hamilton, and thus the royalist party, on the issue, the burgesses and lairds remained solid behind Argyll and carried the day. Negotiations began in earnest about the sending of an expeditionary force to aid Parliament in England. A Committee was established to try Lord Carnwath and Lord Traquair. Nithsdale and Aboyne were declared outlaws and fugitives, and Huntly, Ogilvy, Herries and Banff were ordered to find cautions to keep the peace. The royalists of Scotland had been defeated. On August 7th, commissioners from the English Parliament arrived in Edinburgh to begin the negotiations that established the Solemn League and Covenant. At Kincardine, Montrose made preparations to part from his great estates, from his family, from his friends for the last time in peace. There is no means of knowing whether his wife watched him with anger, or bitterness or merely sorrow. She must have been as much distressed as any woman by the pillaging of her houses while her husband was a prisoner, by his alienation from the great majority of his countrymen, by his determination to cast himself upon the pikes of the enemy at whatever cost to those around him. The Earl and his Countess seem seldom, if ever, to have met again. On this day of 1643, he ordered a small escort to accompany him, including probably his half-brother Harry Graham and one or two personal servants. Then he rode out of the courtyard of Kincardine, across the Ruthven into the Ochill hills on the other side, away southwards to find the King.

Montrose had reached his decision to join himself openly at last to the cause of Charles I by a thorny, tortuous path. He was a good calvinist, a good Scot, and he had shared all his countrymen's anger at the high-handed, distant rule imposed upon them from London since 1603. He was to avow on the scaffold: "The Covenant I took; I own it and adhere to it; bishops, I care not for them; I never intended to advance their interest." But then he added, crucially: "but when the King had granted you all your desires, and you were every one sitting under his own vine, and under his fig-tree, that then you should have taken a party in England by the hand, and entered into a league and covenant with them against the King, was the thing I judged my duty to oppose to the yondmost."

It is possible for the literal-minded to argue that it was only

Montrose's gullibility that led him to join the King, since the
royal promises and concessions that he considered so generous
were never meant to be kept. It is possible to look at the record
of his foolishness and perfidy in Scotland and to argue that
Argyll and the Covenanters were wholly justified, that the
King was a posturing fool who deserved his end.

It is indeed hard to defend the government of Charles I.
But some good and great cavaliers in England and in Scotland
were to ride for him in the Civil War, knowing all his errors and
weaknesses. They simply looked beyond him, at his enemies,
and perceived men bent on tearing down the house about their
heads, who showed the keenest ingenuity in wrecking the
existing machinery of government, yet who offered nothing to
compensate for the vast store of blood and treasure and misery
that was expended in the process. The cold, ruthless revolution-
ary Pym who undid Strafford, and Cromwell who was to
reveal the essential emptiness of his lifework by nominating his
own son to succeed him as Lord Protector, had no appeal to
some of the best men in the two Kingdoms. They knew those
regiments of bigots like the fanatical minister Hugh Peter, who
was to rush to torment the poor Marquess of Winchester even
as he stood among the ruins of Basing House after its fall, chiding
him mercilessly for his support of the cause of the ungodly.
The dazed old gentleman replied with simple nobility that "he
hoped the King might have a day again". The religious
conceits of the rebels were to many decent men even more
distasteful than the extravagances of the King's claims to
Divine Right. In Scotland, the Covenanters gleefully abolished
Christmas as soon as they gained power in the land. "None
suffered to make good cheer or be merry according to the old
custom," recorded the Aberdeen diarist[5] sadly, and the
wretched local fishermen were driven to sea in a storm on
Christmas Day lest there be any suggestion that they were
honouring the occasion as a holiday. Many good Scots' instincts
were repelled by the Covenanters' excesses in the name of the
Lord. The humiliation of the King had only made way for the
melancholy tyranny of Argyll. Where was the new liberty, the
new dignity in any of this? It is characteristic of most revolu-
tions that they unseat one power to make way for another
even worse. When men of such honour and intelligence as
Verney and Falkland had overcome their deep misgivings

about Charles I to die for his cause, then Montrose joined a worthy company. He concluded that the King represented a lesser threat to men's peace and dignity than those who sought to overthrow him. He was one of a host of men who were originally and justly appalled by the excesses of Charles I, but who recoiled from those of his enemies at some point between 1641 and 1660.

Montrose reached Oxford some time in August 1643. There was now "no cause or room left to doubt his sincerity to the King".[6] He at once addressed himself to Henrietta Maria, pleading the urgent necessity of an uprising in Scotland. He brought the first hard news of the Covenanters' plans to move an army into England. But Hamilton's reports from Edinburgh were still sanguine. Montrose made no progress with the Queen. In desperation he rode westwards to the King's headquarters with his besieging army outside Gloucester.

His experience of war had not, as yet, been in any very hard school. In Charles I's great camp around Gloucester, for the first time he met an army that knew the meaning of fighting for its life.[7] They were newly arrived from the storm of Bristol, at which the magnificent Cornish regiments had paid so dearly for the King's victory. The cavalry had ridden through a hundred skirmishes. Already some of the finest gentlemen of the royalist cause—Godolphin, Grenvile, Verney—were in their graves. The King's fortunes were at a high point after Bristol and the battle at Roundaway Down, but those around him were finding the business of civil war bloodier and grimmer than any of them had thought possible. Charles himself held Court every evening at Matson House, while during the day he watched the progress of the siege. Miners from the Forest of Dean were tunnelling deep under the city walls to lay their petards, although Prince Rupert had misgivings that the ground was too wet. A storm had been forbidden for fear of losses as severe as those at Bristol. The Prince himself was living at Prinknash Park, but that pleasant house saw little enough of him, for every day he laboured beside his sappers in the mines.

Montrose and his little personal household probably found quarters in some cottage in one of the nearby villages, like most of the senior officers of the royalist army. He was welcomed by the King. With all his earnest, passionate charm, Montrose began to plead with him to give the signal for action in Scotland. But Charles was receiving the same dispatches from Hamilton as the Queen. He was also preoccupied with the siege. Montrose had no better luck with Rupert. Soon after his arrival came the critical moment of the Campaign. On August 24th Colonel Massey and the Parliamentary garrison were offered a last chance to surrender before the mines were fired under them. They refused, and that night Rupert mustered his storming parties to attack at dawn as soon as the breaches had been blown. But before morning, there was a severe rainstorm. The royalist mines collapsed before the fuses could be lit. The tunnelling had to begin again as Parliament's relieving army drew rapidly nearer. The King and Rupert left their men to their labours, and took horse for a hasty trip to Oxford. Montrose rode with the party, trotting alongside them up the damp lanes, still begging desperately for the chance to deliver what he believed could be a decisive stroke of the war. He could hardly have chosen a worse moment to plead his case.

Rupert[8] knew nothing of Scotland except the troublesomeness of its politicians. He was an energetic, mettlesome officer carrying huge responsibilities, who had just suffered a serious setback. England was the great theatre of war, and the affairs of Ireland and of Scotland impinged only as dangerous diversions, fraught with complications. Every commander is harassed by subordinates and rivals seeking men for their pet projects and sideshows, and it is part of the business of controlling an army to resist such pressures, to concentrate forces at critical points rather than scattering them in penny portions around the map. In the Civil War, the royalists had already allowed themselves to become much too preoccupied with the defence of strongpoints, castles and great houses, each needing a garrison, each drawing men away from the King's army on the battlefield. Montrose's credentials when he arrived at Oxford looked no more impressive than they had at the Queen's Court at York six months earlier. The King might have come to like him and to have a certain respect for him, but there was nothing to suggest that he deserved a place in the highest councils of the war. His grace and his enthusiasm were charming, but Rupert and the King were trapped in agonized suspense, desperate to see their miners blast a way into Gloucester before the relief force arrived. Nothing was done for

Montrose. As the King returned to Gloucester on August 28th to break up the siege and acknowledge defeat, the pale young Scottish nobleman had become merely one of many men who rode with Charles and lavished their suggestions upon him.

It was Montrose's tragedy and Charles's that just as 1642 had been the wrong moment for the Scottish royalists to rise, just as even February would have been premature, the critical moment had now come without being recognized. If Montrose had been able to break through to the north in the autumn of 1643 with the King's commission and a few hundred horse, it is conceivable that he could have enabled Charles to win the Civil War. Now that the Solemn League and Covenant had been signed, now that the Covenanters were openly raising an army to march across the Border, there was no longer any political objection to a royalist rising. There was nothing to lose and much to gain. With Argyll in open rebellion against the King, doubters might be induced to join the royalists. All the advantages that were to work for Montrose a year later existed in 1643, and Antrim's Irishmen might even have been transported in time, had there been sufficient sense of urgency. It was essential that Montrose established himself in the Covenanting rear, north of the Forth, and cause havoc so great as to prevent Leven and his army from going south. If Montrose had already been leading an army in the hills that autumn, it is difficult to imagine that the Convention of Estates in Edinburgh would have allowed their own forces to leave them. It was the Scots army that decided the balance of forces and the fate of the royalists at Marston Moor, and thus in turn sealed the fate of the King's cause. Montrose had to be in Scotland that winter of 1643 to prevent Marston Moor from taking place as it did. After Marston Moor, and after the Covenanting army was established in England, Montrose needed a miracle to alter the course of events in the south. He never commanded a fraction of the force that would have been needed to bring meaningful assistance to the King in England.

It is pointless to dwell too long on the might-have-beens of history. But Buchan, Napier, and other historians have chastised Charles for his failure to give Montrose his head in 1642 or early 1643, which seems unfair. In turn, if one chooses the year that began in September 1643 with the collapse of the siege of Gloucester as the hinge of fate for the King, then

Charles's failure to use Montrose at the critical moment—only indeed to commission him at the twelfth hour as the most forlorn of forlorn hopes—must be singled out as one of his most tragic, if most understandable missed opportunities.

While Montrose was arguing his case with the King in England, in Scotland the Covenanters were bracing themselves for war. In the process they cast overboard at last such tiresome passengers as the Duke of Hamilton. The English Commissioners from Parliament had reached Edinburgh in August 1643. The Convention of Estates received them with self-conscious gravity. Then both sides hastened to business: to reach agreement for the dispatch of a Scots army against the King. Parliament was then hourly expecting the fall of Gloucester, and was in deep alarm about the long succession of royal victories. More and more wavering spirits were worrying, like Manchester, that "if we fight a hundred times and beat him ninety-nine times, he will be King still. But if he beat us but once, or the last time, we shall be hanged." Parliament needed the Scots very badly indeed. The Covenanters, well aware of this, forced a mean, grasping transaction upon the English Commissioners. The Parliamentarians had no difficulty in accepting the abolition of the English episcopate, but they agreed to the Scots demand for imposing presbyterianism in England in such equivocal terms that it was obvious that they had no intention of fulfilling their side of the bargain. The political clauses of their agreement called for the preservation of peace and of the 1641 treaty, together with the securing of constitutional liberties. The English recognized their own role as suppliants and that of the Scots as mercenaries by agreeing to repay the entire cost of the Scots army once peace had been made. Each party undertook not to make a separate treaty with the King. By August 18th matters had gone far enough for the Convention to issue an order for men between sixteen and sixty to muster to the army. On August 26th, the Convention approved the draft of the Solemn League and Covenant. Leven received his commission to command a force of 18,000 infantry, 2000 horse and 1000 dragoons, which together with supporting artillery crossed the border into England on January 19th, 1644. Always a pragmatic and ambitious man, the little old Earl had reached the conclusion that his promise to the King not to serve against him did not extend to the new political situation.

The eternally flexible Lanark allowed the Convention's muster call against the King to be sent out in the King's name. But even he and his brother Hamilton knew that the game was played out at last. On the occasion of Lady Roxburgh's funeral at Kelso a few weeks later, they were among a large gathering of royalists who met, feebly to debate the possibility of an uprising, quickly to dismiss it. Lanark and Hamilton then slipped away southwards, leaving their ferocious mother to muster men for the Covenant on their estates. They arrived at Oxford in the middle of December to face the King's anger. He was always at his most merciless with those whom he had trusted and who failed him, for whatever reasons. Hamilton's sudden conversion from blithe optimism to hopeless resignation was too much for Charles, who bitterly diagnosed treachery. Hamilton had no friends to plead his cause at Oxford, and many enemies. Montrose, Aboyne, Ogilvy and Kinnoul were all eager for revenge on the man who had so injured themselves and the King's cause. They were perfectly sincere in thinking him a traitor. Montrose, according to Wishart, promised Charles that he would emigrate if Hamilton was this time allowed to escape his deserts. But Charles needed little convincing. Hamilton was sent to begin three years of imprisonment in Pendennis Castle in Cornwall. Lanark was also confined, but he escaped, confirming all the worst royalist suspicions of him by fleeing to London and thence to Edinburgh, where he signed the Solemn League and Covenant. In reality, it seems unlikely that either he or Hamilton had consciously betrayed the King. They were merely hopelessly flawed instruments in whom Charles had been mad to place his trust. Hamilton served Charles after his fashion, while tortuously seeking also to serve himself. It was his own and his master's misfortune that he was hopelessly out of his depth in a game with such players as Argyll, Warriston and Henderson.

That winter of 1643–44 must have been a difficult one for Montrose in Oxford. Among so many strange English faces, men to whom Scotland had always been something of a joking matter, he had to make himself respected and earn the right to be taken seriously. He had Aboyne and Ogilvy for company, and no doubt they found cramped lodgings in one of the colleges like the hundreds of other royalist officers who crowded the city. But access to the King was jealously guarded by such

familiars as Digby. Even Rupert himself had perpetual difficulty
keeping in touch with his uncle as he rode tirelessly up and down
England rallying the forces of the Crown. There were endless
place-seekers and favourites and meddlers such as Will Murray
who pursued their own ambitions without thought for the
interest of the cause. Perhaps Montrose sometimes chased
away boredom by riding on Rupert's raids into the Chilterns,
harassing Parliament's positions and supply trains and beating
back to Oxford before enemy horse could be roused against
them. He must have learnt a lot that winter about the strengths
and weaknesses of armies which the war had already revealed.
But it is never much fun to be a hanger-on when everyone else
has his appointed task, and Montrose was neither field officer
nor state official, only a perpetual Scot in waiting, chafing
impatiently in Oxford while, in his own country, hope was
slipping away from Charles Stuart.

Oxford must have been a claustrophobic town, with the
Cherwell dammed and marshes and streams on three sides, and
most of the citizens doing forced labour digging trenches and
raising bastions to seal the weak points on the perimeter. Oxen
and sheep driven in by Rupert's horse grazed in Christchurch
quadrangle. New College Cloisters and the tower of Schools
were armouries. The Queen held her Court at Merton, while
the King's Officers of State held their Cabinets in Oriel. The
city was crowded with royalist refugees and officers, foreign
visitors and emissaries and petitioners, drunkards and duelling
gallants, messengers and servants. The crush and the marshes
caused constant outbreaks of camp fever, and the city was
chronically unhealthy. Pembroke was at one moment housing
more than a hundred guests, including twenty-three women
and five children. There was still a dwindling body of under-
graduates, but it was widely believed that they only kept their
gowns to avoid having to fight, and were despised accordingly.
One familiar face Montrose recognized—Colonel Hurry, the
former Covenanting officer who had so alarmed the Estates in
Edinburgh with his tale of attempted seduction during The
Incident, was in town. Hurry was "a soldier of fortune and
very changeable", as Sir James Turner[9] remarked wryly.
He was constantly to cross and recross Montrose's path between
Oxford and the scaffold. He had been fighting for Parliament
for the past few months, but had now changed sides, not for the

last time, and been welcomed in Oxford as a valuable recruit bringing important intelligence. The city had become a haven for all manner of men around the King—Jeremy Taylor, old Archbishop Ussher preaching in All Saints and St Aldates, Edward Hyde and Endymion Porter. At least Montrose awaited his hour among stimulating company.

That winter, he and the little band of Scottish royalists at Oxford learnt that their estates lay under the hand of the Covenant and their income was confiscated, for their failure to return home to subscribe the Solemn League and Covenant. Montrose himself may have felt some small pang of family shame or anger to learn that of all the royalist peers threatened by the Covenanters, only his own father-in-law Southesk had turned apostate and signed the wretched document.

Argyll, meanwhile, utterly committed to the King's destruction, led the subscribers to the Scots war chest with a loan of £12,000. He had also been appointed President of the section of the Committee of Estates which was to go south with the army. The only embarrassment to his absolute power and influence in Scotland was news that an Irish Catholic chieftain, Alasdair Macdonald, one of the Macdonalds of Antrim, was raiding with 300 men among the Campbell's possessions in the Western Isles, claiming that he swung his sword for the King. Without the ghost of a smile at the absurd paradox, the Convention gave Argyll a Commission as King's Lieutenant to root out the troublemakers. Alasdair retired to Ireland without achieving his main purpose of freeing his father, the great Coll Keitach, and his two brothers, all of whom had been languishing as prisoners of Argyll since 1640. They had been captured on the island of Colonsay to which they had traditionally held title, along with Kintyre on the mainland, until the Campbells seized them on some spurious pretext. The Macdonalds were the Campbells' unrelenting enemies, Alasdair all the more so since his family's injuries at the hands of Argyll. Montrose was soon to make formidable use of that hatred.

Irishmen were beginning to loom large in the affairs of England. In September 1643, Ormonde as King's Lord-Lieutenant in Ireland had signed a truce with the Catholic Irish rebels and begun to send his desperately-needed troops across the water to join the King. The Cessation, as it was called, caused an uproar both in England and Ireland. The

Catholic rebels continued to harass and pillage Protestant
settlers, especially the Scots in Ulster, who were left defenceless
by the departure of the King's men. The alleged truce was
interpreted both by the settlers and by Parliament in London as
a cynical manœuvre designed solely to release troops for the
King's service at the price of abandoning good Protestants to
the wrath of the papists. Even English royalists were dismayed
when Ormonde's Irish soldiers began to arrive in England.
Then, as now, the Irish were regarded as beyond the pale of
civilization, excluded from any claim to truce or mercy. These
men of Ormonde's were mostly Protestants. Future schemes to
bring Irish Catholics into the struggle in England were to
appall English public opinion. Yet it was the prospect of Irish
Catholic aid that persuaded Montrose that he might yet save
Scotland for the King.

The revelations of deceit and incompetence on the part of the
Hamilton brothers together with the disastrous news of the
Covenanters' muster against him, had brought a change of
heart to the King. Montrose, the man who had so insistently
warned him of what was coming to pass, took on a new
importance and respectability. Charles always craved hope, and
liked to surround himself with optimists. Now, when so many
men were shrugging their shoulders despairingly about
Scotland, Montrose offered amazing plans and glittering hopes.
They met several times in public and in private that winter
of 1643. Charles, according to Wishart, "complained that he
had been most grossly betrayed by those to whom he had
entrusted his secrets, his crown, and his life, and earnestly
pressed for his advice. Montrose answered that though matters
seemed in a deplorable state, yet if it pleased his royal master, he
promised either to reduce the rebels to order, or lose his life in
the attempt. The King, not a little cheered by Montrose's
confidence, desired him to take a day or two's grace for full
deliberation, and so dismissed him".

When Montrose returned, he put it to the King that the vital
ingredient for any uprising was a measure of outside aid. An
Irish landing in western Scotland, perhaps some troops of
German horse from the friendly King of Denmark, anyway
arms and ammunition to equip local recruits—it was impossible
to raise Scotland without at least some minimum of resources.
The Covenanters controlled the country: ports, arsenals, castles,

roads. Montrose would need a few squadrons of horse from the Marquis of Newcastle in Yorkshire before he could even cut his way through the Covenanting cordon into Scotland. Then there was the possibility of the Irish.

The Earl of Antrim, buoyant and garrulous and charming as ever, sprung himself back on the Court at Oxford the very week that the Hamiltons returned to face their disgrace in December 1643. Antrim had yet again escaped from his Covenanting captors in Ireland. After calling in on the Catholic Irish rebel headquarters at Kilkenny, he now came to Charles claiming to be their General-In-Chief. He was nothing of the kind, of course, but he was a cheerful soul of boundless optimism and Charles was happy to welcome him back as such. When the project of an Irish descent on the west coast was raised yet again, Antrim assured the Court that he could bring in 10,000 men. Even those who doubted his commission as General-In-Chief knew that he was at least chief of the Macdonalds of Antrim, who had proved one of the most ferocious and bloodthirsty clans in Ireland during the rebellion. Their hatred for Clan Campbell and thus for Argyll, their claims to Kintyre and Colonsay were well-known. At the very least the unleashing of the Macdonalds upon the Campbells promised to cause bottomless mischief for the leadership of the Covenant. As Montrose and Antrim and the King and Aboyne and Ogilvy talked of the prospect for Scotland, the longer they thought of the Irish descent, the more splendid it appeared.

On January 28th, 1644, while Charles's Oxford parliament sat in Christchurch Hall, a document was drawn up embodying the plan that was now agreed between Montrose, Antrim and the King: ". . . the said Earl of Montrose and the rest of his Majesty's party in Scotland engaged shall raise forces to the utmost of their power for his Majesty's service, both in the north, in the east, and on the borders of Scotland, and that what power soever they shall be able to engage in his Majesty's service they shall assemble into a body or several bodies, as shall be most expedient for his Majesty's service, and that they shall therewith declare for his Majesty's service against the rebellious party there in the latter day of March next ensuing the day hereof . . . That the said Earl of Antrim on his part shall to the utmost of his power raise forces in the isles of Scotland as also what forces he can do for that purpose within

the Kingdom of Ireland and with the said forces invade the
Marquis of Argyll's country in Scotland by the latter end of
March. . . . There to endeavour by arms, as far as in him lies,
the reestablishment of his Majesty's just rights . . . and to the
performance hereof they do mutually engage their honours to
one another, as witness our hands and seals, this day and date
hereof. . . ."[10]

The agreement was signed by Montrose and Antrim. Digby
witnessed it for the King, President Spottiswoode, the son of
the late Archbishop for Montrose, and Daniel O'Neill for
Antrim. It is a mark of Montrose's desperation at this time that
he agreed to use Catholic Irish troops. He must have understood
the unspeakable horror with which they would be received
among the Lowland Scots. Even in Oxford, the project was
concealed from several of the King's English advisers, including
Hyde, although naturally all men knew that Montrose was
given a commission from the King to go into Scotland. There
was some little debate about the exact terms of his command:
initially he was to be Captain-General under the King, and a
commission was made out to that effect. But on further consideration—some say at Montrose's own request, fearing the
jealousy of his fellow Scottish peers—Prince Maurice, Rupert's
brother, was named Captain-General, and Montrose as the
King's Lieutenant-General. It was a sound scheme, for Prince
Maurice might come in useful as an eminent figurehead for
dealing with such prickly creatures as Huntly. Maurice, it
was agreed, would come to Scotland at some appropriate
future moment after Montrose had started the rising. For the
present, however, the King's Lieutenant-General was to march
alone.

It is easy to imagine Montrose and those happy few Scottish
gentlemen who were his friends dining together in Oxford
before he rode out to win back Scotland for the King, toasting
their impossible dream with a glow of occasion in their hearts.
To Spottiswoode, to Aboyne, and Ogilvy and a handful of
others, the venture meant so much. To most of the English
officers and courtiers, this was merely one of a dozen desperate
throws that had little substance beside the great realities of
defeating Fairfax in Yorkshire, of checking Meldrum at Newark,
of taking the next round in the endless struggle for the West.
But the Scottish royalists were exiles from their own homes and

estates, ruined men if they could not achieve the impossible task that was being put upon them.

One gleam of hope was already dying as they rode out of Oxford for the north: on March 9th, Sir John Gordon of Haddo raided Aberdeen and seized the Covenanting Provost of the city. Finding the city such easy prey for the royalists, even Huntly at last bestirred himself to occupy it in the King's name. Argyll was forced to quit Leven and the Scots army in England to go north and cope with this new threat in the rear. But Huntly was still as feeble as ever. As soon as Argyll's men were within reach of the city, he handed over all his property to his Covenanting eldest son Lord Gordon and fled by sea without making any resistance. This time, even his own castle seemed too close to the Covenanters for safety. He journeyed on, around the top of Scotland to the Reay lands of Strathnaver. Reay himself was in England with the King, but Huntly established himself in that enchanting refuge the House of Tongue, and settled moodily beside the sea to nurse his grievances against the world. Had Montrose and his party known that even this small flicker of royalist hope in the north was so abruptly to be snuffed out, they would have been even more sober men on their frosty road northwards.

Crawford and Reay, who had ridden out of Oxford with Montrose, left him on the way to take a squadron of horse to join Prince Rupert at Shrewsbury. The King's Lieutenant himself, together with Ogilvy and Aboyne, rode on to York, probably with a small personal escort. On his arrival, he at once sent an officer to the Marquis of Newcastle at Durham, acquainting him with his Commission and with his need of men and money. There was little to be had of either, replied the Marquis gloomily, and on March 13th Montrose wrote to his "good president" Spottiswoode at Oxford to report his disappointment. "So these are the terms we stand on," he said. "It shall be no matter of discouragement to withold us from doing our best. Tomorrow we are to go to the army, which is looked daily to fight. But I hope we shall come in time to bear witness. Argyll, upon the rumour of our coming, is returned to Scotland in haste; but we intend to make all possible dispatch to follow him at the heels, in whatever posture we can . . . from your most affectionate and faithful friend to serve you, MONTROSE." He added a postscript: ". . . I intreat you will keep particular good intelligence with them all, and chiefly Mr Porter. . . ." Many of the King's best servants, Rupert chief among them, suffered from endless intrigue against them at Court, and Montrose had learnt enough in his time at Oxford to guard his rear. Endymion Porter, a royal Gentleman of the Bedchamber as faithful as Will Murray was treacherous, had obviously become a friend of Montrose, and it was vital that he should remain so.

Montrose rode north to see Newcastle, who was encamped at Durham in great perplexity. He was heavily outnumbered by Leven's Scots army a few miles away on the Tyne, around the town of Newcastle. Manchester and Fairfax threatened to bring even heavier forces against him from the south. He was a man of little energy or strategical imagination, who commanded in the north of England for the King out of a languorous sense of duty. With his vast possessions, he held court almost as a monarch in his own right, and he despised the ungraceful mud and powder smoke of the battlefield. At the end of March, Rupert by prodigies of skill and energy had achieved a master stroke in concentrating royalist forces around Newark, and checkmating Sir John Meldrum into surrender. Had Newcastle exploited Parliament's difficulties further south with any show of energy, great things might have been managed. Instead, he wrote with laboured courtesy to Rupert: "I must assure your Highness that the Scots are as big again in fact as ours are, so that if your Highness does not please to come hither, and that very soon too, the great game of your uncle will be endangered, if not lost. . . . Your Highness's most passionate creature, W NEWCASTLE." Newcastle suffered from much of Huntly's weakness and vapouring. Poor Rupert, as he urged his great black horse across England, his scarlet cloak flying behind him, was harried by endless messages from royalist generals each apparently incapable of shifting by himself for a moment. Even the Queen wrote suddenly demanding his presence to escort her personally to Bath for her latest pregnancy. The atmosphere at royalist headquarters at Durham can have done little to increase the confidence of Montrose and his little party.

But Newcastle felt obliged to take some notice of the King's Commission that Montrose carried. He gathered the miserable little force he could scrape together without weakening his line regiments. There were a hundred poorly-mounted cavalry and two small brass artillery pieces. Newcastle ordered the militia of Cumberland and Westmoreland to muster for Montrose, and they brought him 800 men and three troops of horse. There was an unhappy encounter in camp one day, when Aboyne went to Lord Carnwath to present that temperamental peer with a commission as Lieutenant of Clydesdale. Carnwath angrily refused to accept it from the hand of Montrose. He was not alone among the Scottish royalists in resenting the power and title that had been conferred on a man of such chequered career. But Carnwath's people did supply the strangest creature of Montrose's expedition, a lady named Mrs Peirson who claimed to be Carnwath's daughter, but who held a commission as Captain Francis Dalziel, to lead a troop of horse for the King. Her cornet rode behind carrying her grotesque black banner, displaying a naked man hanging from a gibbet and the motto "I dare".

Perhaps the most valuable recruit Montrose acquired at about this time was Major William Rollo, brother to his own Covenanting brother-in-law Sir James, and a man of infinite resource and loyalty. Rollo suffered from a club-foot and had been lame all his life, yet he could ride as far and as fast as any cavalier, and swing a sword with the best of them. He had been serving for some months with the royalist army in the north, but on the arrival of Montrose and his band, Rollo delightedly joined them. In the months to come, he was to be a tower of strength to Montrose, one of the very few men in whom he confided his most private thoughts and fears.

With Crawford, Ogilvy, Aboyne and Captain Dalziel beside him, Montrose crossed the border north of Carlisle at the head of 1300 men on April 13th, 1644. It was a wretched expedition. With his past experience of Covenanting armies and their usual zeal, Montrose's present rabble of unhappy militia, disgusted by finding themselves bear-led into the wilderness of Scotland, must have been a gloomy revelation. Some miles short of Dumfries on the river Annan, there was a mutiny. Many of the conscripts slunk sourly homewards. Montrose advanced to Dumfries with his remaining forces and was welcomed there by the city provost. But it soon became clear that there was precious little the King's Lieutenant-General could look for in south-west Scotland. It was far from his own country, and he knew neither the ground nor the people. Lord Herries and a handful of men came in to join him, but one by one the great lords from whom he had hoped so much—Annandale, Morton, Roxburgh and Traquair—refused his Commission. Montrose later wrote to the King with deep bitterness about those who had failed him. He lingered on in Dumfries, hoping for some word of Antrim and his promised Irish army, but they remained insubstantial as so many fairies. The only encouraging word came from many miles further north, from the brave little band of conspirators with whom he had shared so much, headed by Lord Napier. They had been living at home, closely watched and under constant suspicion, but they had never ceased to work for the King. Montrose's doughty niece Lady Stirling of Keir—Napier's daughter—wrote that Stirling Castle and the town of Perth were open to him for the taking. She sent her own token because Montrose was unlikely to believe the unsupported assurances of Stirling's commander, Lord Sinclair. He was the man who had rifled Montrose's desk for evidence against him on the orders of the Covenant two years earlier. Sir James Turner, the professional soldier who was Sinclair's second-in-command, confirmed in his memoirs that the offer of Stirling was sincere. But for Montrose it was never a realistic option to seize it. With his poor little force and no sign of local support, he would merely find himself a prisoner in Stirling to be isolated and dispatched by a Covenanting army at their leisure.

Any remaining hopes Montrose nourished at Dumfries were dashed by news that Lord Callendar—in his days as Lord Almond one of the Cumbernauld Banders—was on his heels with 7000 men. Montrose hastily marched his little force out of the town and into the hills. He retired to the Border with the Covenanters behind him, ditching his guns in Annandale. His campaign in Scotland had lasted barely a fortnight. Sir James Turner[11] always insisted that if Montrose had shown finer diplomacy and more timely initiative, and if Callendar had kept his ambiguous promises to declare for the King, then the royalists could have had Scotland at the end of this sorry little foray: "By Montrose his neglect and Calender's perfidy was lost the finest occasion that could be wished to do the King service." But Montrose had no men on whom he could rely, he had been disappointed from Ireland, and Huntly was obviously getting nowhere in the north. With his view of Scotland from Dumfries, he had no choice. He celebrated his pathetic little retreat by hearing of his excommunication by the Kirk in Edinburgh, and by receiving his patent as Marquis of Montrose from the King. It was a tragi-comic ending to a hopeless little adventure.

Back on the borders, his chief concern was to keep his command intact until he received word of the coming of the Irish into Scotland. He set about justifying the existence of his little force. First he attacked the strong Covenanting garrison in the town of Morpeth in Northumberland. An assault failed with heavy loss. But he was able to send to Newcastle for cannon with which to batter a breach. During parleys with the defenders, he managed to convince them with his usual fluent charm that Leven's army was in dire straits and their own position isolated. On May 29th, he triumphantly entered Morpeth after the garrison surrendered on terms. Characteristically, that night he entertained the captive Governor to dinner in his quarters.

Morpeth was a useful little success for Montrose, and he followed it all through June by vigorous operations in support of the royalists besieged in Newcastle. He took South Shields, raided Alnwick for supplies and then slipped neatly past the Scots besieging lines to get the food in to the Newcastle garrison. He was still thus engaged, playing his dashing little role as an independent column commander, when he received word from Prince Rupert to march to join him at his utmost speed.

Rupert was hastening north by way of Boroughbridge to relieve the unhappy Marquis of Newcastle besieged in York by a large Parliamentary army. The Prince needed every man he could get, but Montrose was still moving southwards when Rupert encountered the Parliamentary army at Marston Moor on July 2nd. With his usual dash, the Prince had danced gracefully around his enemies and relieved York. Then with his equally characteristic haste and bluntness, he marched smartly out of the city again to attempt the urgent and difficult task of rejoining in the King in the south. He brusquely ordered the Marquis of Newcastle to bring his men at once behind him. But Newcastle was bitterly incensed by the Prince's presumption. He dragged his heels in pique. Rupert lost a great chance of attacking the Parliamentary army before they were ready for him. Instead, he lingered in line of battle until Newcastle's men had at last arrived. The evening light was failing. He decided there could be no battle that day and stood down his men. Cromwell's Ironsides seized their opportunity to attack, and in this their first major engagement smashed into the royalist flank. A bitter struggle ensued along the length of the line, in which Leven and some of his Scots fled the field believing all was lost. But at last the royalists broke in disarray and fled headlong to York. They had been outnumbered 28,000 to 18,000 and their defeat was no disgrace, but it was a disaster of incalculable magnitude for the King's cause. In York that night amidst the chaos of defeat, Lord Eythin met Rupert and asked him what he would do. Rupert, typically, after a day on which he had fought unceasingly to hold his army together, answered briefly: "I will rally my men." Newcastle, also typically, said he would sail for Holland: "I will not endure the laughter of the court." Charles had told Rupert that, "If York be lost, I shall esteem my crown little less." Now the great city was doomed. Rupert rode south with 6000 horse, leaving his personal standard in the hands of his enemies, his little white dog Boy dead on the field of Marston Moor, and his reputation and confidence in ruins. It was at an inn at Richmond two days after the battle that Montrose came upon him.

There never seems to have been any great intimacy between Rupert and Montrose, to judge from the coolness of the few letters between them that survive, and *pace* Margaret Irwin. It is likely that Rupert considered Montrose's wild schemes strategically irrelevant; perhaps Montrose was angered that Rupert was so constantly preoccupied with the demands of his army, and so casual about Scottish lords with no following. Whatever their relationship, that meeting at Richmond must have been tense and awkward. Montrose, his spirit unsullied by the shock of the battle, came once again to beg aid to carry out his Commission in Scotland. Rupert and his officers lay gloomy and angry, the Prince perhaps most of all with himself. He had made culpable errors and been humbled for them. Like some medieval knight at a tournament, he had gone out gaily to joust with Cromwell and test the reputation of his new regiments, and Cromwell had coldly crushed him. War might be a fine game in victory, but the consequences of defeat such as this were incalculable. Rupert, like Jellicoe, had had it in his power to lose the war in an afternoon, and he had just done so, although there were to be many more battlefields before this was generally understood.

In the taproom at Richmond, Rupert impulsively responded to Montrose's suggestions by offering him a thousand cavalry. Tired and unhappy, it might have seemed to him that night that a thousand horse one way or the other mattered little enough now, when so many lay dead at Marston. Perhaps Montrose's passionate optimism made him see a hopeful gamble worth supporting. But Rupert's staff were appalled by the proposal. Sir John Hurry was with Rupert, and may have taken his part in this argument. By morning, the Prince had repented. It was vital that Charles should retain a convincing army in being. Every trooper would be needed if Marston Moor was ever to be avenged. Wearily, he ordered Montrose to hand over the few men he still had under his command. It was neither cruelty nor conceit that drove Rupert, but harsh necessity. He and his squadrons clattered away out of Richmond towards the south, to save what they could from the wreckage of the campaign. Montrose and his little party were left to watch them go, themselves now destitute of men, resources or any apparent hope of executing the King's Commission.

At last they mounted again and took the dusty road north to Brough and through Appleby to Carlisle, passing royalist deserters and avoiding Parliamentary patrols and talking sombrely about the future. It seemed worth investigating the slim possibility that some of the great Scottish lords who had spurned the King's Lieutenant-General in the spring had now mellowed to the cause. Pride made it impossible to slip meekly back to Oxford after promising so much and achieving so little. Montrose settled himself impatiently at Carlisle while, very bravely, Lord Ogilvy and Major William Rollo rode deep into Scotland in disguise to spy out the land. For two weeks they talked, watched and listened to the King's friends and to his enemies. Then they came back to Carlisle to report to Montrose. The situation was hopeless, they said. "They did not find any person who dared to speak with any tolerable reverence or affection of his Majesty." [12] Every pass and road was guarded by the Covenanters. Many waverers like Traquair whose loyalty had always been ambiguous had now declared openly for the Covenant. In their lonely, isolated quarters at Carlisle,

Montrose's little band of friends began to wonder grimly if the moment had not come to look to their own lives.

The King's Lieutenant-General at last emerged from a long reverie. He gave his strange orders. He handed to Lord Ogilvy his reports and letters for the King, and directed him to take command of the party and lead it down to Oxford. Ogilvy set off with Harry Graham, Montrose's half-brother, Sir John Innes, Patrick Melville and a handful of other gentlemen. On their way southwards they ran headlong into a skirmish with a Parliamentary force which captured them all. That October when Newcastle fell, Wishart—Montrose's chaplain and biographer—along with Crawford, Reay and Maxwell were also made prisoner. All of them were handed over to the Committee of Estates and imprisoned in Edinburgh, where they remained until Montrose himself delivered them.

After Ogilvy and the others had ridden out of Carlisle, Montrose was left only with Aboyne, lame Rollo with his club-foot, and an officer named Colonel Sibbald, the same who had once commanded the Airlie Castle garrison when Argyll came calling. Montrose had not previously dared to trust the wild Aboyne with the secret of his intentions. But now the time had come to reveal them. He had resolved to ride alone into the heart of Scotland, into the depths of the Highlands among the clans with their traditional Catholicism, royalism, hatred of the Campbells and love of war and booty. Somehow, amongst them, he proposed to raise an army for the King. He could take nothing with him except the Royal Standard, his Commission as the King's Lieutenant-General, and one of the greatest hearts in Scotland. It was an insane venture which could lead only to the scaffold if he was captured, a scheme epic as the quest for the Golden Fleece or the slaying of the Minotaur. It was as he had written as a schoolboy:

> So great attempts, heroic ventures, shall
> advance my fortune or renown my fall.

Only Rollo and Sibbald were to go with him, and all three of them must be disguised. Aboyne was much too indiscreet for a venture of this sort: "But as that young nobleman was lacking in steady perseverance, he did not urge him to share the hardships of the journey. He found no difficulty in persuading him to stay at Carlisle until summoned by the news of his success . . ."[13]

Rollo and Sibbald took the road north from Carlisle trailing behind them a humble groom on a sorry, broken-down hack. Sewn into the lining of the groom's saddle was the Royal Standard and his Commission. Before they even crossed the border, there was a nerve-racking encounter with one of Sir Richard Graham's men, who took them for Covenanters from Leven's army, and chatted garrulously about his duty, watching the road for any royalist seeking to sneak northwards. It was lucky that the weather was fair for them. They could rest in the open when necessary, out of sight of the constant Covenanting pickets who checked every man for papers lest he be a deserter or a royalist. But one man they could not avoid on their road— a soldier who had served under the Marquis of Newcastle, who accosted them in one of the most famous encounters in the legend of Montrose. He passed by Sibbald and Rollo. Then he appalled them, by saluting their groom by name. The poor servant denied himself. But it was to no purpose. "Do I not know my Lord Marquis of Montrose well enough?" said the soldier, smiling. "But go your way, and God be with you."

It was hopeless to maintain pretences. They gave him a few crowns for his loyalty and begged him to keep what he had seen to himself. Montrose was thoroughly alarmed by the encounter and by the constant danger of exposure. The three men now rode as hard as their horses would carry them to the Forth, and beyond. Their nerves were stretched to breaking point, their horses were as tired as themselves, when they came into Perthshire and Montrose's own country. There was no question of stopping at Kincardine or risking any encounters on his estates. They rode on to the very edge of the high hills, to the house at Tulliebelton, near the Tay, of Montrose's devoted kinsman and friend Patrick Graham of Inchbrakie. Here at last on August 22nd, 1644 they believed themselves safe. Inchbrakie and his son Black Pate—so called because of a youthful mishap with gunpowder which had left its mark—welcomed them warmly but soberly. They sent Montrose to sleep in one of the little cottages on their estates. During the day he had to lie out in the heather lest a Covenanting patrol come by the houses. Rollo and Sibbald disappeared into the countryside in search of news. They returned a few days later to report that matters seemed as black as they could be. Huntly's absurd enterprises in the north had collapsed leaving the Gordons leaderless and without hope. The hand of the Covenant bore ruthlessly and inexorably upon any man who sought to serve the King. It seemed impossible to discover any means of breaking the stranglehold the King's enemies held upon Scotland.

As Montrose lingered unhappily in hiding, desperately at a loss how to begin to save the fortunes of his King, no one has bettered Gordon of Ruthven's enchanting contemporary account of the miracle, the revelation that descended upon him: "As he was one day in Methven Wood, staying for the night, because there was no safe travelling by day, he became transported with sadness, grief, and pity to see his native country thus brought into miserable bondage and slavery . . . and therefore in a deep grief and unwonted ravishment, he besought the Divine Majesty, with watery eyes and a sorrowful heart, that his justly kindled indignation might be appeased, and his mercy extended, the curse removed, and that it might please Him to make him, Montrose, an humble instrument therein, to his holy and divine Majesty's greater glory: While he was in this thought, lifting up his eyes he beholds a man coming the way to St Johnston with a fiery cross in his hand. Hastily stepping towards him, he enquired what the matter meant? The messenger told him, that Coll MacGillespick, for so was Alexander [Alasdair] Macdonald called by the Highlanders, was entered in Athole with a great army of the Irish, and threatened to burn the whole country if they did not rise with him against the Covenant; and he was sent to advertise St Johnston, that all the country might be raised to resist him."[14]

The incredible had happened: Antrim's Irish had swum at last out of the mists, striding into Atholl with the gigantic Alasdair Macdonald at their head and all their priests and women and children and booty behind them. The King's Lieutenant-General had been granted the steel spearhead of an army. Montrose's Year of Miracles had begun.

# CHAPTER SIX

## *The King's Lieutenant-General*

---

In a society in which prowess in battle was esteemed above all things, Alasdair Macdonald had achieved a reputation as one of the most ferocious warriors of his age. As a son of the great Coll Keitach and kinsman of Lord Antrim, he stepped easily into command of a Macdonald brigade in the Irish rebellion. By the time he turned twenty-one, he was already the scarred veteran of a hundred Irish skirmishes and pitched battles, many of them against the Scots Covenanting army in Ulster. "A stout brave fellow," noticed an officer of Sir John Clotworthy's regiment in action against him, "who charged alone to the work but was shot, and after a very severe skirmish the Irish fell back, and took the retreat, where many were slain, and with much ado O'Cahan brought off Macdonald in a horse litter."

There were a dozen episodes of this sort in Alasdair's short, bloody life, hallmarked by his characteristic combination of mad courage and hardheaded stupidity. He was single-mindedly devoted to war and sudden death, and he dealt them out to his enemies with Gaelic enthusiasm. Always eager to improve his technique, he is said to have modified his sword by attaching to its hilt a steel rod which ran parallel with the blade, and upon which a heavy steel apple floated free. Thus when he raised his sword, the weight slid to the hilt. When he brought it down upon the head of some miserable Covenanter, the weight smashed down the blade with irresistible force. It is the only tentative evidence of ingenuity[1] in a life of violent simplicity, tempered by devout Masses between battlefields.

Alasdair sailed from Ireland on June 27th, 1644, with 1600 men, all that could be mustered of Antrim's vaunted 10,000 strong expeditionary force, although the Earl himself claimed that he had been forced to discharge a further seven hundred "for want of shipping". Their passage was an alarming business with Parliament's squadrons everywhere and the certainty of their fate if they were captured. A month earlier seventy men and two women had been thrown overboard in mid-Channel by their Parliamentary captors, for no better reason than that they were Irish. This time, however, the boot was on the other foot. The Irish convoy fell in with three small enemy ships which they made prizes, two carrying useful supplies and the third a party of Covenanters returning from Ulster. Alasdair released all the prisoners except three preachers, whom at the first opportunity he offered in exchange for his father and two brothers held by Argyll. It was hardly his fault that Argyll let two of the preachers die in captivity rather than surrender his Macdonald prisoners.

On the fifth day after leaving the Irish coast, Alasdair's little convoy made its landfall in the Sound of Isla on the west coast of Scotland. Going ashore for news, he learned to his delight that only a day's sailing away stood two Campbell castles that were lightly garrisoned and vulnerable. On July 5th, the Irish expeditionary force, greedy for plunder and glory, disembarked on the Scottish shore at Ardnamurchan. "Their landing was accompanied by some confusion arising from an extraordinary prodigy which occurred," noted the Catholic chronicler Father James Macbreck,[2] "for although the sky was cloudless and there was no sign of any disturbance of the atmosphere, there was suddenly heard a terrific explosion, so loud as to be heard in every part of Scotland, the effect of which was to make everyone feel as if his ears were stunned by a report from behind him, from an enormous brazen cannon of unheard-of dimensions."

In the years to come, the omen would be remembered along with all the others that had presaged Scotland's bloody distemper: the monster that had swum up the river Don, the disappearance of the seagulls from the lakes around Aberdeen, the loud tucking of drums in Mar, the unearthly trumpets, bagpipes and bells at Peterhead. The judgement of the Lord had descended upon the Kingdom in the dreadful shape of the Macdonalds of Antrim.

As soon as they landed, Alasdair and his army set about capturing the two Campbell castles of Mingarry and Kinlochaline, and both soon fell to them. Garrisons were left to guard the booty while the main force of Macdonalds advanced up the coast, sacking and burning Campbell property wherever they found it. Their ships were ordered to move north to Loch Eishort in Skye, and wait there for further instructions.

But in the month that followed while Alasdair and his men pursued their pleasurable raiding across the countryside, Argyll and the Covenanters bestirred themselves mightily. Every available man was moved north-westwards to meet the Irish. Day by day a ring closed around the Macdonalds. Alasdair had counted on his Royal Commission to bring the clans flocking to fight beneath his banner, but the men of north-west Scotland knew him much too well for that. He had come now, as the Antrim Macdonalds had always come, to raid and plunder. He had brought with him this new cloak of political respectability to mask his depredations, but his chief interests were the harrying of the hated Campbells and the capture of the alleged Macdonald lands in Kintyre. There was no strategy, no grand design behind Alasdair's wanderings. It is unlikely that at this stage he had any serious intention of seeking out Montrose. The clan chiefs to whom he applied for support did not examine their own royalism, they merely pondered the likelihood of his survival or destruction. They saw him blundering into the net that Argyll was already casting for him, and they declined to join him in his plight.

Even Alasdair himself gradually became aware of his own loneliness and peril. He was already considering a hasty withdrawal to Ireland when word reached him of disaster: a Parliamentary squadron had surprised his ships at Loch Eishort and burnt them to the waterline. The Macdonalds' escape homewards was cut off. Their fate was to be decided in Scotland. In growing desperation Alasdair now turned to Seaforth, chief of clan Mackenzie, from whom he had expected much when he first landed at Ardnamurchan. Seaforth coldly declined to join his rash adventure. But when he found himself confronted by the Macdonald war band in a mood for any enormity, he reluctantly offered them supplies sufficient to take them out of his territory. With these slim provisions, Alasdair rambled away eastwards, away from the avenging Campbells. He took hostages and threatened fire and the sword against the smaller clans in his path to induce them to join him, and somehow he added a few hundred swordsmen to his ranks. It was becoming obvious throughout the Highlands that the

Macdonalds in this mood offered a prospect of endless purpose-less blood and misery unless they could be destroyed. It was not only the Covenanters who were mustering against Alasdair now, but every clan in his way. The Grants and the Moray gentry held Strathspey against him. Seaforth raised 1000 men to prevent him from threatening the Mackenzie country once more. Argyll was afoot in the West and Lord Elcho was arming in Perthshire. It was only a matter of time before the Macdonalds were hunted down.

Alasdair had no more ideas. In an outbreak of uncharacter-istic humility, he could think of no other course but to beg advice and orders from the King's Lieutenant-General for Scotland, the Marquis of Montrose at Carlisle. He wrote a letter—or more likely had one of his priests write one for him—and gave it to a royalist who could start it on the long precarious journey down the length of Scotland to Montrose. The messenger knew nothing of the whereabouts of the King's Lieutenant. But he was well aware of the ardent royalism of Black Pate Inchbrakie. To Tulliebelton, where Montrose lay in hiding, went Alasdair's desperate plea. The Irishman must have been bewildered and astonished to receive, as he lay with his hungry tribe in the hills, a speedy order from the Lord Marquis himself to march at once to meet him at Blair Atholl in Glen Garry. He still had no hint of Montrose's movements. But in his desperate situation he had no plan of his own. He was grateful enough to be offered one, however hazardous it seemed.

A Clanranald man guided the straggling Macdonald force down to Blair, a very necessary aid in lieu of maps or compasses in the trackless passes. At last they poured thankfully down the hill into the mellow green valley above the Garry. They seized the castle and pitched camp around it in the midst of the glen to await fresh news of the King's Lieutenant-General. Now, they were utterly in his hands. Unless he could somehow save them they were doomed. From every corner of Scotland armies were moving against them. Even in Atholl itself, royalist country, the Stuarts and the Robertsons were standing to their arms within musket shot of the Macdonald camp, enraged by this alien descent upon them and determined to drive out the intruders at the first opportunity. The Macdonalds huddled bitterly around their half-starved women and children, their priests and their booty, and like so many trapped wolves, snarled defiance at the hostile hills around them.

On the morning of August 29th, the men of Atholl and the Macdonalds had reached breaking point with each other. They mustered in their companies with swords and matchlocks in their hands, resigned to battle. Many of Alasdair's men must have been bitterly wishing they had never left their own Antrim glens, and paled for the fate of their women and children if the day went against them. Each side nerved itself to begin the onslaught to have it out for possession of the valley.

Then in the distance across the dusty heather, the rival armies perceived two lonely figures hastening towards them. The Atholl men were the first to recognize their old friend Black Pate. Then, beside him, they saw the slight, astonishing figure of the Lord Marquis of Montrose, the King's Lieutenant-General in Scotland. Montrose walked into Atholl as a Highlander, as one of themselves, in trews and plaid, a bonnet on his head, a studded target on his arm and a sword at his side. He had come twenty miles alone across the hill with Black Pate to reach the appointed rendezvous, and they arrived in the nick of time to prevent the battle that would have dashed the last hopes of the King's cause in Scotland. The Atholl men hailed their coming with a great cry of surprise and delight.

Then it was the turn of the astounded Irish. They had never seen Montrose. They must have expected the King's Lieutenant in courtly splendour, riding upon them with his banner before him and cavalry behind. Instead he came armed only with his dreams and his Commission. They had imagined him still at Carlisle, too far to protect them from their impending fate. Now, come what might the spectre of immediate disaster was banished from them. The Irish, too, fired off the last of their powder with characteristic improvidence to salute their unexpected saviour.

The Atholl men and the Macdonalds drew apart, and their chiefs began their first long and eager consultations with Montrose. That night, he and Black Pate slept in the House of Lude, across the river Tilt from Blair castle. The following morning the Atholl chiefs came to him with the welcome news that they were putting their 800 men at the disposal of King Charles. Then the whole camp rose to walk behind their commanders to a little mound named the Truidh a short distance from the castle, looking down upon the whole soft sweep of Glen Garry. There Montrose solemnly raised the Royal Standard that he had brought north in the lining of his saddle. In the still summer air, his voice carrying down the ranks of his silent regiments, he read aloud before the army the declaration that he had prepared for this moment:

WHEREFORE to justify the duty and conscience of His Majesty's service, and satisfy all his faithful and loyal hearted subjects, I, in His Majesty's name and authority, solemnly declare that the ground and intention of his His Majesty's service here in this Kingdom (according to our own solemn and national oath and covenant) only is for the defence and maintenance of the true Protestant religion, His Majesty's just and sacred authority, the fundamental laws and privileges of Parliaments, the peace and freedom of the oppressed and thralled subjects; and that in thus far, and no more, does His Majesty require the service and assistance of his faithful and loving hearted subjects, not wishing them longer to continue in their obedience than he persists in maintaining and adhering to these ends. And the further yet to remove all possibility of scruple, lest—while from so much duty and conscience I am protesting for the justice and integrity of His Majesty's service, I myself should be unjustly mistaken—(as no doubt I have hither-to been, and still am) I do again most solemnly declare, that knew I not perfectly His Majesty's intention to be such and so real as is already expressed, I should never at all have embarked myself in this service . . . which I am confident will prove . . . able to satisfy all true Christians, and loyal hearted subjects and country-men who desire to serve their God, honour their Prince, and enjoy their own happy peace and quiet.

MONTROSE.

In the year that had passed since Montrose rode to join the King, he had become a harder, surer man. His declaration at Blair bore witness to his continued devotion to the Covenant, but his understanding of the King's desperate plight had made him ruthlessly pragmatic about the nature of the tools with which he served the King's cause. Irishmen, Catholics, MacGregors, renegades and outlaws, clansmen and freebooters

—all were alike to be dignified as soldiers of the King. During his year in England, Montrose had been battered and bruised by fate. Never again does he seem impetuous and hot-tempered as in the days of his Edinburgh politicking. He had lost none of his optimism and daring and appetite for the impossible, but at the age of thirty-two he had also gained an extraordinary mastery over the men around him, an evident genius for leadership. In the clean, clear air of the hills he now stands serene, playing his impossible hand with cool brilliance. Patrick Gordon[3] described him amongst his army, sharing his wit and calm sense with the clansmen, offering his quiet charm to any man who would have it: "A presence graceful, courtly and winning upon the beholder as it seemed to claim reverence without sowing for it. For he was so affable, so courteous, so benign as seemed verily to scorn ostentation and the keeping of state, and therefore he quickly made a conquest of the hearts of all his followers. . . ."

On this, the eve of his great campaign, he had committed himself to saving the King's cause in Scotland with a Celtic army. He had been spurned by the great Lowland lords, the descendants of the Saxons and Normans. He had turned instead to their natural hereditary enemies, the wild hillmen whom they hated and feared. By raising his Standard in the Highlands, Montrose put himself beyond the pale in the eyes of Lowland Scotland. It was as if he brought the plague upon them. By employing Irish Catholics he was betraying his own civilization as surely as if he had raised an army among the Cannibal Islanders. From this moment he had no more political options open to him in Scotland. Far away in Oxford, the King was to weave wild fantasies of alliances between Montrose and the Covenanters against Parliament, unions of Highlander and Lowlander against the English rebels. But on the battlefield itself, Montrose was utterly dependent on the fickle, emotional, mercurial Highland clans. Whatever the constitutional niceties, it was the King's Lieutenant who was now seeking to use them to begin a rebellion against the existing government of Scotland.

To the clans, warfare was a way of life. Their chiefs held absolute power over their lives and lands by virtue of the feudal charters granted to them in the Middle Ages. When Macdonald of Keppoch was asked the size of his income, he answered proudly that he could summon five hundred fighting men.

But the Highlanders were accustomed to fight in their own way, on their own ground, in their own time. Generals through the centuries had discovered the difficulty of marshalling a Highland army to fight a concerted campaign for any length of time, of uniting the chiefs for any common political purpose. By habit and inclination they were raiders in their own cause and had little interest in anyone else's. Since time immemorial they had fought bloody feuds against their clan enemies and neighbours. Alasdair Macdonald and his men, after all, had come to Ardnamurchan not for King Charles, but to strike a blow against the Campbells.

In the reign of James VI, Highland warfare had diminished. In 1608 the Scots Privy Council had ordered the destruction of all "houses of defence, strongholds, and crannates", and made efforts to force the wildest chiefs to send their heirs south to be educated among the civilizing influences of the "in country". But in the mid-seventeenth century, scores of Scottish lairds and lords still depended for their influence, even for their survival, on possession of some thick-walled stone tower armed with a pair of falconets with which they could command access to their own private passes through the mountains. The pattern of Highland life and Highland loyalties was dictated by the rivers and passes, for between them lay only the hills, respected as natural barriers rather than natural beauties.

Father Macbreck,[4] reporting to Rome, painted a grim picture of northern Scottish life: "In this country noblemen of the highest rank, and those of the middle and lower orders, as well as people of all classes, do not generally reside in towns, but are scattered all over the land, in their own fortified dwellings, or castles, or palaces, or smaller buildings according to the custom of their nation. . . . Besides, the country is cut up by innumerable torrents, streams, and rivers, the necessity of crossing which constitutes by far the greatest of our difficulties, added to the nature of the ground and the hostility of our opponents, especially in the rigour of winter, when icy winds, with fast-falling snow and the raging fury of the storm seem to blend sky and earth and sea in a chaos of confusion. . . ."

The clans lived in a misty, mysterious mountain world rich in songs, battles, fairies, superstitions and strong passions. They were not industrious, and cared nothing for exploiting their great forests or improving their poor fields. They accepted their

Montrose by
Honthorst

Montrose as a
young man in
1629 by Jameson

ARCH⁰. LORD NAPIER I

Archibald, 1st Lord Napier, by Jameson

The Marquis of Argyll in 1652

cruel lives fatalistically, even with pride. Their chiefs were famed for their hospitality. They kept open house in their draughty towers for a host of relations, warriors and pensioners. In autumn they took to the hills with their shaggy hounds and their clansmen for the great deer drives. Their sons might go south to learn Latin, but they had little future in their own lands unless they could leap a burn, drop a deer, and wield a claymore as surely as any of their clansmen. Just as Scottish kings lived much more closely with their nobles than their English cousins, so did Highland chiefs and their tenants enjoy the intimacy of common hardship and strife. There was obedience and loyalty, but there was none of the formality and mannered servility of an English tenant to his lord. Patrick Gordon[5] wrote scathingly of those Scottish peers who attempted to bring English social ways into the glens: "For once that English devil, keeping of state got a hold among our nobility, then began they to keep a distance as if there were some divinity in them. . . . It is true that in England the keeping of state is in some sort tolerable, for that nation (being so often conquered) is become slavish. . . . But our nation, I mean the gentry not the commons, having never been conquered, but always a free-born people, are only won with courtesies and the humble, mild, cheerful and affable behaviour of their superiors."

The Highlanders rejoiced in a great tradition of Gaelic song and poetry kept alive by their bards. By the fireside they played their harps; on the march to the battlefield they followed the pipes which since the sixteenth century had become feared across Scotland as the herald of the clans on the warpath. To the Saxon Lowlanders, Highlanders seemed as moody as the seasons in their violent country. In the far north the sun scarcely set in the long June days, the purple heather bloomed wonderfully in the clear bright light, the endless game provided food for every man, families took to their summer sheilings in the hills to tend the black cattle. But then, in winter, came the terrible melancholy of grey days, endless mists and drizzle, snow clogging the passes for months on end, and an awful death for any man who lost his path on the hill. They bled the cattle to support themselves, and as a result their beasts were invariably mangy. They kept a few sheep only for their milk. In the seventeenth century they had not even the doubtful salvation of the potato. They huddled around the fires of their miserable turf huts, the

F

wind checked only by a wicker door, their animals sharing the stinking, smoking atmosphere beside them.

The dress of every Highlander of every age was the belted plaid, the great length of rough, thick cloth that could be adjusted at will to become a cloak, slung over the shoulder on a brooch, or wrapped as a blanket in the night chill on the hill. The first duty of every newly-wed Highland wife was to weave her man a plaid. Underneath it, summer or winter they had only their long shirts down to the knee, such as they wore unadorned to the charge at Kilsyth. To the horror of visiting Englishmen, the women and children usually went barefoot. Such shoes as there were went to the men who had to walk the hills.

Even by the standards of seventeenth-century England, it was a life of miserable poverty. There was ale, and whisky on special occasions. There were games in summer and dancing in the winter. Otherwise a Highlander had only his clan and his relationship with it to sustain and protect him. A man with sixty cows was rich, but his wealth could buy him little comfort in the glens. Money was scarcely seen—barter was the chief means of exchange and booty the usual hope of en-richment. Highlanders cared very little for what went on beyond their own hills. The old religion was still strong among many clans, and the tradition of superstition and magic ran deep. There was little political awareness or enthusiasm, only a dedication to the clan chief, wherever he chose to lead them.

A Highland army, a gathering of these clans, was always the most delicate of plants, sensitive to the slightest shifts of mood or confidence. There is a barbed jest about Highland troops through the ages: "They run very fast both ways." Under the right leader on the right day, their exultant headlong charge upon the enemy was devastating. A change in the climate however, might send them slipping away into the hills to hide their booty, or suddenly flying headlong from a battle line because they scented a stricken field. Highland bards wove great legends around their warriors and their battles, but there seems some cause to suspect that on some of these great occasions there was more noise than bloodshed. The greatest number of casualties in a Highland battle usually occurred after the issue had been decided, during the pleasurable pursuit of the vanquished, when they could be slaughtered at leisure.

Highlanders had certain great qualities to offer any commander: fitness and startling speed in covering country; strength and dash in the charge, marksmanship and utter intimacy with their weapons. They possessed all the historical vices and virtues of lightly armed guerilla forces. The general who wished to lead them, to mobilize them for war, needed the skills and serpentine subtlety of a salmon fisher: he had to sense the changes in the weather and the colour of the water, to spot the pools that held fish and the moment to try them with a fly; he had to choose his lures with care and instinct, to give line at the critical moment. No man could simply give a Highland army an order and expect to be followed doggedly wherever he led. Instead, he had to conjure them along beside with him skills few magicians possess.

"They could not be kept longer than they were laden with plunder," wrote Gordon of Ruthven[6] of Montrose's army, "for they got no other pay, and therefore could not be sworn to their colours. The Irish he only was sure of because they had no place of retreat."

As Montrose reviewed his forces in the valley of the Garry below Blair in those dying days of August, a lesser man would have despaired. His little army was without cannon, without cavalry, and pitifully supplied even with swords and matchlocks and ammunition for them. Alasdair Macdonald's original strength of 1600 Irish had been eroded, by the garrisons he had left on the west coast and by casualties and sickness, to 1100. They must have looked a fearsome crew with their stinking plaids, straggling beards, their short swords and crucifixes, their glittering eye for plunder. A muster roll survives that was taken before they sailed from Ireland, full of the wildest names in Celtic legend: McQuillan, O'Sheil, MacHenry, MacColl, MacClen, MacCana, MacAlister, O'Hara, O'Neill, O'Cahan. . . . Colonel James McDermott's company numbered 100 men; his captain was Lieutenant Sorley Macdonnell, his Ensign John MacHeoghin, his Sergeants William MacKearn and Hugh O'Kealte. Only a few of the outstanding soldiers of the force are mentioned by name in any of the Scottish accounts of the campaign, most notably Magnus O'Cahan. O'Cahan was probably a cousin of Alasdair's and had fought with him throughout the Irish rebellion—it was he whom Clotworthy's officer had watched drag off the wounded Macdonald under fire. O'Cahan was second in command of the Irish expeditionary force with Montrose, and at the end was to prove himself certainly a more loyal and possibly a more skilful soldier than Alasdair himself.

Besides the Irish, there were the Atholl men with their sturdy tradition of royalism. But it was vital to Montrose to recruit much more widely across the Highlands if he was to have any chance of striking an effective blow for the King, and already the Macdonalds' ravages had poisoned the atmosphere among half the clans in Scotland. Montrose had an uphill struggle before him to overcome the misgivings and jealousies of the chiefs. Above all, he had to convince them that he had some hope of success, that his adventure would not simply crumble away to dust, leaving those who had shared it to face the avenging mercy of Argyll.

"Montrose," wrote Wishart[7] cheerfully, "being now provided with an army and relying not upon his numbers but on the providence of God in the protection of a just cause, wished for nothing more earnestly than an opportunity to try his strength, even with the stoutest of his enemies."

Yet in reality his task was to fight his way out of the cage that his enemies had already constructed around him. He must have pondered for a moment the possibility of striking north-eastwards, towards Aberdeen, in search of support in the Gordon country. But Lord Burleigh was already in arms there for the Covenant. Huntly was a fugitive and his remaining sons pawns of Argyll—Aboyne, of course, was still in England. Aberdeen, then, was fraught with uncertainties. But Montrose dared not remain a moment where he was. Each of the forces mustered against him heavily outnumbered his own tiny army. If he allowed them to unite to overwhelm him, he was doomed. He had to fight a battle, to begin at once the piecemeal destruction of the enemies threatening him. To a man of Montrose's heroic temper, it was a challenge at last worthy of his steel. There was the exhilaration of setting forth to win or lose it all. He had a romantic cause, a noble purpose, the tools and the setting to match them. On August 30th, 1644, less than twenty-four hours after he had walked into Blair with Black Pate, he marched away southwards with something over two thousand men at his back. He had determined first to try his destiny against Lord Elcho and the nearest host of the Covenant, mustering against him behind the walls of Perth.

The Highland army possessed three horses, and the Lord Marquis himself may have sat one of them at the head of his army as they advanced across the hill for Blair, the Royal Standard fluttering above him in the breeze, the clan pipers' fierce music echoing down the ranks behind. The army skirted the north bank of Loch Tummel before turning south once more, leaving Shiehallion on their right as they wound up the steep pass towards Aberfeldy and the Tay. In the fine summer weather on the hill, their passing must have stirred every sheiling for miles, as with a clatter of arms they trudged along the dusty droving tracks, sometimes trampling through the high heather, matchlocks across their shoulders, short swords at their sides, the occasional great two-handed battle sword slung down a man's back and tied on his neck. At three or four miles an hour they could easily outmarch the swiftest Lowland regiment in rough country. Behind them, because there was no safe refuge in which to leave them, came the miserable rag and bobtail of women and children, ragged and ill-kempt, the wives sometimes carrying their man's weapon or equipment. And amongst them too, strode the Irish priests who celebrated their unfailing Masses at every nightly halt around some poor hut upon the hill. It was a tribe rather than an army on the march. At times as Montrose looked back over his shoulder down the hill at his followers, he must have sighed deeply.

Towards evening of that first day, they dropped down the pass into the valley of the Tay. Montrose had sent a herald ahead to bring word to the Menzies laird of Castle Weem, above the river, that the King's army was at hand. But that sorry gentleman was Argyll's man, and canny enough to notice that the royalists had no artillery. Within the safety of his thick stone walls that Montrose had no means of battering down, he had the herald beaten half to death before hurling him out. Then he sent his men to harass the royalist rear and pick off any stragglers footsore enough to fall behind in the failing evening light. Turning in anger, Montrose's men fired such houses and granaries as they could find on Menzies's land. Then they bivouacked, no doubt with strong pickets, around the Tay itself, their advance guard on the south bank. The Menzies must have sent riders hell for leather towards Perth to keep

*Montrose*

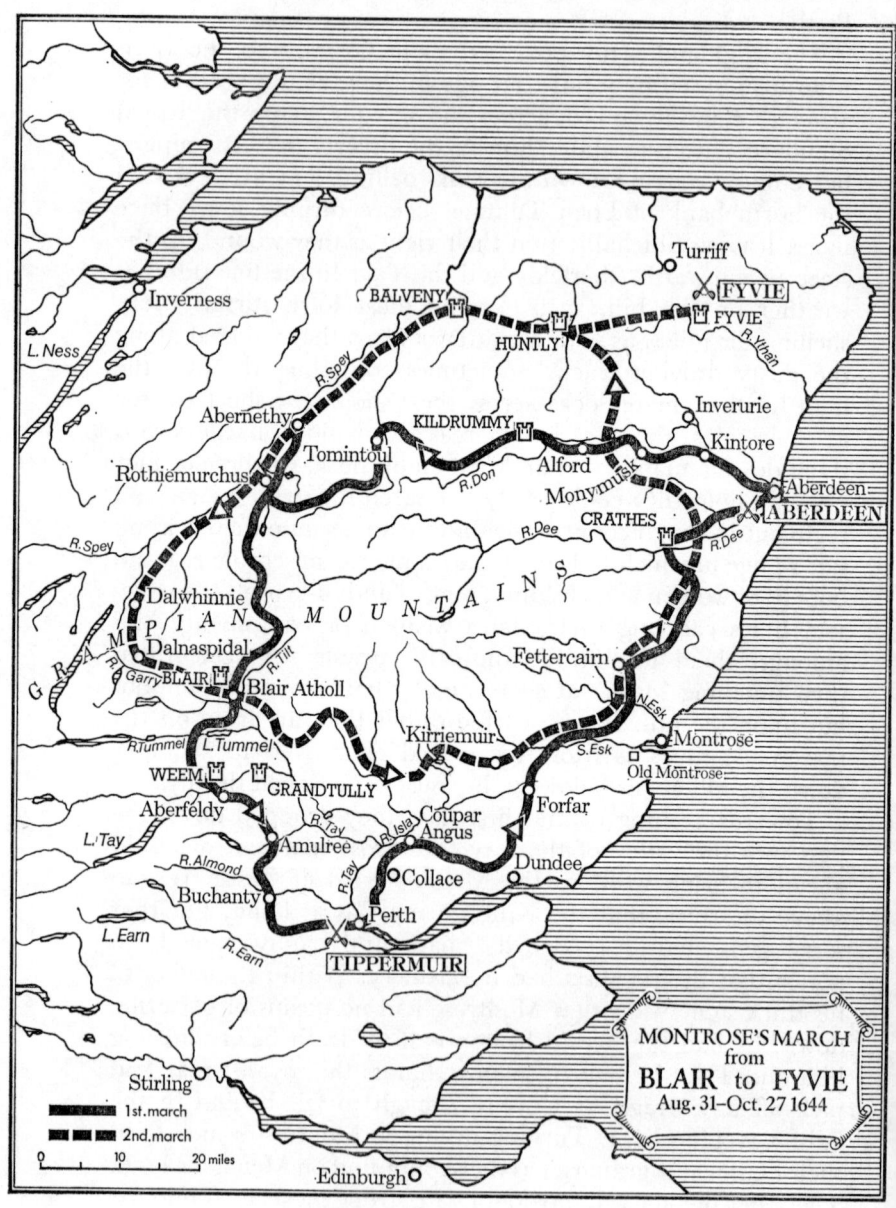

Inverness

L. Ness

Turriff

BALVENY  FYVIE

HUNTLY  FYVIE

Abernethy  KILDRUMMY  Inverurie

R. Spey  Tomintoul  Kintore

Rothiemurchus  Alford  Aberdeen

R. Don  Monymusk  ABERDEEN

R. Spey  CRATHES

R. Dee  R. Dee

M O U N T A I N S

Dalwhinnie  R A M P I A N

Dalnaspidal  Fettercairn

G  R  Garry  BLAIR

R. Tummel  L. Tummel  Blair Atholl

WEEM  Kirriemuir  Montrose

Aberfeldy  GRANDTULLY  S. Esk  Old Montrose

L. Tay  R. Tay  Forfar

Amulree  R. Isla  Coupar Angus

R. Almond  Dundee

Buchanty  Collace

L. Earn  Perth

R. Earn  **TIPPERMUIR**

MONTROSE'S MARCH
from
**BLAIR** to **FYVIE**
Aug. 31–Oct. 27 1644

Stirling

1st. march
2nd. march

0      10      20 miles

Edinburgh

Elcho abreast of Montrose's movements. But the city felt little enough alarm. Her citizens had faced Highland raiders before. They had seen enough of the Graham's tender conscience and political vacillations to feel confident that their only urgent requirements were for sufficient gallows to deal with the prisoners.

On the second day of Montrose's march, Black Pate skirmished ahead with an advance guard of 300 Atholl men who had specially begged that he command them. Probably early in the afternoon, they were moving down the Sma' Glen to the Almond when they saw before them, drawn up on the Hill of Buchanty in their path, 500 bowmen headed by Lord Kilpont, the Master of Maderty—who was married to Montrose's youngest sister Beatrix—Sir John Drummond and a bevy of Perthshire gentlemen. It was a critical moment for the royalists. A premature encounter battle now would delay their march, disorder and tire the men, and possibly seriously weaken them before they even met Elcho's regiments. Yet fight they must if necessary, to clear the road to Perth. The army closed up for action.

But Montrose never opened a battle in these first days of his campaign without attempting a parley. The knot of Covenanting officers standing amongst their men on the hillside were amazed when they learnt that it was the Lord Marquis who commanded the clan army below. They came hastily down to where he stood beneath the Royal Standard, and heard with astonishment and respect of his Commission from the King. They had been mustered by the Covenant to meet a marauding Irish raiding band, not to fight the King's Lieutenant-General. The tension of confrontation ebbed away as Montrose spoke. Within the hour, as the regiments gathered to march on towards the south-east, Lord Kilpont and his bowmen fell in alongside the Macdonald and the Athollmen, in the ranks of King Charles.

It was a gayer army that forded the Almond and pressed on towards Perth. Montrose had left Carlisle with two men at his back. Now—as he might have reckoned in an expansive moment—he was nearing his first battlefield with almost 3000. That night they made their camp on Fowlis moor north-east of Crieff, ten miles or so from Perth and Lord Elcho, almost in Montrose's own country of Kincardine where

he had spent so much of his boyhood. Some of his old friends
and neighbours were around him now, and he was on ground
that he must have known well. Perhaps that night he walked
among the camp fires as did Henry before Agincourt, listening
to the murmuring Gaelic voices in the darkness, gazing down
upon the heaps of huddled bodies asleep in their plaids by
whom, on the morrow, the King's cause in Scotland would be
immeasurably advanced or irrevocably destroyed.

Few men of either army slept much that night. In the early
hours of September 1st, 1644, Montrose and his men were afoot
once more, striding along the gently undulating road to Perth,
two hours' march to make up between themselves and Lord
Elcho. In the city, the Covenanters sounded reveille at first
light. They had news that the Highlanders would be upon
them that day. Elcho led them out, up the long hill above
Perth, over the crest and on until they reached the broad open
country just short of Tippermuir, three miles west of the city.
Here they began to deploy on a wide front across the royalists'
line of march.

There were 6000 infantry—the levies of Angus, Fife and
Perthshire, for the most part—to take post in three divisions.
Elcho himself commanded on the right, the experienced
professional Sir James Scott of Rossie took the left, and Lord
Murray of Gask the centre. On each wing stood some 400
cavalry, with open ground before them across which they could
smash into the Highland line with maximum impact. Forward
of the infantry were the seven light artillery pieces with which
the Covenanters expected as usual to sow terror and confusion
among the undisciplined hillmen. But Elcho's men had precious
little experience of standing shoulder to shoulder in close-
quarter battle: "Freshwater soldiers, never before used to
martial discipline", they were local militia not to be compared
with the regiments of the main Scots army in England and
Ireland.

But outnumbering their enemies almost three to one, this
scarcely seemed to matter. They were more or less trained, they
were incomparably better equipped than their enemy. They
stood rested and relaxed in a strong position their own commanders had chosen. A considerable crowd of spectators walked
up the hill from Perth to watch the slaughter of the royalists.
Now, the bystanders stood behind the Covenanting lines, on

Methven hill and other vantage points at a safe distance from the enemy, waiting for their bloody amusement to begin.

For the Highlanders it must have been a daunting moment when they topped the horizon and saw before them the host of the Covenant drawing up for battle: the great array of musketeers and pikemen, horse and guns, the sun shining on breastplates and helmets and harness such as hardly a man in Montrose's army could boast of. They could expect no mercy in defeat from these enemies, so certain of their rectitude, of doing the work of the Lord. They would be hunted down, and they would find no refuge in the valleys of southern Perthshire. But the Irish were agog at the prospect of the rich booty of Perth. The notion of fighting for it held no terrors for them. It was second nature. The little Highland army drew up for battle in good heart, armoured by fierce contempt for the soft Lowland peasants and apprentices who filled the ranks of their enemies a few hundred yards distant.

Montrose made simple dispositions, for he had little enough to deploy. He could not risk having his flanks turned by the wide front of the Covenanters. They stood six deep. He chose to meet them on a similar front of perhaps a thousand yards, but with his own men in three ranks. Kilpont and his bowmen took the left wing of the thin line, opposite Elcho. A company of Lochaber men armed with their deadly slashing axes moved up in support. Alasdair Macdonald commanded his Irish in the centre. They were reduced to a single round of ammunition a man for their matchlocks, but too much has been made of this. In a Highland battle, neither side had time for more than a volley or two before they closed and fought it out "at push of pike" or claymore. Sir James Turner in his military manual *Pallas Armata* says that many regiments carried only three rounds as standard issue, and he himself was considered exceptionally cautious to insist on twelve.

Montrose himself, target on his arm and half-pike in his hand, commanded on the right opposite Sir James Scott. Many of the Atholl men in his division had no arms of any kind. He simply ordered them to fire at the enemy as many volleys of stones as they could find ammunition on the rocky hillside under their feet. He must have made up his mind before the first shots were fired that come what might, it must be his men who launched themselves to the charge before the Covenanters. The royalists,

without pikemen, had no hope of standing to receive a headlong assault by their enemies. When the time came, they must
seize the initiative and hold it.

While the armies prepared themselves, their officers briefed
them for the battle. The Covenanters believed that they were
performing an act of vermin control this fine Sunday morning.
Their ministers stood among the regiments exhorting them to
hew mightily for the Lord. "If ever God spoke certain truth out
of my mouth," cried out the Reverend Carmichael of Markinch,
of all of them the most devout, "in his name, I promise you
today, a certain victory." The battle cry given out to the
Covenanting army was uncompromising in its simplicity:
"Jesus and no quarter!"

For every soldier in battle before the twentieth century, it
was a nerve-racking, cold-blooded business deploying for hours
in full view of an enemy doing the same. Then, at last, the two
armies stood face to face in a moment of explosive stillness
before the word was given to advance. Montrose, punctilious
as always, sent forward his brother-in-law the Master of
Maderty, mounted upon one of the army's three poor nags, as
herald to observe the courtesies of war. Under a flag of truce, he
rode out to Elcho bearing a declaration from Montrose. The
Lord Marquis expressed his horror at the prospect of bloodshed: "All he desired was that in God's name they would at
length give ear to sounder counsels, and trust to the clemency,
faith, and protection of so good a king. . . . If notwithstanding
they persisted in rebellion, he called God to witness that their
stubbornness forced him into the present strife."

With a teasing irony which it is delightful to think was
intentional, Montrose begged Elcho at least to postpone the
battle a day to avoid shedding blood on the sabbath. But at this
point the Covenanters rudely cut short all these courtesies.
Spurning convention and Maderty's flag of truce, Elcho
ordered him seized and sent to the rear. He was to be hanged
as soon as the day's work was done. The ministers declared the
Lord's day a fine one for doing his work. Around midday the
Covenanters fired the first shots of the battle of Tippermuir.

Seeing Montrose's division in the midst of shifting ground,
Elcho ordered out a body of horse and foot from his own left to
engage and disorder them. Lord Drummond led them forward,
the best of his cavalry amongst them, probably moving at a

steady trot. It was Alasdair Macdonald who saw the Covenanting movement develop, and pushed forward a company of his own men at their customary ferocious charge, sending Drummond's force reeling back in confusion against their own positions. Montrose seized the moment. He ordered a general advance along the length of his line while the enemy stood bewildered before him. With a great cry the Highlanders raced forward, ignoring a single feeble salvo from the Covenanting cannon which roared emptily over their heads, sweeping past the gun line itself to check in front of the massed infantry of the Covenant. As Montrose had instructed, the Irish paused to empty their single volley of musketry into Elcho's horrified regiment.* Nothing had prepared them for the ruthlessness and determination of the royalist charge. They were already reeling as the Irish closed to grapple their enemies with matchlock butts, swords, axes, clubs.

On the left of the Covenanting line, Sir James Scott forced a hard fight upon Montrose and his men. The cavalry charged the royalist right to be met with volleys of stones. As the Highlanders advanced, Scott's men retreated doggedly back up the ridge behind them, struggling to hold back the surging mob of clansmen. But the terrified levies were overwhelmed by the raw violence of the Highland onslaught. It was now, in the midst of their difficulties, that their lack of training told fatally against them. They lacked the confidence in themselves, in each other, in their commanders to fight patiently where they stood. Along the length of the front Lord Elcho's army began to crumble as desperate men broke in knots and handfuls from the heaving ranks and fled away down the hill towards Perth, hurling arms and helmets into the ditches as they ran. The cavalry, as usual, were best equipped to fly. They turned eastwards and rode almost to a man for safety, abandoning the foot to their fate. Now the battle began to collapse rapidly. The royalists drove the remains of the Covenanting line stumbling backwards in front of them. Already exulting Highlanders were dragging round the captured guns to rake the horde of fugitives. The Lord Marquis himself, cool now as before battle began, ordered them to hold their fire. The day was won, and

* A charge must have been very difficult for seventeenth-century musketeers burdened with their musket rests, and it is possible that the Highlanders dispensed with them in a situation like this.

there had been killing enough. The Lord had shown his mercy to his hopeless little army. He was willing enough, in his turn, to show it to the wretched broken regiments of the Covenant.

But his men were not. Savouring their triumph in the usual Highland manner, the blood-hot victors pursued their flying enemies one by one across the hill, hacking them down and stripping their bodies, cutting off pockets of stricken Covenanters and dirking them relentlessly, wounded or not. Soon the battlefield was strewn with naked men, and the litter of pale bodies with the clothes stripped from them by the ragged Irish reached grimly down the hill to Perth itself. Only a handful of Covenanters died in the battle, it was said, and just two royalists. It was a brief business. But hundreds were slaughtered in the course of that long, dry afternoon.* It can only be said that the Covenanters themselves would have done more, and with infinite self-righteousness and hypocrisy around the gallows, had the fortunes of war gone otherwise.

Tippermuir cannot rank as one of Montrose's greatest battles, for the qualities it demanded were those of his Highland rank and file rather than of himself as a master tactician. Courage, élan, mad determination broke Elcho's line. These were the virtues the clansmen possessed in plenty. Yet it was Montrose's marvellous energy and purpose that pushed his army on Perth at lightning speed after their precarious rendezvous at Blair Atholl, and which put it in position to strike a decisive blow. The defeat of Lord Elcho brought arms, ammunition, money, clothing and new hope to the royalists' frail forces. Before Tippermuir, Montrose's only thought had been for how to preserve his army, how best to

* The contemporary authorities for Montrose's battles give casualty figures which must be treated with the utmost caution. First, it is difficult to believe that the royalist losses were as negligible as they usually claim. It may be that they count only the better-known casualties and not the anonymous clansmen. It also seems certain that some, if not most, of the wounded died later. As for the losses of the enemy, it is absurd to imagine that anyone was able exactly to count them. One modern writer has soberly totted up the Covenanting losses given by Wishart and Gordon for Montrose's battles, and talks of his army having killed 16,000 of the enemy in all. This carries respect for contemporary sources to the frontiers of absurdity. I believe that one can only reasonably assume that in a given battle losses were either light, or heavy. Light, to me, means less than 50 killed. Heavy means well into the hundreds of dead. I have cited Wishart's or Gordon's figures as they are given. But a decent scepticism is essential.

avoid extinction. Now, he had at least won for himself a breathing space.

The city of Perth, where in the previous century John Knox had laid the foundation stone of the Scottish Reformation by preaching his sermon "vehement against idolatry", surrendered herself meekly to the victors that evening. The Lord Marquis of Montrose received the keys of the city from the magistrates at the Highate port. He must have smiled to see those sombre men of the Covenant, who only that morning had made such a brave show in the streets with their swords and boasts, now trembling and bowing before him. He took formal possession with a regiment of his victorious army, probably the Atholl men. The City Fathers had begged as a condition of their prompt surrender that none of the Irish be permitted to enter the walls. Alasdair and his men bivouacked across the river at Kinnoul. They were sufficiently sated with the plunder of Elcho's army to allow themselves to be denied the rape of Perth. Montrose was eager to win good will and support in Perthshire, not hatred and fear.

He lodged for the next three days at Margaret Donaldson's house in the city. Her home became the first Court of the King's Lieutenant-General in Scotland. Through her doors processed an endless throng of officers and suppliants, friends and local gentlemen to wait upon the Lord Marquis: there was Alasdair of course, the "general-major' of Montrose's army, as he was now to be styled; The Master of Maderty, saved from the gallows by victory; William Hunter of Balgayes, complaining of his corn being flattened by heavy-footed clansmen; Graham of Fintry; and most welcome of all, two days after the battle John and James Graham, at fourteen and eleven Montrose's two eldest sons, ran joyfully into Mistress Donaldson's house to their father's embrace. He had sent urgently to Kincardine after missing them for so long, and Sir John Graham of Braco escorted them to Perth. Of his wife Magdalen, there was no word. Perhaps he did not even trouble to send for her. If he did, she declined to come. Perhaps there was still one great sadness deep in his heart in the midst of this great triumph in arms.

He must have felt deep satisfaction as he held court in the second city of Scotland. He had been in the wilderness for so long, mistrusted and disdained, racked by fear that his King might judge him to have been an empty boaster, that he might end his days exiled from his country and his estates, dismissed as a political wastrel. Now all that was behind him. He had set his mark on the story of Scotland and it could never be rubbed out.

There was yet another touching reunion at Perth: Montrose called for his old tutor, Master William Forrett. The teacher who had guided him through Caesar and Raleigh, who had conjured up for him his first visions of Alexander, who had guided him until he succeeded to his father's title, now came to bow before his pupil in his hour of fierce triumph as the King's champion. Forrett became Secretary to the army and tutor to the young Graham boys.

Montrose must have faced immense paperwork in Perth, his first real headquarters. There were reports to be sent to England to the King, and urgent letters for every corner of Scotland. He drafted written orders for every movement of his army like any modern commanding officer. To several Perthshire gentlemen he believed might be able to muster men in his support, he dictated hasty notes: "Right Honourable Sir, Being here in arms for his Majesty's just authority and service, these are to require you, in his Majesty's name, that you will repair here, or where I shall be for the time, with all the force possible you can make, as you will answer to his Majesty, and for what may ensue. So I am your most loving friend, MONTROSE."

Perhaps it was now, when his campaign at last assumed dignity and he had the means for formal correspondence, that he wrote the letter to Argyll which survives undated among his papers:

MY LORD—

I wonder at your being in arms for defence of rebellion, yourself well knowing his Majesty's tenderness, not only to the whole country, whose patron you would pretend to be, but to your own person in particular. I beseech you therefore to return to your allegiance. . . . But if you shall continue obstinate, I call God to witness that through your own stubbornness I shall be compelled to endeavour to reduce you by force. So I rest

       Your friend, if you please,
       MONTROSE.

Montrose did his uttermost to deal kindly with the citizens of Perth. He observed every courtesy with the Provost, prevented looting and entertained the ministers to dinner—one of them was afterwards interrogated with some asperity for having said grace at the excommunicate James Graham's table. But it was fear, not sympathy, that induced so many God-fearing citizens to speak fairly to the royalist general. He made few converts and collected few recruits in Perth. After he left the city, the Covenanting authorities conducted a characteristic witch hunt to discover those who had had dealings with the enemy, and they bore down hard upon Mr Balneaves, the minister of Tippermuir, when he admitted that on the morning of the battle he had given the Marquis of Montrose a drink of water as he rode by. But Balneaves, for all that he was a Covenanter, had no patience with hypocrisy: "When reproved by the brethren for his hospitality, he answered them in expressions more coarse than were fit to be recorded in the register. The purport of his answer was that however they might now find fault with those who had shown any civility to the Marquis, yet there was not one of them who about the time of the battle durst have refused to kiss—in the meanest manner—the Marquis, if he had commanded them to do so."[8]

Montrose dunned the citizens of Perth for £50 in ready cash for Alasdair Macdonald, and enough cloth to supply the whole Irish brigade. Arms and ammunition he now possessed in tolerable plenty, but to his dismay he found his army already ebbing away from him. Four hundred of the Atholl men announced that they were going home with their booty in the customary Highland fashion. They made lame excuses about getting in the harvest, and about rejoining the army in due season. None of this spared the Lord Marquis the brutal fact that he must now march out of Perth (for he could not linger until his enemies gathered a new army to trap him) with a poorer army than that with which he had fought Tippermuir. The Perthshire gentry had ignored his letters and imprecations. One victory against Elcho's soft levies convinced them of nothing. Montrose was too weak to be able to threaten them, and they could safely ignore him. After all the stir of his great descent upon Perth, he could not even hold the city but must shift once more to skulk in the hills. There must have been moments when the Lord Marquis himself, as well as his enemies, wondered to what purpose he might pursue his wanderings across Scotland with a clutch of Covenanting armies endlessly hounding him.

But as Montrose began to assemble his little army to march away from Perth, the news of Tippermuir was echoing southwards across Scotland and into England, sending a great thrill of excitement through every royalist camp, and a stir of alarm and fear through those of the Scottish Covenanters. Baillie wrung his hands at news of this "lamentable disaster" brought upon them by these "most desperate and cruel villains". The English Parliament found the Scots the most intolerant and intolerable of allies, and mutual affection and confidence was already low. Now, this news of Montrose dealt a crippling blow to Scots prestige, and deepened the rift between the allies in a way that made the Court at Oxford rejoice hugely. If Montrose had achieved so much with one battle, what might he not gain in a campaign?

But the King's Lieutenant was still a hunted man, and Argyll's army was lumbering dangerously behind him. Montrose ferried his army across the Tay from Perth, and then destroyed all the boats along the riverside to hamper pursuit. It was time to try the north-east, the Gordon country, which might still yield men and support; there was Lord Burleigh's Covenanting army at Aberdeen to be dealt with, and the possibility of capturing fortresses and booty along the way. With his slender force, Montrose could do nothing else. He needed more, much more of everything—men, supplies, horses, arms—before he could think of marching south into the rich Lowlands far less of offering any aid to the King's cause in England. For the present, he could seek only to wreak havoc in the Highlands and create a serious diversion for the men and the plans of the Covenant. "We are for the time under a great and very black cloud," wrote Baillie[9] gloomily.

On September 10th, almost a week after the royalists had marched north, Lord Lothian clattered hotfoot into Perth at the head of 800 horse, the vanguard of Argyll's army which reached the city the following day. Their quarry, in the manner that was to become the hallmark of the campaign, was already many miles away and preparing a new thunderbolt.

"The year 1644 was fruitful in new surprises and events, and an unlooked-for mode of warfare inaugurated fresh slaughter

and fresh and unexpected victories," recorded Father Macbreck[10] as he looked back later at the great doings of the
campaign. Scotland was already bemused. She was now to
be astounded by the "unlooked-for mode of warfare" of the
Lord Marquis of Montrose.

# CHAPTER SEVEN
## Aberdeen and Fyvie

It was to be the Gordon country now, through the great fertile coastal strip of green fields and gentle hills that stretches around eastern Scotland, in the past the heart of such bitter opposition to the Campbells and the Covenant. There was Lord Burleigh's Covenanting army to be crushed at Aberdeen before it could unite with that of Argyll. There were recruits to be looked for, towns to be summoned. There was also, of course, Montrose's pressing need to be on the move away from Argyll. At least now the little royalist army was rested and tolerably well-equipped as its men strode along the dusty summer road north-east from Perth towards Coupar Angus, clutching the booty of Tippermuir.

Their first camp, however, was marred by a tragedy that struck a bitter blow to the King's cause. The army stopped for the night at Collace, in the valley beside the little stream below Dunsinane Hill. Early on the morning of September 5th "before the drums had beat to march, the whole camp was in an uproar, the men all running to arms, shouting and storming like madmen in their rage and indignation. Hearing the disturbance, Montrose, who thought that it was some brawl between the Highlanders and the Irish, threw himself into the thickest of the throng. There he found that a most horrible murder had just been committed. On the ground lay Lord Kilpont, foully slain."[1]

Kilpont had been stabbed by one of his own lieutenants, James Stewart of Ardvoirlich, who had been sharing his own bed that night. Ardvoirlich escaped in the confusion and eventually came safe to Argyll, who rewarded him with a free pardon and a majority in his own regiment. Notice was thus served across the breadth of Scotland that any man who would rid the Covenant of its enemies, even by the foulest means, could be sure of a welcome in Argyll's bosom. A week later the Covenant put its price upon the carcase of Montrose himself: £20,000 to the man who delivered him dead or alive.

The truth about the killing of Kilpont has never been established. Some said that he was murdered because he learnt of a plot by Ardvoirlich to kill Montrose himself; others, that he became involved in some hasty campfire quarrel. It seems unlikely that his death was part of any pre-arranged plot by the Covenanters. Ardvoirlich had only joined Montrose's army because he chanced to be with Kilpont on the Hill of Buchanty, arrayed against the royalists, the day before Tippermuir. The most plausible explanation of the murder is that Kilpont learnt that his man proposed to defect, tried to prevent him, and was killed in the ensuing scuffle. For Montrose, the personal loss was eclipsed by the military one: Kilpont's bowmen took possession of their chief's body and bore it away for burial among the family graves at Menteith. The army shrunk once again by 500 men. Sadder and fewer, the royalists marched on towards the north-east.

The townspeople of Dundee closed their gates in Montrose's face, and rested secure behind their fortifications when the King's Lieutenant summoned them to surrender. The Earl of Buchan and Lord Coupar had mustered the townspeople and rounded up many of the stragglers from the Covenanting army at Tippermuir. Confident of Argyll's army not many days away from them, they rejected Montrose's call. He could not linger to start a siege, nor risk the casualties of a storm. After camping overnight on Dundee Law outside the town while he reviewed the situation, the next morning he marched on northwards towards Aberdeen.

In front of him, the Covenanters began to rally their forces. The citizens of Aberdeen were no more enthusiastic followers of the Covenant than they had been seven years earlier when Montrose came with Alexander Henderson at his side to plead with them to subscribe it. But much water had flowed down the Dee since those days, some of it bloody. Argyll had ruthlessly crushed Huntly's rising that spring, and many of the chief royalists lay in jail. The Provost and most of the Baillies were Covenanters. The hand of the Forbes, the Earl Marischal and other prominent Covenanting lords of the north-east lay heavy on Aberdeen. When the Covenanters called for a muster of every citizen between sixteen and sixty to drill on the links for war, a reluctant quota of able-bodied Aberdonians reported for duty. The levies of Banff and Aberdeenshire were ordered out along with the Fife regiment stationed in the area since the spring.

A more difficult problem was that of command. The first thoughts of the Covenanters turned to young Lord Gordon, Huntly's eldest son who was now totally under the influence of his uncle Argyll. As chief of his clan in his father's absence in Strathnaver, Lord Gordon ordered a muster at Kildrummy. But he was curiously half-hearted about the business, and it soon became apparent that the Covenanters could look neither for his presence nor even for his clansmen in their battle line at Aberdeen. His younger brother Lord Lewis Gordon rode in with eighteen troopers to serve as a gentleman volunteer, and there was brief talk of asking him to assume command. But Lord Lewis was a wild young man still in his 'teens and utterly unreliable for any serious purpose. Grudgingly it was decided that it must be Lord Burleigh, president of the provincial committee of Aberdeen, who assumed control. A forceless man at the head of less than dedicated soldiers, his position was unenviable. But even without the Gordons his army mustered 2500 infantry and 500 horse. Surely, given a strong position of their own choosing and a two-to-one advantage of numbers, they must be capable of destroying Montrose and his slender force of half-naked cut-throats.

As the royalist army advanced northwards, a stream of local gentlemen rode warily out to pay their respects to the King's Lieutenant and to assess his prospects of survival before committing their loyalties. Most were unimpressed by what they saw. They knew of Burleigh at Aberdeen and of Argyll somewhere not far behind in Perthshire. Kilpont's murder had cast a new and ugly stain over the royalist progress. Most of the visitors to the camp spoke fairly with Montrose and left promising to return as soon as they had armed themselves and put their affairs in order. Instead, they went home and shut their doors until the royalists were far away. Knowing the hard road that lay ahead, Montrose shed one of his private responsibilities by leaving his second son Lord James at the family home of Old Montrose, to continue his education out of reach of the Covenanters, as he may have hoped. His eldest son John, Lord Graham, rode on beside him.

But as they advanced there were a few really valuable reinforcements to be welcomed. One day a fine little squadron rode up to meet the army, headed by old Lord Airlie and his two younger sons Sir Thomas and Sir David Ogilvy. Airlie was a haughty-looking man, already over sixty and in poor health. But he had the heart of a lion, and he devoted it to the service of his King. It was his eldest Ogilvy son who had shared so much with Montrose in England and who now lay a prisoner in Edinburgh Tollbooth. He brought with him forty horsemen, providing Montrose with his first respectable cavalry troop. Then came Nathaniel Gordon, the tough, able freebooter who had proved himself a fine soldier in the Bishops' Wars and had lived by his wits on the edge of the law ever since, fuelled by a passion for action and a contempt for Convenanting ministers. He brought with him another thirty horsemen. Nat Gordon was to prove one of the toughest, most resourceful, most loyal cavaliers in Montrose's army, a gay spirit game for any adventure. The coming of himself and of the Ogilvies went far to make up the loss of Kilpont and his bowmen.

On September 11th, the royalist army reached the Dee south of Aberdeen. Montrose made no attempt to repeat his success of five years before, when he forced the Bridge of Dee, the main approach to the city, against Aboyne and the royalists. It was now strongly held by a detachment of Burleigh's army. Instead he led his force rapidly upriver to a lightly-guarded ford near the Mills of Drum. Having crossed the water, he camped that night around Crathes Castle, home of Sir Thomas Burnet of Leys, a courteous gentleman who managed to reconcile friendship with Huntly and devotion to the Covenant. Montrose and his officers dined with Sir Thomas in his hall and declined his offer to ransom himself and his property for 5000 merks. They marched away the following morning leaving his estates unscathed, having commandeered only his arms and horses for their own urgent needs.

On September 12th Montrose and his men advanced a short distance towards Aberdeen. Then at the Two Mile Cross outside the city, they pitched camp once more. The King's Lieutenant ordered them to prepare for battle the following day. They rested, cleaned their matchlocks and foraged for the precious horses while Montrose himself gathered intelligence about the strength and intentions of his enemy. The Irish priests set up their altars in their usual fashion, and the herd of women and children gathered around their Macdonald men. Sir James Turner, strangely enough, who was in all things a diligent professional soldier, believed that the presence of women in camp was good for any army: "At the long siege of Breda," he remarks,[2] "it was observed that the married soldiers fared better, looked more rigorously, and were able to do more duty than the bachelors." To the Covenanting scouts watching the royalist camp from a safe distance, the Macdonald's presented a strange, perhaps deceptively domestic spectacle.

The Covenanting army, which had arrayed itself for battle outside Aberdeen on the Wednesday, September 11th, withdrew again into the city when it became obvious that the royalists would not be on them until the Friday. On this occasion Montrose's preliminary summons to the city to surrender seemed to him much more than a formality. He may have cherished real hopes that Aberdeen, which had resisted the Covenant so strenuously when he himself had been one of its soldiers, might now declare freely for the King.

> Loving Friends [he wrote to the City Fathers],
>
> Being here for the maintenance of Religion and Liberty, and his Majesty's just authority and service, these are in his Majesty's name to require you, that immediately upon the sight thereof, you render and give up your town, in the behalf of his Majesty; otherwise that all old persons, women and children, do come out and retire, and that those who remain may expect no quarter.
>
> I am as you deserve,
>
> MONTROSE.

On the morning of Friday September 13th, he sent his messenger accompanied by a drummer boy under flag of truce to the city walls, bearing his letter. They were admitted, and led through the streets to the house of Alexander Fyndlater. They were shown into the room where the City Fathers and the chief Covenanting peers of north-east Scotland were holding their sombre Council of War. Civilly enough, the envoys were offered a drink while the Covenanters considered their reply to Montrose's summons. One of them even tipped the drummer boy a piece of silver. But the letter they returned to the Lord Marquis offered him only Aberdeen's defiance:

Noble Lord,
We have received yours with a gentleman and a drummer, whereby your Lordship signifies to us that you are for the maintenance of Religion, Liberty, and his Majesty's just authority; and that we should render our town, otherwise no quarter except to old persons, women and children. We acknowledge likewise our obligation to maintain the same which your Lordship professeth you are doing; and we shall be most willing to spend the last drop of our blood therein, according to the Covenant subscribed and sworn by us. Your Lordship must have us excused that we will not abandon nor render our town so lightly; seeing we think we deserve no censure as being guilty of the breach of any of the aforesaid points; and specially of that latter article; but have ever been known to be the most loyal and dutiful subjects to his Majesty; and by God's grace, shall to our lives' end strive to continue so; and in the meantime to be,
> Your Lordship's as ye love us,
> PROVOST AND BAILLIES OF ABERDEEN,
> In name of the burgh.

Soon after 11 a.m., as Montrose's envoys were returning from the city with the Baillies' reasonable but unyielding reply, the Covenanting army drew up for battle. As the two royalists passed the ranks of the Fife regiment, a musketeer coldly shouldered his piece and picked off the drummer boy. The child dropped dead in full view of Montrose's army, standing to their arms a few hundred yards away. The royalists seethed to see the flag of truce dishonoured by their enemies yet again, to see their own Gaelic blood once more despised. It may have been now, in the heat of his own anger before the battle, that Montrose promised his army the sack of Aberdeen if they won the day.

It seems to have been one of those damp, overcast Scottish autumn days on which the musketeers worried a little about keeping their matches alight. The Covenanters marshalled their 2500 infantry in three divisions on the face of the gentle hill that looked down upon the royalists. On each flank they

deployed 250 cavalry. Although Lord Burleigh held the
nominal supreme command, each of his subordinate officers
seems to have begun the battle with his own idea of how he
proposed to fight it. The Covenanters' cannon were mounted
as usual in front of their positions, and firing downhill began
the battle at some advantage against the royalists below.

Montrose's three Irish regiments took the centre of his own
line, a few hundred yards in front of the How Burn that ran
behind their positions. Half his horse rode on each flank, Nat
Gordon and Colonel James Hay commanding those on the left,
Major Rollo and Colonel Sibbald those on the right. Each
cavalry squadron was supported in the Swedish fashion by 100
musketeers interspersed between the troops, those on the left
commanded by Captain Mortimer. The cannon captured at
Tippermuir were mounted in front of the Irish at the centre
of the line. Montrose himself rode with Lord Airlie and his
officers in the classic manner of command. The royalist army
at Aberdeen was smaller than that at Tippermuir, but it was
also a much more respectable-looking fighting force. One last
little ritual had also been observed: for the sign of the day
Montrose had ordered all his men to pluck a handful of
oats from the cornfields around them and stick them in
their bonnets, just as the cavaliers wore a green bough at
Newbury, a white band at Marston Moor. Thus distinguished
from their enemies, they stood to await the opening of the
battle.

Some time around noon Lord Lewis Gordon began the
Covenanting attack in his own inimitably disorderly fashion.
With his score of clan troopers behind him, he trotted forward
against Montrose's right flank, and fired volley after volley
"in caracole" from the saddle. It was a dashing, old-fashioned
and ineffectual style of warfare: each man fired his pistol then
wheeled to seize another while the following rank fired. Each
trooper carried several weapons on his saddle, so the fusil-
lade from the circling horsemen sounded deafening enough.
But it was impossible to shoot accurately under such conditions,
and there was a real risk of blowing one's horses ears off. The
little charge appealed to Lord Lewis, "whose forward and free
disposition had not learnt the court way of temporizing"[3]
Patrick Gordon's way of explaining that the boy was wild,
rash, and intemperate. But Rollo's men stood unflinching

before the ill-aimed hail of fire. Lord Lewis's troops galloped away again when they had emptied their pistols.

The Gordon charge was followed by that of the entire left flank of the Covenanting horse under Lord Fraser and Lord Crichton of Frendraught. But they too showed little spirit in pressing home their attack. Their lancers trotted to within range of the royalist line and then halted to fire their carbines. Rollo's supporting musketeers answered them with rolling volleys that caused confusion in their ranks, and then the royalist cavalry hurled themselves uphill on them. The Covenanters were driven back in disorder. They made one more half-hearted attempt to attack, were again repelled, and proved then to be broken for the day. Throughout their action the rest of the Covenanting army made no attempt to use their weight of numbers to launch simultaneous assaults the length

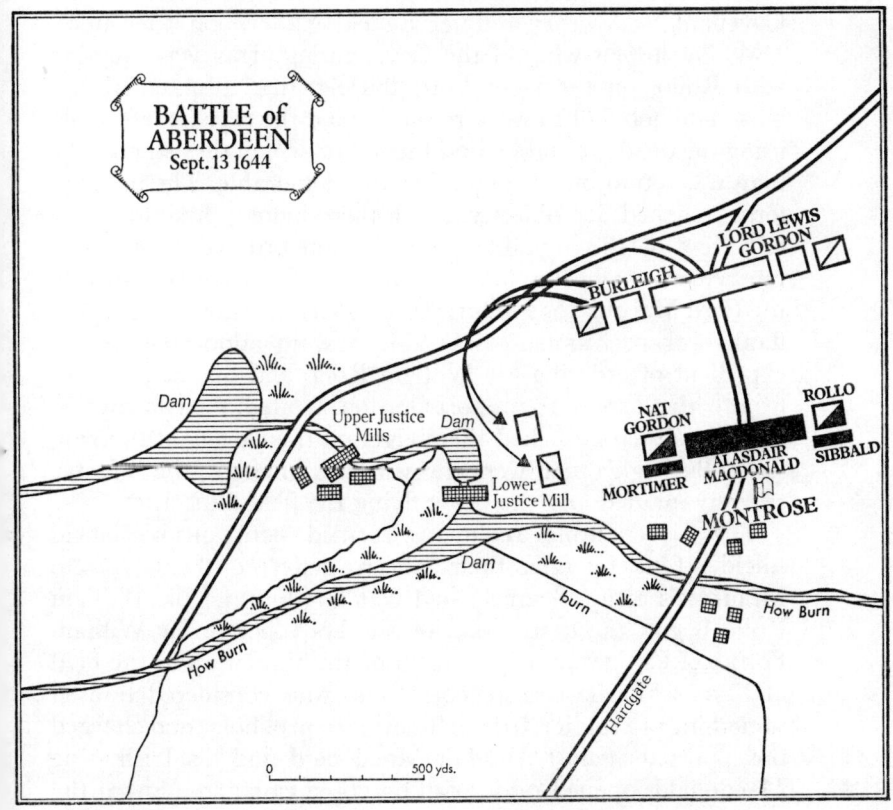

of the line. Instead they stood hesitant, passive while their left
was beaten back. The best chance of the day had slipped away
from them.

Aberdeen appears to have been a battle fought in slow motion
for several hours, with the bulk of both armies standing inactive
while local actions were disputed with angry violence. It is a
mistake to imagine their cavalry charges being fought out with
the speed and ferocity of Balaclava. The Highlanders' horses
were almost certainly the shaggy little garrons of the hills rather
than the big chargers of English armies. Nat Gordon's horsemen
probably advanced at a clumsy canter, the men's legs dangling
absurdly under the bellies of their tough little beasts. Neither
side could maintain a continuous blast of musketry when each
man needed a minute or more to reload his matchlock after
firing. At Aberdeen, unlike Tippermuir, Montrose spent the
first hours cautiously parrying the clumsy thrusts of the
Covenanters. A weary and nerve-racking afternoon it became.

While the left wing of the Covenanting army was tangling
with Rollo, on the right Lord Burleigh had dispatched 100
horse and 400 foot to work round behind the royalist left flank,
using the dead ground behind the hill on which they stood. The
plan was sound but its execution was deplorable. The flanking
force reached its objective and then halted, hesitating, in
full view of the royalists. Nat Gordon ordered Mortimer's
musketeers to wheel to face the threat, and sent urgent word to
the Lord Marquis for support. Having seen the Covenanting left
flank broken, Montrose was able now to adopt the drastic
expedient of ordering Sir William Rollo and his men to shift
front with all speed to support Gordon. United, the two royalist
regiments then launched themselves on the Covenant flanking
force. Burleigh's men were thrown back in chaos, the infantry
severely mauled and the horse flying the field altogether.

The Covenanting regiments seemed bent on piecemeal
suicide. One by one, their officers delivered themselves to
Montrose's army. Scarcely had Nat Gordon and Sir William
Rollo begun the destruction of one body before Sir William
Forbes of Craigevar, who had "brought himself up in the field
of Mars while he was abroad"[4] and thus considered himself
something of a soldier, led out his own troop of horse and charged
unsupported against Alasdair Macdonald and his Irish. The
Macdonalds opened ranks with practised ease and allowed the

Covenanters to sweep harmlessly through them. Then they delivered a devastating volley at the wretched horsemen's backs. Craigevar's troop was shattered, and he himself was wrenched from his saddle by the Irish and made prisoner.

For two hours now, Montrose's army had been blunting the attacks of the Covenanters successfully. But Burleigh's regiments still stood unbroken along the ridge, and the Macdonalds were suffering severely from the heavy cannonade that still blasted down upon them where they stood. One Irishman's leg hung by a shred where it had been struck by a cannon ball. "Ha, comrades, such is the luck of war," he remarked phlegmatically as he took out his knife and cut away the last of the limb. "As for me, sure my Lord Marquis will make me a trooper now I am no good for the foot."[5]

But the Irish were shifting restlessly under the ceaseless fire, and Montrose knew that merely to hold his ground was no longer enough. Calling down the ranks to settle matters at close quarters, he ordered the general charge. Alasdair's regiments swept yelling up the hill, through the little cluster of cottages and gardens held as an outpost by the Covenanters, past the gun line and into the massed ranks of the Covenanting pikemen. At Aberdeen as at Tippermuir, it was too much for poorly-trained, ill-led levies to bear. Battle in the seventeenth century must often have resembled a gigantic, bloody, heaving rugger scrum. Steadily and surely the Covenanters were pressed back, giving ground, trampled under the rush of men and metal, fear giving way to panic as one by one they saw their officers swing their horses and spur away towards Aberdeen. Burleigh and his staff escaped along with almost all the cavalry, hurling away their lances as they fled. The Aberdeen militia threw away their banner and ran desperately for their homes in the city. The battle dissolved into rout.

The royalists hurled themselves into the pursuit of the fugitives with their usual enthusiasm. Scores were killed on the road to Aberdeen, stripped of their clothes and left naked. Even at the gates of the city there was no attempt to check the royalist torrent: the Macdonalds and the Highlanders poured headlong into the streets clutching their bloody swords and pikes, seeking out every fugitive from the battlefield and laying them dead upon the cobbles. Montrose allegedly lost only twelve men killed and twenty wounded at Aberdeen. The

Covenanters, in the battle and the slaughter that now took place, reportedly had 1000 men killed. The victors set about the sack of the city.

Contemporary Covenanting propagandists and later historians have made much of the sack of Aberdeen as a blot on the honour of Montrose. The great Gardiner has written: "It was impossible to restrain an unpaid army composed of such wild materials as his own. This defence, however, is in reality his condemnation. He made use of a force strong enough to slay and plunder, but entirely incapable of founding a political edifice."

Montrose's Irish certainly needed booty to assuage them. It was chiefly for this that they fought at all. But what they did at Aberdeen was no worse than a hundred incidents in the English Civil War, much less than was routinely done by officers and gentlemen in the Thirty Years' War, and very much less than was done to any Irish captured by the forces of the Covenant. Argyll carried fire and the sword against royalist families and properties whenever it suited him to do so. The number of innocents killed in cold blood at Aberdeen, as distinct from fugitive Covenanting soldiers hunted down, was not very great—probably less than a hundred. Some women were raped and others were carried off to the royalist camp, but even the British Army in Germany in 1945 considered this a fair portion of victor's rights. Montrose's conduct throughout his campaign was generally extraordinary for its courtesy, mercy and discretion. It is hard to feel that the pillage of Aberdeen was by any contemporary standards a very wicked or dishonourable business. It was simply seized upon by enemy propagandists in much the same manner as the Black Prince's sack of Limoges three hundred years before.[6] In each case, the generals concerned achieved fame as the pattern of chivalry. Their momentary fall from their own standards was only held against them because their usual conduct was of such a high order, as was to be seen in Montrose's refusal to take reprisals for the Covenanters' orgy of judicial murder after Philiphaugh.

But on practical, political grounds, the sack of Aberdeen was a serious blunder. Montrose hoped to win the Gordon country to his side, to persuade Aberdeen and other cities of Scotland to declare for the King. The spectacle of drink-maddened Irishmen tearing the clothes off women and corpses in the streets did untold damage to the image he sought to create. Spalding, the Aberdeen chronicler, was himself a royalist, but he compiled a bitter list of those who were killed: ". . . John Canarell, fencing master; Thomas Webster, piper; Robert Reid, advocate; Robert Milne, miller; Vice Thomson, scholar. . . . These persons were not Covenanters, but hurled out sorely against their wills to fight against the King's Lieutenant."[7]

Montrose himself entered Aberdeen on the morning of Saturday, September 14th, the day after the battle. He was deeply distressed by the misery and terror that he found all around him, the unburied bodies lying naked in the streets, the plundered merchants' houses, the drunken Macdonalds still prowling dangerously in search of fresh blood and booty. Like Wellington at Badajoz, he was confronted by the frightening spectacle of his own army become a rabble. Conscious of the damage to his cause, he ordered his officers to shift the entire force a few miles northwards to camp around Kintore and Inverurie. He instructed the city baillies to set about burying the dead and clearing up the debris of battle. Belatedly, he had read the royal proclamation, together with an order in his own name calling forward every loyal citizen to subscribe his allegiance. It must have seemed a hollow little ceremony at the Market Cross, and the Lord Marquis himself cannot have expected much from it under the circumstances. He must have felt very conscious, suddenly, of the loneliness of his struggle. The only recruits he won from Aberdeen were the Gordon prisoners lodged in the tollbooth since the failure of Huntly's rising in the spring, and now set free by the royalist victory.

It was fortunate for Montrose, that autumn, that he was a a man of dauntless optimism. After the battle of Aberdeen, his simpler officers must have been agog with excitement and conceit at their own invulnerability, their eyes glittering gaily in the candlelight of their dinner tables as they argued in their cups whether to go next for Glasgow or Edinburgh. Only the shrewder men around Montrose understood his own hesitation, his thoughtful silences and brooding moments amidst the hubbub of the army's headquarters. Even now, with two amazing victories won, there was no prospect of making a move directly to aid the King. He was still hunted. Behind him Argyll was still trudging in pursuit. There was no prospect of lingering in Aberdeen, far less of holding the city, for once again there was news of the Covenanting army. Their powerful forces, at least 4000 strong, were less than two days' march away at Brechin. On Monday, September 16th, Montrose and those of his men remaining in Aberdeen moved north to Inverurie, leaving the city sullen and bitter behind them. Even at this late hour, Spalding recorded, stragglers were still at work: "Many runagate Irish bade behind, rifling and spoiling the old and new towns pitifully, and nae durst bury the dead. Yea, and I saw two corpses carried to their burial through the old town with women only, and not a man amongst them."[8] As long as any portion of Montrose's army remained in Aberdeen, not a man dared to venture out of doors. Nor were the city's troubles over even after their departure. Two days later, on Wednesday, September 18th, the vanguard of Argyll's army marched belatedly in, to be lodged at free quarter in the houses of the citizens. The coming of their deliverers proved an expensive business for the Aberdonians in the next few weeks.

The royalists were camped on the Don a few miles below the legendary battlefield of Harlaw, where some two hundred years earlier the clans had fought, and lost, their epic confrontation with the Lowland knights. The Macdonalds, in their simple way, were perfectly happy: "The riches of that town hath made all our soldiers cavaliers," wrote one of their officers as they lay surrounded with the booty of Aberdeen. Montrose sent dispatches to the King with news of his latest triumph. For Charles at Oxford, the campaigning season seemed set to end full of bright hopes, with the surrender of Skippon at Fowey, the dissensions between Parliament and the Scots in London, and now Montrose's great deeds—"stupendous" as the admiring Hyde noticed them—bringing the promise of great events in Scotland. Faithful Rollo carried Montrose's dispatch south, but he had ridden that road once too often. He was captured on the journey and brought before Argyll to face that subtle and vengeful nobleman in person. The King's Lieutenant had some weeks to wait before he had news of his devoted officer.

With Argyll and his army at Aberdeen, Kintore became unsafe. The royalists broke camp and withdrew cautiously up the valley of the Don to Kildrummy, burying their cannon in a marsh along the way to lighten their progress. Guns were never to be much value to such an army as that of Montrose, and they were a fatal encumbrance on the trackless broken ground of the hills. At Kildrummy, some thirty miles west of Aberdeen, they paused to take stock. It was a matter of urgent importance to try the temper of the Gordons, if possible to make some contact with Huntly himself. Montrose began the first of endless attempts to catch the ear of the temperamental Marquis, skulking in his lair in Strathnaver. Even lacking the presence of the clan chief in person, the royalists nursed some hopes of raising Gordon recruits. From Kildrummy the Lord Marquis sent out Nat Gordon to tour Strathbogie and parley with every Gordon laird he could reach.

To Argyll at Aberdeen, it was also apparent that the Gordon country held the key to the campaign. If Montrose could raise support among that powerful clan, he might make north-east Scotland the hub of a revolt which would bring the Covenant to its knees. Once the royalists grasped vital territory, built a base for their rising, all the waverers in Scotland might rally to their banners. Without the Gordons, however, for all Montrose's military genius he and his army were only an isolated guerilla force, mere nomadic brigands to be hunted down in the fullness of time.

So at all costs the Gordon country must be held against the royalists. Argyll wasted no time on persuasion. As he set out with the bulk of his army in pursuit of Montrose, he detached regiments to march the length and breadth of the Gordon lands burning, threatening, garrisoning, crushing every seed of dissent. He ignored the bitter protests of young Lord Gordon, at his side, about this destruction of his inheritance, this terrible reward for his loyalty to his uncle. Brusquely pleading the exigencies of state, Argyll set about the wreck of Strathbogie and the harrying of Montrose.

The royalist army gathered once more, and moved lightly westwards in the face of the advancing Argyll until they reached Rothiemurchus, the great gentle forest just below Aviemore on the Spey. Nat Gordon was back from his ride around the Gordon lands, bearing news of a string of dour refusals from every man of Huntly's. Without the word of the clan chief they would not move. At his camp beside Loch An Eilan, Montrose wearily accepted the inevitable: until a new opportunity presented itself to strike on his own terms, he and his army must keep running from Argyll.

They planned to cross the Spey, but to their dismay found the western bank held by a powerful force of Grants backed by the levies of Moray, Ross and Caithness—the same army that had mustered only a few weeks earlier to drive away Alasdair and his marauding Macdonalds. The Grants spoke fairly enough to the King's Lieutenant, assuring him that they were royalists at heart, and needed only the encouragement of seeing others beneath the King's banner to join it themselves. When, for instance, they saw the Earl of Seaforth and his Mackenzies armed for the King, then the Grants and all the others would be close enough behind them. Meanwhile, however, they and their allies regretfully denied passage to Montrose. The royalists slipped hastily away northwards to the forest of Abernethy, still on the eastern bank of the Spey, before they could be pincered between the Grants and Argyll.

But while Montrose danced up and down the Spey, Argyll and his army were in the very heart of Gordon country, burning the parishes for miles around Huntly, Cromar, Auchtersoul and Abergeldie, destroying the corn that sustained life and hope through the winter, seizing arms and horses, sapping the fighting power of the clan and burning its houses around its ears. To the Campbell regiments of Argyll's army, it was a mission after their own hearts, a fine chance to wreak private clan havoc in the name of the Covenant. The strength of the Gordons was ebbing as they lay leaderless. Huntly, at Tongue, icily declined to move a muscle in alliance with the upstart Montrose who had brought humiliation on his family five years before. Without word from Huntly, no Gordon laird would move. If Argyll's depredations continued much longer, the Gordons would be too weak to assist Montrose even if they should change their minds and accept a call to arms.

Montrose could not offer battle to Argyll, but he could at least lead him out of the Gordon country. At the end of that eventful September, he began the long strenuous march up the Spey, through the heart of the Grampians, high into the hills, before dropping once again towards the soft valley of Atholl where the great adventure had begun a crowded month earlier. It was a journey displaying all the heady magic of Montrose's campaign, at breakneck speed through the high heather,

George, Lord Gordon

George Gordon, 2nd Marquis of
Huntly

1st Earl of
Airlie

Lord Ogilvy,
later 2nd Earl
of Airlie

bear-leading his sluggish enemies panting hopelessly in his wake. The army slept heaped in their plaids on the hill beside the chilled burns that provided their drink. Each man carried his sack of oatmeal to cook in the evening with a chunk of venison shot by some clansman while the army marched. Some men had the knack of tickling trout from the streams and perhaps even of spearing a salmon or two from the Spey. The evenings were chilly, for it was that Highland season when the weather is bracing itself for winter, when the first squalls mar some of the days and the rain, when it comes, soaks doggedly through the thickest plaid. Montrose and his officers shared everything with their men, because there was nothing else for them to do. Occasionally they struck some house or tower where the laird could be encouraged or frightened into setting his table for them, but the King's Lieutenant had to wade every burn, leap every peat hag, slide down every hill amongst his men. With so small an army, he must have known almost every man by name very quickly. His charm and his eloquence were constantly at play, soothing the latent tensions between Irishmen and Highlanders, cheering his officers when they despaired of this apparently futile Highland merry-go-round, smiling sweetly on men who had begun to wonder whether they were too tired to march more miles that day. It is his extraordinary achievement in holding together his motley army on so many marches of such difficulty and danger that marks Montrose as a leader of genius.

Somewhere in the hills the Lord Marquis frightened his men very much by developing a serious fever from exhaustion and overstrain. The Covenanters pursuing him even cherished a rumour for a time that he had died of it. But he recovered to march onwards. On October 4th, he led the royalists into Atholl. Argyll, alarmed by the possibility of Montrose's descent upon the Lowlands which had been left exposed by his absence, broke off his devastations in the Gordon country just as Montrose had hoped, and marched south in pursuit, ravaging royalist property wherever he could find it in his path.

Montrose paused in Atholl to pick up supplies provided for him by John Stewart of Schierglass, a friendly local laird. He shed his prisoners and his own wounded by garrisoning Blair Castle and making it his prison and his hospital: it became his only fixed base for the rest of the campaign. Any dilemma

G

about what next he might attempt was now rudely resolved by the impetuous Alasdair Macdonald. Not for the last time in the campaign, Alasdair announced his intention of turning aside from the King's business to pursue his own: word had reached him that the Campbells were threatening his cherished captured castles on the west coast, Mingarry and Lochaline. He was most anxious to relieve them and to deposit the booty of Aberdeen in safety. There was also the prospect, as he lamely reminded his exasperated general, that he might yet recruit men from the Clanranald for next season's campaigning. Montrose must have been appalled by Alasdair's defection with the great risk that he would never return. Even if the Macdonalds proved willing to come back, there was a considerable danger that the Covenanters would cut off and destroy their blundering commander once he was left to his own devices. But Montrose could not stop Alasdair. He had to watch him march away westwards over the hill from Blair with the best grace he could muster. One Irish regiment, under the devoted Magnus O'Cahan, remained with Montrose. All told, he now had perhaps 800 infantry and his 80 horse left. Once again, he could not remain passive in Atholl with so small and vulnerable a force. He was obliged to run very fast in order to stand still, to press on with his mad dash around eastern Scotland merely to avoid extinction. It was getting late in the year for war, but he must once more march out of Atholl to do what he could to keep alive the flickering flame of the King's cause in Scotland.

It had become imperative to do something to frighten the Covenanters in their homes as badly as the depredations of Argyll were unnerving the royalists. On the second day of his march out of Atholl, Montrose reached Dunkeld, and gave the men the welcome order to destroy Covenant property wherever they found it. Then he swung eastwards, towards Kirriemuir and Angus and the coast. Colonel Sibbald took half the army up Glen Ardle on a recruiting foray, while Nat Gordon led a squadron of horse into Strathmore. Gordon's men brushed with—of all people—Montrose's brother-in-law Lord Carnegie. Carnegie's men managed to pick off two of the royalist column before the whole force turned in anger and chased him to the very gates of Dundee, where they burned a few houses before withdrawing to rejoin Montrose. The army was now once again approaching long-suffering Aberdeen, and the Covenanters in the city made hasty preparations to receive them: "We have been watching the Bridge of Dee foolishly with about fourteen troops, living idly, destroying the country and their corns pitifully," wrote Spalding[9] in disgust.

While the Earl Marischal and his cavalry stood at the Bridge of Dee, on October 17th Montrose once again marched up river to avoid them, and crossed over at the Mills of Drums to seek the hospitality of Sir Thomas Burnet at Crathes. On the night of the 19th they stayed at Monymusk with Burnet's daughter, who was married to a Covenanting Forbes. Her husband was away, but Montrose spared the castle "upon fair conditions". Still burning and plundering Covenanting property, the royalists advanced onwards into Strathbogie. On October 21st, they reached Huntly Castle, and for five days Montrose made his headquarters there while he sought in vain once more to communicate with the recalcitrant Huntly. The help of the Gordons remained the best hope for Montrose's cause, and he seemed doomed to wander Scotland hopelessly until he could obtain it.

His latest dash into Huntly territory went for nothing. The Marquis resolutely declined to stir from his northern fastness, or to send a word of help or encouragement to the King's Lieutenant-General. The Gordons were immovable. Some of them, at least, were now well cowed by the visit of Argyll. Montrose raised 200 half-hearted recruits in Strathbogie, but they were a poor return for so many desperate marches that autumn.

It is hard to understand the motive behind his next move. On October 27th, he marched fifteen miles eastward from Huntly to the castle of Fyvie, the ancestral home of the Earls of Dunfermline. Montrose's brilliant scouting was normally in vivid contrast to the very poor standard of intelligence-gathering in the Civil War. But on this occasion he was dangerously badly-informed about the movements of Argyll. He may have been preparing for some new descent on the coast to replenish his failing supplies of ammunition. At any event, he and his small force were resting unsuspecting beside the little river Ythan when their pickets came racing towards the castle to report that Argyll's army was two miles away and closing fast. It was the morning of October 28th.

It is easy to take for granted Montrose's dispositions in these moments of crisis, to assume that his actions were the automatic reflexes of any seventeenth-century commander. They were not. They displayed a speed of thought and an eye for ground that were the wonder of the age. At Fyvie Montrose instantly rejected the notion of shutting himself in the castle with his army. It was a poorly-fortified place, and it would be disastrous to allow himself to be besieged at leisure by Argyll's far superior army. Nor was there time to make a cool retreat. The royalists must make a stand, and in such a position as to keep their options open to march again when they chose. They were also desperately short of ammunition, and a party was at once set to work melting down all the pewter in the Dunfermline halls to make bullets. As the Highlanders prepared for battle, jokes about the qualities of Fyvie's chamber pots were running the length of the line as they were hastily cast into shot.

The ground upon which Montrose chose to make his stand was a steep bluff behind the castle, broken up by thickets, stone walls and ditches that lent themselves ideally to firing positions. His men began digging furiously to improve the natural defences. Only a small screening force was left to hold the castle itself. The horse were held in reserve somewhere in the rear, while the infantry officers called along the hillside to their men to make every precious bullet count.

Argyll began his attack by sending forward a regiment of Lothian's tough, dogged infantry to assault the bluff. The whole Covenanting army was weary after its long and fruitless game of grandmother's footsteps around the hills after Montrose for a fortnight, and their heavy armour and equipment made hard going of an uphill attack. But to Montrose's dismay, as the Covenanters broke upon his forward defences the Gordons he had so recently recruited in Strathbogie threw down their arms and fled in panic back up the hill. Fierce skirmishes developed on the hillside as yard by yard the Covenanters pushed the shaken royalists from their positions.

But the Covenanting attack gradually lost momentum as the tired attackers puffed stumbling uphill. Montrose called on Magnus O'Cahan and Donald Farquharson to gather every man they could muster and counter-attack. The Irish charged madly down the hill in one of their irresistible onslaughts, sweeping the Covenanters helpless before them. They cleared the hill and then lingered in triumph cutting the powder flasks and bandoliers from their vanquished enemies to replenish their own critical supplies.

A Covenanting cavalry charge up the hill was now broken up by cool royalist musketry among the trees and ditches. Volleys of Fyvie chamber pot cut down trooper after trooper. Had the inexperienced Atholl men not fired prematurely, Montrose had planned to lure the whole regiment deep into his positions and annihilate it. It was clumsy of Argyll to try a cavalry attack unsupported, against an enemy entrenched on such difficult ground, but the Campbell never showed a spark of tactical instinct. Another flanking attack by his cavalry was checked by musketry and then dispersed by Nat Gordon's cavalry. At nightfall the royalist positions stood unbroken. Argyll's bruised army withdrew two miles to make camp.

The Campbell was a proud man, and that day's work must have been wormwood to his soul. Ever since their youth, he and Montrose had enjoyed a grating, eternally antipathetic relationship. Argyll had found much about Montrose's politics and popularity unjust and intolerable. Now he found himself thwarted, even humiliated, on the field of battle also. With a far superior army, he had caught the Graham after a long, almost absurd pursuit. Having done so, the pride of the Campbells was being humbled before his eyes. He would have been less than human had he not retired to his bed seething that night, after sitting his saddle all through the long day watching attack after attack falter and break amidst the fierce little ripples of smoke on the royalist positions. By rights he should have been in London or Edinburgh or with Leven's army, steering the great debates and great events that were being decided between the two kingdoms. Instead, he stood here on a Scottish autumn hillside playing a losing game of cat and mouse with the mischief-making Montrose and his band of brigands.

The following morning, his army returned to the attack, but with no better success. They never showed the slightest prospect of breaking through the royalist positions. Charge after charge painfully gained a little ground, only to lose it with substantial loss against the unceasing sniping and ferocious counter-attacks of the Irish and the Highlanders. The Earl Marischal's brother, Alexander Keith, was killed at the head of one Covenanting attack. The hillside was now strewn with the broken bodies of Argyll's men, hung over the walls and trenches they had struggled so bitterly to seize. That night of October 29th, dispirited and hungry with the failure of their attack and the shortage of their provisions, the Covenanting army once again drew sulkily off to make camp and nurse their defeat.

Early on October 30th, word reached Montrose of a vital development: the errant Marquis of Huntly, the man who held the keys to the north-east, had suddenly returned from Strathnaver and was expected hourly in Strathbogie. It was time to move. The Lord Marquis had conducted a brilliant defensive action for two days, inspiring a Highland army in the kind of battle that so often proved beyond its spirit and patience. But he could not forever resist an army outnumbering him five to one. Deftly he disengaged his little force from the positions they had held with such success, and hastened to Huntly Castle to find its Marquis.

Yet again, however, a fleeting hope for the royalist cause was dashed. The report of Huntly's coming was false. His clan still showed no disposition to stir. Momentarily at a loss once again as to what course to pursue, Montrose paused in Strathbogie. The action at Fyvie had at least alarmed Argyll. The Covenanting army plodded wearily after Montrose to Huntly, but finding him strongly entrenched to receive them, they declined battle and pitched camp at a safe distance under the watchful eye of Montrose's scouts. For the next three days, a series of wary parleys appears to have taken place between the two armies. It is impossible to believe that Argyll seriously intended to offer mercy to the Lord Marquis himself. He merely wanted to divorce every man he could from the royalist standard.

Montrose now welcomed the sudden and unexpected return to his camp of Sir William Rollo, his old Major newly knighted by the King. But he was disgusted to hear upon what terms his friend had been permitted to leave Argyll. The Campbell had offered his prisoner freedom in return for a promise that he would attempt to murder Montrose at the first opportunity. Not unreasonably, Rollo felt it less dishonourable to break this odious bargain than to keep it. But Argyll's other subterfuges at Huntly were not without effect. Montrose had already sent off his baggage and was preparing a night march to disengage himself once more from the clutches of the Covenant when he was alarmed to learn that Colonel Sibbald, the officer who had ridden north with him at the outset of his adventures, had deserted to the enemy. Sibbald was privy to all Montrose's plans. He hastily countermanded his order for the march and had the baggage brought back. He lingered in Strathbogie until November 6th when, feeling at last that he might catch Argyll off-guard again, he slipped away by night with his army leaving camp fires burning and his little cavalry force screening his rear.

Free of Argyll at last, Montrose and his officers took stock. It seemed too late in the year for much more campaigning, with the first heavy snows already on the tops. Argyll had offered passes to any man who left the royalist army. It was agreed between Montrose and Nat Gordon that the latter should take advantage of this offer to linger in the Gordon country and see what could be done with young Lord Gordon and some of his lairds before the spring. To the disgust of the honest Covenanting gentlemen of Aberdeen, Montrose's dashing cavalry colonel was soon to be seen walking the streets of the city a free man, and making some ambitious recruiting plans for the spring.

Some of Montrose's officers left him unbidden. They had had enough of his epic marches across the hills, of the excesses of the Irish and the wild gambles with fortune. The King's Lieutenant found himself in the heart of the Grampians with only Black Pate, Lord Airlie and his sons, Magnus O'Cahan and his 1000 or so infantry, as the harsh Highland winter came on. He made one more amazing attempt to achieve a coup against Argyll: knowing that the Covenanting cavalry had been sent to the winter quarters while their infantry lay unsupported at Dunkeld, he suddenly launched his little army on a race across the hills to fall upon them. It was a terrible journey through the ice and snow, across the frozen burns, covering twenty-four miles of broken country in a single night, slipping and sliding along the passes. Had it succeeded, the southward dash through Atholl would have been remembered among Montrose's great achievements. But as they reached Blair and prepared to drive on the last few miles to their target, the royalists learnt to their frustration that Argyll was for once in front of them. Hearing that Montrose was afoot and wisely putting no trust in his own weight of numbers, he ordered his men to withdraw at once on Perth, out of Montrose's reach. He himself, along with Lord Lothian, then felt free to post thankfully south to Edinburgh, the Marquis to resign his commission before the Committee of Estates. That sour body was sufficiently respectful of Argyll to vote him their thanks. But they were also sufficiently scornful of his failure to deal with Montrose to add a heavily ironical word of congratulation that he had completed his campaign with so little bloodshed. Next season, they intended, matters would go differently. They had summoned William Baillie, one of Leven's ablest officers from the army in England, to assume command of the expeditionary force against Montrose. Until he could begin his operations, the Estates could only linger in bitter frustration. It had not yet proved necessary seriously to weaken their army in England to deal with the royalist uprising (although some regiments had been brought back from Ireland). But Montrose's doings had brought about a disastrous loss of confidence in the Covenant by the English Parliament. Until the excommunicate Graham could be hunted down, there would be precious little peace of mind in Edinburgh.

That November in Blair Atholl, however, Montrose himself must have reached the depths of despair. He had failed to raise the Gordons. Alasdair and two-thirds of the Irish brigade had vanished into the western mists in search of plunder. Perth and Aberdeen, two of the greatest towns in Scotland, had received him with cold hostility and offered him not a man for his cause. That early winter of 1644 must also have been desperately boring for a man of Montrose's impatient, urgent spirit. Day after day he was obliged to linger at Blair Atholl, wandering among the draughty tents and huts of his army, pacing the turrets of Blair Castle and looking out over the snow-covered hills in vague hope of seeing the errant Macdonalds appear by some magic. He might occasionally have hunted the deer to relieve the monotony. He had his son beside him for the first time for many months. He could talk to him and at last learn to know him after so many absences. But always, always there was the knowledge of Argyll plotting his destruction over the hills, the sense of time running out, of the weeks going by against him, of the new army mustering to fight him in the new campaigning season. In England, Newcastle had fallen and the north was lost for the King, but the Second Battle of Newbury had been fought in October without a royalist disaster, and the prospect was still bright in the west. There seemed to be hope, a chance of accomplishing so much if only he could do his part and march southwards out of Scotland at the head of a royalist army. Impatiently, anxiously, Montrose lingered into December at Blair, awaiting another miracle to add to all those he had been vouchsafed already.

Some time in the second week of December, God's mercy granted him the impossible once more: over the hill from the west, through the snow and across the Garry ford and up the slope towards Blair Castle, came Alasdair Macdonald, leading not only his two regiments but another 800 men of the western clans. Alasdair had reached his western castles to find that they had already been relieved by no less a chief than John Moydartach, the captain of the Clanranald. After watching for weeks while the Campbells besieged Mingarry, Moydartach had found the opportunity to bring vengeance upon them too much to resist. First leading out his men on a great raid against the unguarded Campbell lands, he then sent supplies to succour the beleaguered Macdonalds in their strongholds. His own future was thus ordained. Argyll would wreak vengeance for all this against the Clanranald as soon as he had the force and the opportunity. They had nothing to lose and much to gain by joining the royalist banners and seeking to undo the Campbells before they could do their worst. The Macdonalds of Keppoch, the Camerons, and the Stewarts of Appin fell in behind them. Among the Highland clans at least, news of Tippermuir and Aberdeen and the great toll of plunder and glory that had been won from them roused the keenest warlike instincts.

An eye-witness in Atholl that December,[10] amidst the great muster that was now assembled, marvelled at the men united beneath the King's banner: "There were young men from Orkney . . . and from Uist. . . . There were men from the English border, and from Lothian, from Galloway in the south-west . . . from the neighbourhood of Stirling, Menteith, Perth, Strathearn, Angus, Ireland, from the Highlands, Ardnamurchan, Knoidart, and Moidart, Lochaber, Badenoch, Glencoe, Mar, Strathavon, Strathspey, Strathisla, and Glenesk. The island of Skye, the largest of the Hebrides, sent the flower of the youth of the Macdonalds, and Moray and Buchan, in the east and north, furnished a number of noble young men, full of ardour and goodwill, though little accustomed to excursions in the Highlands."

With their jewelled brooches on their plaids, their studded targets and claymores and dirks and matchlocks, their beards and bonnets and pikes, there were now almost 3000 of the finest fighters in Scotland in Atholl. The King's Lieutenant had an army once again.

There was no question of remaining in the valley all winter waiting for the snows to melt. With 3000 men to feed, Montrose had to march, and march quickly. It was a great opportunity. Lightly-equipped and incredibly hardy, the Highlanders could move in winter with an ease impossible for a conventional Lowland army. Argyll's forces were dispersed and unprepared. Fortune gave Montrose the chance to strike a devastating blow, by moving against the Lowlands with all his men when he was least expected. It would be hard for the Committee of Estates even to summon reinforcements from England at any speed in winter weather. As soon as the Macdonalds and the new recruits from the clans had settled down and the first greetings and chattering were over, the Lord Marquis called a council at which he proposed that they march at once for the south.

But here at Blair, the fatal weakness of his army was revealed. His plan was met with blunt rejection. Instead, the Lord Marquis found himself confronted with a concerted counter-proposal from Alasdair and all the clans who had had so many weeks in which to mull it. Argyll, the Campbell himself, was their enemy. It was against him and all his that they wished to strike. Now, in December, the Campbells lay idle and un-suspecting in their fastnesses, convinced that no man could touch them behind their great wall of icy mountains. Alasdair demanded that the royalist army embark on an immediate crossing of Scotland to fall upon Inverary and the heart of the Campbell country.

Montrose was horrified. His grand strategy for breaking the power of the Covenant was to be dashed aside in favour of a mere predatory clan plundering expedition. Alasdair argued that to attack the power of Argyll was to attack the heart of authority of the Covenant, but this was his apology, not a justification. Montrose replied that not only did he disapprove of the proposal, he was also appalled by the difficulties of carrying it out. The snows; the range of mountains shielding

Inverary; the passes held by Campbell garrisons between Blair and Loch Awe; the danger that Argyll could muster a great army of his clansmen to oppose them; their certain starvation in the hills if the attack on the Campbell granaries failed: all these perils Montrose graphically outlined for his officers. Airlie and the young Ogilvies, Black Pate and Donald Farquharson grimly supported their general.

But the clans and the Antrim Macdonalds had made up their minds before the council began, and where they wished to march, the King's Lieutenant must of cruel necessity march with them. It must be to Inverary, to harry the Campbell in his lair. Montrose, resignedly, fixed his steadfast eye on the Glencoe man who promised that he could guide them across the pass. Was he certain that he knew the way? Were there really victuals and shelter in the depths of the snows for an army of 3000 men? Angus MacAlain Dubh answered calmly that "if tight houses and fat cattle to feed upon in them would answer their purpose, that they would procure them".

One of Alasdair's Irish priests offered one further reassurance. Sniffing the wind, he turned to the King's Lieutenant and promised him that as long as it blew from the east, the weather would hold. There would be no fatal blizzard to drown the royalist army on its march.

For Montrose, it was a matter of making the best of a sorry business. A great chance to further the King's cause was being lost. The army was to hazard everything upon one of the most dreadful marches ever attempted in Scottish warfare. They could only carry enough food for a few days, and when it was exhausted they must capture cattle and corn to survive. There was the ghastly ragtag of Irish women and children to follow them through the snows. There was the uncertainty of what force they would find arrayed against them in the west. But, on December 11th, 1644, armed with only his iron will and indestructible zest for the impossible, Montrose led his army out of Atholl to assault Clan Campbell in its fastnesses.

# CHAPTER EIGHT

## The Day of Clan Donald

SOME TIME LATE on the morning of December 11th, 1644, such chilly souls as were afoot around the north shore of Loch Tummel lifted their heads to hear the fierce skirl of the pipes drifting down the wind towards them. Pounding along the waterside from the east, a dark stream flowing along the white hillside, footsteps muffled by the snow, came the first soldiers of Montrose's army. The column stretched a mile or more behind them with its pack animals, the handful of riding horses and the usual tail of stragglers.

The deer brought down to the low ground by the hard weather bolted out of their path as they came on: south from Blair then west along Tummel until they forded the head of the loch; then south again on the track that had taken them to Tippermuir scarcely three months before, that a hundred years later was to become one of Wade's military roads. Only the harsh panting of the men and the dull clatter of weapons and equipment broke the great silence of the hills as they made the long, heavy climb up the pass south of Tummel that afternoon. Each chieftain came on with his ghillies, his shield-bearer and clansmen behind him. In the midst of the army, beneath the Royal Standard, marched the Lord Marquis and his staff. Old William Forrett had been left behind on this savage march, but the aged Airlie had scorned the hardships and the freezing hillside. Now he strode uncomplaining beside Montrose. There too, extraordinarily, was young Lord Graham. The legs of a fourteen-year-old, even a boy raised in the hills, are ill-matched to covering twenty miles a day through the snow, but somehow the child managed it. Probably he rode a pony at least part of the way. Even the Lord Marquis may have availed himself of a seat in the saddle when there was a chance of one. But through the worst of the going it would have been impossible to ride a horse, even the toughest little Highland garron. The King's Lieutenant marched on foot beside his men. Even with all his experience of privation, this expedition into Argyll must have been a terrible ordeal for him. There was still a great distance between the brutal fitness and condition of the clansmen, and that of himself bred as a gentleman to sleep under a roof. No doubt he still joked as he marched, and laughed beside his men, because he was that kind of commander. But there can have been little private gaiety in the hearts of himself and of his staff. They were marching now to do or to die as literally as any army in history.

It is ironic that it should be this stroke, the great winter thrust into Argyll, that is remembered as Montrose's most extraordinary, most romantic adventure. The expedition had been undertaken against his passionate wishes. It was a wild clan raid that offered pitifully little to King Charles or to his cause, yet risked the extinction of royalism in Scotland. Across the centuries it catches the imagination even amidst the host of astonishments that jewelled Montrose's career. To beard Argyll in his lair was an epic fit for the bards. For so many years, the Campbells had been stretching their probing, grasping fingers deeper and deeper into Scotland. One by one, the little clans and septs around their borders had been pinched out or subdued, their towers and lands added to the Campbell empire. Their power, their wealth, their pride and greed and command of the tremendous Campbell battle line were already written deep into Scottish life and Scottish history. For Montrose and his men to march against Argyll, their chieftain, was an undertaking worthy of the Argonauts.

When the royalist army descended into the valley of the Tay, this time they did not wait upon the defiance of Alexander Menzies, who had so imprudently taunted them on the march to Tippermuir. Somehow the castle which had protected him in August was now laid open to expose the Laird of Weem to the royalists' revenge. He was made prisoner and his lands laid waste. Then, probably on the second day after leaving Blair, Montrose turned west once more and began to drive up Loch Tay.

The Lord Marquis himself took the northern shore. The Captain of Clanranald, John Moydartach, forded the Tay with his men and swept the southern bank parallel with the main army. At Taymouth, the harrying of the Covenant began in earnest. It is a little difficult to discern which path Montrose personally followed, and which were taken by the flying columns sent out from the main force at his orders. Parties hastened up Glen Lyon burning every village in their way. As news slowly travelled up the loch shore of the coming of the clans, a terrified herd of peasants and their women and livestock must have struggled desperately ahead of the royalists, the columns of smoke from their miserable homes burning black against the snow, the screams of the victims echoing back and forth from Clanranald's men to Montrose's across the mile of gunbarrel-blue water between them. Corn and animals were gratefully plundered. The royalists drove relentlessly on, skirting the endless marches and morasses where they could, or trusting to the ice to carry them over the treacherous masses of reed and scrub where there was no other road. Their poor shoes were little protection against days of stumbling through the snow, the great muddy puddles of ice, the half-frozen burns that crossed their path. Soon many men were walking with only strips of cloth bound around their feet. For the few precious ponies, it must have been a terrible journey, pressed on unsparingly, for to allow man or beast to linger would have been to waste precious food. By the third day, at the end of Loch Tay, they were marching within sight of the mountains that sheltered the dragon himself.

The approaches to Argyll have a mystic, Tolkienesque air of empty dread hanging upon them in winter. The days are short. They must have marched out before dawn to make any distance, thankful for the grudging grey light that fell on their path after eight o'clock or so. The sun rose, described its low arc across the sky, and then sank red before them to vanish abruptly by four in the afternoon. Then the snow and the moon lit them for an eerie hour or two more, before they sought such barns and empty hovels as they could find to shelter at least their officers. The men huddled in heaps in their plaids, soaking them in water so that they might somehow steam through the night. However terrible their exhaustion, each night the priests set up their altars as soon as the columns came to rest: "They placed a quantity of sheaves of corn in such a position as to form some kind of table, and breaking down the door-post, put it upon such pieces of wood as were smooth and well-fashioned, as a resting place for a portable altar stone which was laid upon them, and hung up their plaids at the back, and on both sides, to prevent the wind, often very violent in the hollows at the base of the hills, blowing the fabric away."[1]

They were now deep in Argyll's country, entering those mountains whose passes he believed impenetrable. He had often been heard to say that he would rather lose 100,000 florins than have their exits and entrances betrayed. "In summer and early autumn," wrote Father Macbreck,[2] "they are frequented for the purpose of hunting the stags and shooting the wild fowl, and men of rank engage eagerly in these pursuits, but in winter they are covered with immense masses of snow, through which it is impossible to find even a footpath. Argyll is the wildest country of all, and there is a proverbial saying that it is far enough to follow plunderers to Loch Tay, for that is the first obstacle encountered, and seems to have *Ne Plus Ultra* written upon it. . . . There are few trees to conceal or adorn the landscape. There is no track which the traveller can follow, except along the shore, and this is frowned upon by rocks, and interrupted by pools of water alternately spreading and subsiding, and the whole region seems to devour the wayfarer rather than carry him through it. The soil is full of caves and holes, or covered with mosses, with innumerable bog-holes of black and brackish water. . . . In short, it is scarcely possible to find a practicable pathway."

Even for such a Highland army as that of Montrose, it must have been a daunting experience to march into oblivion, utterly at the mercy of their guides. Three miles an hour would have been fast going under such conditions, even for the clansmen. The grouse started from the snow-covered heather under their feet, the snow buntings danced their fleeting ballets where in summer the larks spring and fall. There were dogs among the column to course the endless blue hares as they sprang up the hillside, and men to kill them if they ran among the marching regiments. It was the worst of omens for a timid hare to be allowed to pass alive between the ranks of a Highland army. Always, too, there were the crows hovering black, bleak and watchful over the army, picking the poor crumbs of each night's bivouac and waiting expectantly for richer, human prey.

Between the poor hamlets, Breadalbane and Argyll were a vast wasteland offering neither mercy nor comfort to man or beast in the midst of winter. When the clansmen struck a handful of the half-starved black cattle, their friendly fringes of hair falling lank over their faces, there was no lingering to bleed them. They were instantly slaughtered and thankfully cooked over such fires as Campbell roof timbers could fuel. Winter in the seventeenth century was an infinitely grimmer business than even the chilliest Scottish December today. It was a period that seems to have seen much sharper extremes of climate than those to which we have grown accustomed, in which the chamber-pots froze solid under country house beds, and great sheets of ice were a commonplace upon the sea lochs. Today, for a fit man in good boots and with the best of equipment, that march into Argyll in winter is still a tough undertaking. But Montrose's Highlanders, ah, they were men of iron. . . .

Probably about the fourth day, the scouts ran back to the head of the column with disturbing news. A narrow pass ahead ran by the south shore of Loch Dochart. In the midst of the loch on a little island stood a gaunt tower, mounting several field pieces, and garrisoned by a score or more of Argyll's Campbells. This was the postern gate to his mountain fastness. Even if the royalists could face a long detour round the back of the hills through the deep drifts to avoid the castle, it would be a terrible risk to leave the keys of the pass in the hands of the enemy. They could not storm it, nor by-pass it along the shore, for from the battlements the garrison could rake the army at will as they approached.

The column halted well out of sight of Castle Dochart while Montrose and his staff pondered the problem. But as they were in the midst of a sober conference, a group of local men were led forward who announced that they were seeking an audience with the Lord Marquis. There were a dozen of them, Macnabs, part of a tiny local sept which bore a deep grievance against the Campbells: "Witty, bold and active men, as men that of old had possessed much land in those parts, but the strength and power of the Campbells had dispossessed them".[3] If the Lord Marquis would grant them title to the castle when he had gained it, they said, they would show him the way to its capture. Montrose was at first sceptical of the Macnabs and their promises. But every hour lingering beside Castle Dochart was an hour in which Argyll might be mustering an army against them. The Macnabs must be trusted. Their ruse must be tried.

Before dawn the next morning, the Macnabs hailed the sentries on the castle wall. They bore letters from Argyll

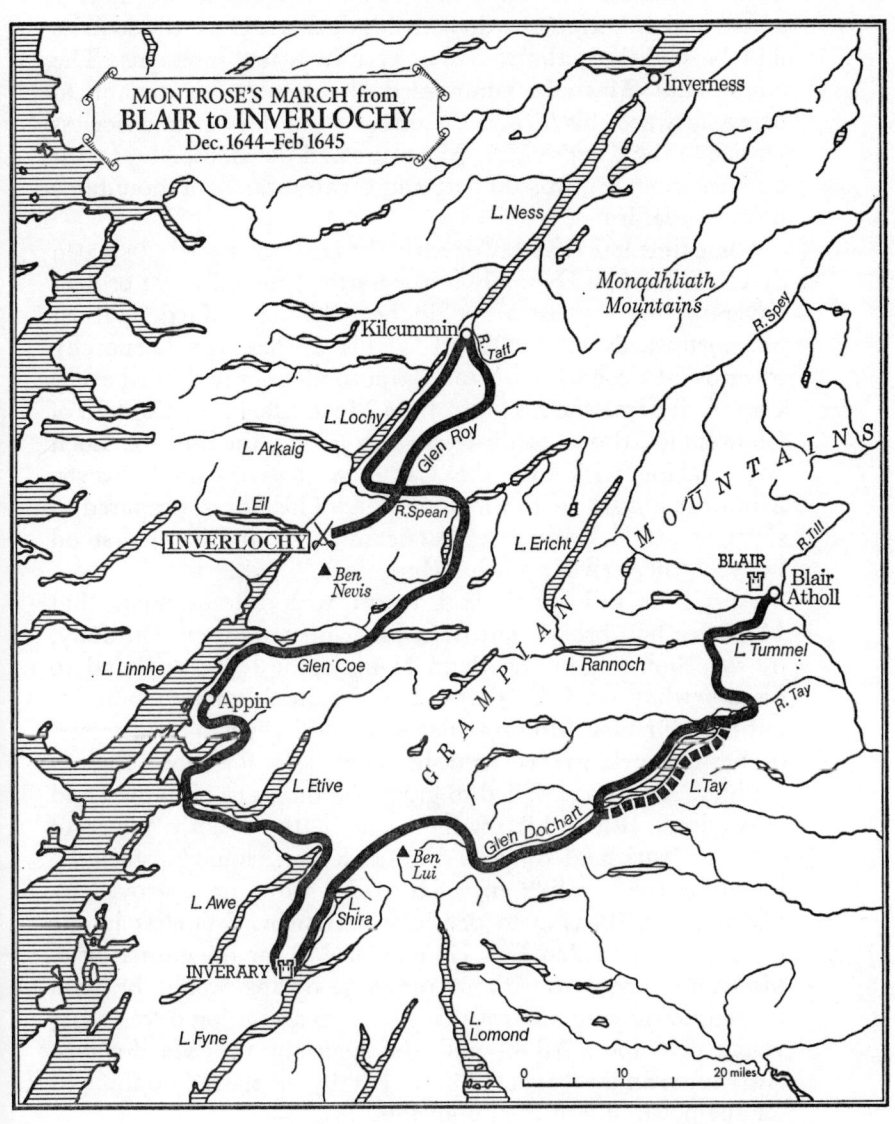

MONTROSE'S MARCH from
**BLAIR to INVERLOCHY**
Dec. 1644–Feb 1645

Inverness

L. Ness

Monadhliath
Mountains

R. Spey

Kilcummin

R. Tarff

L. Lochy

Glen Roy

L. Arkaig

L. Eil

R. Spean

**INVERLOCHY**

Ben
Nevis

L. Ericht

M  O  U  N  T  A  I  N  S

BLAIR

Blair
Atholl

R. Till

L. Tummel

L. Linnhe

Glen Coe

L. Rannoch

R. Tay

Appin

G
R
A
M
P
I
A
N

L. Etive

L. Tay

Glen Dochart

Ben
Lui

L. Awe

L.
Shira

**INVERARY**

L. Fyne

L.
Lomond

0          10          20 miles

himself for the garrison, they said. Unsuspecting—for the men were well-known in the area—the Campbells let them row across and unbarred the door to admit them. Once the sentries had been dirked, the rest was over in a few moments. The triumphant Macnabs summoned the King's Lieutenant to bring forward his army. Saluting them for their priceless service to the King's cause, Montrose and the clansmen pressed on once more towards the last and greatest range of mountains before Inverary.

Some time late that day or early the next, somewhere between Strath Fillan and Dalmally to the north of the hills that protect Inverary, the royalist army divided. Alasdair Macdonald set off northwards at the head of his Irishes, up Glenorchy towards Glencoe with a commission to plunder and burn every Campbell hamlet in his path. John Moydartach, the Captain of Clanranald, drove south-westwards along the line of Loch Awe, taking with him the Camerons and Appin Stewarts. Montrose himself, with the remainder of his forces, prepared to surmount the last bitter miles of snow, rock and ice that stood between themselves and the Marquis of Argyll.

Argyll in Edinburgh had learnt with astonishment that Montrose had broken out from his winter quarters. Dutifully, he took horse across Scotland to his castle to be on hand to discuss what need be done. Yet despite his long wretched autumn pursuing Montrose across the hills, even after a season of battles such as Scotland had not seen for more than a century, Argyll now failed to grasp the threat to his power and possessions. Before his own fireside in the mighty tower of Inverary, surrounded by his devoted servants and clansmen, he imagined the royalists engulfed in the snows or destroyed by his outposts, starving to death or wallowing guideless in the ghastly drifts on Ben Lui. He gave orders for the gathering of his clan army, but without urgency. Spring would be soon enough to mop up any royalist survivors and bring devastating vengeance upon Atholl and the glens of the Macdonalds. Argyll was an over-rational man. Fatally, he spared no thought for the possibility of the impossible.

Montrose had been able to divide his forces because he was assured that Argyll had not yet mustered the Campbell army. The royalists were setting forth to bring death and destruction to every corner of Argyll's empire. Three divisions would find it easier to feed themselves in the midst of winter than one great body of men. It was arranged that the army would concentrate once more at Inverary when its task was done. Thus confident of his dispositions, Montrose led his men upon the last terrible stretch of their great march.

Only a lonely eagle or snowy owl watched them as they struggled up the mountains north of Loch Shira,[4] more than two thousand feet of painful climbing before they passed the watershed. The frozen burns created near-vertical sheets of ice along the face of the hill, fit to maim or kill the man who slipped and fell. Old wounds ached and muscles screamed as they stumbled towards the crest, the great icicles hanging from the rocks above them, the north end of Loch Awe glittering coldly far behind. Troops of lean deer sheltering from the wind in the corries broke and cantered away as they passed. The pipers can have had little breath left by now to give the marchers a tune.

At last, they stood in the midst of the hills beside Loch Shira, where the Shira burn begins its long breakneck descent to Inverary nine miles below. The royalists must have been probing every inch of the horizon now, searching for the Campbell scouts whose presence seemed inevitable. Yet still, incredibly, there were none. Unremarked, thrilling to the prospect before them, Montrose's men set forth on the steep downhill race through Glen Shira, slipping and running, leaping and twisting amongst the trees and poor hovels that marked the path to Inverary. There, now, they saw Loch Fyne glinting before them. Still there was no shout of warning, still no sign of Campbell claymores. In the narrow, sheer fold of Glen Shira two hundred, even a hundred men led by a determined chieftain could have stood for hours against an army. Montrose's men surged onwards, braced at every bend of the pass for a blast of gunfire that never came.

The royalists were already fanning out onto the softly sloping meadows at the foot of the glen when Argyll's men burst upon their chief to report their coming. They were half an hour from his gates. Argyll did not hesitate. Logic directed him to sweep up his family, his servants and dearest possessions and hasten to the loch shore where his personal galley lay tied up. "A well-guided reason, without prejudice to a man's honour, may justly countermand a rash and inconsiderate resolution," he wrote sagely to his son many years later, counselling him against foolish acts of courage. "A well-guided reason" now persuaded him that to linger in Inverary promised at best useless months besieged in his castle, at worst his own death or capture. The Campbell was never a man to think much of martial glory, to feel guilt at the betrayal of his clan bards who yearned for great deeds of which to sing. As the first of Montrose's howling clansmen burst upon Inverary, sending the great swans flapping fearfully from the loch beside the castle, the chief of clan Campbell was already speeding away up Loch Fyne. His men shut themselves up in his castle and watched, impotent, as the Royal Standard was borne aloft into Inverary, as the King's Lieutenant ordered it to be planted on the steep hill overlooking the village and the sea and set up his headquarters below.

"The world believed that Argyll could have been maintained against the greatest army, as a country inaccessible," wrote Baillie,[5] appalled, in London. "But we see there is no strength or refuge on earth against the Lord!"

"Montrose used to acknowledge that never had he experienced the singular providence and fatherly mercy of God in a more remarkable manner that at this time, in bringing him and his men safe out of those parts," wrote Wishart. "Had the passes been defended by only 200 resolute men, his forces would either have been annihilated or easily prevented from invading the country. If only the herds had driven their cattle out of reach, as they might easily have done, they would have perished with hunger in that barren land. Had the winter proved as hard and stormy as usual in those parts, they would have foundered in snow or been frozen to death. But God had deprived his enemies of courage and the season of its usual severity; and in place of bread, had given them great abundance of cattle."[6]

That mid-December day as they stood at last by the icy shore of Loch Fyne, Montrose and his officers must have laughed from their hearts for the first time in many days. They could embrace each other to celebrate an astounding achievement. They might have sent for that Irish priest who had promised them they would reach Inverary without the risk of new snowfall, to join the heady congratulations. Most of the Campbells of Inverary must have fled for the hills as their chief took to the water, and the jubilant clansmen were rushing from house to house stripping every bolt of cloth, hoard of valuables, stand of arms. Old Airlie might grin his leathery grin to see his great score against the Campbells repaid at last, to stand watching the Campbell capital ravaged just as Campbells had ravaged and burnt his own houses five years before. Lord Graham, gaunt with the strain the march had imposed on his young bones, could collapse at last before a fire, under a roof, and begin to recover his strength. Men chose their billets and marked houses to shelter themselves so that they might be temporarily spared from the torch.

The invasion of Argyll had been achieved at the cost of great hardship amongst Montrose's army. In the weeks that followed, the victors had their reward. Alasdair Macdonald in the north, the Clanranald in the west and Montrose's division around Inverary looted and burnt villages, seized cattle and cut down such men as they met of military age across all the vast expanses of the Campbell empire. If there was little killing, it was only because the Campbells fled to become starving fugitives, cowering freezing and impotent in the hills while the royalists swept the passes. The injuries of generations were being revenged, the years of Campbell punitive expeditions and raiding parties repaid twenty-fold.

The men of Montrose's army must soon have become a strange spectacle, burdened with every kind of weapon and knick-knack, oddments of armour and clothing and cooking pots hung about them like Christmas tree decorations. Their ideas of loot must have been modest enough. In Inverary itself there may have been some rich pickings, but in the tiny bailes across Argyll there can only have been the pathetically poor household possessions that were common to all the Highlands in the seventeenth century. The only real booty worth having to men not feverish with blood and destruction, was the four-footed kind—the cattle that stood beyond any other wealth in Highland society. To the satisfaction of the royalists Argyll was rich in cattle above all things.

Whatever misgivings Montrose and his officers had suffered about the expedition before it set forth from Blair, they now knew the grim pleasure of wreaking havoc across the lands of the chief apostle of the Covenant. As the regiments trickled in from all over Argyll to the camp at Inverary, they left behind villages in ashes, ruined for a generation. Montrose himself may have found the killing and pillage a tasteless business, but he had seen enough of Argyll's handiwork in Atholl and Angus during the Bishops' Wars, and in Perthshire and Aberdeenshire the previous autumn to brush aside any scruples about the humbling of the Campbells. Through a winter in which mere mortals would never have thought of waging war, he and his army had kept the flame of the King's cause burning brilliantly in Scotland. There was now no more to be done or won in Argyll. It was time to choose the next battlefield.

Through the weeks in which his army had revelled with simple delight in their triumph, Montrose himself had been thinking coolly. The first freshness of spring would bring the regular army of the Covenant out of Perth to pursue him once more. There was already word of forces mustering against him in the north, at Inverness. He could be certain that the sullen, furious Argyll was already lurking somewhere at hand, nursing his rage and preparing revenge for the rape of his empire. Montrose must begin again his endless struggle to recruit his army, to create a fighting force powerful enough to lead south to aid the King. He must also strike out against the enemies mustering against him before they could unite. He dared not remain any longer in Argyll, or the strongholds his men had plundered with such relish would become death traps when their rightful owner returned to claim them with an army.

Montrose's problems, then, were precisely those that he had faced the previous autumn. They must be met in the same way. He must march fast to raise men and then to join battle against the enemy of his choice. The great mountain of loot, the herds of cattle were gathered together. The houses of Inverary were put to the torch. Some time around January 14th the royalist army marched away, striking north towards Inverness.

The clansmen left Argyll in the style in which they had entered it, burning and plundering their way up Glen Aray, round the north end of Loch Awe and up the Pass of Brander to Loch Etive. Alasdair Macdonald savoured a moment of sweet personal triumph at a Campbell castle on Loch Awe where he found his father and two brothers, held prisoner for so long by Argyll. The castle was seized and they were joyously unchained. It was a great hour for the Macdonalds of Antrim, and for

Alasdair himself of whom the bards would sing into eternity. In the Pass of Brander, tradition has it that Montrose saved an old Campbell woman who defied his army, a scythe in her hand, and killed the first man who tried to pass her. The Lord Marquis himself stayed the hands of his blood-hot soldiers when they would have dirked her.

But as the army approached the south shore of Loch Etive near its narrow outlet to the open sea, the men's spirits were waning. The weather broke at last. They trudged on through a boring gale, sheeting rain, dark skies and melting slush underfoot. As always, parties of clansmen temporarily sated with plunder and hardship were breaking away every day to walk home with their spoils. With each defection the army seemed to lose a little more of its impetus and fragile cohesion. It is easy to imagine the Lord Marquis himself slipping calmly to and fro, up and down the long column, the rain streaming down his long locks, saluting the chieftains, joking with the clansmen, somehow making each man feel himself proud to be amongst a chosen company. Through the streaming rain by the shore of Loch Etive, men searched the inlets anxiously for boats with which to cross the channel. They found none. Reluctantly Montrose was compelled to order his army to make what shelter it could, and pitch camp. Scarcely a mile or so westward through the murky haze stood the threatening tower of Dunstaffnage Castle, a Campbell stronghold. Much more serious, they could see lying close offshore a Campbell sloop sent to harass their march. Its guns could prove fatal to the army if the royalists had to run the gauntlet to cross the loch.

But now, as so often during this Year of Miracles, fortune favoured the brave. Clumsy seamanship or the heightening of the storm drove the Campbell warship ashore that night, to be dashed to wreckage by the breakers. Early the next morning the acquisitive Macdonalds were cheerfully stripping it of its brass cannon to make them their own. Then there was the matter of finding boats. Campbell of Ardchattan, whose mother had been a Macdonald, was appalled by the prospect of his kinsfolk devastating his lands around Loch Etive. He came before Montrose and appealed to him for mercy to his estates. In return, he produced for the royalists four boats. Three of them were small skiffs that held only five men apiece. The other was a damaged but barely serviceable craft capable of holding forty. Montrose's men quickly set about repairing the big boat. Within a few hours the long, tedious shuttle began across the loch, the army constantly wary for a sally from Dunstaffnage, an attack from more Campbell warships, even the coming of a new Campbell army. For two days and nights the crossing went on, a nerve-racking, temper-testing business of men wading and splashing in the shallows around the boats, driving the horses and captured beasts to swim beside them, ferrying equipment into and out of the boats, cursing freely, working hour after hour soaking wet and bitterly tired. But at last it was done. The army hastened forward once more, out of the jaws of Argyll at last.

Now they entered the Appin Stewart country, and they were among friends again. One hundred and fifty of those doughty warriors joined the column, stirred by the spectacle of the plunder the royalists carried and the unbroken tale of victories the King's Lieutenant could proclaim. It was a modest replacement for the steady drain of men still breaking away home with their loot. Refreshed a little, the army marched in the rain by Glencoe, skirted Loch Leven and drove on through the great wilderness of rivers and hills until at last at Kilcummin, the modern Fort Augustus, they paused once more to take stock.

Montrose marked his army's stay at Kilcummin with the the drawing-up of one of those documents so dear to his heart, "ane band" by which the chieftains of his army pledged themselves to support the King's cause "with our lives, fortunes and estates". He sought to match the power of the Covenant not by creating a rival religious bond, but simply by a formal union of the King's supporters. If a Band such as that of Kilcummin caused a chieftain to pause even for a day before breaking his oath and changing sides with characteristic readiness, then it was worth something to the King's cause. At Kilcummin, after Montrose himself the Band was signed by young Lord Graham his son, by Alasdair, Airlie, Keppoch, Maclean of Duart, the Macpherson, the MacGregor and every important chieftain in the army. Later the Gordons and others added their names to make fifty-three signatures in all. Montrose had done what he could to bind the Highlands in formal allegiance to the King. Now, in the last days of January, he stood at Kilcummin pointed to strike up the great glen to Inverness, against the army of the Covenant mustering against him under the fickle Earl of Seaforth. He still had no inkling that, behind him, much greater events were stirring.

Since the day Argyll's black-sailed galley had fled away up Loch Fyne to escape the royalist invasion, the brooding Marquis had been striving mightily to organize his revenge. In England the contempt of the parliamentary soldiers and politicians for their Scottish allies was now unbounded. "If we get not the life of these worms chirted out of them, the reproach will stick on us forever," wrote Robert Baillie[7] in London, wringing his hands at the latest tidings of disaster from Scotland. The Committee of Estates in Edinburgh craved the destruction of Montrose and his villainous band with something near to desperation. It was no longer a matter of waiting patiently for spring, for the formal opening of the new campaigning season. The royalists must somehow be rooted out wherever they could be found.

The man formally charged with this thankless task was Lieutenant-General William Baillie of Letham. When Argyll had resigned his commission as Commander-in-Chief of the army in Scotland at the end of the 1644 campaign, Baillie had been appointed by the Committee of Estates to succeed him. He always afterwards claimed that he had only reluctantly accepted the job, having been seized upon by the Committee while he happened to be in Edinburgh on private business, on leave from Leven's army in England. Born the illegitimate son of Sir William Baillie of Lamington, like so many other men with precarious prospects in life, he had sought his fortune abroad in the army of Gustavus Adolphus. More recently, he had served with distinction in Leven's army, and fought at Marston Moor. It is easy to believe that after so many years of serving among professionals in the greatest wars in Europe, Baillie was disgusted now to be drawn aside to lead half-trained militia and unwilling conscripts against a band of mountain brigands.

His chief asset as he prepared to take the field was a force of 1100 infantry, sixteen companies sent north to him by Leven. These veterans would be the backbone of his army against Montrose, and he was glad of them as he laboured to organize for war with his cavalry commander, none other than that "very changeable" officer, Sir John Hurry. Hurry had deserted back to the Parliamentary army when captured soon after Marston Moor. He and Baillie were now to bear the brunt of the year's

struggle against Montrose. Turncoat or no, Hurry was an able
soldier, and Baillie was grudgingly glad to have him as he
struggled with the endless conflicting demands of the politicians,
ministers and amateur soldiers around his headquarters.

In the midst of all Baillie's troubles came a peremptory
summons from the Marquis of Argyll, to wait upon him at
Dumbarton. On his arrival, he found to his dismay that while
the Marquis was quite willing for Baillie to be titled
Commander-in-Chief, he cared not a fig for his needs or his
wishes or his strategy. The MacCailein Mhor was in an icy
rage after his humiliation by Montrose. Despite all those who
have sought to justify him before history, at this moment
Argyll was seen at his worst. Brushing aside murmurs about
the interests of Scotland, he informed Baillie of Clan Campbell's
intentions to have its revenge on those who had done such awful
injury to its own. Baillie's services would not be required. The
Campbell himself would ride at the head of his clan with a
Campbell general. However, Baillie was to send forthwith his
cherished sixteen companies of foot to stiffen the Campbell
battle line. At that moment, Baillie's commission was not worth
the paper on which it was written. He was being addressed by
the Marquis of Argyll, the greatest nobleman in Scotland. He
and Argyll resolved that day to hate each other thoroughly, and
were to do so with sorry consequences for the Covenant. But
Baillie gave the order for the release of his sixteen companies,
and rode off to Perth in a fine rage to join Sir John Hurry
organizing the army still in winter quarters there. Argyll,
meanwhile, had recalled from Ireland a captain of his own
name to lead the clan's army. Sir Duncan Campbell of Auchinbreck, a good soldier who shared the horror of all Campbells at
the deeds of Montrose and his brigands, hastened to report to
his chief and gladly accepted the commission. Side by side,
Argyll and Auchinbreck rode northwards at the head of more
than three thousand men to destroy Montrose.

For many miles through the Campbell lands, they could
follow the royalists' trail from blackened village to blackened
village, the starving wretches scratching in the ashes well able
to testify to Montrose's passing. The army and its leaders must
have been appalled to see proud Campbells come to such
straits. Argyll seems to have travelled with them like some
English Crimean general, his personal galley sailing the coast

parallel with the army carrying the comforts to soften his journey. He had dislocated his shoulder falling from a horse, and thus was suffering pain to fuel his anger as the army moved northwards. They crossed Loch Leven by the Ballachulish Ferry, boasting to an old woman by the way that they would soon be back to tell her how Montrose met his end. Fixing them with her staring eye, she answered grimly that perhaps they would not be returning that way. For a moment, an icy wind of superstition blew over that Scottish army. Then their certainty of invincibility asserted itself once more. Spurred on by word that they were closing upon Montrose, they pressed forward. On February 1st, 1645, they pitched camp around the castle of Inverlochy, at the eastern end of Loch Eil just north of the modern Fort William. They knew that they were thirty miles behind the royalists at Kilcummin. They studied their distant prey, measured the distance to the Covenanting army at Inverness, pondered their moment to smash Montrose's army between their hammer and the anvil of Seaforth.

It is said that it was Ian Lom Macdonald, the bard of Keppoch in person, who walked to tell Montrose at Kilcummin the news of the Campbell army at his back. Montrose at first simply did not believe him. He had heard nothing to suggest that any Campbell force was anywhere within days of him. His own army had dwindled to barely 1500 men. All the others, the Atholl men and most of the Clanranald amongst them, had retired home with their plunder. He knew that there were at least 5000 levies under Seaforth at Inverness. He had few doubts of his ability to defeat them. His concern was that whether he did so or not, after fighting one major battle he would be in no condition instantly to turn and grapple the Campbells in another.

It was one of a hundred critical moments in Montrose's campaigns, when the hinge of fate turned solely upon the quality of the intelligence he was receiving. Again and again, he was able to defeat or out-manœuvre his enemies because his scouting and information was vastly superior to theirs. But the previous autumn he had come close to disaster once, at Fyvie, when he had received no warning of the coming of Argyll. His later misfortunes were to stem directly from failures of intelligence. It is not easy today to perceive how acute was his dilemma at Kilcummin. Again and again, almost every

day of his marches, men must have been brought before him
with word of Campbells here and Frasers there, of Argyll's
legions in the west and vague rumours of Baillie on foot in the
east. Out of all this to piece together some portion of the truth,
to gauge instinctively the enemy's likely intentions, calls for
the highest genius in a commander and is one of the qualities
that marks him out for greatness.

"Almost every soldier can tell you that in all armies intelligence is the life of action," wrote that canny old soldier Sir
James Turner,[8] himself a great admirer of Montrose. "But
how to get good intelligence to which a general or any commander may trust is an art yet to be found out, and I say more,
it will never be found so long as that remains true . . . that all
men are liars." The word of country people is useless, he
continues, and even that of prisoners is of limited value:
"They can tell you how strong your enemy is, where he was
yesterday, and where he was this morning, but cannot tell
you where he will be this night or tomorrow."

Montrose questioned Ian Lom Macdonald with deadly
patience, for the fortunes of the King's cause in Scotland hung
upon his answers. He asked him about the paths over the hills
and the state of the drifts on the higher ground, about the
strength of the Campbells and the slightest clues as to their
intentions. If Macdonald lied, said the Lord Marquis coldly,
he would hang for it. Stubbornly the poet insisted that he told
the truth. The critical moment had come. Montrose ordered
his officers to rouse the army and prepare to march against the
Campbells.

"I was willing to let the world see that Argyll was not the
man his Highlanders believed him to be," he wrote cheerfully
to the King in his later dispatch, "and that it was possible to
beat him in his own Highlands."

Montrose reckoned that, left to his own devices, Argyll
would dog his footsteps until he was entangled with Seaforth,
and then fall upon him from the rear. Such a strategy suited
perfectly the Campbell's temperament. It was essential that
Montrose destroy his southern, most dangerous enemy, before
moving on at his leisure to deal with the vacillating Seaforth.
His first move was to plant strong pickets along the main track
southwards through the Great Glen, to prevent Campbell
scouts moving forward or informers going back to report that

the royalist army was gone from Kilcummin. Then he led his men from their billets to begin one of the greatest flank marches in the annals of warfare.

The weather was worse than on the hardest stages of the descent on Inverary. The army must move fast to have any hope of achieving vital surprise. Montrose had chosen once again to attempt the impossible in order to confound his opponent. Instead of approaching Argyll down the passes of the Great Glen like any lesser mortal, he planned to take to the mountains and march parallel with the main road south-westwards, hidden by the intervening range of hills. The going, naturally, would be a thousand times more difficult. The snow-drifts lay virgin upon the hillsides. The very deer floundered clumsily in their midst. The steep faces were untrodden even by cowherds and deer hunters since winter began. The cold was appalling. Even if somehow Montrose could lead his army to confront Argyll without benefit of maps or compasses through the wilderness, his exhausted men must then do battle against odds of two to one.

Yet Montrose's utmost genius flowered when faced by the challenges mere mortals declined. One imagines a smile on his lips, a glitter of excitement in his eyes, the promise of action filling his heart: "As Alexander I will reign, and I will reign alone. My spirit ever did disdain a rival near my throne. . . ." The huge clansmen must often have wondered at these moments how his slight frame bore the punishing demands upon it. But old Airlie was there beside him as they began the climb up the little Tarff burn into the hills. And his eldest son, Lord Graham, was close behind. The boy was almost broken by the endless marching, the shivering nights, the slender rations. But Montrose dared not leave him, so powerful a hostage to the Covenant. He must march where the army marched, if he died in the attempt. Up the valley of the Tarff they laboured, high into the hills towards the fierce summit of Carn Dearg. That first day of the march, Friday, January 31st, they had well over two thousand feet to climb before they were over the shoulder of Carn Dearg and could begin the descent into Glen Roy. Once over the watershed, somewhere high in the pass they may have rested for a few hours on the first night. But they had little enough time to spare, and to many of them it must have seemed worse to lie endlessly shivering in their plaids than to stagger on through the snow. Clumsily improvised deerskin sandals and ragged clothes worn to shreds by weeks of exposure under intolerable conditions offered little protection against the freezing January night. For those who were thirsty there was only the shocking chill of the burn water. If some of the men managed to bring down a deer, they ate their chunks of bloody flesh unsalted. They had no bread and only a little oatmeal.

As they marched along the western face of Glen Roy the next morning, the scouts caused a flush of alarm by reporting a Campbell raiding party in front of them. This was Keppoch country. The Campbells were savagely revenging themselves upon every village in their path for Montrose's march through Argyll. Hastily the royalists made for the higher ground, and passed far above the burning hamlets, concealed by the brow of the hill. The scouts must have studied the valley of the Spean with eagle-eyed caution before the army slipped down to ford the river: it would have been fatal for them to meet Campbell clansmen as they crossed the pass, yet while they did so they were visible for miles if there was any man to look at them. Miraculously they waded the river unnoticed. Then they were once again climbing thankfully into the safety of the hills, up the course of the Cour burn, two miles above the modern Commando Memorial. The last six miles of their march lay around the skirts of Ben Nevis. They could only trust to luck that no passing Campbell would notice the long swathe of beaten snow in their wake that proclaimed with such certainty that a large body of men had passed that way.

Somewhere on these last stages of the march, Montrose's vanguard suddenly found themselves face to face with a small party of Campbells. There was a startled, brutal little struggle in which most of the Campbells were cut down. But a few escaped. Away they fled, down the hill to report to Argyll's leaguer at Inverlochy that an enemy was afoot, close at hand. Around the friendly Campbell camp fires on the loch shore, it was unthinkable that Montrose and his army were anywhere nearby. They were known to be thirty miles further north at Kilcummin. It was obvious that this must be some clan raiding party on the loose, perhaps skirmishers sent by Montrose to harass the advancing Campbells. Auchinbreck was a cautious man, so he strengthened his pickets and pushed out patrols to probe the hills, but he left the bulk of his army to its food and sleep.

Montrose's clansmen reached their objective on the hillside above Inverlochy just as night was falling on that Saturday, February 1st. As the order was given to halt, men slipped into the shelter of the burn beds and the folds of the hill to rest their aching limbs. Montrose's officers fell in around him to report: the army was utterly exhausted, and the tail of stragglers stretched dangerously for miles behind them. It would be hours before they were all assembled. They were hungry, although there was little enough to be done about that. They could mark Argyll's camp fires below them well enough, but they had no clues as to his dispositions. It was unthinkable to attack immediately. "So be it then," said the Lord Marquis calmly. "We will take them at dawn."

For the royalists crouching shivering on the hillside, it must have seemed that that night could never end. There was no fuel for fires, and it would anyway have been dangerous to light them. It was all but impossible to sleep when there was the cold, the constant movement of men and confused coming of stragglers, the murmur of orders and arguments. A huge moon hung over the mountains, bathing royalists and Campbells in the eerie grey light that seems to promise dragons and fairies whenever it lights Lochaber in winter. Many men must have lain silent, watching the flicker of Campbell fires far below, computing grimly how many claymores lay around each one. Montrose himself will have been one of these.

It was on such a night as this that he must have felt the full loneliness of his command, of his isolation from his own army by the burden of responsibility. To his clansmen, the campaign was a matter of glorious, lethal simplicity. They stood tonight on the eve of battle with their hereditary Campbell enemy, to kill or be killed, to plunder or to have the brooches and targes stripped from their own naked bodies on the morrow. If they won, they might go home with their loot or fight on for a few more months in search of greater riches yet. If they lost, then the bards would sing of them in their own glens through the long winter nights for generations to come. Amongst all his army, perhaps only Airlie and his sons and a handful of others could watch Montrose pondering his decisions, able to understand the great duty that he bore.

The Lord Marquis must have sat in his cloak above Inverlochy that night, his wild clan army around him and his desperate gamble before him on the morrow, thinking of that serene, mannered, desperate man at Oxford who took so much for granted and yet needed Montrose so much if he was to save his Kingdoms. Perhaps the Graham remembered that brave, shy parting dinner with Spottiswoode, Ogilvy and all his other close friends in Oxford before he rode out—was it really less than a year ago?—to win Scotland for the King. He will have smiled to think of the glories of that court and of the schemes of Digby and of the well-ordered armies that were struggling for possession of England, while the fate of Scotland hinged on his own handful of vagabonds. Lord George Goring would scarcely have troubled to lead out a cavalry flying column as feeble in numbers as Montrose's "army" at Inverlochy. Rupert had scorned to wait for Montrose's mere thousand men before fighting Marston Moor. This Highland army knew no engineers, no proper cavalry, and had only a nodding acquaintance with cannon. No English army had ever seen such a Sergeant-Major-General as Alasdair Macdonald. Yet Montrose loved these men, and here in the snow below Ben Nevis he was at peace with himself as he had never been at Kincardine, in Edinburgh, at Oxford, or commanding his rabble of militia on the Borders. This campaign was his manifest destiny. Few men are fortunate enough to find one.

At dawn on the morning of February 2nd, Sir Duncan Campbell of Auchinbreck was rousing his army to fight, still uncertain whom he faced. All night his pickets had skirmished indecisively against the mysterious enemy on the hills, exchanging occasional shots and cries in the darkness, marking the dark shadows flitting across the hill in the moonlight. The Marquis of Argyll announced that he was taking to his galley. It lay offshore, ready to hand as usual. Argyll was rowed out with his companions, amongst them the tiresome Covenanting minister Mr Mungo Law, and Montrose's own brother-in-law Sir James Rollo. With his arm still disabled from his fall, Argyll would be of no practical value on shore, as he could point out with his usual unanswerable logic. His capture would be a disaster for the Covenant. The MacCailein Mhor felt no romantic compulsion to stand beside his clan army in battle to offer his moral support in their struggle to the death. As the grey light brightened reluctantly, the Campbells on the shore and their chief on his galley stood silent, gazing curiously upwards at the hillside to discover what this day would bring.

As the first shaft of sunlight appeared in the sky, the sound of the fanfare saluting the raising of the Royal Standard echoed down upon the Campbells with the majesty of the last trump. The presence of the Standard signified the presence of the King's Lieutenant, of Montrose himself at the head of his army. A shock of dismay and astonishment ran down the ranks. Then as the trumpet fanfare died away, the pipes took up the tale. They were playing the terrible Cameron pibroch, "Sons of dogs come and I will give you flesh". Duncan Campbell of Auchinbreck steeled himself to fight for his life.

On the hillside as the royalists deployed in their clan regiments, Montrose, Airlie and the rest of his staff crouched in the snow eating a mess of oatmeal and water off the point of their dirks. This was all the breakfast the army could look for that morning. Their supper still lay in Campbell pouches. They prepared themselves to go and fetch it. Impatiently the Irish took up their positions, half under Alasdair's command on the right, the rest under Magnus O'Cahan on the left. The order of battle for the centre of the army reads like a rollcall of the great names of Highland history: the men of Glengarry, of Maclean, Keppoch, Glencoe, Atholl, Appin, Lochaber: each contingent headed by its chieftain and eager to outdo its rivals. Behind them stood a reserve of Irish musketeers. Thomas Ogilvy's handful of horse gathered around the Royal Standard. Their poor beasts were already on the verge of collapse, hopelessly lame and constantly underfed. But this day they would be driven to their utmost, if they collapsed under their riders at the end of it.

The priests walked before the ranks blessing the men, and the Catholics knelt to pray, their arms at their feet. Alasdair was dismayed to see Ian Lom Macdonald, the bard of Keppoch who had guided them through such hazards to reach this battlefield, now walking alone away from the army. "Ian Lom, wilt thou leave us?" he cried. "If I go with thee today and fall in battle, who will sing thy praises and thy prowess tomorrow?" called back the poet calmly. He turned again, and walked away up the hillside until he reached a knoll

H

from which he could see Loch Eil and Inverlochy fairly below him. There that lonely figure stood unmoving through the morning, watching the ebb and surge of the battle beneath.

Sir Duncan Campbell of Auchinbreck drew up the Campbell battle line to face the royalists with half the Lowlanders seconded from Baillie on each flank, and half-a-dozen cannon to strengthen his position. Knowing so well the shock of a Highland charge such as he expected, he placed a vanguard forward of his main positions to break the force of the attack. If the majesty of titles alone won battles, its commander Gillespie son of Gillespie Og, Laird of the Bingingeadhs, must have vanquished the royalists single-handed. On the left flank in front of his positions, behind the massive walls of Inverlochy Castle, Auchinbreck disposed fifty musketeers to enfilade the royalists as they attacked. To his irritation, he found himself forced to begin the battle without one contingent of his army, which was camped across the Lochy river and unable to reach the main force in time. But Auchinbreck's forces still formidably outnumbered the royalists. He faced them in a strong position of his own choosing. The Campbells, even Wishart later grudgingly conceded, were "very brave men, worthy of a better chieftain and a better cause".

Inverlochy was a battle like Tippermuir, in which Montrose's genius had been employed to create the circumstances in which the encounter could take place. Once the first shot had been fired, it disintegrated into a bloody mêlée in which the superior skill and courage of his warriors decided the outcome. Magnus O'Cahan began the struggle with a headlong charge upon Gillespie's vanguard. Gillespie's men leapt forward to meet them. Axe and sword and pike crashed headlong in the snow. Gillespie's men reeled back, appalled by the wave of slashing steel and point-blank musketry from O'Cahan's downhill attack. As they fell back on the main Campbell position, Alasdair's men threw themselves on Auchinbreck's left. Then the whole royalist army poured down the hillside and drove madly at the Campbell battle line. The Lowland musketeers were trained to fight like-minded regiments of their opponents. For a few minutes they rhythmically loaded and fired by ranks as they were accustomed. Then the Gaelic fury broke upon them, and all their experience and discipline lapsed into chaos. Their ranks disintegrated. A company which attempted to withdraw to the castle was picked out and charged by Thomas Ogilvy's horse. A musketeer brought down Ogilvy himself as he spurred forward at the head of his men, but then the Covenanters were broken, flying towards the hopeless loch shore along with so many other desperate men, to drown or to await extinction at the hands of the victorious clansmen now encircling them. Already the Campbell army was in desperate trouble.

But in the centre, at the heart of Auchinbreck's line, there was no such easy triumph for the royalists. Clan Campbell stood at bay upon the ridge of Inverlochy, cut off and now unsupported, flanks shattered. But its warriors chose to die where they stood, and they fought to the end. Montrose's men had to carve a painful, bloody path through their ranks, hacking onwards as through some teeming forest, to gain their victory. Those who believe that modern warfare is a barbarous business can never have pictured a battle in which men seek literally to cut each other to pieces, face to face. There is none of the comforting distance between rifleman and target. Each man cuts and thrusts through gristle and bone. Montrose's army may have suffered few fatal casualties in their battles, but any clansman who did his part manfully expected to be scarred in almost every encounter. Two hundred royalists were wounded at Inverlochy. A man like Alasdair Macdonald, after a hundred battles bore a hundred wounds. It was a terrible way to kill and a terrible way to die.

The wretched Campbells had no living bards to write the tale of how they died on the shore at Inverlochy, of how their standard at last tottered and fell with Auchinbreck himself and a galaxy of Campbell chieftains dead and dying around it like the stricken ring at Senlac. The terrible slaughter of fugitives went on all day for miles along Loch Linnhe and Loch Eil. Some were driven into the water and hacked down, others were pursued across the hills. Montrose's army lost scarcely a dozen men, yet claimed to have felled fifteen hundred Campbells. Even if the toll was not quite so vast, the fighting power of the clan was broken for a generation. Among the most miserable losses of all were those Campbells who drowned in the loch, struggling hopelessly to reach the galley of their chief, the MacCailein Mhor, as it sailed swiftly and silently away to the sea and safety.

The army sang a *Te Deum* in the surrendered castle that

night, amidst the host of prisoners who surrendered on quarter, including some of the greatest of the Campbell name. With a full heart, Montrose wrote his dispatch to his King.

... When I had the honour of waiting upon your Majesty last, I told you at full length what I fully understood of the designs of your Rebel subjects in both kingdoms, which I had occasion to know as much as anyone whatsoever being at that time, as they thought, entirely in their interest. Your Majesty may remember how much you said you were convinced I was in the right in my opinion of them. I am sure there is nothing fallen out since to make your Majesty change your judgement in all those things I laid before your Majesty at that time. The more your Majesty grants, the more will be asked, and I have too much reason to know that they will not rest satisfied with less than making your Majesty a King of straw. I hope the news I have received about a treaty may be a mistake. . . .

As to the state of affairs in this kingdom, the bearer will fully inform your Majesty in every particular. And give me leave, with all humility, to assure your Majesty that, through God's blessing, I am in the fairest hopes of reducing this Kingdom to your Majesty's obedience. And, if the measures I have concerted with your Majesty's other loyal subjects fail me not, which they hardly can, I doubt not before the end of this summer I shall be able to come to your Majesty's assistance with a brave army which, backed with the justice of your Majesty's cause, will make the Rebels in England, as well as in Scotland, feel the just rewards of Rebellion. Only give me leave, after I have reduced this country to your Majesty's obedience, and conquered from Dan to Beersheba, to say to your Majesty then, as David's General did to his master, "come thou thyself lest this country be called by my name". For in all my actions I aim only at your Majesty's honour and interest, as becomes one that is to his last breath, may it please your Sacred Majesty,—

Your Majesty's most humble, most faithful, and most obedient Subject and Servant,

MONTROSE.

Inverlochy in Lochaber,
February 3rd, 1645.

The romance between the monarch and his servant had come
a long march since that day at St. James's on which they had
first met with such coldness. Montrose had made the King his
idol, at whose feet he laid his marvellous achievements. This
day of February, Charles Stuart needed to be a great King indeed to be worthy of his servant.

When the battle was over, Ian Lom Macdonald came down
from his post on the hillside above Inverlochy. He was true to
his promise. To honour this Candlemas of 1645, he wrote
one of the greatest of all Gaelic odes. Montrose and Alasdair
and the royalist army had joined the immortals.

Heard ye not! heard ye not! how that whirlwind the gael—
To Lochaber swept down from Loch Ness to Loch Eil—
And the Campbells to meet them in battle array
Like the billow came on—and were broke like its spray!
Long, long shall our war-song exult in that day.

'Twas the sabbath that rose, 'twas the Feast of St Bride,
When the rush of the clans shook Ben Nevis' side;
I, the bard of their battles, ascended the height
Where dark Inverlochy o'ershadowed the fight,
And I saw the Clan Donald resistless in might.

Through the land of my fathers the Campbells have come,
The flames of their foray enveloped my home;
Broad Keppoch in ruin is left to deplore,
And my country is waste from the hill to the shore—
Be it so! By St Mary there's comfort in store!

Though the braes of Lochaber a desert be made,
And Glen Roy may be lost to the plough and the spade,
Though the bones of my kindred, unhonoured, unurned,
Mark the desolate path where the Campbells have burned—
Be it so! From that foray they never returned!

Fallen race of Diarmed! disloyal—untrue,
No harp in the highlands will sorrow for you;
But the birds of Loch Eil are wheeling on high,
And the Badenoch wolves hear the Camerons' cry—
"Come feast ye! come feast where the false-hearted lie!"*

* Mark Napier, after the Gaelic of Ian Lom Macdonald.

Montrose's army marched north from Inverlochy leaving the shore strewn with the naked bodies of their enemies. None came to the battlefield to bury the dead. The Camerons had fulfilled the ghastly promise of their pibroch. The dogs came down to feast upon Campbell flesh.

# CHAPTER NINE

## *Auldearn*

---

IT IS STILL a magical experience to hold in one's hand one of the letters written by Montrose from the hills during his great campaign. The handwriting is the characteristic spidery scrawl of the seventeenth century. The parchment has become browned and worn by its many travels, and the folds have been cut deep by innumerable openings and closings. But Montrose's seal is still there as it was the day he took a candle to the wax somewhere in the depths of the Highlands, the shouts of Alasdair's boisterous Irishes and the cackling of the women around the camp fires echoing outside, his cuirass beside him, the latest long-delayed packet of letters from England on the table. Standing today on the hills above Inverlochy, Montrose and his triumph still seem very close.

It is easy to become drunk with the exhilaration that he shared with his men at that moment. For their invincible brotherhood nothing was impossible. Such a succession of victories as they had achieved must surely unlock the conquest of Scotland. Montrose had begged the King to brook no compromise. He and his little band of royalists had suffered so much to bring triumph within sight. It would be intolerable to have it betrayed by politicians. It was the cry of a soldier, such as soldiers have given from the Punic Wars to Vietnam.

Argyll and the Campbells had been brought to their knees. The opposition in the north, Seaforth and his friends, held no terrors for the royalist army. There were encouraging promises from Huntly's country where Nat Gordon had been singing Montrose's song all winter. Nor was it only in Montrose's camp that the future seemed so sure: "This disaster did extremely amaze us," wrote Robert Baillie[1] lugubriously after Inverlochy. "I verily think that had Montrose come presently from that battle, he should have had no great opposition in all the Highlands, in the Lennox, and the sheriffdom of Ayr, Glasgow, Clydesdale, scarcely till he had come to Edinburgh."

On February 12th, 1645, Argyll reported before Parliament
in Edinburgh that his efforts to crush the rebels had met with a
temporary setback. Balmerino added an aside on the Marquis's
behalf, explaining that the Campbells had lost only thirty
men, and any rumour of more serious misfortune was the
product of mere royalist malice. Argyll walked the streets of
the capital with manful dignity, "having his left arm tied up in
a scarf as if he had been at bones breaking", as Guthrie
recorded scornfully. But the other survivors of Inverlochy had
told their tale, and Scotland was not deceived. Alarm and
dismay were universal. When the Kirk proposed executing
every royalist prisoner held in Edinburgh, Parliament thanked
the men of God for their "zeal and piety", but tactfully deferred
wholesale judicial murder until Montrose "could be brought
lower". They had seen the list of important captives the
royalists now held at Blair and Inverlochy, and flinched from
any exchange of executions. They confined themselves to
proclamations of the forfeit of prominent Scottish royalists'
estates. They had their coats of arms publicly torn asunder and
condemned them to death in absentia. Montrose was never to
be called by his title amongst the gentlemen of the Covenant.
He was merely "James Graham, that viperous brood of Satan".

But James Graham's winter thunderclap now yielded the
most encouraging dividend for the royalist cause in England:
a further 1500 men from Leven's army in the south, along with
1400 more hastily recalled from Ireland, were at once ordered to
Perth to reinforce Baillie's army. Relations between the English
Parliament and the Scottish Commissioners in London plumbed
the chilliest depths. Natural catastrophe compounded the
gloom in Edinburgh. A serious outbreak of the plague was
spreading across the principal towns of Scotland, hastened by
the constant movements of the marching armies. An epidemic
of private lawlessness was also causing concern, as independent
free-booters took advantage of the government's preoccupa-
tions. For many months to come, Scotland was troubled by such
gentlemen as Lord Kenmure in Kirkcudbrightshire, who
hoisted a brandy barrel on a stave for his standard, and
plundered the countryside declaring that he fought for the
King. Taxation was becoming ruinous and trade was severely
hampered. The Uxbridge negotiations between King and
Parliament for a compromise peace, which had been stalemated

for weeks, were finally broken off two days after news of
Inverlochy reached Oxford on February 19th. The Covenanters
quailed at the prospect of an apparently endless war from which
they seemed to stand in danger of ruin.

Yet the morning after Inverlochy, Montrose was no closer to
winning Scotland than he had been on that August day he
crossed the border with Sibbald and Rollo. His army was still
a Highland army unshakeably hated and feared in the Lowlands, unalterably prone to melt away as soon as its soldiers
had won their plunder. In one of his supremely optimistic
moments some years later, when planning another Highland
campaign, Montrose computed that the clans of royalist
leanings were capable of fielding an army of 20,000 men, a vast
fighting force even by English standards. Notionally, of course,
this might have been so. But mutual jealousies ensured that it
would never be possible to assemble all of them together in a
single battle line. Even amongst the clans actively aiding
Montrose at the height of his success, for every man who came
forward to fight beside him there were two who preferred to
remain at home or were left behind to guard the glens and the
wives and tend the cattle. Montrose's efforts to build an army
capable of marching south to aid the King were akin to chasing
mercury with a fork. His Year of Miracles earned its name
because it was incredible that he succeeded even as far as he
did.

Yet for all the fine logic of Argyll, history has not made much
of him, while Montrose has passed into legend because he
reached for the stars. His unquenchable optimism was one of
his most enchanting characteristics. The portraits of him in his
later years suggest sadness, but it is impossible to accept that he
was a melancholy man in those days when he led his Highlanders across Scotland. The much younger, Jameson portrait,
with those pleasant warm eyes and gentle smile, seems to
suggest Montrose much more surely as he must have been. His
style and his achievements suggest wry humour, a rich fund
of nervous energy, of sympathy, of inspiring passion. He was
convinced that he could conquer Scotland for the King. The
men who followed him came to believe that they would live to
see him walk on water.

A few days after Inverlochy, he led the army up the east bank
of Loch Ness to investigate the intentions of Seaforth and his

purported Covenanting army. Robert Baillie, of course, was talking nonsense when he suggested that the royalists might now have marched directly on the Lowlands. It was essential to gather up all the clansmen who had gone home during the winter, and to recruit far more widely before Montrose could think of an adventure in the south.

Finding Inverness strongly held against him, he passed on eastwards towards Elgin. As he marched, a dour procession of peers and lairds trickled in day after day to make their peace, chief among them the redoubtable Seaforth. That nobleman's enthusiasm for action had ebbed away rapidly on the news of Inverlochy. His interest was to safeguard his clan and his estates. With his usual sense of expediency, he now signed Montrose's Kilcummin Band, along with the Laird of Grant who had been one of those mustered against the royalists on Speyside the previous autumn. Their pledges served their turn. Montrose left their lands unscathed. The Grants' change of heart took place just in time for the clan to share in the pleasurable sack of Elgin.

None of this much advanced the royalist cause, but there at Elgin in the heart of the Moray plain, one of Montrose's most exciting hopes was fulfilled. Some of the most prominent members of the great Clan Gordon rallied to the King's cause. Lord Gordon, Huntly's eldest son, had for years been in thrall to his uncle Argyll. But the previous year Argyll's army had ruthlessly savaged the lands that were the young man's birthright. Then through the long winter months, that engaging buccaneer Nat Gordon had patiently worked upon his wavering allegiance.

For weeks Lord Gordon had been waiting at Gight Castle for news of Montrose. Now, hearing that he was at hand, "he leapt quickly on horse, having Nathaniel Gordon, with some few others in his company, and that same night came to Elgin, saluted Montrose, who made him heartily welcome, and they sup joyfully together; his brother Ludovic [Lord Lewis] came also to Montrose, and was graciously received".[2]

Patrick Gordon of Ruthven was at his most sycophantic when he wrote of Lord Gordon "the brave and gallant youth, being the miracle of his time for all the excellencies both of body and mind, and having naturally and most pregnant witty and solid judgement for about his age. . . ."[3]

In reality Lord Gordon seems to have been rather an impressionable young man, and his brother Lord Lewis was well-known to be quite unpredictable and uncontrollable. But in the absence of their father Huntly in the north, Lord Gordon was the chief ornament of his clan, and had considerable influence over it. He rode into Elgin at the head of two hundred priceless cavalry, horsed from his father's rich stable. There was no telling how many of his clansmen might flock to the Standard on the news that he had declared for the King.

Lord Gordon, a little like Montrose himself in his younger days, came forth seeking a hero. He found him in his general. He was entranced by Montrose and henceforth devoted to his service. He and Lewis signed the Kilcummin Band, and then invited Montrose to make his next headquarters at Gight Castle. There they rode from Elgin in the first days of March. Montrose was delighted to have young company of his own background and tastes with whom to laugh, and talk, and build dreams. The whole army remarked how the Lord Marquis and the Gordon heir rejoiced in each other's society. For a brief space, every omen seemed auspicious.

But at Gight on March 4th, a wretched new chapter of tragedy and frustration opened for Montrose. His son Lord Graham caught fever and died at the age of fourteen, weakened by the terrible demands of the winter campaign at Montrose's side. It was a cruel blow, not least because it must have cost his father agonies of self-reproach. Montrose's relations with his wife Magdalen had never been close. When the news of this loss reached her, the gulf between the Lord Marquis and his lady must have deepened still further.

But the boy was scarcely buried in the little churchyard near the castle walls when another mishap struck the army. The old Earl of Airlie fell ill. After a few days it became apparent that his condition was unlikely to improve for weeks to come. He was sent with all the care and attention the army's predicament could contrive to Huntly Castle in Strathbogie. Montrose, who had been rejoicing at the accession of another 500 foot and 150 horse to his army from the Gordon lands, now dispatched almost as many men to guard poor Airlie. He loved the old man too well to grudge the escort, but it was another sorry blow to his plans.

The army had moved camp to Kintore, on the Don a few

miles above Aberdeen. Montrose sent Colonel Nat Gordon at
the head of a cavalry escort to receive the keys of the terrified
city, to empty its arsenal and release the royalist prisoners
from its tollbooth. They retired to Kintore having collected
substantial quantities of arms and given Aboyne a good fright.
Four days later, on the evening of March 12th, the dashing
Colonel and some of the gayer royalist officers decided that it
would be a fine thing to ride down to the city again, this time
in search of some entertainment. They trotted boldly into the
town, tied up their horses, and settled down for a night of the
best eating and hardest drinking Aberdeen could provide. A
few hours later, they were still lolling cheerfully around their
tables when they heard the furious clatter of hoofbeats in the
street. Leaping up, they dashed out onto the swords of Sir
John Hurry and a hundred and fifty of his dragoons. Hurry's
camp lay only a few miles outside the city. The moment he had
word of Nat Gordon's rash picnic, he gathered every man he
could put into the saddle, galloped for Aberdeen and fell on
the bewildered royalists. In the ensuing mêlée, several were
wounded and taken prisoner. One man, Colonel Donald
Farquharson, was shot dead as he ran into the street. Farquharson, who had so distinguished himself at Fyvie and was one of
Montrose's ablest and most popular officers, was a bitter loss.
To add insult to injury, Hurry ran off with all the royalists'
horses, including the pick of Huntly's stables.

It was probably one of the prisoners from Aberdeen who also
informed the Covenanter of young Lord Graham's death.
Montrose's second son James, living quietly with his tutor at the
family home of Old Montrose, was now his father's heir. Hurry
rode hard for the house, seized the boy, and sent him under
guard to join the sad company of royalist prisoners in
Edinburgh Castle.

Montrose was furious. The army had suffered a grievous loss
through wanton carelessness. Perhaps, too, he was disturbed to
find that in Sir John Hurry he was now fighting an officer of
unusual drive and dash, qualities the Covenant leadership had
so signally lacked for so long. Half the royalist army was
dispatched to cover Aberdeen from the Bridge of Dee and Two
Mile Cross, while the Lord Marquis rode into the city with
Lord Lewis Gordon for Farquharson's funeral. The terrified
City Fathers paid £10,000 in blood money for Hurry's escapade,

to save Aberdeen from the wrath of the clansmen. Only a
handful of Alasdair's wily and greedy Irish slipped against
orders into the city, "lurking behind him, abusing and fearing
the townspeople, taking their cloaks, plaids and purses from
them on the street. No merchants' booth daredst be opened. The
stable doors were broken upon the night and the horses taken
out. But the major [general] hearing this returns that same
Monday back, and called all their rascals with sore skins out
of the town before him."[4]

It is a marvellous picture: the enormous Alasdair Macdonald
moving off with the army, hearing of the stragglers' misdeeds,
running back to chase them through the streets of Aberdeen,
kicking and lashing them half-drunk in front of him down the
road to the Bridge of Dee.

It was March 18th when the royalist army marched from
Aberdeen. They moved destructively down the east coast of
Scotland, plundering and burning every Covenanting estate
and town. On the Lord Marquis's orders, Montrose itself was
spared, but the Earl Marischal watched powerless from his
castle as his barns burnt at Dunnottar. At Halkerton, a few
miles from Fettercairn, the doughty Hurry overreached himself
in his efforts to harass Montrose's progress and, having charged
what looked like a royalist cavalry outpost, found himself
meeting volley after volley of musketry from a classic Montrose
ambush. He was lucky to get away across the South Esk
river. The Lord Marquis moved on to Brechin, which was
sacked.

It was some time about now that Montrose received word
from the King that a critical juncture in the royalist fortunes
had been reached. A Scottish gentleman disguised as a beggar
got through to the army with a dispatch from Oxford revealing
that Charles himself intended to try to reach the Border
country, and that he was sending 500 horse ahead of him to
reinforce Montrose's army. Both these intentions were to go
unfulfilled, but to Montrose it now seemed vital that he seize
the moment and march southwards to link up with the King.
His army numbered 3000 infantry and more than 300 horse.
This would suffice. It was only necessary that he secure his rear
before he moved. Baillie and Hurry must quickly be brought to
battle and destroyed.

But Fortune, having smiled so sweetly upon Montrose, now

seemed utterly to have abandoned him. He had become the hunter and Baillie the quarry, but his attempts to bring him to bay petered out in helpless frustration. On March 29th the two armies came within sight of each other across the river Isla, and Montrose tried desperately to goad Baillie by sending him a teasing formal challenge to fight. But the Covenanter replied curtly and properly that he would fight when he pleased. As Montrose meandered on south-westwards, Baillie shadowed him cautiously. The Covenanter's business was to keep his army in being at all costs. With prudent modesty, he declined to match his skills against those of the Graham in open battle until the time suited him. For the present, his army's mere existence thwarted all the royalists' hopes. Montrose rambled onwards to Dunkeld, for once wholly at a loss.

His position now deteriorated rapidly and dangerously. After all his painful efforts to recruit it, his army was once again shrinking. The Covenanters in the north-east were threatening the Gordon country, and many of the clan retired abruptly homewards to protect their own. After the latest round of sack and destruction, other clansmen were melting away to the glens as usual with their booty. Impatience and boredom eroded the ranks of those gentlemen of the army who "although they were young and lusty, seeing no appearance of fighting, but continual watching and unmeasurable travel, necessities and want of provisions, both for horse and man, they wearied and shrunk away daily".[5] Montrose numbered his depleted companies and found himself reduced to 2000 men. Once again, the prospect of an early dash for the border had collapsed.

He ordered most of the army, along with the sick and wounded and the baggage, to retire on Brechin. There was no help for it, they must once again take to the north-east where they could be sure of friends and shelter. There the painful building of a fresh army, a frail new house of cards, might begin. But there was one chance of striking a body blow at the Covenant before pulling back. Montrose's scouts and informers reported that Baillie and the Covenanting army were certain the royalists were making for the Lowlands. They had pulled back southwards to guard the Forth crossings against their coming. Dundee, the rich Covenanting city which had defied the royalists the previous autumn, lay open for the taking. While the main body of Montrose's army moved to Brechin, the Lord Marquis himself could not resist this chance of a quick, punishing thrust. With 300 Gordons, 300 Irishes and 150 horse—the fittest and best-armed men in the army—he moved on Dundee.

Montrose summoned Dundee on the morning of April 4th, 1645. As usual his messenger was hurled into the tollbooth for his pains. The royalists then stormed the walls of the city at three points. Against the stout-hearted but ineffectual local militia, they soon won command of a breach. The Irishes rushed the chief Covenanting battery on Corbie Hill, seized it and swung its guns to bombard the town. The defence collapsed piece-meal, and the attack disintegrated into an afternoon of fitful street fighting and intensive looting. In the maze of alleys and narrow streets around the market place, Montrose's officers lost control of most of their men, who were soon breaking into houses and cellars as fast as they had cleared them of the enemy. Drunk on the vast quantities of alcohol they discovered, overwhelmed by the rich plunder on every side, they lost all thought for their general's hopes and plans. They failed even to carry the tollbooth where the army's unfortunate envoy languished forgotten after his capture that morning. Montrose's officers shrugged their shoulders helplessly, yet without great concern. The next morning would be soon enough to round up the men after their appalling debauch. There was no threat of a rally by the Dundee militia. The royalists had the town, at least as tightly as was necessary in the circumstances. They relaxed and waited for the army to tire of drink and loot.

The afternoon was already far gone when Montrose's pickets galloped hell for leather into Dundee crying out for the Lord Marquis himself. All the reports of Baillie's withdrawal to the Forth had been utterly false. At this moment he was marching on Dundee at the head of the Covenanting army. The dauntless Hurry was flying ahead with all the horse, and would be at the gates within half an hour.

"To make a retreat from an advancing enemy is not at all difficult, if he who is to make it have so good intelligence that he may begin in time," observes Sir James Turner.[6] "But if it be bad or uncertain, or that his scouts and parties disappoint him, nothing is more difficult . . . when an enemy is near, orders are given and obeyed with so great haste and confusion

that the march looks rather like a flight than a retreat, and this
hath ruined many armies, and loaded their generals with
dishonour and disgrace."

Montrose's officers despaired. Their men lay unconscious
or incapable around the cellars and parlours of Dundee.
There was no hope of rousing them in time to escape Hurry,
nor of holding out against the Covenanter when he came. The
coolest heads urged Montrose to ride for it himself with the
horse. The hottest called for a last glorious dash on to Baillie's
pikes. The argument for Montrose's personal flight was very
strong: the rest of the army was at Brechin. He would lose only
the 600 foot at Dundee. What were these against his own life,
the very life of the royalist cause in Scotland? Argyll, in such a
pass, would not have hesitated for a moment.

But here at Dundee Montrose's spirit soared as always in the
face of the impossible. Alone amongst his officers, he swore that
it could be done, it would be done. With his impassioned orders
in their ears, his captains scattered running through the streets,
kicking and cursing men from the houses, dragging them from
under tables and beds, bawling them from the alleys. Few
soldiers of the seventeenth century would have believed it
possible, but by sheer force of personality, Montrose dragged
his army from the mouth of destruction. A handful of men were
left behind to be taken prisoner. But though they staggered
bewildered as they marched, though some were supported by
comrades and others hauled by their belts, the royalist army
was through the Eastport gate of Dundee as Hurry raced
through the Westport at the head of his dragoons. The clansmen were dumping plunder by the wayside, now. They were
marching for their lives.

There were perhaps two hours before darkness fell and
Montrose's men could hope for a respite. At all costs they must
gain time. The Lord Marquis himself took command of the
horse, detailed a company of the fittest of the musketeers to
support them, and waited patiently at the rear of the army for
Hurry to come up. The Covenanter was soon enough upon him.
He had orders from Baillie to harass the royalists while the main
body of the army marched to cut off their line of escape to the
hills. Hurry had only to hold them against the sea for a few
hours and their fate was sealed. At last Montrose was at bay.
There must have been intense excitement in the Covenanting

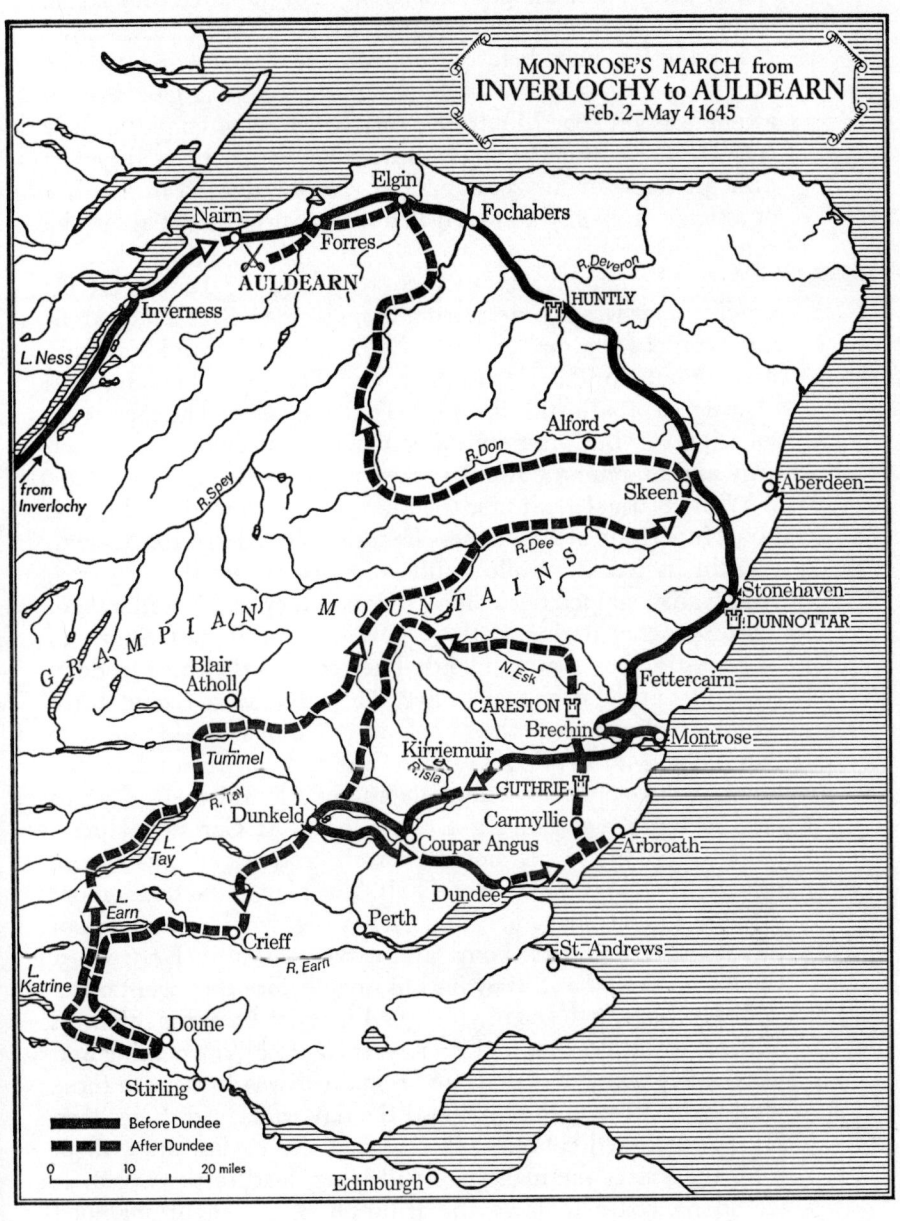

MONTROSE'S MARCH from
**INVERLOCHY to AULDEARN**
Feb. 2–May 4 1645

ranks. They knew the pathetic strength of the force they faced.
They were to meet James Graham on their own terms.

For the last hour before dark, Montrose coolly directed the
fire of his rearguard against Hurry's persistent charges. As each
attack was broken, Montrose's men wheeled to continue their
retreat. As night came on, Montrose achieved one of the most
difficult feats for any commander. He disengaged in the face
of a superior enemy and vanished from Hurry's sight along the
coast.

But although he was momentarily safe, he knew that his
predicament was still desperate. Somewhere on his left, marching parallel with him further inland, were Baillie and his army,
waiting only for dawn to destroy him. The royalist column was
nearing Arbroath still pinned against the coast. The men were
sobering up. But after storming Dundee, surviving a drunken
orgy and marching ten miles, they were also tiring.

With his usual genius for the unexpected—how that phrase is
taxed in writing of Montrose—he suddenly ordered the army to
turn in its tracks. While Baillie plodded on north-eastwards,
the royalists slipped back along the road they had just marched.
Through the darkness they hastened until just short of
Carnoustie, they swung inland. They crossed the track trodden
by Baillie an hour or two earlier. Then they were racing north
with all the speed their exhausted limbs could muster:
Carmyllie went by, then Guthrie Castle, then Melgund. As the
bleak dawn came up before them, they found themselves at
last, incredibly, within sight of the hills. At Careston House,
a Carnegie house an hour's march from safety, Montrose
reluctantly allowed his army a halt. The men could do no more
until they had rested a few hours. They had travelled more than
fifty miles in thirty-six hours and sacked Dundee. Even when
their lives hung on it, they had to sleep before they went on.

There was one piece of vital good news at Careston: the rest
of the army at Brechin had been warned of Baillie's coming and
were safely away. All that now remained was to stagger those
vital three miles to the hills, and the day was saved. Yet, when
Hurry's lathered column was reported closing fast upon them
from the south, the men were still lying dead to the world. It
would be bitter to have the triumph of the night snatched
from them now, yet Baillie was already marching furiously to
overtake them. Hurry had only to delay the royalists an hour

with his dragoons. Then the Covenanting infantry would be up to finish the job.

Jabbing the rumps of the supine clansmen with their sword points, shouting and kicking the sleep-walkers into life, Montrose's officers drove them to their feet for a last supreme effort. Stumbling through the last few thousand paces they went, their general still behind them, tirelessly ordering the rearguard holding Hurry's horse at bay. Load, fire, wheel, march—the musketeers backed slowly towards the hills, the cavalry covering them in turn as they withdrew. Then, at last, they were into the marshes and reeds and soft turf and bog at the foot of the hills. Hurry's tired cavalry stood disconsolate, frustrated behind them, unable to manœuvre around the royalists and unable to follow them up the narrow pass in the face of Montrose's rearguard. Somehow the clansmen staggered upwards into the heather, most men bowed by utter exhaustion, supporting themselves on their matchlocks; a few still twisted anxiously to gaze back at the column of Covenanters watching them helplessly in the distance. Incredibly, the royalists were safe.

"Whether such an account will be believed abroad, or in after ages, I cannot pretend to say," wrote Wishart.[7] ". . . But I have often heard officers of experience and distinction, not in Britain only, but also in Germany and France, prefer this march of Montrose to his most famous victories."

The Dundee attack, so nearly Montrose's undoing, under-lined the critical importance of accurate intelligence to a campaign being fought with such slender resources. Its outcome was an escape, not a victory. But it was a dazzling display of Montrose's powers of leadership and tactical brilliance. No man who knew what the Lord Marquis did to save his army at Dundee could ever afterwards wonder why his men loved him so dearly.

Yet in the weeks that now followed, as the army lay recovering its strength in the hills, Montrose must often have pondered to what purpose Divine Providence had saved him at Dundee. Ever since he left the north-east his army had been haemor-rhaging, losing men in a steady daily seepage. In the wake of the nerve-racking Dundee encounter, he found himself abandoned by the entire Gordon contingent. Lord Lewis appears to have stormed away in one of his frequent outbursts of pique and intemperance, taking some of the clansmen with him. Soon afterwards, Lord Gordon himself begged Montrose to be allowed a brief leave with his men in order that they could secure their threatened lands in the north-east from the local Covenanters. The Lord Marquis sadly gave his consent. Had he not done so, he might have been obliged to watch the Gordons go without it. He could scarcely blame them for their well-grounded fears.

But without the Gordons there was no prospect of fighting a major action. Until the army could reassemble, Montrose must waste time in the most profitable fashion that he could devise. Black Pate was sent down to Atholl to recruit once more. Alasdair was dispatched north-west to raid and gather men. The Lord Marquis himself retained 500 foot and 50 horse around his person. It was not an army, only a raiding force. He could merely seek to lead Baillie a merry dance and keep alive the seeds of royalism across the Highlands. He had word that Aboyne and a handful of horse had at last escaped from the siege of Carlisle and were riding fast to meet him. He may well have appointed a rendezvous with them, for they can have had little chance of effecting a random junction with him in the midst of the hills. He must have made some arrangement with Alasdair and Lord Gordon to meet their forces again, though military necessity was in the event to precipitate the union. But whatever plans he made for the future in those first weeks of April, it is difficult to see any useful strategic purpose in his movements when he marched away with his 550 men in the direction of Dunkeld. There was only his perpetual need to remain in motion. Unless he moved south-west hoping for news of the King's promised 500 horse coming north from the Border he was killing time until the Gordons had settled their affairs.

It was now the middle of April. The heather was still in its dark winter plumage, but the snow was gone and the burns were swollen with its melting. The days were lengthening, and the worst privations of the winter were forgotten. From Dunkeld the royalists marched onwards to Crieff, where they camped just east of the village, near Inchbrakie Castle. Baillie, at Perth, was galvanized by the news that his quarry was only seventeen miles away and so weak in numbers. Rousing his army, he drove them all night to strike the

royalists at dawn. But Montrose was not to be surprised twice
in a month. He rode out in person to watch the Covenanters
coming on, probably looking for some chance to ambush and
discomfit them. But the odds against him were far too great.
Returning to the camp, he sent his infantry marching at their
best speed westwards up Strathearn. He himself took command
of the cavalry squadron, and deployed it to cover the march
from the Covenanting horse. When the infantry reached Loch
Earn, they turned to move up its south shore. In the narrow
pass at the foot of the loch, the royalist rearguard had no
difficulty in blocking the Covenanters until the main body were
well away. Then at last they disengaged and left Baillie fuming,
empty-handed after all his troubles. Such little actions may not
win wars, but they greatly upset enemies.

Beside Loch Earn, the royalists burnt the house and barns of
Kilpont's murderer, at Ardvorlich. Then they marched on by
Lochearnhead and Balquhidder, at last swinging southwards
into the Trossachs.[8] On April 19th, two days after they had
broken the camp at Crieff, they achieved a delighted reunion
with Aboyne and his little troop of horsemen, safe at last after
their hair-raising dash north from Carlisle. To add to their
gay fellowship, the same day they were joined by Montrose's
twenty-year-old nephew the Master of Napier, and by young
John Alexander, one of Stirling's sons, who had together escaped
from house arrest at Holyrood.

Yet when they had exchanged news and gossip on the
thousand things to be spoken of between them all, when they
had destroyed the homes of the prominent local Covenanters
and listened to the latest reports from the scouts and the
informers about the movements of the enemy, Montrose and
his party must have sensed the futility of their immediate
activities. It was now apparent that the King's promise of 500
horse, like so much else, had been mere fantasy. Montrose
remembered all their talk of getting help from abroad, of
shipping arms into the north. He had told Charles that without
these things a rising in Scotland was impossible. In the event,
he had wrought wonders alone and unaided. But now in the
midst of this meaningless ramble around the hills with his
raiding party, he suddenly felt very weary.

"Had I but for one month the use of those 500 horse, I
should have seen you (before the time this can come to your

hand) with twenty thousands of the best this Kingdom can afford," he wrote to the King from Doune on April 20th. It was the first time in all his dealings with Charles that the faintest note of reproach had crept in.

> Though I may justly say I have continued things this half year bygone without the assistance of either men, arms, ammunition or that which is the nerves of war; so that had we not been supported by Divine Providence our army could not have subsisted, and I cannot choose but think it strange that this unhappy country which had been the bane and cause of all your woes, being now in so fair a way of reducing, that not only the ordinary but easy means should have been neglected. Howsoever though you have not assisted me, I will yet still do my best to bar all assistance coming against you, and to the better. . . . And so I will cast me into your hands and sign myself,
>
> Your Majesty's most faithful and humble servant,
> MONTROSE.

This letter never reached Charles. Its bearer, James Small, who had carried so many vital papers between the royalists of England and Scotland, was captured and executed by the Covenanters on his way south. It is remarkable that so much correspondence got through from Oxford to the hills and back. It must have been an appalling undertaking to locate Montrose and his army, far less to reach them to deliver dispatches. But the loss of the letter from Doune probably mattered very little. Even had it reached the King, it is unlikely that he could have expedited his efforts to support Montrose. And even had he done so, the Lord Marquis was at his most romantic when he suggested that 500 English cavalry would have enabled him to recruit 20,000 Scots for the King. The letter is significant only as a *cri de cœur*, evidence of one of the rare moments when Montrose gave way to tiredness and depression. No one could have blamed him.

But now, suddenly, all his doubts were dispelled, his dilemmas resolved. As he lay in the hills around Loch Katrine, decisive intelligence was brought to him from Lord Gordon with his clan in the north-east. The Covenanters had divided their army: Baillie, who was expecting heavy reinforcements,

was burning the royalist recruiting grounds in Atholl, and
threatening Blair Castle itself. But Sir John Hurry had marched
with two regiments of foot and one of horse to raise a new
northern army to suppress the Gordons. He had reached
Aberdeen on April 11th. After delaying there for a few days to
settle a mutiny, he was now advancing northwards once more,
more than 1000 foot and 600 horse at his back. Lord Gordon
was withdrawing before him.

Montrose was mustering his own column within the hour.
They would move at once by forced marches to the north-east.
He could not risk the possibility of the Gordons being defeated,
and he saw an opportunity to bring Hurry to battle while his
force was cut off from that of Baillie. He must anyway have
made plans for the army to regroup before long. In the new
situation, it was merely a matter of hastening every intention. In
great strides across the Highlands, he raced for the north-east
to meet the Gordons: back through Balquhidder and up to
Loch Tay, along that shore where his army had survived such
nightmares four months before; up by Tummel to Atholl,
where he gathered up Black Pate and his men. Baillie might
have checked him in the passes had be been so minded, but the
dour Covenanter had allowed himself to be drawn off eastwards
in futile pursuit of Alasdair Macdonald, who was burning in
Angus. Montrose pressed on unhindered—by Glen Isla and
Glen Muick would have been his natural line—until at last,
he called his column to halt at Aboyne Castle, high on the Dee.
Lord Gordon rode to meet him at the head of his clansmen.
Alasdair swaggered in with his marauding Irishes, 300 new
recruits behind him. On April 30th, ten days after leaving
Doune, Montrose had concentrated an army of 2500 foot and
250 horse, after marching more than a hundred miles across
some of the worst country in the Highlands to reach the
rendezvous.

They were chronically short of ammunition. Before they
could move against Hurry, it was essential rapidly to remedy
the situation. Aboyne was still suffering from a shoulder injured
in his escape from Carlisle, but after months of inglorious
confinement, he was thirsting for great deeds. At the head of a
cavalry column, he was sent flying down the Dee to Aberdeen.
Amongst the ships in the harbour, he and his raiders found
twenty barrels of powder. Thus laden, they rode cheerfully

back to Montrose. On May 2nd, the whole army marched in pursuit of Sir John Hurry.

The Covenanter had now recovered from his initial amazement at the news of the royalist concentration. He moved with careful deliberation. On his orders, powerful reinforcements were being assembled at Inverness to join him. He had only to survive a week of marching with Montrose at his heels before turning, with a strongly superior army, to bring the royalists to battle at a disadvantage. Back across the Spey Hurry led his men, into Moray, through Elgin and Forres, making for Nairn and friendly Covenanting country. The royalist horse hung on his flanks, striving to delay him just as he had snapped around Montrose's army on the road from Dundee. Hurry's veteran regiments fought a series of sharp rearguard actions day by day along the road. Montrose must have viewed his enemy's progress with reluctant admiration. He was handling his forces as deftly as the Lord Marquis might have done himself.

But the royalists, crucially, knew nothing of the reinforcements at Inverness. Montrose believed that time was on his side, that he had only patiently to pursue Hurry until he brought him to battle. On the evening of May 8th, when his army pitched their camp by the tiny village of Auldearn, less than two miles short of Nairn, he believed that the following day he would be continuing his pursuit of Hurry towards Inverness, seventeen miles westwards.

In reality, the gleeful Hurry that afternoon achieved his vital junction with the Convenanting reinforcements outside Inverness. He was now master of six regular Covenanting regiments, amongst them Lothian's, Lawers's and Buchanan's, which were reckoned the equal of any in Leven's army. Supporting them were the mass of local Covenanting gentlemen headed by Seaforth, Sutherland, Forbes and Crichton. In all, his army numbered 4000 foot and 600 horse—odds of two to one against Montrose. There was no need to fear for the quality of this force against the clansmen, as at Tippermuir and Aberdeen. Many of these men were veterans of Marston Moor, trained to stand against any enemy in the two Kingdoms. Hurry, the soldier of fortune, stood poised to make his fortune. The Lords of the Covenant would grant any prize in Scotland to the man who rid them of James Graham and his horde.

As soon as his men had rested a little and a council of war

had been held to ensure that his orders were perfectly understood, Hurry set his army on the march. Through the darkness
they moved back along the road to Nairn, rejoicing in the
royalists' ignorance of the thunderbolt about to descend
upon them. Rain poured down on the sodden troops as they
plodded through the heather and muddy grass, long lines of
shouldered pikes dimly silhouetted against the sky. To avoid
any risk that Montrose's outposts might hear them, they were
ordered to clear their matchlocks of damp powder before they
reached Nairn. The musketeers emptied their weapons into
the air and carefully reloaded, ready for the attack at dawn.

But by some merciful trick of the wind, Montrose's outposts
had heard that ragged volley. They hastened back through
the rain to the cluster of cottages at the centre of Auldearn.
They reported to the Lord Marquis the astonishing news that
the enemy was advancing upon them. Amidst general confusion
and sleepy anger, reveille was sounded. The army was ordered
to muster. Officers fumbled through the darkness calling for
their men amidst musketeers loading their pieces, pikemen
searching for their regiments, horsemen struggling to harness
and saddle. Montrose had perhaps an hour in which to prepare
to receive the Covenanting army.

As soon as he knew the Covenanters' strength, he toyed
with the prospect of retreat, only to reject it. If Hurry with
his new army survived to unite with Baillie, it was all over for
the royalists in Scotland. If there was to be any slim hope of
saving the King's cause, he must fight Hurry, and do it now.
As dawn came slowly up over the Moray Firth, stretching out
into the North Sea a mile north of his positions, Montrose had
his first opportunity to look at the ground on which he must
fight.

Auldearn, a cluster of cottages and gardens, stood on a low
ridge facing westwards, across the plain on which Hurry must
advance. On the right stood the steep mound of Castle Hill,
site of some forgotten tower. Beyond this, at the foot of a shallow
valley ran a burn feeding marshes all around itself. The ridge
was the natural position for Montrose to hold against Hurry.
The great Royal Standard was boldly planted in its centre. A
screen of musketeers was posted in the cottages and gardens.
Below them and to their right, Alasdair Macdonald and a
mixed force of 600 of his own Macdonalds and Gordon levies,

deployed to hold a thin line along the ridge. His position was strengthened by the mess of fences, walls and vegetable patches in front of his men. His right flank was secured by the burn and its attendant marshes, ensuring that the Covenanters could only attack on a narrow front.

Hurry's first glimpse of the royalist position from the plain must have disappointed him a little. They were deployed ready for him. Surprise had been lost. But at last the moment had come to revenge himself upon General Baillie for the months of quarrelling between them, most recently when Baillie accused Hurry of making possible Montrose's escape from Dundee. It was a brisk May morning, the ground underfoot still soggy after the heavy rain. Hurry ordered forward

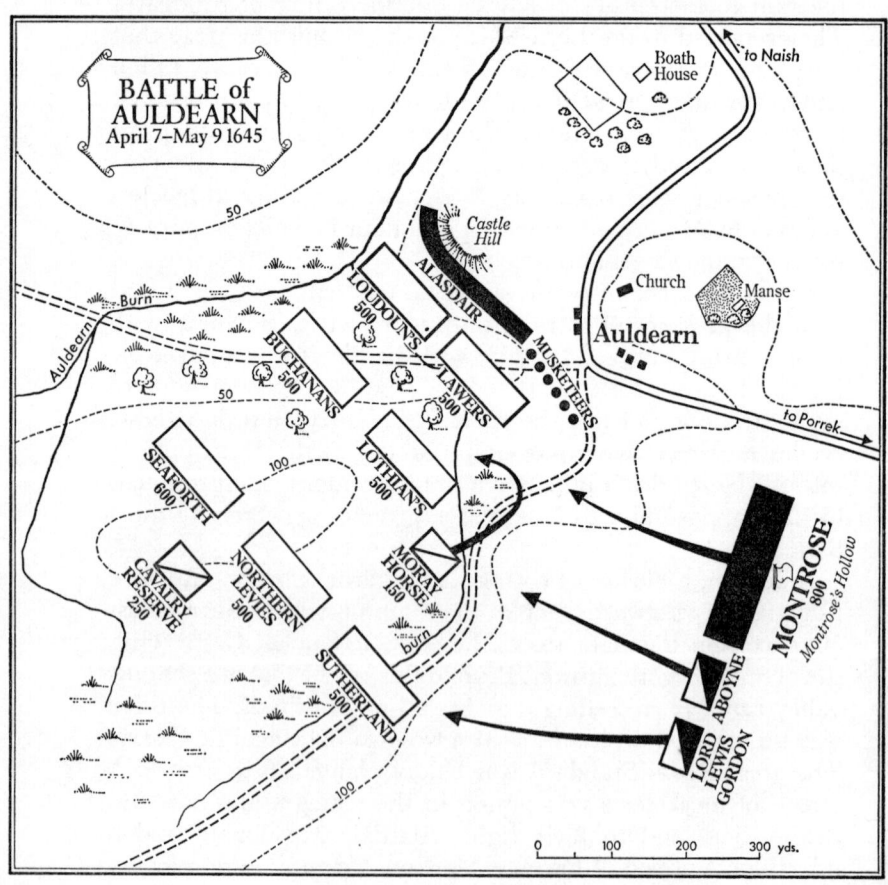

his four veteran regiments, Lawers's having the honour of the van. He placed those of Seaforth and Sutherland in the rear with the northern levies. He held the bulk of his cavalry in reserve to charge when the royalist line had been broken—there was nothing for them to do against such a ridge as that upon which Alasdair and his clansmen stood.[9]

Lawers's men, their colonel Sir Mungo Campbell before them, marched boldly to the foot of the ridge, pikes presented, supported by a hail of musketry and arrows from their comrades in their rear. But as they scrambled up the broken ground, they found their handsome formation sadly disarrayed. Alasdair and his men grappled them piecemeal as they reached the royalist line. For a space the heaving mass of men swung to and fro around the crest of the ridge then, Lawers's regiment, the pride of the Covenant, found themselves falling back in confusion to the base of the hill. Hurry watched with growing impatience as his regiments pressed forward again, only to be once more repulsed. Doggedly they struggled on. Still there was no hint of a breach in the royalists' bristling battle line.

But although Hurry could not claim to have contrived the manœuvre as did Duke William at Hastings, he was suddenly amazed to see the battle transformed in his favour by a moment of mad indiscipline from Alasdair Macdonald. To Alasdair's simple, murderous intellect, the spectacle of the Covenanters falling back down the ridge after their latest repulse proved irresistible. With a great cry he leapt down, leading his Macdonalds and his Gordons behind him, to drive home his advantage. The Covenanting pikemen snapped with iron discipline into their ranks to face them. This kind of attack, from so slender a force, was a gift for them. Alasdair's men were in deep trouble, yard by yard being driven back up the ridge, Hurry's army pressing forward with a surge of new confidence.

The Macdonalds fought like tigers, Alasdair utterly in his element in this man to man butchery. His great sword whirling about his head, his target pierced with pikeheads like some giant's dartboard, he clove the heads of every Covenanter who dared close on him. His blade at last snapped with the fury of his great blows, and for an instant time stopped: his life seemed forfeit. But beside him his brother-in-law Davidson of Ardnacross, coughing out his lifeblood amidst the great mass of struggling men, saw Alasdair's plight. He had strength enough to toss his own redundant blade to the Macdonald before he collapsed dying on the hillside. Alasdair seized it and plunged once more into the fray.

The Macdonald bards sang for generations afterwards about Ranald Macdonald son of Donald son of Angus MacKinnon of Mull. He stood alone, at bay before a ring of Covenanting pikemen, an arrow through his cheeks, his sword hilt broken and the blade jammed in its scabbard. He emptied his pistol to kill his first man, and tore out his blade as a row of pike points touched his breast. Slashing through their shafts, he leapt free of his persecutors. Cleaving one man's head from his shoulders as he fell back, he reached the Macdonald line once more, bloody but still on his feet with his sword in his hand. The royalists needed him, and every man still alive on the ridge. Their position was critical. But through this devastating struggle around Castle Hill and the ridge of Auldearn, Montrose himself had been a passive, secret spectator a quarter of a mile away. Well out to the left of the Macdonald position, behind a long gentle slope, lay dead ground invisible to the Covenanting army. Ever since that May morning of 1645, it has been called Montrose's Hollow. In that depression stood more than half Montrose's army, almost 1000 foot and all of his 250 horse. He had planned this battle with extraordinary daring. Alasdair and the clansmen were only the holding force, intended to drag the Covenanting army into chaotic commitment to the struggle around the ridge and the Royal Standard. The weight of the royalist army still stood poised to deliver a devastating flank attack on Hurry's regiments at the critical moment of the battle.

It was a brilliant disposition, probably the greatest in all Montrose's battles. Countless years of training and experience cannot give a commander that instinctive eye for ground that is part of military genius. Montrose had conceived his plan in the few moments he was able to study his position in the half-light before deploying his regiments to face Hurry. There are those who read the stories of the mad clan charges at Tippermuir and Inverlochy and conclude that there was little room for finesse in his great campaign, that once the battle began he lost all power to influence its outcome and was compelled to trust everything to his undisciplined troops. But Auldearn is the example to all those who seek proof of Montrose's tactical subtlety. The principles that he employed at Auldearn would have served him as well at the head of 20,000 men. Marlborough and Wellington would have been proud to have thus ordered a battle.

But in the midst of that bloody May morning, Montrose must have been inwardly fulminating at the risk that Alasdair Macdonald's insane rush from the ridge had wrecked all his hopes. Alasdair had been instructed to hold his position at all costs, and no more. If he now lost it, if the centre of the royalist line collapsed, then all was lost. From his vantage point on the hill, Montrose was forced to act hastily, concealing his terrible anxiety. As his officers began to fear that Alasdair's destruction was imminent, the Lord Marquis walked back down the slope into the hollow where the horse waited, harness jangling nervously, arms clattering as the men shifted restlessly in their stirrups.

"Come my Lord Gordon, what are we waiting for?" he cried gaily. "Our friend Macdonald on the right has routed the enemy and is slaughtering the fugitives. Shall we look on idly and let him carry off all the honours of the day?"

For the first time in his campaign, Montrose had the thrill of watching royalist cavalry charge by squadrons. Breasting the ridge behind which they had lain hidden, they stampeded down upon the shocked Covenanting infantry still waiting to engage. Major Drummond, the Covenanting officer commanding a squadron of horse on the right, closest to the advancing Gordons, yelled to his men to wheel and charge them. But incredibly, in the heat of the moment, he appears to have ordered them to swing left, rather than right. In panic they galloped into the ranks of their own infantry, throwing the companies into chaos as the Gordons crashed into the line, and Montrose led forward his powerful infantry flanking force to the charge. In panic the Covenanting levies in the rear broke and ran. Even Hurry's veteran regiments began to crumble. The Gordons reformed to charge again, sweeping all before them. Hurry's broken companies fled in terror from the field up the long road to Inverness. On the ridge, at last Alasdair's moment had come. Rallying his remaining clansmen, he sprang forward to the charge, driving the ruins of Lawers's regiment into a grim, doomed circle. The Covenanting pikemen held their ground and died on it. Lawers's regiment was almost wiped out, Sir Mungo Campbell of Lawers at their head. Sir John Murray and Sir Gideon Murray, nine nephews of Douglas of Cavers, seven captains and five lieutenants were among the Covenanting dead at the foot of the ridge of Auldearn. Montrose's clansmen set about the triumphant butchery of the fugitives, racing for miles across the hill to hack them down. The wreckage of Hurry's army littered the long road through Nairn to Inverness.

Sir John Hurry himself, whatever else was said of him, was no coward. He stayed on the field until it was certain that all was irretrievably lost. Then he rode for his life with the horse. Montrose's cavalry might have had him, but for an exasperating misunderstanding. The exuberant Aboyne came charging towards the royalists with his squadron, proudly waving the standards they had seized from the Covenanters. They were mistaken for a new Covenanting cavalry force, and in the painful minutes of disentangling themselves, Hurry and his escort made good their escape, along with Seaforth and Sutherland and most of the local gentlemen, safe in possession of mounts. Hurry's misery and rage went with him as he rode. Once sure that he had outdistanced the pursuit, he halted his men for an abrupt little ceremony. Major Drummond, the officer who had wheeled his squadron into the Covenanting line, was ordered to stand in the middle of the road. A file of musketeers doubled forward and halted. On Hurry's merciless order, Drummond was shot where he stood. Then the defeated and humiliated Covenanter mounted his horse and rode fast to join General Baillie.

Auldearn had cost the Covenant up to three thousand dead. Wishart supposes that the royalists lost 15 men. Gordon of Sallagh reports that the royalists lost 22 gentlemen and 200 private soldiers, in addition to hundreds of wounded. This total is much the more convincing. The great majority of the casualties were men of Alasdair's division on the ridge, and many of them might have been spared but for his folly. It must have tried Montrose very hard indeed to congratulate the Macdonald without bitter words of reproach. Alasdair's passion for personal glory might one day be the undoing of them all.

Auldearn must rank among the foremost of Montrose's triumphs. Yet it was only an overture. Hurry's destruction had merely cleared the way for a trial of strength with Baillie.

# CHAPTER TEN

## *"A Company of the worst men in the earth"*

---

ON MAY 11TH, 1645, two days after Auldearn, Montrose led his army once more into Elgin, trailing behind them the train of litters and carts loaded with wounded from the battle, together with the few of Hurry's men who had had the good fortune to be taken prisoner. The Covenanting townspeople, plundered once already by the royalists, lay sullen and frightened behind their doors as they saw them come again, still victorious. For the wounded, suffering the effects of pike stabs, sword slashes and musket balls, there was little comfort and every prospect of gangrene. But they were distributed among the houses and halls while the army took up quarters for a brief pause. As usual, some clansmen were already drifting away. Others amused themselves by visiting nearby villages that had escaped their earlier attentions, looting and burning Covenanting homes. After nine months of devastation by both armies, the glens and bailes of north-east Scotland presented a sorry spectacle. Their inhabitants nursed deep bitterness towards King and Covenant. Aside from the usual strategic considerations, Montrose's army could never linger long in one place because of the need to range constantly in search of supplies.

During all these months of marching to and fro across the Highlands, the Lord Marquis himself was not always poring over dispatches or communing with chieftains. At a moment of anticlimax such as that in Elgin, there must have been fire-lit evenings of songs and dancing, gay dinners and exuberant speeches from Gordons and Macdonalds. Montrose was the lone star of his extraordinary campaign, and never for an instant was he out of the spotlight of his army's fascinated attention. In England, the royalist armies looked above all to the King. In Scotland, they had only his Lieutenant, the man on whom every decision hung, the pivot of every hope and fear. It must have been a great strain for Montrose. As he walked amongst the horse lines or talked to O'Cahan outside his quarters, ate breakfast or went for a morning ride, every man's eye was upon him. His army was never as large as that of any of the great captains in England. He lived trapped in perpetual intimacy with his men. He must have handled them with endless quiet tact and patience. Blustering arrogance achieved nothing when they were free to come and go at will. He had learnt a great deal in a few months about the Highlands and about the clans. When he was young, he had enjoyed the luxury of being hot and impetuous. Now he had to keep his temper as clansmen casually abandoned him at critical moments of his campaign, smiling gently as they marched away, begging their chieftains to honour him again with their presence at their convenience. He laboured under many of the handicaps of a British officer parachuted to the Resistance in Occupied Europe during the Second World War. Admittedly he was a Scot, but he was no Gaelic tribal chieftain. He could lead, persuade, advise, and beg. But he could not order them. By this early summer of 1645, following Auldearn, his strongest card in the struggle to maintain and enlarge his army was the prospect he could offer of plunder and limitless glory. Never had the Highland clans, the Gaels, inflicted such humiliations on their Lowland enemies. Montrose's name and deeds were the marvel of northern Scotland, celebrated to the very outermost Hebridean islands as men returned home laden with their booty.

But as he struggled to prepare his army for a decisive encounter with General Baillie, his difficulties with his mercurial followers were still as great as ever. Aboyne, who was as moody and irresponsible as his brother Lewis, went on sick leave, taking a strong troop of Gordons as a personal escort. Even the Irish contingent, on whom he had always relied because they had no villages to which to return, exasperated him by persistent desertions to set up homes for their families in any glen which would receive them. On June 6th Montrose was writing to his commander at Blair Castle, Robertson of Inver:[1]

> I have ofttimes written to you before, anent the Irishes who straggled to your country, and for punishing of them; and it is only the neglect of my orders which makes them so

insolent. Wherefore these are to will and command you, that immediately after sight hereof, you pursue all such Irishes as can be found in the country, with fire and sword; and that you burn of the houses of all those who resist them; as you will answer on the contrary at your highest peril. . . .

Montrose was merciful but he was not soft. Nelson was as willing as any captain in the fleet to flog recalcitrant seamen. So Montrose readily hanged those who defied his orders when they were marching under his banner.

On May 14th, the royalists transferred their camp to the Bog of Gight, and began raiding Covenanting outposts and villages from Gordon Castle. They were thus occupied when news reached them that Baillie was once more on the march. The Covenanter had been blundering about in Atholl on orders from Edinburgh. Now he marched north to cross the Dee and threaten Huntly Castle. Montrose moved rapidly to cover the castle. For several days the royalists stared defiantly out at their enemies from behind a hastily-dug range of trenches and earthworks. Montrose hoped to tempt Baillie into attacking him here, in a carefully-chosen and prepared position. The royalist numbers were already so shrunk after Auldearn that he felt unable to risk a battle with the Covenanter on even terms.

Sir John Hurry had managed to slip through to the Covenanting army with a squadron of horse saved from the wreckage of Auldearn. There was unbounded jealousy and dislike between himself and Baillie, but when the general had heard the details of Auldearn, he felt no inclination whatever to rush upon the royalists until a moment carefully chosen by himself. When Montrose became bored with inactivity, broke camp and moved away westwards, Baillie followed with the utmost circumspection. The Covenanters paced the royalists through Balveny to Glenlivet, and there was a series of minor skirmishes and ambushes. Up amidst the purple bloom of the heather and the innocent charm of the summer hills, Baillie avoided all Montrose's attempts to bring him to battle on unfavourable terms. He merely shadowed him until his own supplies ran down and he was obliged to fall back on Inverness to replenish them.

I

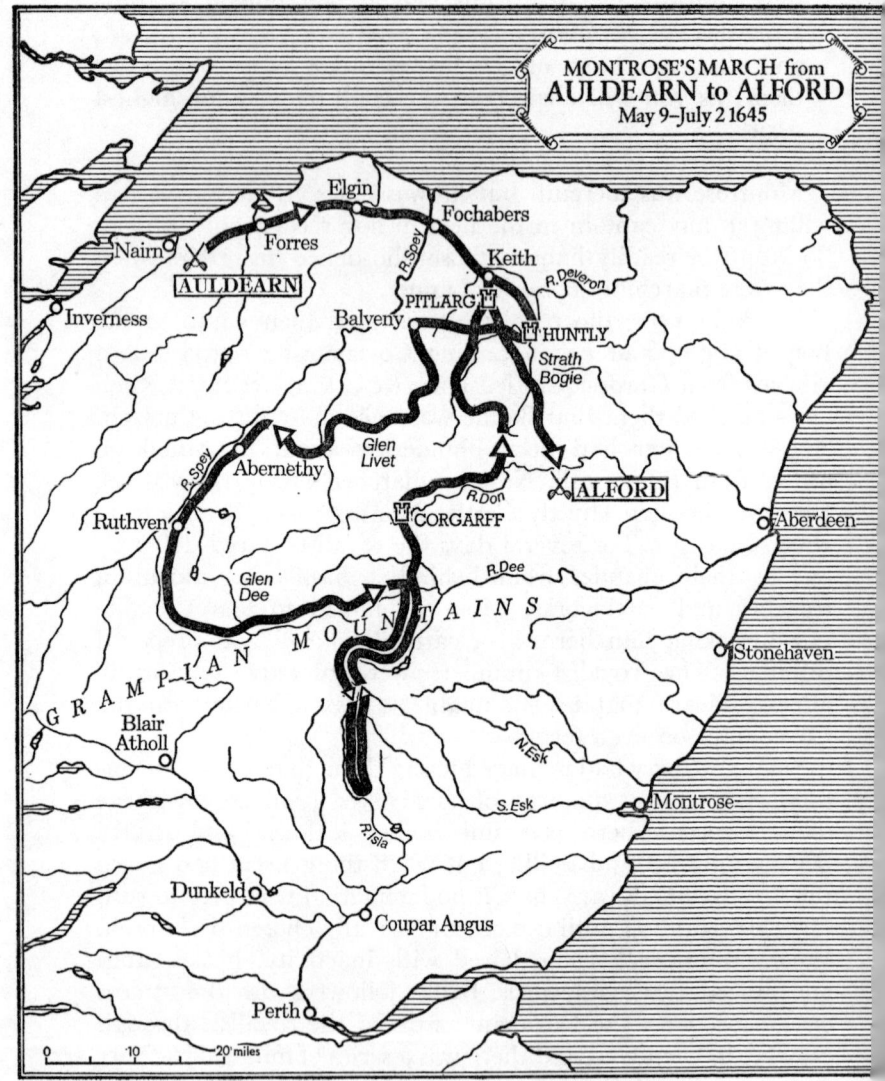

Montrose was not sorry to break off contact. He now had word that Lord Lindsay of the Byres, the egregious Covenanter who had been a close friend in their St Andrews' days, had formed a new army in Angus. Lindsay was a vain man of negligible military talent, who had won a command simply because he stood second to Argyll in the councils of the Covenant. The latest Lowland levies, intended to reinforce Baillie, were given to Lindsay to create a second force between Montrose and the South. Lindsay was now sitting vacillating at Newtyle of Angus, a few miles from Kirriemuir. Montrose moved down the Spey to Rothiemurchus, then struck east to the Dee. He had decided on a rapid thrust to remove Lindsay's small force from the reckoning before he once again faced up to the problem of Baillie.

In June in the Highlands, the days seem to go on forever. Through the warm heather of Glen Muick Montrose briskly marched his army, over the watershed and down Glen Clova, along the bank of the South Esk river. Unusually among Montrose's marches, this must have been a pleasant expedition, marching to deal with feeble opposition in the kindliest of conditions. He expected to fall on Lindsay with one of his unheralded thunder-bolts. He was seven miles from the Covenanter's unsuspecting camp when fatal dissension within his own army brought the column to an abrupt halt.

The entire Gordon contingent announced that they were returning home. Young Lord Gordon and Nat Gordon were amazed and appalled, and pleaded desperately with the men to stay at least until Lindsay had been disposed of. But it seems that some directive had arrived from the distant, incorrigible Marquis of Huntly, chief of clan Gordon. His words overruled all his son's urgent pleas. Wishart suggests that Huntly thwarted Montrose out of malice, arising directly from their old antagonism. In reality, Baillie's presence at the head of his army within striking distance of the Huntly estates probably had much to do with the Gordon's behaviour. It may also be that Aboyne was making mischief on his own account, or on the instructions of his father. "Lord Gordon was in the camp, and no one was more deeply incensed at this treachery," wrote Wishart,[2] "in so much that Montrose could with difficulty restrain him from punishing with death those of his own followers who had deserted."

The attack on Lindsay was abandoned. Montrose could only console himself, as the army turned in its tracks up the South Esk, with the knowledge that it had been strategically irrelevant. It was Baillie's army which remained the critical factor, the principal obstacle to the royalist dash for the South. Once again, Montrose addressed himself to his eternal problem, that of recruiting. Alasdair Macdonald was sent west with a regiment of his Irishes to raise men among the Macleans and Macdonalds. Lord Gordon and Colonel Nat Gordon rode off towards their own country to try to resolve the clan's internecine feuds and reassemble their forces. Montrose himself, having moved northwards, pitched his new camp in the ruins of Corgarff Castle on the river Don, strategically placed either to move deep into the Gordon country or to make for the hills. There he sat down to wait for news and for men.

One of his chief fears, as he lingered impatiently at Corgarff, was for the safety of the prominent royalists in the hands of the Covenant. With each of his victories the ministers' thirst for their blood increased. It would be tragic if so many of his dearest friends and relations were murdered on account of his triumph. James Small had already been executed for carrying messages to the King. Just before Auldearn, John Napier of Easter Torrie, Lord Napier's elder brother and a man well into his seventies, was arrested and charged with the same offence. The entire Napier family was now confined, including the young Master's wife Lady Elizabeth Erskine; eighteen-year-old Lady Lilias, Montrose's niece; and Sir George Stirling of Ker. Poor Lord Napier himself, a broken old man of seventy, was briefly released on May 27th, to raise the huge fine of £10,000 Scots levied on him by the Covenant for the escape of his son to join Montrose. As soon as he had collected the money, he was returned to solitary confinement in his dungeon. Lord Ogilvy, Harry Graham, George Wishart and Lord Graham were also, of course, still in the Covenanters' hands. Only Montrose's younger son Robert was free, released with his mother after a brief inquiry in April. Lord Southesk's influence with the Committee of Estates, together with Lady Montrose's alienation from her husband, sufficed to keep them out of the net. There are apologists for Southesk and his daughter who notice that he voted against the confiscation of Montrose's estates, and argue that the lack of evidence about Lady Montrose should not be used to damn her. But Southesk was always a trimmer, and his concern for Montrose's estates was probably a matter of dynastic self-interest rather than generosity to his son-in-law. As for Magdalen Carnegie, left under her father's influence for so much of her married life, had she ever shown great enthusiasm for her husband or his cause, there would certainly have been a chronicler to notice it. It is impossible to believe that Wishart ignored her existence in his biography of her husband by chance or as a matter of male chauvinism.

Southesk had secured the safety of his daughter and one grandson at the price of some dishonourable disavowal of Montrose. But for the other royalist prisoners in Edinburgh, the prospect looked grim and Montrose knew it. He could only thank providence for his own rival collection of hostages, locked up in Blair Castle under the watchful eye of Robertson of Inver. The Covenant had dispatched a succession of armies to wreak havoc in Atholl, the birthplace of Montrose's campaign. Each one must have hungered to seize Blair, the royalists' only permanent base through the campaign. It may well have been only the promise of misfortune falling upon the Covenanting prisoners in its dungeons that restrained them from attacking it. After each of his successful battles, Montrose dispatched his chief captives to Blair with a note to Inver such as this: "These are to will and command you, that, immediately after sight hereof, you receive Captain Mortimer within the castle of Blair, and keep him close; whereanent these shall be to you a warrant; as you will answer on the contrary to your highest peril."

Now, as the fate of the royalists in Edinburgh appeared to hang in the balance, Montrose wrote to his garrison commander at Blair:

INVER,
   I received yours and have directed along ammunition unto you. You will be careful of all that concerns your charge, until my coming into that country, which I hope shall be shortly. Also, you will hasten the exchange of prisoners; and show Crinnen [Campbell of Crinnen whose brother Colin was held in the castle] that I am informed

that there is one Mr Napier, brother to my Lord Napier, a prisoner with them, against whom they intend to proceed in a seemingly legal way; which if they do, let him assure them from me that I will use the like severity against some of their prisoners; and you will acquaint me with what answer you shall receive from them thereanent. Also, let me hear from you, with diligence, all such intelligence as you can learn from the border; and concerning Lindsay. . . .

Montrose's threats, together with the persuasive reality of his continuing triumph in arms, stayed the hand of the Covenant. John Napier was released in mid-June, and negotiations continued about an exchange of prisoners. To his eternal credit, young James, Lord Graham, refused to be party to an exchange lest his release cost his father a vital Covenanting prisoner. But he was alive and safe. At least, that is, for as long as his father was winning victories.

Late in June, Montrose was still at Corgarff debating his next move, when the Covenanters once again acted with astounding foolishness. Lord Lindsay met Baillie at Mills of Drum, and ordered him to hand over 1200 of his veteran infantry, offering in exchange 400 raw recruits from his own column. Lindsay then disappeared to indulge himself by devastating Atholl once more. Baillie moved sullenly north to besiege Gordon Castle in the Bog of Gight.

Montrose learnt of Baillie's movement and of the sudden weakening of the Covenanting army on June 25th. He broke camp and marched out at once to follow the enemy northwards. At least a proportion of the Gordon levies had rejoined his army, although Aboyne had disappeared once more with another troop of horse after a brief visit to the camp. Alasdair Macdonald was still in the north-west. But with Baillie's strength eroded and his best men gone to Lindsay, Montrose was convinced that given a fair chance at the Covenanter, he could defeat him.

The two armies first glimpsed each other once more on the hills near Keith. Baillie's scouts had watched Montrose's pursuit closing upon them. The Covenanter drew up his army in a very strong position on a hilltop at the head of a narrow pass commanded by his cavalry and guns. Montrose had not the slightest intention of attacking him uphill at such a disadvantage. He camped that night, June 27th, a short distance away on lower ground. The next morning he sent another of his teasing challenges to the Covenanter, defying him to come down and fight it out on level ground. Baillie once again contemptuously declined. Montrose turned about, and marched his army away southwards towards the Don. On July 1st, he crossed it at the Boat of Forbes. He ordered the army to make camp on Gallows Hill, a mile above the river crossing, by a tiny village named Alford.

This was the second time that Montrose had conducted a tactical retreat in the hope of bringing Baillie to battle on favourable terms. On the earlier occasion, beside the Spey, the prudent Covenanter had kept his distance. But the pressure upon him to grapple with James Graham and settle the royalist menace without delay had become intolerable. Urged on by those meddling representatives of the Committee of Estates who travelled with the army, he marched southwards in the wake of Montrose. As they went, they were vastly encouraged to learn that Alasdair Macdonald and many of his feared Irishes were still away in the north-west. The more confident of Baillie's officers talked exuberantly about Montrose's head-long retreat from Keith. There was now a priceless opportunity to catch him off balance. On the morning of July 2nd, as the Covenanters marched down the Suie Road and crossed the Don at the Boat of Forbes, they saw with intense excitement the royalist rearguard ahead of them on Gallows Hill. To the officers of Baillie's van, it seemed an extraordinary chance: if they moved fast, they could swing left-handed round Montrose and pin his army against the Don for destruction. In reality, from the moment they forded the river, their fate was sealed.

At Alford alone amongst his battles, Montrose was able to choose his own ground on which to fight. He planned Baillie's destruction with meticulous care. First, he reconnoitred the Don east and westwards to confirm that the Boat of Forbes was the only point at which the Covenanters could reasonably cross the river. He placed the bulk of his own forces behind the crest of Gallows Hill, where they were invisible to Baillie's vanguard as they descended the Suie Road to the river.[3] Marshes and a fast-flowing burn west of the Boat, on Baillie's right, made it all but impossible for him to manœuvre on that side. It was most unlikely that he would choose to attack the royalists up the long slope of Gallows Hill. It was almost certain that the Covenanters would attempt a flanking move on their left, despite the bogs behind them.

Each side probably numbered around 2000 infantry, and thus for once Montrose and his opponents faced each other at something like equal strength. Baillie had 600 cavalry commanded by Sir David Lindsay of Balcarres against the royalists' 250, but there was no comparison in the quality of the troops on each side. The Covenanters were for the most part half-trained levies who had never fought a battle. Wishart is unfair in saying that Baillie's army "were listed from amongst the lowest class of people, and fought for pay, having little discipline and far less honour to excite them". But Montrose's seasoned clansmen expected to eat them alive. Once he had so brilliantly manœuvred Baillie into committing himself to battle at Alford, it would have been outrageous had he failed to defeat him. He had achieved the aim of every field commander in war: he had arranged matters so that the first shots of battle were fired under overwhelmingly favourable circumstances. It is nice to notice that Montgomery, three hundred years later a past master in this art, quoted lines from Montrose in his orders on the eve of D-Day.

The Covenanters were already across the river when they saw that far from being a rearguard, the forces now revealing themselves over the brow of Gallows Hill were Montrose's regiments drawn up for battle. Balcarres's squadrons, already pressing forward on their hopeful flanking march, were hastily halted. Poor, doomed Baillie drew up his army as best he could with a marsh at his back and the foot of Gallows Hill in front of him. The country around Alford is green, soft and gentle by Highland standards, the banks of the Don lined with trees, the slope of Gallows Hill perfect ground for a downhill charge. Baillie's infantry took post in a long, thin line, one cavalry regiment on their right, Balcarres and his troopers still on the left, where they had halted when their advance was countermanded. Baillie had done all he could. He stood impotent, awaiting his fate.

Montrose's clansmen stood in the centre of the Highland battle line led by Eneas Macdonald of Glengarry, in the absence of Alasdair. They were the usual exotic company of

Irishes and Gordons, Athollmen and Macphersons, Macdonalds and Farquharsons. On each flank stood half the Gordon cavalry, Lord Gordon commanding the right, Lord Aboyne and Sir William Rollo the left. Magnus O'Cahan led a picked force of musketeers supporting Aboyne, Nat Gordon a similar company with Lord Gordon. The Master of Napier,

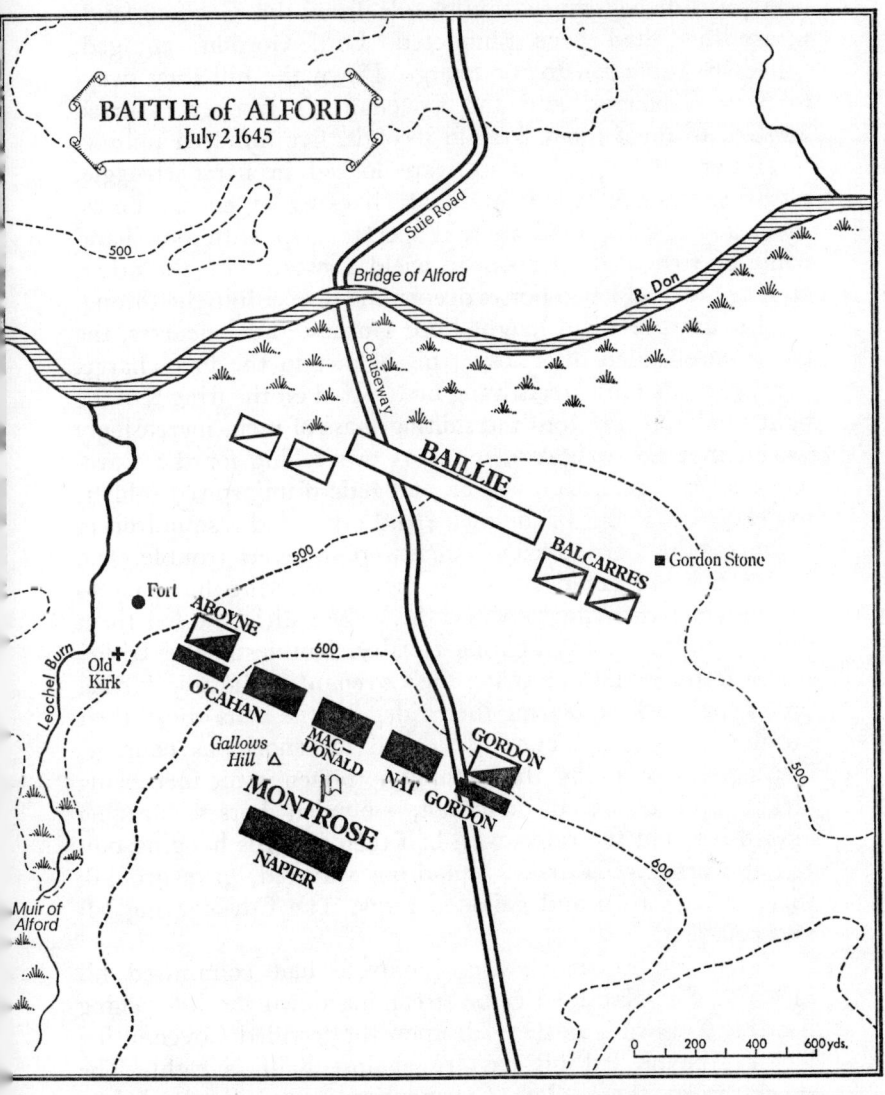

BATTLE of ALFORD
July 2 1645

who had earned warm praise for his courage and dash at Auldearn, commanded the reserve, which was still held invisible behind the crest of Gallows Hill.

The battle began in the usual precipitate fashion of Scottish engagements. The Gordons noticed the cloud of dust thrown up around a great herd of cattle behind Baillie's army. Every beast had been driven southwards from the Gordon lands where they had been plundered. Lord Gordon, enraged, called his squadron to the charge. Down the hill they swept towards Balcarres, and the Covenanter's troopers spurred forward to meet them. Within seconds, five hundred milling, thrashing horses and riders were locked in fierce struggle, pistolling each other point blank, hacking at enemy limbs, each man's reins held in a desperate grip with one hand while he struggled for room to wield a sword with the other, kicking the maddened horses deeper and deeper into the throng. In the midst of them fought Lord Gordon and Balcarres, the latter bareheaded after losing his helmet in the first charge. Nat Gordon's musketeers hung bewildered on the fringes of the fight unable to fire into the shifting mass of men, increasingly fearful that the weight of numbers was telling for the Covenanters. Balcarres, who was an energetic if uninspired soldier, somehow broke out of the mêlée and organized a squadron to charge again. Lord Gordon's men were in severe trouble.

Nat Gordon could stand no more. Ordering his men to throw down their muskets and draw their dirks, he led them into the midst of the fighting cavalry. Ruthlessly the Irishes began to hack and hamstring the Covenanters' horses, darting under their bellies, tearing their riders by the belts out of their saddles. It was a tactic that called for enormous courage, leaping on foot amidst the seething horsemen, some men being kicked and trampled underfoot, wounded horses charging crazed through the ranks with half their innards hanging out. But it worked. Balcarres's squadrons wavered, gave ground, then at last broke and galloped away. The Covenanting left had collapsed.

Meanwhile in the centre, Montrose had committed his infantry. The clansmen came streaming down the hill yelling horribly as always as they fell upon the terrified Covenanting levies. Aboyne led his cavalry against Baillie's right. The shock broke them. The Covenanting army dissolved into wisps of flying fugitives, poor pockets of desperate men struggling to hold back the rings of homicidal clansmen at their throats, knots of horsemen riding for their lives, Baillie and his officers amongst them. To their credit, some of the levies fought hard. Montrose's Standard-Bearer was wounded. When the reserve charged to complete the rout of the Covenant, the young pony boys and servants rushed down amongst them in search of loot and glory, and several of them were cut down for their pains, at the very moment of victory. The royalists claimed to have killed 1600 Covenanters at Alford and in the usual long, bloody pursuit that followed it. According to Wishart only two royalist gentlemen and not a single private soldier were killed at the battle, which is unbelievable. It can only be assumed that Montrose's losses were very slight.

Yet in that moment of victory, news suddenly flew from man to man through the army of an incalculable disaster: Lord Gordon, spurring madly into the ranks of the enemy— some said to seize General Baillie himself—had been shot and mortally wounded.

"Conquest and plunder were forgotten as they crowded round his lifeless body, kissing his face and hands, weeping over his wounds, praising the beauty of his person even in death, and extolling a nature as noble and generous as his birth and fortune. They even cursed a victory that was bought so dearly."[4]

Lord Gordon's death bitterly distressed Montrose. He had delighted in the young man's company for the few months that they had ridden side by side. Lord Gordon's confidence in Montrose had been unshakable, his soaring optimism a tonic to the Lord Marquis when frustration and difficulty bore hardest upon him.

"Never two of so short acquaintance did ever love more dearly," wrote Patrick Gordon of Ruthven[5] in his most heroic vein. "There seemed to be a harmonious sympathy in their natural dispositions, so much were they delighted in a mutual conversation. And in this the Lord Gordon seemed to go beyond the limits which Nature had allowed for his carriage in civil conversation. So real was his affection, and so great the estimation he had of the other that, when they fell into any familiar discourse, it was often remarked that the ordinary air of his countenance was changed from a serious listening to a certain ravishment of admiration of the other's witty expressions. And he was often heard in public to speak sincerely, and confirm it with oaths, that if the fortune of the present war should prove at any time so dismal that Montrose, for safety, should be forced to fly into the mountains without any army or any one to assist him, he would live with him as an outlaw, and would prove as faithful a consort to drive away his malour, as he was then a helper to the advancement of his fortune."

The loss of Lord Gordon was not only a bitter personal loss for Montrose, it was also a political disaster. The royalists must now depend upon the fickle Aboyne to recruit and command the men of Clan Gordon who were so vital to the King's cause. The sweet taste of victory at Alford soured for Montrose. At every feast, the gods seemed bent on snatching the cup from his lips.

On the evening of the battle, the royalists marched with the setting sun behind them down the Don to Craigton, where they camped. The next morning Montrose rode to Aberdeen with an escort, bearing the broken body of Lord Gordon. The young man was buried with due ceremony alongside his Campbell mother in the city's cathedral. Montrose took his beloved friend's French servant into his own service. Sombrely, the royalists rode away to their camp. It was fortunate for the spirits of the general and his army that it would be some days before it became fully apparent that the victory at Alford and the death of Lord Gordon had been wholly in vain. Covenanting forces still straddled the road south, to the King.

Montrose remained at Craigton protecting his wounded and awaiting the return of Alasdair Macdonald. He sent Aboyne northwards to recruit, and Black Pate set out once again on his familiar road into Atholl. It was a time of agonizing impatience. The urgency of moving to support the King was acute. With a heavy heart, Montrose learnt of the battle in Northamptonshire on June 14th: Naseby, the little village was called by which it was fought. All the King's infantry and most of his horse had been destroyed by a vastly superior army. The royalist cause was in desperate straits. It might truly be said that the King's Lieutenant-General in Scotland and his Highland army offered the last chance of resurrection. While in England the Parliamentary army swept all before them, Montrose's

victories in Scotland caused the King's enemies to quake.
Robert Baillie wrote in his most apocalyptic manner: "We are
amazed that it should be the pleasure of God to make us fall
thus the fifth time before a Company of the worst men in the
earth." The Scots Commissioners in London lifted their eyes
to heaven in despair: "We pray the Lord to discover the cause
of his great wrath, manifested by the continued heavy judgements of pestilence and sword, and why our forces there have
received defeat upon defeat even these five times from a
despicable and inconsiderable enemy, while the forces of this
nation obtain victory upon victory."

Montrose must have chafed bitterly through these weeks
that he was compelled to squander in idleness. Speed had always
been essential in his campaign to compensate for his weakness
in numbers. Yet Aboyne returned to the camp at Craigton
with only a handful of men, and had to be sent off once more
with cold courtesy to raise more. Each day brought news of the
Covenant's frenzied efforts to recruit a fresh army. Baillie and
most of his horse had escaped south after Alford. Sir John
Hurry was still in the field with some cavalry. Lindsay had the
regiments he had stripped from Baillie. New levies were
coming in from Fife and the Lowlands. All these forces were
concentrating south of the Earn. It slowly became apparent
that yet another battle must be fought before the road to the
Lowlands was open, and the Highlands secure behind the
royalist advance.

Montrose moved slowly south, collecting his scattered
forces as he went. Black Pate joined him with the Athollmen.
Then one fine July morning at Fordoun, in the Mearns half-
way between Montrose and Stonehaven, Alasdair Macdonald
marched triumphantly into the royalist camp at the head of
1500 glorious fighting clansmen. Alasdair had done marvellously to raise such a force in the north-west, justifying all his
weeks of absence. There were 500 men of the Clanranald;
Macleans, Camerons, Appin Stewarts, Macnabs and Mac-
Gregors and MacPhersons. The royalist battle line now boasted
terrible teeth.

But Montrose's army, although swollen to more than 4000
foot, still possessed only 100 horse. It was unthinkable to move
south without an effective cavalry screen. Lacking cavalry
support, the army's movements would be hopelessly slow, as

Covenanting horse skirmished around them. Yet it was also intolerable to drag their heels much longer waiting for reinforcements. Montrose decided on a tactical compromise. He would take the army slowly south, so that they stood poised to strike into the Lowlands the moment the cavalry came up with them. Amidst a flurry of messages to Aboyne to make all speed with his Gordons, the royalists broke camp and moved by Dunkeld, across the Almond, to halt in Methven Wood five miles west of Perth. They were close to their old battleground of Tippermuir, in gentle rolling country that Montrose knew well from his boyhood. He now had word that in the city of Perth, the Scottish Parliament was meeting on July 24th. That august body had been driven first from Edinburgh, then from Stirling by the rising tide of plague that was causing such grief in Scotland that summer. In Perth, they were now being guarded by Sir John Hurry and 400 horse. General Baillie, who was utterly weary of the campaign and had just attempted to resign his command for the second time, was still camped a few miles south at Kilgraston near Bridge of Earn.

Montrose had no desire to attract Hurry's hostile attentions at such a delicate moment of his advance, but something had to be done to keep the Covenanter at arm's length. In Methven Wood, he gathered a detachment of his clansmen, and mounted them on every four-footed beast he could muster from the wagon lines, a wild round-up of ponies and cart-horses of every shape and size. Then he ordered them out to sweep the countryside west of Perth and south of the Earn, raising dust clouds on the horizon that caused agonies of apprehension among the watching Covenanters on the city walls, just as he had planned. For the best part of a week, Hurry's squadrons lay idle in their quarters, fearing to risk any encounter with such a formidable array of royalist horse.

But as the days went by and still Aboyne did not come, inevitably Montrose's bluff collapsed. Hurry's first cautious patrols revealed the royalists' weakness in cavalry. As the Covenanter ordered every man into the saddle to ride on Methven Wood, Montrose reluctantly gathered the army for another retreat northwards. He could not risk being pinned by Hurry while Baillie advanced to attack him. His rearguard held off the Covenanters while the baggage train rolled hurriedly out of the camp. Twenty picked marksmen were

sent forward to snipe at the enemy from cover, and keep them
at a distance during the withdrawal. Hurry's first eager
troopers suffered a bad ten minutes at their hands. But then
the Covenanters were sweeping forward, overrunning the
abandoned royalist camp. By some tragic accident, they fell
on a party of Irish wives and camp followers who were
straggling away northwards in the wake of their men. The
Covenanters hacked down every woman without mercy. It is
not surprising that Macdonald's Irishes were seldom moved to
give quarter. First at Naseby, then at Methven, the King's
enemies had revealed their own barbaric notions of godliness.

Montrose, having withdrawn ten miles northwards to
Little Dunkeld out of reach of Hurry's mischief-makers, was
now compelled to linger for another long week, waiting
helplessly on the coming of Aboyne. It must have been very
hard for him to maintain the morale of his mercurial clansmen
under such conditions. Alasdair had brought them across
Scotland with the promise of plunder and glory, yet so far
they had only rambled aimlessly around eastern Scotland,
fleeing like frightened fishwives from a Covenanting general
the Lord Marquis had defeated once already.

But now, at last, came Aboyne. He rode into the camp at
the head of 200 cavalry and 120 musketeers mounted on ponies,
equipped as dragoons. It was less of a force than Montrose had
hoped for from a clan capable of putting 1500 men in arms,
but it would have to suffice. And as the army prepared to
move once more, there was another delightful reinforcement.
Lord Airlie, at last recovered from his illness, presented himself
to Montrose at the head of 80 horsemen, beside him his son
Sir David Ogilvie, and Alexander Ogilvie of Innerquhartie.
The Lord Marquis was enchanted to see the faithful old
royalist, at a moment when he himself stood so short of constant
friends fit to share his confidences. He now commanded more
than 4000 foot and 500 horse, the largest army he had yet
led into the field. The decisive moment had come. If he was to
meet the King before all was irretrievably lost in England, he
must march for the Lowlands and "put it to the touch".

His army moved south, fording the Almond and the Earn a
few miles west of Perth. From a discreet distance, Montrose
studied Baillie's lines around Bridge of Earn. The Covenanter
had dug himself into a strong position to await reinforcements.

He was expecting three hastily-recruited regiments of Fifeshire
levies to join him. Montrose had no intention of attacking the
Covenanter in his entrenchments. His patrols brushed with
the Covenanting horse, but the main body of the royalist
army had now moved rapidly down Glenfarg to Kinross and
Loch Leven without attempting to engage the enemy.
Montrose may have hoped to encounter the Fife levies on their
way to reinforce Baillie. But having reached Kinross without
intercepting them, he took a vital decision. He would leave
Baillie to pursue him, as he surely would. He himself would
strike directly for the Lowlands, crossing the Forth.

Montrose now knew that the Earl of Lanark had raised
1000 foot and 500 horse among the Hamilton estates in
Clydesdale, and was marching to join Baillie. Further west,
Cassilis and Eglinton, two of the greatest of the Covenanting
lords, were mustering another army. Montrose proposed to
march between all these forces and Baillie. He was also
determined no longer to be diverted from his principal
strategic objective, the descent on the Lowlands.

Baillie's unwillingness to continue in command of the
Covenanting army had resulted, ludicrously, in the appointment of a new committee of sixteen of the lords of the Covenants
to advise him. They were headed by such military wizards as
Argyll, Burleigh, Elcho and Lindsay. Goaded by their nagging,
Baillie abandoned his camp at Kilgraston and hastened down
the road to Kinross in pursuit of Montrose. He was joined on
his march by the Fifeshire levies, raw troops who were now to
be dragged miserably behind his Standard half-way across
Scotland. What his army possessed in numbers, it glaringly
lacked in training and enthusiasm. There had already been a
succession of mutinies in the ranks. When to these were added
the dissensions in command, it was a sullen and unhappy
column that trudged off in pursuit of Montrose. They were
still on their way to Loch Leven when they learnt that he had
already swung westwards and was marching hard for Stirling
and the Forth crossings. The long pursuit began.

It was the fulfilment of all the nightmares of the King's
enemies. Montrose had broken out of the hills in which he had
been contained for so long. He had the bit between his teeth,
all Scotland before him, his ferocious army of plunderers at his
back. The clansmen were entering lands of milk and honey

MONTROSE'S MARCH from
**ALFORD to KILSYTH**
July 2–Aug. 15 1645

that inspired them to ecstasies of greed. At Dollar they burned Castle Campbell—"Castle Gloom", as it was known. Around Alloa they looted and destroyed everything in their path. The Earl of Mar entertained Montrose at Tullibody Castle while the Irish were devastating his estates outside the gate. Lady Elizabeth Erskine, his daughter, was married to young Napier, but the royalist army was in no mood to be restrained from plundering friend or foe.

Montrose skirted Stirling to the north, partly to avoid the plague raging in the city, but partly also to avoid the risk of having his army trapped in an orgy of looting like that at Dundee. Above Stirling, he led his army across the Forth. It must have been an emotional moment for him, this fording of the Rubicon, the final commitment to battle for the Lowlands. If his army now came to grief, there would be no escape, no friendly hills to which to flee. This was the fulfilment, at last, of all his promises to his King. He passed west of the field of Bannockburn and crossed the Carron. On the evening of August 14th, 1645, he pitched camp on a wide meadow northeast of the village of Kilsyth, scarcely a day's march from Glasgow.

Baillie's army lumbered after Montrose, delayed by orders from Argyll to burn the Graham house of Airth and Lord Stirling's castle of Menstrie in revenge for the sack of Castle Gloom. The lords and their general bickered incessantly. With every mile further from their homes, the Fife levies dragged their feet more reluctantly. But Lanark was known to be approaching rapidly with his powerful reinforcements. When the army of the Covenant halted for the night of August 14th, at Hollanbush, four miles east of Montrose's camp at Kilsyth, the Covenanting lords believed that once again, they had brought James Graham within reach of destruction.

There is no reason to suppose that Montrose in fact expected to fight a battle at Kilsyth, because no commanders save the Committee of the Covenant, armoured by their unassailable moral conceit, would have chosen to launch their assault without waiting for the arrival of Lanark. The Earl and his 1500 men were only twelve miles from the royalist camp that night of August 14th. Whatever the excuses of their apologists, it is a mark of the gigantic arrogance of Argyll and his colleagues that when they reached Baillie's camp early on the morning of August 15th, after spending the night amidst the dubious comforts of Stirling, they witheringly dismissed their general's objections and insisted on an immediate advance. Incredibly, even after Tippermuir, Aberdeen, Inverlochy, Auldearn and Alford they still set out to deal with the royalist army as "a despicable and inconsiderable enemy".

When he awoke on the morning of August 15th to learn that the Covenanters were advancing upon him, Montrose's position at Kilsyth was perfectly sound. But instinct suggests that it was not the ground on which he had expected to fight Baillie. An uphill attack has always been a difficult business from Senlac to Cassino, however easy the subsequent victory may make it appear. Montrose merely made the best of his situation with his customary brilliance. Calm and resolved as always, he ordered the army to muster. Then he made his dispositions to fight the battle that made him ruler of Scotland.

# CHAPTER ELEVEN

## The Equipoise of Fortune

ON THE EVENING of July 15th, 1645, as his men wandered the battlefield in the failing light stripping the dead and dirking the dying, the Lord Marquis of Montrose surveyed his victory. Argyll and his creatures had fled the country. Word soon came that Lanark had disbanded his army and ridden for his life as soon as he heard the news of Kilsyth. Leven and the chief army of Scotland were still in England fighting the King. If Montrose was granted just a few short weeks, he believed that he could gather the reins of Scotland into his own hands and recruit an army to smash the dour old mercenary. For the present, there was only the fantastic intoxication of this victory. Now there need be no more skulking in the hills with only the heather for a bed: every palace in Scotland was the Lord Marquis's for the taking. Every armoury and castle, the cities of Edinburgh and Glasgow, the rich recruiting ground of the Lowlands—all these now fell to the King.

The implications for Montrose himself were awe-inspiring. In his younger days he had been a noisy political enthusiast, hot for the Covenant. But he had never commanded real power in Scotland. All through these last months he had been leading an army for the King, but his high-flown Commission as the King's Lieutenant had not been worth the paper on which it was written in dignity or power. It was only his own military genius which had clothed it with some semblance of reality. Yet now his old friend Sir Robert Spottiswoode, the Secretary of State, somehow reached him from Oxford with a new Commission: Captain-General and the King's Lieutenant-Governor of Scotland. This time, the great title had great substance. Montrose was transformed overnight, from an outlaw to the most powerful man in the kingdom, successor to Archibald Campbell, the fugitive Argyll. He could wield political power such as he had never dreamt of: dispense patronage, receive suppliants, appoint justices, order the affairs of Scotland. It is evident, and not surprising, that after Kilsyth the Lord Marquis's sudden great burden of responsibility bore heavily upon him. He had accomplished a military miracle in bringing down the old order. Could he now accomplish the greater one of establishing a new order capable of replacing it?

Two days after Kilsyth, he led the royalist army triumphantly down the road to Glasgow. The trembling citizens opened their gates and the burghers came forth with their steeple hats and nervous smiles to offer tribute of £500 sterling to save themselves from sack. It was a sober moment both for Glasgow and for Montrose. His clan army bayed for the fantastic plunder of the Covenanting city. They were unhesitatingly denied it. The campaign was no longer a business of bringing fire and the sword upon the hosts of the Covenant, but of bringing a nation back to its loyalties. There could be no more looting, no more orgies of destruction. Montrose ruthlessly hanged the first men of his army to try his temper by seeking booty in Glasgow. He ordered the citizens to appoint their own garrison for the King, and then he took his army six miles down the dusty road to Bothwell Brig. There, a safe distance from temptation, he pitched his camp and set about governing Scotland.

Alasdair Macdonald was sent westward to deal with the Covenanters reported to be raising armies against the King. He found that the news of Kilsyth had withered the enemy in their tracks. Cassilis and Glencairn fled to Ireland. Eglinton disbanded his levies. The Irishes returned in self-conscious triumph, bewildered by their new status as servants of the ruling power. Alasdair had been entertained in princely style by the Covenanting Countess of Loudon, the Chancellor's wife herself. Her husband had fled to England. Resourceful as every Scottish chatelaine had to be in the seventeenth century, she set about protecting the family possessions with ruthless gallantry. It was said that she greeted the conquering Macdonald with a kiss. After Alasdair's return to Bothwell, Montrose paraded all his army to honour the most distinguished of his officers. With the authority of his Commission from the King, he dubbed Alasdair a knight before the exulting Irishes. The great bandit, the son of Coll Keitach, had achieved

incongruous respectability. Who could grudge it to the giant
who had held the ridge at Auldearn, who had led the clan
charge at Inverlochy? In his blundering, massive way, he had
done as much as any man in Scotland to bring the King's
army to Bothwell Brig.

From the moment that Montrose reached Glasgow, half the
lairds and lords of Scotland who had rejected him for so long
were riding in procession to make their peace at his table. The
King wrote to announce that Home and Roxburgh would do
all in their power to assist him, and that 1500 horse commanded
by Sir John Belle were on their way to meet him at the Border.
The Douglas, Charteris, Traquair, Fleming, Wigton, Airth,
Carnegie, Maderty, Drummond, Erskine, Seton and Hartfell
were foremost among the suppliants, offering their swords or
purses. The towns and the shires sent representatives to beg the
King's mercy for their citizens who had fallen from their
allegiance under the guidance of evil men. Sure sign of a
change in the wind, that sensitive sailor Sir John Hurry chose
this moment to lay his sword at the feet of the Lord Marquis.
Montrose must have been grateful for the aid of Spottiswoode
in dealing with the army of sycophants and frightened men,
trimmers and traitors who came to stand so sweetly before the
King's Captain. His own officers had to take their turn to see
him now, behind the queue of suppliants and whiners and
place-seekers. Some, who had shared a bivouac in the heather
with the Lord Marquis for so long, were bitter and sullen about
the new, so much more distant relationship. Amidst everything
else, Montrose somehow had to make plans for his drive to the
Border to raise an army and to arrange a junction with the
King. The pressure upon him was immense. As he understood
so well, he had ceased merely to be one servant of the King's
among many. He had become the focus, the chief desperate
hope of the failing royalist cause in England.

But he found time to write the orders for one vital mission:
Nat Gordon and young Napier were sent with two hundred
horsemen to rescue the royalist prisoners still in the dungeons
of the Covenant. First they sped to Linlithgow, where old
Lord Napier and his son-in-law Sir George Stirling of Keir
were being held with their families. There was a joyful family
reunion with the young Master of Napier before the column
mounted again, this time to ride for Edinburgh. It must have

been an extraordinary moment for that adulterous, gay
buccaneer Nat Gordon and for the Napier boy at his side.
They stood before the principal city of Scotland and demanded
that the gates be opened in the name of the King. Opened they
were, and forward came a deputation of the City Fathers to
stand shaking at their stirrups to plead for mercy. With an
ingratiating show of humility, such as came easily to sons of the
Kirk, they explained that they had been seduced from their
duty by evil men.

Gordon and Napier cared little enough for the burghers.
They watched as 150 royalists came blinking and stumbling
out of the Edinburgh tollbooth into the sunlight of the stinking,
plague-ridden city. They were weak with fever, emaciated
with hunger and privation, even half their gaolers dead of
plague. Some were scarcely recognizable at first, but one by
one their rescuers were able to pick out Crawford, Wishart,
Ogilvy, Reay, Drum and Ogilvy of Powrie. Heart-breakingly,
young Lord Graham was not amongst them. He was held in
the castle above, where the garrison still kept the walls for the
Covenant. The freed prisoners went to join Montrose as soon
as they were fit. Ogilvy, who had been among the sickest,
amazed them all by the speed of his recovery. Within a
month of his release, he was recruiting on the Borders for
Montrose.

As the Lord Marquis strove to secure his base before marching southwards, he faced the unpalatable reality that his men
were everywhere being received, not as liberators, but merely
as conquerors. Terror of his wild army secured a measure of
obedience to his commands, but this was no basis for a political
settlement. The old poet Drummond of Hawthornden had
offered him some essays he had written in vindication of
monarchy. Montrose wrote begging him to send them at once.
He must fight a vigorous propaganda campaign to undo the
ghastly image of himself and his band of excommunicate
outlaws created by the ministers in the minds of most of
Scotland. He prepared and published a personal Remonstrance, drafted for him by old Lord Napier. He was now as he
always had been, a staunch supporter of the true Covenant,
he proclaimed. He had broken with the Covenanting government of Scotland only because of their political greed and
pretension.

Traitors we are not, to God, or King, or country [he declared]. Not to God, because we stand or fall by God's assistance, for the reformed religion. . . . Traitors to the King we are not, for we go about His Majesty's expedition according to his express mandate. . . . Traitors to our country we are not but we endeavour the liberties thereof. . . . And as for the shedding of blood—we would by all means shun the same; neither ever did we shed the blood of any but of such as were sent forth to shed our blood, and to take our lives, whose blood we shed in our defence.

It was a proclamation entirely characteristic of Montrose: decent, honest, moderate, reasonable. But his efforts were hopeless. He had been excommunicated by the Kirk. The tale of the sack of Aberdeen had been broadcast and multiplied a hundred-fold across Lowland Scotland. His Irishes were the army of the damned. However humble the surrender of so many peers and lairds and burghers and merchants, the terrible power of the ministers remained unbroken, and all of it was directed against James Graham. If his vision of a new Scotland was ever fulfilled, their tyranny would be ended, as well they knew. Their influence over their congregations was enormous, and they used it unstintingly. Men as yet might be afraid to lift their hands against Montrose and his royalist army. But pitifully few of them were willing to join him. An overwhelming majority waited, nursing their hatred, to see his downfall.

Montrose had believed with his usual all-conquering optimism that after Kilsyth the people of Scotland must quickly see the light, cast off the chains of bigotry and declare for the King. He had shown that Argyll was a paper tiger. He had achieved power at a moment when the empty promises of the Solemn League and Covenant had already been exposed. Yet now he was floundering, making no political ground when he needed to secure his rear with desperate urgency before moving south. It must have been a deeply frustrating experience for him, to discover in those weeks of August and early September that victory on the battlefield is easily won compared with that in the closet and the conference chamber. In this it is interesting to compare Montrose with the great captains of later centuries. Marlborough might have looked back at the

Lord Marquis with some cynicism, conscious that he himself possessed the political experience and diplomatic genius that the Graham so signally lacked. Yet even Marlborough was broken, in the end, by political failure. Wellington proved a political disaster when he left off commanding armies. Cromwell, in Montrose's own generation, was able to rule England only by the power of his regiments. He created a military dictatorship rather than a political edifice. Much has been made of Montrose's naïveté and political innocence. Yet it is difficult to think of any great soldier in modern British history who has shown complementary success in politics. It was part of Montrose's tragedy that having done his part brilliantly, having achieved the impossible of generalship, he was at once called upon to attempt a parallel feat of statesmanship. Inevitably he failed.

Even as he sat at his desk surrounded by petitions, dispatches, plans, letters—trying to secure his grasp on the machinery of government of Scotland when he had scarcely a handful of reliable officers, never mind an army of loyal administrators—Scotland was slipping away from him. First, the clansmen who had carved his path to Bothwell Brig began to desert in their hundreds. Every day while he talked in his headquarters, troops of Highlanders impatient of a campaign which offered no more booty but had yet to offer any pay, gathered such loot as they had won and began the long walk homewards. The Athollmen had gone, and the Macleans, making their usual vague promises of return when they had attended to their affairs at home. The Lowlands were alien territory to them, and all their instincts recoiled at the talk of a march into England. They hungered for their hills. All the proclamations about the King and the Government of Scotland were as dust to them. Only their glens and their cattle and plunder and war and deer and the snows were real. They saluted Montrose, who had given the Gael a day on the battlefield such as the bards would sing of for a thousand years, and they slipped away.

Then, incredibly, Sir Alasdair Macdonald announced that he was taking all of his Irishes who would follow him, to renew his war against Clan Campbell for possession of Kintyre. Montrose was appalled. Alone among his army, the Irishes had been a constant factor. They had been the spearhead, honed by bloody experience, to which the shaft of the Highland clans had been affixed. Montrose begged Alasdair to remain, told him how much depended upon him and his men, promised the earth when the war was won. But to that slow-witted, narrow-minded, bloodthirsty, obstinate Macdonald none of this mattered. Perhaps his jealousy had been aroused by Montrose's easy command over his clansmen. Perhaps he was so drunk on the great chain of victories that he had begun to imagine that he might win such battles for himself. Certainly he cared nothing for the King's cause unless the fight for it happened to coincide with the interests of his clan. Alasdair dishonoured himself by his defection, exposed his small mind and petty ideas and trivial loyalties to the eye of history. Had he remained, he could have died for a cause, a royalist, like Magnus O'Cahan and the 500 of his men who chose to stay with Montrose rather than wander away to Kintyre. O'Cahan and his regiment may have begun the campaign as plundering outlaws, but they chose of their free will to end it as loyal soldiers of the King. Alasdair, instead, blundered away across Kintyre until at last the avenging Campbells had their day. He was driven out. His father and most of his warriors were executed with the utmost brutality after surrendering. He himself was saved to die in November 1647 in a wretchedly obscure little Irish battle, shot down by Inchiquin's troopers, some say after yielding on quarter. Perhaps it was a fitting end for Montrose's major-general. He had spurned the chance of a better.

On September 4th, 1645, Montrose broke camp at Bothwell. His army was already shrunk to half the force that had fought at Kilsyth, perhaps 2000 men. Those of his Highlanders who remained still sulked about the lack of loot. Even the £500 Montrose had received from the city of Glasgow had now been given back to the burghers. He had summoned the Parliament of Scotland to meet in the city on October 20th, and the money was needed to cover its expenses. Among the gentlemen of the army, there was deep restlessness. Argyll's spies had been moving unceasingly through the lines at Bothwell, dealing out promises, threats and bribes, fostering the tensions that were already sadly apparent.

Even for the most devoted followers, it had been a chastening experience to see the gulf widen between themselves and their general after Kilsyth. The affairs of state consumed his days. He received and made much of newly-won converts to the King's cause who would have seen them all hanged a month earlier. There was now little time for the long talks beside the fire in some cottage commandeered as a headquarters, nor for the jokes with the clansmen, and the morning rides. Some of his shrewder officers, such as Nat Gordon, understood the strains on the Lord Marquis. But others, above all the chronically jealous Aboyne, did not. Aboyne professed to be bitterly wounded by a pamphlet written by Sir William Rollo, which he considered did less than justice to the Gordon role in the campaign. He protested to Montrose, who made soothing noises but declined to repudiate the pamphlet. Probably, fatally, among all his other responsibilities Montrose found it exasperating to be bothered with so trivial a matter, and brushed it aside too lightly. Aboyne's resentment redoubled when Crawford, newly released from Edinburgh Tollbooth, was given command of the cavalry instead of himself.

There seems to have been some friction between the group of Montrose's officers who had ridden with him through the Highland campaign, and the band of old friends and comrades fresh from the horrors of the Tollbooth, who now took their places by his side. Aboyne, especially, was enraged that Ogilvy seemed to be usurping his place beside Montrose, although it is hard to believe that Montrose had ever confided deeply in the Gordon. It is a mark of Ogilvy's exceptional modesty and discretion that he noticed the danger and wrote to Aboyne: "Argyll leaves no wind unfurled to sow dissension among you and draw your lordship off . . . notwithstanding of any oaths or promise that he will seem to make to you [he] does intend nothing but your dishonour. . . . I know your Lordship's gallantry to be such that I will not presume to go further faithfully than render up my commission to you."

It was all useless. Aboyne was prey to appalling pettiness and temperament, without even the excuse of Alasdair's rude origins. He cared nothing for the fate of kings if his own pleasure was denied. On September 5th he left the army at Calderhouse and rode away north, declaring that his father, who had at last returned from exile in Strathnaver, had summoned him home. All the Gordons, including most seriously their cavalry, went with this spoilt wastrel. Montrose's army was reduced to 700 foot and 200 mounted gentlemen, most of these last being newly-joined recruits and newly-declared royalists. Nat Gordon, Lord Airlie and Sir William Rollo remained. Each was worth several regiments. But the spell of Kilsyth had been broken. Already, victory and the government of Scotland were fading into nothingness before the eyes of the unhappy royalists. The magic had lasted scarcely two months. The tragedy had begun.

Montrose and his sadly shrunken army were at Cranstoun Kirk just south-east of Dalkeith on September 6th, when they received word that David Leslie was at Berwick with a Covenanting army. It was a terrible blow. Leslie, Leven's cavalry commander, was a tough, capable officer. He was leading the pick of the Scottish army, hardened by years of battle in England, trotting northwards to save their homeland from Montrose and his company of the ungodly. They moved fast, 5000 horse and 1000 foot, perfectly ordered ranks of steel, each man fully helmeted and armoured: Eglinton's Horse, Fraser's and Kirkcudbright's Dragoons, Middleton's Regiment and several brigades more behind these. Middleton, that same Middleton who had fought with Montrose on the Bridge of Dee an age ago, was riding north now with murder in his heart. His aged father had been cut down in his own home by Alasdair's Irishes not six months since. At Berwick, Leslie's column was joined by Argyll, Lindsay and Lanark, each man nursing his private rage against Montrose and the humiliations he had brought upon him. The Covenanters were coming north in search of a terrible reckoning. Montrose was ill-prepared to receive them.

It was the Scottish royalists' misfortune that while the King in England now counted on Montrose to save his throne, he lacked the strategic perception and unselfishness to make his Captain's task possible. As his fortunes flagged, so his projects became increasingly fantastic and irrelevant. Digby was already persuading himself and his royal master that Montrose and the Covenanters might soon unite against the armies of Parliament. Prince Rupert, with his superb strategic judgement, had been in disgrace since Naseby and now stood accused by the King, incredibly, of betraying Bristol. The one useful task of which the King's army was still capable was that of preventing any portion of Leven's army from returning north, as it was certain to attempt to do. Afterwards the Covenanters freely admitted that there was a moment, at Rotherham, when Leslie's army halted exhausted on their forced march northwards to face Montrose. They were within reach of the royalist army and might easily have been attacked. Montrose could have used every day free of Leven and Leslie to "fix" his victory in Scotland. Yet it never seems to have occurred to the King and his advisers to assist him in winning it. They seemed to function as if Montrose's campaign, splendid though it might be, was part of some entirely separate war from their own. Sir John Belle's 1500 horse had, of course, already disappeared back into the mists of fantasy from which they had sprung. Montrose, at Cranstoun Kirk, knew that he must seek his own salvation.

Many of the officers around him urged immediate retreat northwards as soon as they heard of Leslie's coming. In the Highlands he might make his peace with the Gordons, recruit the clans once more, gather Alasdair back into the fold, then march in his own time to tackle Leslie. But the Lord Marquis

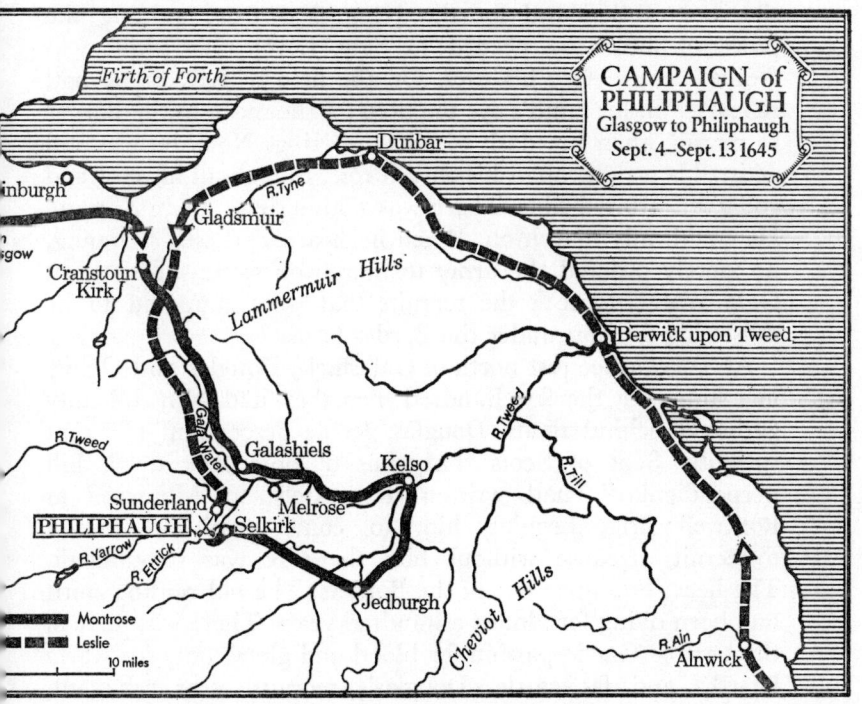

himself perfectly understood that this was impossible. When he began his campaign just over a year before, the King's cause had been ailing. It seemed that there might just be time to save it. Now, the King's situation was desperate. There was quite simply no more time to spare. If Montrose retired now, by the time he emerged from the hills again, there would no longer be a royalist cause for which to fight.

And even with his incurable optimism, he would have been more than human had he not doubted whether he could do it all again. Herculean efforts and staggering good luck had generated the momentum to win Scotland. If he fell back now, it was asking too much of Providence to offer him another Tippermuir, another Auldearn. Some say that after Kilsyth he became impossibly over-confident. It seems more likely that by the time he reached Cranstoun Kirk he was riding through his pre-ordained part in his great drama with a kind of courageous madness. He must have come to understand, through the weeks of July and August, that he had failed to win the soul of Scotland for the King. Far from gaining the powerful forces he needed to fight Leven, his army was fading away before his eyes. On the field of Kilsyth he had rehearsed in his mind's eye the plan for the move to the Border to recruit, then the dash to join the King. Now, he was still acting his way through his chosen role, though all his cast had collapsed around him. There was nothing else for him to do. He could only march on. When he heard of Leslie's coming, he merely ordered the army to march on southwards, down Gala Water, to seek the recruits that were supposed to be mustering for him under the Border lords.

At Torwordlee just north of Galashiels, Douglas and Ogilvy met him with the few hundred men they had with difficulty gathered behind them. Douglas, feeble descendant of "that sprightly Scot of Scots that runs o' horseback up a hill perpendicular", had written desperately to Montrose at Bothwell Brig, begging him to come south in person to recruit, because without him the task was so difficult. The heart had gone out of the Borders. The old raiding spirit had been dying for almost a hundred years. There was none of the terrible Gaelic passion for blood and glory, only for warm hearths and fat cattle. Douglas's recruits were reluctant, untrained, unhappy. They deserted in a steady, sordid trickle from the rear of the royalist column. At Galashiels Lord Linton, Traquair's son, arrived to join them with a well-armed troop of horse, but it would be time enough to be sure of the Traquair family's loyalty when the shooting started. Around September 8th, Montrose moved twenty miles eastwards across country to Kelso, where he had arranged to rendezvous with Home and Roxburgh. Even at a time of many gloomy tidings, the Kelso news was among the worst. The two lords had been taken by the Covenanters the previous day.

It was said that they had arranged their own capture by Middleton's men with cynical cunning, putting themselves safe amongst the Covenanters without publicly betraying their loyalty to the King. Wearily the royalists turned south to Jedburgh. They had gained not a man, and were losing many. This was fanatical Covenanting country, where old women spat at the passing column, and one old hag boiling a sheep's head cried boldly that she wished it was that of Montrose, and if it was she would hold the lid of her pot on. There was a slim chance of finding men in Annandale, on the Douglas estates. Once again the column moved northwards. On the evening of September 12th, they pitched camp at Philiphaugh, across the Ettrick river from the village of Selkirk, in times gone by famous for producing the finest archers in Scotland.

Sir Robert Spottiswoode carried in his pocket the letter he had just written to Digby, vividly describing their predicament:

You little imagine the difficulties my Lord Marquis hath here to wrestle with. The overcoming of the enemy is the least of them; he hath more to do with his own seeming, friends. . . . He was forced to dismiss his highlanders for a season who would needs return home to look to their own affairs. When they were gone, Aboyne took a caprice and had away with him the greatest strength he had in horse. Notwithstanding whereof he resolved to follow his work and clear this part of the Kingdom of the rebels that had fled to Berwick, and kept a bustling there. Beside he was invited here unto by the Earls of Roxburgh and Home; who, when he was within a dozen miles of them, have rendered their houses and themselves to David Leslie, and are carried in as prisoners to Berwick. Traquair has been with him and promised more than he hath yet performed. All these were great disheartenings to any other but to him, whom nothing of this kind can amaze. With the small forces he has presently with him, he is resolved, to pursue David Leslie, and not suffer him to grow stronger. . . .*

For all Spottiswoode's brave words about pursuing Leslie, it was evident to Montrose at Selkirk that his own position was now desperate. In the Highlands his clansmen had been as fish in water, fighting in their element, in conditions ideal for guerilla warfare. They had never been able to hold any town they seized, but they had exposed all northern Scotland to their raids and forced the Covenant to send armies against them in their own country. And whatever their fickleness and temper, the clansmen had never betrayed Montrose and his cause.

Now, however, he stood in the midst of enemy country with an army of which only a few companies could be trusted. If it had been possible for him to win his war in the Highlands, then his victory would have been assured. His misfortune was that it had been essential for him to descend from the hills, to carry his campaign into the Lowlands with their hostile population. The time had come to turn his troops from guerillas into a conventional army, and he could not do it. There were too few of them, they were ill-equipped and lacked cavalry and proper artillery. He himself was qualified to command any army in the world under any conditions. But he was now being forced to fight in circumstances from which the Gods and Heroes themselves would have flinched.

He must have yearned for the clean air and exalted spirit of the hills as he led his dejected column through the grim, hostile villages of the Borders. It was as if his crusade had somehow been corrupted by contact with the dour, intriguing, treacherous Lowlands and their politics. It was as if he was beginning again where he had begun before Marston Moor, leading a ragtail army shambling vainly on a mission to nowhere. It was as if his great victories had never been. The fire was ebbing from him, the glitter in his eye that signalled a brilliant plan, a sudden dash, a prospect of impossible glory. That evening at Selkirk, he retired to his quarters overlooking the camp in the valley, leaving instructions that he was not to

* The letter was still in his pocket when he was captured the next day.

be disturbed. He had dispatches to write to the King. As he closed his door that night, he had cast aside every tactical precept of his own campaign, every vital rule of soldiering.

Montrose's army had achieved its brilliant successes largely through superb scouting and intelligence work. Only once had his intelligence seriously failed him, at Fyvie, and it nearly led to his undoing. At Selkirk he knew that David Leslie was somewhere in the offing, yet he did not trouble to arrange his own pickets, and he certainly failed to ensure that reliable men carried out the vital duty. Captain Blackadder, his scout-master, appears to have chosen local recruits on the grounds that they knew the country. So they did, but they knew nothing of soldiering, and their loyalty was very doubtful.

It was yet another precept of that cynical old soldier Sir James Turner[1] that a good general must endeavour "to trust but few and yet seem to trust all; he should have a wary eye (without seeming jealous) on all the inhabitants of the place, upon the officers and soldiers of his garrison, especially on such as are known to be revengeful, discontented or of avaricious inclination".

Tradition has it that it was Traquair who sent word to Leslie at Gladsmuir of Montrose's movements. It was in keeping with his family's fine record of treachery. Leslie had marched northwards along the east coast from Berwick, and was intending to move on westwards, reasserting the Covenant's mastery over the Lowlands and cutting off Montrose from the Highlands. Now, hearing that the royalists were somewhere around Jedburgh or Selkirk, he crisply changed his plans. At the head of his army, he sped down Gala Water, on the road Montrose had marched a week before, to seek out and destroy the enemy. Leslie knew that the royalist force was very small, and he had complete confidence in his men. They forded the Tweed late on September 12th, and halted around Sunderland Hall for the night. They were three miles from Selkirk, and they were now perfectly informed of Montrose's dispositions at Philiphaugh. Some time during the night, Lord Linton gathered his troop of horse and rode quietly out of the royalist lines. The stage was set.[2]

Montrose's pickets should have given him ample warning of Leslie's advance. In the middle of the night a troop of cavalry posted in Sunderland under Charteris of Amisfield was

K

suddenly attacked and driven out with loss. Charteris escaped, but when he reported to the Captain-General's headquarters, his news was dismissed, as a matter of some brush with hostile villagers. Montrose himself was not woken. Early the following morning, scouts rode out at first light. They returned to report that there was no sign of the enemy within ten miles. It was a brisk autumn morning, and mist lay heavy in the hollows. It would be charitable to assume that the patrols of local levies were too inexperienced and unobservant to do their job properly. But all the circumstances suggest that there was treachery before Philiphaugh. Traquair or some other traitor among the royalists had certainly sent word to Leslie at Glads-muir. It is highly probable that he would have continued his betrayal by arranging the bungling of the pickets.

Montrose's foot were camped on a soft green meadow beside the Ettrick, with the Yarrow burn behind them and steep hills rising on their left flank, perhaps a quarter of a mile from the waterside. It was a comfortable, sheltered bivouac. Early on the morning of September 13th the men were cooking breakfast amidst the dull clatter of cooking pots and the echo of muffled voices in the still air. The gentle wood smoke rose from a hundred fires. The Irishwomen slipped to and fro along the riverside filling the pans for their men's meal. Trenches had been dutifully dug to shield the perimeter of the camp as usual, and the cannon taken at Kilsyth were mounted covering the approaches. The horse lines were across the river, below Selkirk village where the cavalry were mostly quartered. It is extraordinary, treachery or no treachery, that Montrose's army did not hear Leslie's army advancing down the Ettrick to attack them early that morning, for 6000 armed and mounted men in that valley must have made noise enough to waken the dead. Yet they were not heard. It was not until the first squadrons of the Covenanting horse were already thundering down on Philiphaugh, swords drawn, that Captain Blackadder burst upon the Lord Marquis's breakfast of boiled sheep's head to report that Leslie was upon them.

Buchan and other writers have tried to suggest that Philiphaugh somehow does not count among Montrose's battles, that it was a surprise in which the odds were impossible for anything but disaster. Yet Montrose seems to deserve much greater blame, and David Leslie much greater credit than

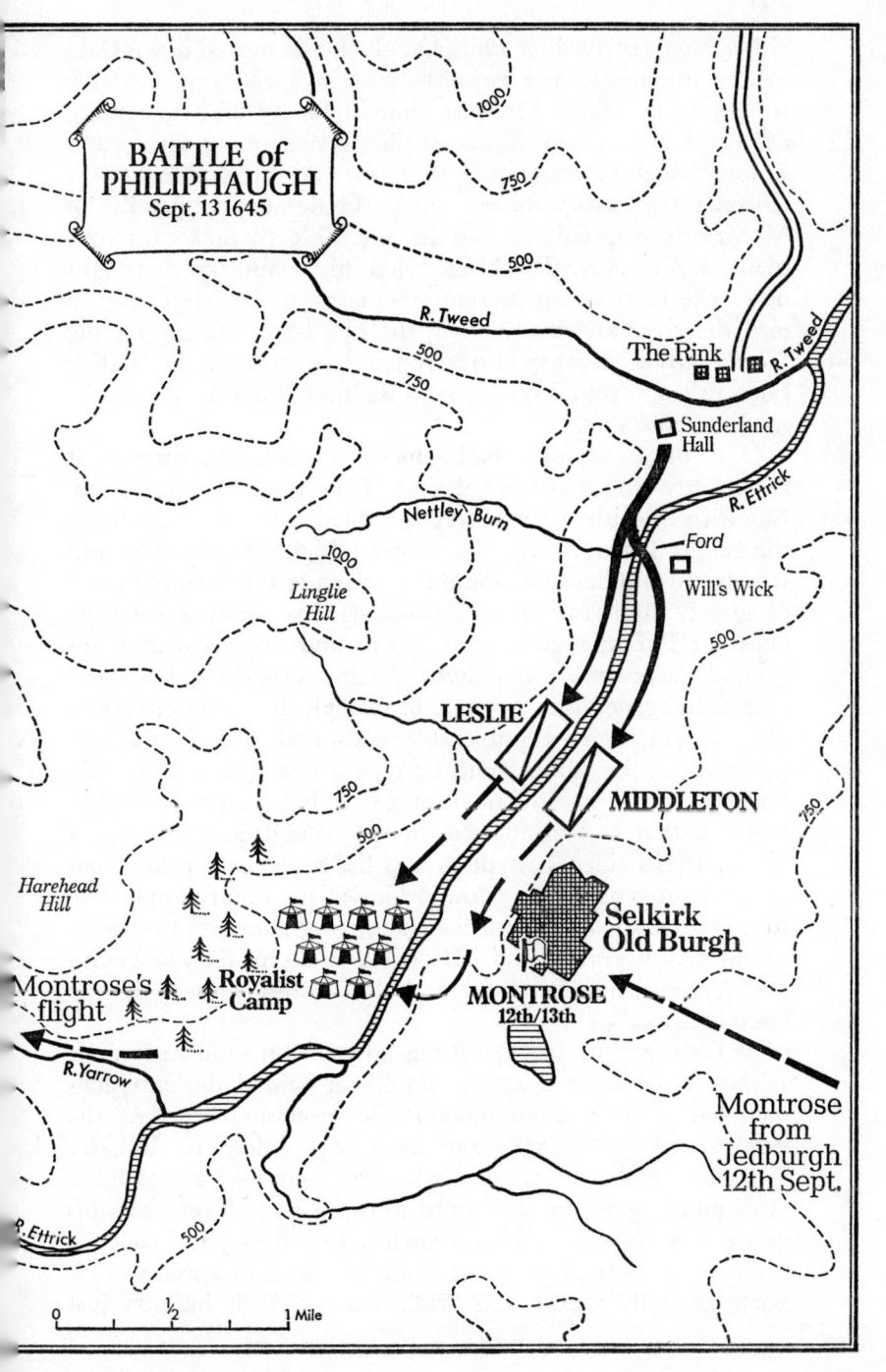

**BATTLE of PHILIPHAUGH**
Sept. 13 1645

1000
750
500

R. Tweed

500

The Rink

R. Tweed

500

R. Tweed

Sunderland Hall

R. Ettrick

Nettley Burn

Ford

Will's Wick

1000

Linglie Hill

500

LESLIE

MIDDLETON

750

500

750

Harehead Hill

Selkirk Old Burgh

Royalist Camp

MONTROSE 12th/13th

Montrose's flight

R. Yarrow

Montrose from Jedburgh 12th Sept.

R. Ettrick

500

0        ½        1 Mile

either have received for Philiphaugh. Leslie moved down Gala Water to engage the royalists with a speed and decision worthy of the Lord Marquis himself. Plenty of Covenanting officers had pursued Montrose in overwhelming force, and simply failed to bring him to battle. At Sunderland, local Covenanting sympathizers gave Leslie exact details of Montrose's dispositions, and he was able to make his own plans accordingly. He himself led his main body straight down the Ettrick, but he sent 2000 horse under Middleton to ford the river and move along the east bank, cutting off the enemy retreat. He may also have sent some men up the Nettley burn to come round on the royalists from Linglie Hill. Leslie made no mistakes.

Once the Covenanter had achieved his stunning surprise, it is perfectly true that the outcome of the battle was ordained. But with or without treachery it is incredible that Montrose, the genius of Inverlochy, the master of lightning marches and wondrous thunderbolts, should have made the cardinal error of grossly underrating his opponent. The position that he chose at Philiphaugh was no better and no worse than his ground, for example at Kilsyth. Against reasonable odds and with skilful generalship, it could be strongly defended. However, like Kilsyth, against intolerable odds and with inadequate generalship, the camp could become a death trap. The only possible conclusion about Montrose's behaviour at Philiphaugh is that he had allowed the strains and disappointments of the weeks since Kilsyth to sap his acute perceptions and military judgement. He allowed himself the luxury impossible to a general in the face of the enemy of giving way to gloom, tiredness and even despair. He failed to do his duty as a commander, and now his army and the royalist cause paid the terrible price.

As Leslie's glittering squadrons advanced up the valley, the Irishes seized their weapons and fell in behind the entrenchments with their usual indomitable professionalism. As the first ragged volleys rang out from both sides, the Douglas levies bolted for the woods, flying for their lives abandoning arms and possessions. The Lord Marquis himself ran from his quarters in Selkirk, hurled himself onto a horse, and rode for the river like a man possessed. Somehow he and as many of his horse as could saddle and bridle reached their infantry just before Middleton's advance cut off the camp from the village. Now there was no need of generalship, no plan to seize upon. Montrose drew his sword and spurred his horse at Leslie's cavalry, to fight as he had never fought in seven victories, to slash and stab beneath the Royal Standard for the honour of the Grahams and the salvation of his poor army. Guilt and dismay brought a madness to his courage, as he rallied 150 of his horse and led them flying at the Covenanters, sending the enemy reeling for a moment as horses and men crashed upon them. The Irishes counter-attacked in two great charges before they were driven back inch by inch upon their tents, men dropping everywhere as Middleton's dragoons enfiladed them from the east with their ruthless, galling musketry. Covenanters were now fording the Ettrick and forming up on the west bank covered by their comrades' fire. The enemy were 6000. Montrose's army was scarcely a tenth of that force. Leslie's unbroken front of steel bore in upon the royalists' shrinking perimeter, swords clashing, musketry rippling along the line. Now, for the Covenanters, it was becoming a matter of mere methodical butchery. Somehow Montrose's officers dragged him by main force from the mass of seething swordsmen. They implored him to ride for safety while there was still time. The army could be replaced. The King's Captain-General could never be. For a few wild moments he dallied with a last, death dash upon the pikes of the Covenant. Perhaps he remembered Dundee and that miracle. But no, this was a thousand times worse than Dundee. He looked down on the line of Irishes, still cutting and slashing, shoulder to shoulder, giving ground with grudging fury amidst the great tide of Covenanters around them. Perhaps he saw Magnus O'Cahan at their head, and caught the doomed eye of that gallant officer for the last time. Then he swung his horse and galloped away up that Yarrow burn, the last fifty of his cavalry behind him.

Up the soft wooded valley of the Yarrow they rode, then they swung north up the steep bare hill onto Minchmuir, heading north-west. They turned for a moment to close with a handful of Covenanting horse who had pursued them, cut them down, and then rode hard for Traquair. They halted the lathered horses outside the Earl's house, and sent in to ask last week's royalist for urgent help and fresh mounts. There was no answer. Traquair skulked in the shadows behind his thick walls until the unhappy horsemen hastened on empty-handed. Somewhere beyond Peebles—perhaps at Biggar, Buchan suggests—Montrose and his men halted for the night. But there was nothing now for any of them in the Lowlands of Scotland. There could be no safe refuge until they had crossed the Highland line once more. Montrose must have named a rendezvous with his officers, for the next morning after he had forded the Clyde, he met the faithful Airlie and the Douglas, still leading 200 horse between them. Gathering up more fugitives as they went, they hastened on across the Forth, across the Earn. On September 19th, they halted at last, at Buchanty. They had come full circle. Barely a year before, Kilpont and his bowmen had come joyfully down the hill to join the army as they marched to the field of Tippermuir. Now Montrose sat desolate beside the Almond, contemplating the ruin of his dreams and the tragedy of some of his dearest friends.

On the field of Philiphaugh after the horse rode away, the Irishes fought with stubborn, snarling courage for an hour more, their dead piling bloody around their feet, their warriors weakening from the pike thrusts and the sword cuts, their women already in the hands of the Covenanters plundering the baggage. It was an utterly hopeless position. When Leslie cried to Stewart, the army adjutant and senior officer, to offer quarter, the survivors wearily, bitterly accepted. The Irishes, who had proved themselves among the finest fighters in Europe, threw down their arms and stood nursing their hopeless rage amidst their captors. As the last fighting died away, they could see at last what was being done to their families and to the baggage boys.

The Covenanters had never been able to bring themselves to regard Irishes or Catholics as human, nor the women and children that went with them. Among the great flock of camp-followers behind the royalist lines at Philiphaugh there were Highland girls carried off from Aberdeen, pony boys who had marched with the clans, cooks recruited in the Lowlands. Now, in a terrible moment of butchery, Leslie's men slaughtered 500 of them where they stood or cowered, screaming or begging for mercy, clutching their babies or running for their lives. They were stabbed or shot without pity until the green meadow was blotted with ghastly puddles of blood and the Ettrick's course was hideously stained with the vengeance of the Covenant. Eighty more women and children were marched northwards to Linlithgow where they were thrown over the bridge into the Avon. Those that did not drown were run through by lines of pikemen waiting on the bank to defeat their struggles to save themselves.

On the field of Philiphaugh, David Leslie was beset by the enraged ministers of the Kirk accompanying the army. His offer of quarter to the Irishes threatened to cheat them of their cherished prey, of the righteous vengeance of the Lord upon hosts of the ungodly. Surely, they argued with oiled cunning, mercy had been granted only to Stewart, not to his men? Leslie, on this first occasion among many that were to blacken his military career, yielded to their whining imprecations. The surrendered Irishes, clutching their ragged bandages and limping from their wounds, cursing the Covenant for the fate of their women and muttering their own preparations to face Judgement, were marched up the valley to the castle—

> where Newark's stately tower looks out
> from Yarrow's birchen bower.[3]

There in the courtyard they were shot in batches and their bodies dragged out to be thrown into a massive grave dug below the walls. The spot passed into history as Slain Man's Lee. All that can be said about the fate of that band is that despite their courage and fidelity, they had never been forward in offering quarter to their defeated enemies. They could not be truly surprised to find it denied to themselves, especially when a man like Middleton, whose family had suffered so brutally at their hands, now stood in the ranks of their executioners. True pity and outraged sensibility must be saved for the Irishes' wretched wives and children and camp-followers.

Enough has already emerged in these pages about the nature of the Covenant and of the ministers of the Kirk for the vigour of their vengeance to cause no surprise. Magnus O'Cahan and Colonel Lachlan were hanged without trial from the south wall of Edinburgh Castle. Any soldier in history would be happy to salute those Irish officers who led their men so gloriously to the bitter end.

Among the distinguished prisoners taken at Philiphaugh, Sir John Hay bribed Lanark to buy his freedom. Hartfell and young Drummond were spared. One of the most extraordinary stories to attach to the legend of Montrose is that of Lord Ogilvy. The unlucky officer had his horse badly wounded at Philiphaugh. It foundered a few miles from the battlefield as he rode for safety, and he was betrayed by a cottager with whom he took refuge. There was never any doubt about the penalty for him. He was condemned to death. But on the night before his execution, he was visited by his wife, mother and sister in his cell at St Andrews. The girls of those days were tigers compared with the modern siblings of Women's Lib. His sister got into his bed while Ogilvy hastily pulled on her dress and bonnet. When the gaoler let the weeping family party out of prison, he shuffled away, face muffled by sobs in his handkerchief, to ride free to join the Lord Marquis. Even Argyll was unable to avenge himself on the girl as he would have wished, on hearing the news of the escape. There was one other successful flight: Stewart the adjutant, who quickly perceived that his turn at the Maiden would soon come. He slipped his captors and eventually reached Montrose once again.

But these were the lucky few. Archibald Johnston of Warriston, chief fanatic of the Covenant, led the great howl for royalist blood that followed Philiphaugh. Mercy, he argued with impassioned eloquence before the Estates, would be a violation of the sacred oath of the Covenant and would bring the wrath of God once more upon the land. The executioners were already at work. At the end of October, Sir William Rollo, Sir Philip Nisbit and Alexander Ogilvy of Innerquhartie were hanged at the Market Cross in Glasgow. Rollo's death was a special tragedy. He had been with Montrose from the beginning, scorning his own lameness, riding beside him through the whole of the great campaign. David Dickson, that ardent apostle of the Covenant, passed into legend that day when he rubbed his hands below the scaffold, cackling horribly: "The work gangs bonnily on." On January 26th, 1646, "the work" began again. Sir Robert Spottiswoode, who had never borne arms in his life, was murdered under the Maiden. He had only joined Montrose after Kilsyth. It was impossible to associate him with even the mildest excesses of the royalist army. As the duly appointed Secretary of State for Scotland, his only crime had been to carry to Montrose his royal commission as Lieutenant-Governor. Andrew Guthry and Nat Gordon, the gallant Colonel, died with him. Gordon seems to have exhausted every trick in his large repertoire to save his neck from the block. At his trial, accused of denying mercy to Covenanting soldiers in battle, he gave evidence that he had given quarter to Captain Nat Moncrieff, Ensign Brown, and Lieutenant Dunbar. After he was condemned, he signed a solemn declaration repenting his adulterous, drunken and misspent life. He was a trier to the end, and Montrose and his staff must have smiled sadly to hear of his subterfuges. No doubt he would cheerfully have entered a monastery had he believed that it would serve to keep his head on his shoulders. But the ministers may have detected the unwholesome gleam in his eye as he fell on his knees before them. He might have saved his breath and his dignity. The Covenanters would as soon have given mercy to a wild dog as to one of Montrose's most distinguished colonels. Poor Nat Gordon, he was one of the most colourful and faithful of the Lord Marquis's band of brothers. The day after his death, nineteen-year-old William Murray, Tullibardine's younger brother, was also executed.

Spottiswoode left a last letter for Montrose, recommending his children to the care of his general and dear friend, and nobly pleading that the Lord Marquis pursue the cause for which he died "by fair and gentle carriage to gain the people's affection for their prince, rather than to imitate the barbarous inhumanity of your adversaries".

It was the end of a terrible chapter. Henceforth, the last of the gaiety was gone from the royalist struggle for Scotland. The last traces of civility, the King's absurd notions of reconciliation between Montrose and the Covenanters had been savagely exposed. The battle between Montrose and the tyranny of Argyll and the Kirk could end only in his death or their destruction.

> Unhappy is the man, in whose
>         breast is confined
> The sorrows and distresses all of an
>         afflicted mind;

The extremity is great—he dies if
　　he conceal—
The world's so void of secret
　　friends—betrayed if he reveal.
Then break, afflicted heart, and
　　live not in these days,
When all prove merchants of their
　　faith none trusts what other says.
For when the sun doth shine, then
　　shadows do appear,
But when the sun doth hide his face
　　they with the sun retire;
Some friends as shadows are, and
　　fortune as the sun—
They never proffer any help till
　　fortune hath begun;
But if in any case fortune shall
　　first decay,
Then they, as shadows of the sun,
　　with fortune pass away.

Montrose, "On Faithless Friends".

# CHAPTER TWELVE

## *"This at first may startle you"*

---

MONTROSE DID NOT waste a moment mourning dead friends
or lost opportunities beside the Almond. The death of 500
Irishes and the flight of as many Douglas levies were tragic but
by no means fatal, he believed. All through that three-day
ride north from the field of Philiphaugh, he had been weighing
prospects, planning, thinking furiously.

Many of his finest officers were still around him: Crawford,
Airlie, Erskine, young Napier, Black Pate; and beside them
such old friends as Wishart and Lord Napier. One of the few
Irish survivors had struggled to reach him, incredibly, with the
great Standard wrapped around his body under his plaid.
Montrose received him with all the honour due to a brave man,
and promoted him to his life-guard. William Hay, Morton's
brother, eventually rejoined him after escaping to England
with the cavalry ensign. Perhaps 500 men of the army that
camped at Philiphaugh rallied to the royalist camp in
Perthshire, almost all his horse among them.

Montrose tasted a moment of bitterness when he now received
the belated letter that the King had written to him on
September 9th from his refuge at Raglan on the Welsh
marches. "... Indeed it is no small part of my misfortune
(though the more for your glory)," wrote Charles, lamenting
his failure to dispatch his vaunted cavalry column to join his
Scottish Captain, "that this shall be as yet all my song to you;
and it were inexcusable if real impossibility were not the just
excuse." But there had been so many disappointments of this
kind that one more scarcely seemed important. All that
mattered now, while autumn was still young, was the gathering
of a new army, retribution upon Leslie, and the safety of the
royalist prisoners in the hands of the Covenant. Erskine rode
for Mar, Airlie and Douglas into Angus on Montrose's urgent
orders to raise men. Messengers set out across the hills to find
Aboyne and Alasdair to beg them to return to the Standard.

The Lord Marquis himself went back to his old headquarters of Blair, probably accompanied by Black Pate, once again to urge the Athollmen to march with him. Some pleaded the necessity of staying to get in the harvest. But 500 clansmen fell in behind him as he moved northwards once more, into the heart of the Gordon country.

On October 7th, at Drumninor Castle near Strathbogie, Aboyne and Lord Lewis Gordon marched to meet him with 1500 foot and 500 horse. The Marquis of Huntly had returned from his long exile in Tongue when he received news of Kilsyth, and Montrose wrote with exquisite courtesy to ensure his good will, promising to regard himself as the Gordon's "son and faithful servant". The omens were auspicious once more. Alasdair Macdonald could not be induced to leave his private war in the west, but already the Lord Marquis commanded 3000 men, as many as David Leslie could muster in Glasgow after detaching Middleton to Turriff with 800 horse. Montrose felt the old thrill of excitement and expectancy surging in his veins. Philiphaugh might yet be avenged while the King's cause lived in England. Nat Gordon and Spottiswoode were not dead. They could be saved, they *must* be saved. His eyes might sparkle once more as they had sparkled at Kilcummin before he turned back on Inverlochy, at Auldearn as he saw Hurry's regiments marching steadily into the trap he had prepared for them. The King might still have his day in Scotland.

For twelve glorious months, Montrose had demonstrated the truth of Napoleon's famous precept that in war the moral is to the material as three to one. But now he was to be compelled to watch this law work inexorably against himself. He could still muster an army big enough to promise miracles once more. But the certainty, the aura of serene invincibility around his person that had bewitched the Highlanders, was gone. He had shown, to the amazement of many in Scotland, that he was but mortal clay. The worm of doubt gnawed deep into the minds of many of the clansmen; perhaps also, fatally, into his own. The more a general agonizes, the more sure becomes his doom. For a year Montrose had somehow risen above the turmoil of deceit and intrigue and indecision and petty rivalries that dogged the King's cause so fatally in his two Kingdoms. Calm confidence in his own powers had been indispensable to

enable him to do this. Now, in the last wretched months of the
Civil War, he was dragged down into the mire which had
already engulfed the great Rupert. His last, fatal defeat took
place not on the battlefield but in the halls of the great nobles
of Scotland and in the conference chambers of the King and
of the Covenant. The fortunes of Montrose and of the King's
cause in Scotland now began twelve months of halting,
unhappy progress towards extinction.

One morning in the second week of October, the Lord
Marquis and his army marched away southwards on the long
road to Glasgow. They left Middleton at Turriff, for it would
have been all but impossible to trap his fast-moving cavalry
force unless they chose to fight. Soon after setting off, Lord
Lewis Gordon defected once more from the royalist army. He
took with him several troops of horse. The following day, a
much more devastating blow fell: Aboyne was ordered by his
father Huntly to return home with all the Gordon forces. At
Alford, where his nobler brother had died in the royalist
triumph only three months before, the maddening young man
marched away leaving Montrose to nurse his icy, impotent
rage against the false Gordons. Lord Reay, Huntly's son-in-law
and the master of Tongue where he had lived in exile, hastened
to Strathbogie once more with Irving of Drum to try to
reason with him. Perhaps partly in fear of the lurking
Middleton, but mostly out of his own hopeless pride, obstinacy
and stupidity, Huntly remained quite unmoved.

On October 22nd Montrose gave up hope of Aboyne and
moved wearily on down Glenshee, then by Lochearnside
towards Glasgow. It was growing cold again now, and the hills
were turning black against the dull grey skies. All the news
was bad. Somewhere in Perthshire Ogilvy of Powrie reached
the column with yet another letter from the King, informing
his Captain that Lord Digby, the elegant courtier himself, was
on his way north to join him at the head of 1500 horse.
Unbelievably, this phantom force, the promise of which had
haunted Montrose's plans for so long, had actually set out for
Scotland, on October 14th. But they were broken before
Montrose even knew of their existence. Digby himself reached
Dumfries before turning back to flee to the Isle of Man.
Montrose sent Powrie on to Strathbogie to try to stir Huntly
with the King's promise, but by now he himself can scarcely

have counted much on news of this sort. It was always the same: he could trust only the men he could see marching at his back at the beginning of each day. All else was fantasy.

The Glasgow venture was hopeless. He dared not engage Leslie, and now that he had been "brought lower" as the ministers had so earnestly desired, they and Parliament no longer feared him sufficiently to deny themselves the thrill of shedding royalist blood. They had already spurned all offers of an exchange of prisoners, shrewdly counting on Montrose's chivalry to deter him from taking reprisals. Rollo and Nisbit were gone, and Gordon and Spottiswoode would soon follow. Montrose lingered impotent beside Loch Lomond for a fortnight before he despaired of his friends and of striking southwards. Then he marched sadly back to Atholl. According to the diary of a Glasgow baillie named James Burns, it was one November day after he had abandoned the drive on Glasgow that he learnt of the death of Magdalen Carnegie, his Marchioness of Montrose. He left his army to ride to Kinnaird for her funeral. Whatever there had been between them was gone now. Guiltily, he might even have felt conscious of the release of one of the great weights upon his shoulders: now, there was one less sad soul to reproach him for the misery he brought to those who shared his name. He returned to Atholl to learn that another face from the past was gone: old Lord Napier, seventy years old and very tired, had died at Fincastle. They buried him at Blair. His son later had to pay the Covenant 5000 merks to prevent its creatures from digging up and seizing the old man's bones.

There was another letter from the King, consoling his Captain for Philiphaugh. As Charles's desperation increased, he displayed a remarkable intensity of feeling in his troubled soul for Montrose, the most constant of his servants. Partly perhaps, Charles had appreciated the ferocity of his Scottish Captain's opposition to any compromise with his enemies. The coolest heads around the King, including Prince Rupert, had been begging him for months to make the best terms he could. But Montrose, with his simple vision of right and wrong, truth and falsehood, had always beseeched the King from his distant hills to maintain the spirit of his crusade unsullied. Charles drank deep of uncritical loyalty and respect. There had been too many men around him lately who had confused him with unwelcome advice and blunt counsel.

As it hath been none of my least afflictions, nor misfortunes, that you have hitherto had no assistance from me, so I conjure you to believe that nothing but impossibility hath been the cause of it [he now wrote]. Witness my coming here [to Newark] (not without some difficulty) being only for that end; and when I saw that could not do, the parting of 1500 horse under the command of Digby to send unto you. And though the success (which I have here ever since expected, and that with some inconvenience to my other affairs) hath not been according to my wishes, yet that, nor nothing else, shall discourage me from seeking, and laying hold upon, all occasions to assist you; it being the least part of that kindness I owe you for the eminent fidelity, and generosity you have shown in my service. . . . No hardness of conditions shall ever make me slacken my friendship towards you; . . . upon all occasions and in all fortunes you shall ever find me your most assured, faithful, and constant friend,

**CHARLES R.**

Even Charles, however, had now dropped the pretence of being able to assist his Scottish Captain with anything more than fair words. In December Montrose led his half-starved army through the frozen passes, in conditions as terrible as any they had known at Inverlochy, to force a confrontation with the intolerable Huntly. It had become apparent that the royalist cause in Scotland was doomed without his assistance, and yet he showed no sign of moving. In iron humour, Montrose rode up to the gates of Huntly's castle at Strathbogie, his little personal escort hunched in their saddles behind him, huddled in their plaids against the icy wind. To his exasperation, he learnt that the Gordon had ridden panic-stricken out of his postern as soon as he heard of the coming of Montrose. But the King's Captain was determined to have it out with Huntly now. Hastening onwards, he finally trapped his man at his castle of Bog of Gight. It was time for some straight talking.

Montrose dealt with Huntly with firm courtesy, elaborate good manners such as the Marquis seemed to expect from him. The Gordon was cornered, wary, crudely cunning at this meeting with the man who towered above him in all things except the power to rouse the clans. Montrose wanted an honest explanation of the Marquis's hopes and intentions. Agreement to do anything was better than apathetic passivity. When Huntly showed signs of willingness to march on Inverness, although bitterly reluctant to allow his men to march southwards where they might be of real service, Montrose seized upon the proposal. Inverness was not a vital strategic objective, but it was a useful port. If Huntly did his part and led his army through Moray while Montrose moved up Strathspey, between them they might achieve a useful little success. There was also news of that changeable creature Seaforth, who was considering changing sides again, and might be about to declare for the King. A royalist attack on Inverness, so close to his own Mackenzie country, might prove decisive in making up his mind. Montrose left Bog of Gight encouraged. Having at last talked to Huntly face to face, it seemed that great consequences might flow from the meeting.

The royalists spent that Christmas of 1645 shivering in Strathspey, waiting on news of Huntly's advance. There were perhaps 1000 of them, and it must have needed all the Lord Marquis's calm inspiration and charm to prevent men from creeping away through the snow to their homes at such a moment of the King's fortunes. He could hearten them only with the promise of the plunder of Inverness and the encouraging news that Huntly was definitely on the move. But by January 10th, his impatience and anger now scarcely concealed, he was writing to the Gordon: "My Noble Lord, It being necessary that we should now take the opportunity of the season and employ the time that so favourably offereth unto us. . . . For it concerns us now really to fall to work. . . ."

Huntly had embarked upon a mad, meandering tour of north-east Scotland besieging minor castles and searching for supposed secret stores of gold. He had no intention of joining Montrose in any move against Inverness. Now he was even questioning Montrose's authority as the King's Captain, reasserting his own old, simmering claim to be the King's Lieutenant in the North. It is arguable that Huntly was almost a madman in the medical sense. It is impossible to find any rational explanation for his behaviour. He allowed his lands to be laid waste and finally he gave his life for the royalist cause. Yet he would do nothing effectively to serve it. He was certainly a huge fool. He seems to have been consumed with a jealousy that went far beyond the bounds of rational behaviour. In this early spring of 1646, his lunatic posturings caused the last royalist hopes in Scotland to die still-born.

In England, fighting was coming to an end. One by one, the remaining royalist strongholds were taken. Hugh Peter the fanatical preacher had already given glory to God for victory: "Oh, the blessed change we see, that can travel now from Edinburgh to the land's end in Cornwall, who not long since were blockt up at our doors. To see the highways occupied again; to heare the Carter whistling to his toiling team; to see the weekly Carrier attend his constant mart; to see the hills rejoycing, the valleys laughing." It seemed almost as if the Scottish Covenanters were no longer disposed to trouble about Montrose: Leslie's cavalry had proved able unaided to defeat him. When matters in England had been decided, all Leven's army would be available to root the remaining royalists from their mountain fastnesses.

The Scottish royalists passed the spring in futile little skirmishes. Black Pate Inchbrakie and Drummond of Balloch led 700 Athollmen to defeat a Campbell raiding party which had descended on Menteith, but this was a matter of old-fashioned Highland war, not a fight for King or Covenant. Young Lord Napier had been sent to garrison Montrose's own Kincardine Castle with fifty men. Middleton besieged it with a powerful army and siege artillery. After a fortnight of incessant bombardment, the castle well dried up. One night among the camp fires of the besieging army, there was a sudden thunder of hooves, a few muffled cries and pointless shots as Napier, Drummond and the Laird of Macnab rode for their lives over the Covenanters' entrenchments. Then they were away, galloping safely into the night, leaving the garrison to surrender the next morning. Thirty-five of them were sent under guard to Edinburgh. The rest were put up against the wall and shot in customary Covenanting style. Kincardine itself, Montrose's great family home beside the Ruthven where he had spent his boyhood, was reduced to a ruin. It was thoroughly plundered by Middleton's men and then abandoned. Soon, the country people began to carry off the stones to make their walls and build their cottages. The brambles and saplings grew up over the mews and the kennels and the great hall and stables. Today, only a crumbling corner of wall remains, unmarked by any memorial. The modern lords of Kincardine, perhaps ignorant of its great past, have planted young conifers in the ruins. Argyll would thoroughly have approved of their instincts.

At the end of April, after Huntly had rejected a new proposal to act in concert with him, Montrose alone invested Inverness with his little army. He had forced Seaforth, Sutherland and some of the other wavering northern chieftains to sign a Bond of Confederation to support the King's cause, and some of the Mackenzies were now giving half-hearted aid to his forces. But the town was strongly garrisoned by the Covenanters and it would almost certainly have cost Montrose heavy loss to take it. In the event, he was denied the opportunity to try. He had sent three troops of horse to watch the Spey crossings lest Middleton and his 2000 men sally from their base at Aberdeen to attack him, but when the Covenanter came, they missed him. It was even suggested that Lord Lewis Gordon had betrayed them. In any case, on May 5th Montrose's army found themselves retreating hastily up the Ness with Middleton pressing on their heels, fighting a series of sharp rearguard actions to hold him off. They had abandoned all their baggage and ammunition and their only two cannon in the entrenchments around Inverness. Huntly, typically, took advantage of the confusion to launch a blundering attack on Aberdeen, which he finally carried with heavy loss and to no useful purpose. Montrose somehow disengaged from Middleton in the hills, and marched back to Speyside by way of Strathglass and Errick. On May 27th he paid a last visit to Strathbogie to try to reason with Huntly. Inevitably, he failed. His pride and anger would allow him no longer to humble himself before the Gordon. He perceived in Montrose a lesser Scottish nobleman seeking to rise above his station and give orders to himself, the greatest magnate in northern Scotland. He despised the Graham's ambition. Perhaps he echoed that legendary Etonian precept that "Gentlemen are never *seen* to *try*". There was something indecent, demeaning, about Montrose's intimacy with his rude clansmen and fantastic marches across the mountains, sleeping beside them in the heather in his plaid. Montrose himself had also had enough of Huntly. Now, at last, he abandoned the mad, damned Gordons to their fate, and looked to his own.

He was no longer waging a coherent campaign with useful strategic objectives. He did not have the means with which to do so. He was merely leading guerilla raids whenever he saw the opportunity to cause mischief for the Covenant. His spirit was unbreakable. He would fight on in the hills for the King alone, if need be. But most of those around him were now aware of the futility of their sufferings. When Sir Robert Kerr rode into the royalist camp on Speyside on May 31st to announce that he came from Newcastle with a letter from the King, it was already apparent that all hope for Montrose's crusade was ended.

"MONTROSE," wrote Charles, "I am in such a condition as is much fitter for relation than writing. Wherefore I refer you to this trusty bearer Robin Kerr for the reasons and manner of my coming to this army; as also what my treatment hath been since I came, and my resolutions upon my whole business. . . ."

As Montrose read the sorry tale by the bank of the Spey on the cool May morning, his heart must have chilled to understand the import of the King's words. Charles had delivered himself, of his own free will, to the Covenanting army, Montrose's implacable enemies.

". . . This shall therefore only give you positive commands and tell you real truths, leaving the *why* of all of this to this bearer. You must disband your forces and go to France, where you shall receive my further directions. This at first may startle you; but I assure you that if for the present, I should offer to do more for you, I could not do so much; and that you shall always find me, Your most assured, constant, real, faithful friend, CHARLES R."

The story that Kerr told Montrose did nothing to relieve his sense of horror and dismay. As the royalist cause in England drifted helplessly towards collapse, Charles had dallied with a succession of tortured schemes to save his own throne. In the early months of 1646, he became more and more attracted by the prospect of reaching an accommodation with the Scottish Covenanters. They were already close to an open breach with Cromwell and the English Independents. They seemed to retain much more sincere reverence for the dignity of their King than the leaders of the English New Model Army. Above all, fantastically, Charles still nurtured hopes of bringing about a union between their forces and those of Montrose under his own standard, in which Montrose's strength and genius would give Charles the ascendancy. In most of these hopes he was encouraged by the young French Ambassador Jean de Montreuil, who had been sent from Paris by Cardinal Mazarin specifically to try to save something from the wreckage of Charles's fortunes. De Montreuil had been the principal intermediary in the months of secret negotiations between the King and the Covenanters.

Perhaps haunted by the memory of Strafford, Charles throughout the discussions showed deep concern for the fate of Montrose: "He wished to be not only securely but honourably reconciled to him, and went so far as to say he would in future consider him as one of his children, and that he wished to live with him henceforth as a friend rather than as a King."

The future of Montrose proved one of the most sensitive issues at stake between the King and the Covenanters who so ardently desired his death. But de Montreuil reported smoothly to Mazarin that he was sure that a reasonable agreement could be reached: "As for Montrose, terms will be made for him at the army, but he will be obliged to leave the country for a short time, and it is promised that on his engaging to do so, he will have his estates and all his offices restored to him. . . ."

The irony of the negotiations between the King and the Covenanters was that each believed to the end that they possessed an absolute monopoly of religious principle. The King was content to be persuaded by de Montreuil that the Scots cared more for political power than for fulfilling their absurd fantasies about a presbyterian England, which nobody wanted. The Covenanters were convinced in their turn that once they had Charles in their power, they could soon induce him to yield to their religious demands in return for saving his crown. Charles made no attempt to reach a written agreement with them before throwing himself on their mercy, or even to ensure that the views of the Scots Commissioners in England were shared by their brethren in Edinburgh. He wrote a memorandum before he rode out of Oxford reminding himself that ". . . before I take my journey, I must send to the Marquis of Montrose to advertise him upon what conditions I come to the Scots army, that he may be admitted forthwith into our conjunction and instantly march up to us". The King even drafted a letter for de Montreuil to send to Montrose, ordering him to march to join him at the Covenanters' camp as soon as it was apparent that they had declared for his cause. Of course the letter was never sent.

Charles left Oxford disguised as a servant on April 27th, 1646. On May 6th he surrendered himself at the Scots camp at Southwell. He was appalled by the reception he received: "There did the Earl Lothian as President of the Committee, to his eternal reproach, imperiously require His Majesty (before he had either drunk, refreshed or reposed himself) to command my Lord Bellasis to deliver up Newark to the Parliament's forces; to sign the Covenant; and to command James Graham to lay down arms; all of which the King stoutly refused, telling him that he who had made him an Earl had made James Graham a Marquis."[1]

But for all his outraged Majesty, as the guards closed in upon him, as the gilded cage was erected around his person, as the ministers of the Kirk began to rail at him to sign the Covenant, the King sadly began to understand the hopelessness of his own predicament, the collapse of his ludicrous hopes. He ordered his garrison at Newark to yield. When he was taken northwards to Newcastle as a prisoner on May 9th, he wrote to Montrose and ordered Sir Robert Kerr to ride to him with the order to disband. There was nothing else to be done.

On June 2nd Montrose replied from Strathspey with a calm courtesy that did not conceal utter turmoil of his private thoughts:

MAY IT PLEASE YOUR SACRED MAJESTY,

I received your Majesty's, by this bearer Lieutenant-Colonel Ker, carrying your Majesty's being at Newcastle: Together with your Majesty's pleasure for disbanding of all forces: And, my own repair abroad.

For the first, I shall not presume to canvass; but humbly acquiesce in your Majesty's resolutions.

As for that of present disbanding, I am likewise, in all humility, to render obedience; and never having had, nor having, anything earthly before my eyes, but your Majesty's service; as all my carriages have hitherto, and shall at this time witness; Only, I must humbly beg your Majesty to be pleased consider, that there is nothing remembered concerning the immunity of those who have been upon your service; that all deeds in their prejudice be reduced, and those of them who stay at home enjoy their lives and properties without being questioned; for such as go abroad that they have all freedom of transport; and also that all prisoners be released; so that no characters of what has happened remain. For, when all is done that we can, I am much afraid that it shall trouble both those there with Your Majesty, and all your servants here, to quit these parts:

And as for my own leaving this Kingdom, I shall, in all humility and obedience, endeavour to perform your Majesty's command: wishing—rather than any should make pretext of me—never to see it again with mine eyes; willing, as well by passion as action, to witness myself your Majesty's most humble, and most faithful, subject and servant,

MONTROSE.

Kerr had emphasized to Montrose that it was vital that he and his army do nothing that gave the Scots an excuse to bear even more hardly on the King. But the moment Kerr had left his camp with his reply to Charles, Montrose drafted a private note: Was all this really true? Was the King not writing under duress when he ordered his Captain to disband? Would the King soon not need his army once more? And what of all his officers who had given everything to his cause and would now be left destitute unless they were granted terms by the Covenant? The Lord Marquis gave his message to his own courier and sent him hastening to Newcastle.

Charles soon issued another public order to all his forces in Scotland to disband. He followed it, on June 15th, with another private letter to Montrose:

. . . I assure you that I no less esteem your willingness to lay down arms at my command for a gallant and real expression of your zeal and affection for my service than any of your former actions. But I hope that you cannot have so mean an opinion of me that for any particular or worldly respects I could suffer you to be ruined. I aver it is one of the greatest and truest marks of my present miseries that I cannot recompense you according to your deserts. . . . For there is

no man (who ever heard me speak of you) that is ignorant
that the reason which makes me at this time send you out of
the country, is that you may return home with greater
glory; and in the meantime to have as honourable employ-
ment as I can put upon you. . . . Wherefore I renew my
former directions of laying down arms unto you, desiring you
to let Huntly, Crawford, Airlie, Seaforth and Ogilvie
know. . . .

The surrender terms published on July 7th offered no hope
of pardon for the excommunicate royalists in Scotland, and
Montrose was obliged desperately to plead once more with the
King. But there was nothing that Charles could do for him:

The most sensible part of my many misfortunes is to see my
friends in distress, and not be able to help them. And of this
kind you are the chief. Wherefore, according to that real
friendship that is between us, as I cannot absolutely command
you to accept of unhandsome conditions, so I must tell you
that I believe your refusal will put you in a far worse estate
than your compliance . . . for if this opportunity be let slip,
you must not expect any more treaties; in which case you
must either conquer all Scotland or be inevitably ruined . . .
if you take another course you cannot expect that I can
publicly avow you in it . . . I shall be in a very sad condition,
such as I shall rather leave to your own judgement. . . .

On July 22nd Montrose met Middleton alone in a meadow
beside the Isla in Angus. As he had begun with Henderson
beside the Forth, so he now ended with Middleton by another
river, in another condition. The Covenanter gave him better
terms than the ministers of the Kirk in Edinburgh would have
chosen. Airlie and Ogilvy and most of the royalists could go
home. The Irishes such as were left with Montrose could return
to Ireland. It was one of the few recorded displays of mercy
by an officer of the Covenant.

At Rattray, beside Blairgowrie, Montrose paraded his army
for the last time. He thanked them for their great sacrifices for
their King, "Their present submission was, he told them, as
essential to the King's cause as their past achievements. . . His
soldiers fell at his knees and besought him with tears . . . to take

them with him where he would. They were ready to live, to fight, and, if it pleased God, to die under his command. ..."2 But it was all finished, and they all knew it. It was an extraordinary, heart-breaking parting from old Airlie and from Ogilvy and Napier and Crawford and the others who had risked so much and shared so much beside him. It was the ending of one of the great brotherhoods in the history of arms. The clansmen broke up into little parties to walk away home. Their officers swung into their saddles and saluted Montrose for the last time. It was over.

Crawford led the few Irishes to Kintyre and personally arranged their transport homewards before taking ship for exile in France. The Lord Marquis himself took his little personal following to the port of Montrose. He had been granted leave to set his own affairs in order, and he had time to visit his poor ruined mansion at Old Montrose, perhaps to see his youngest children at Kinnaird.

Charles wrote to him once more:

MONTROSE,

In all kinds of fortunes you find a way more and more to oblige me. And it is none of my least misfortunes, that all this time I can only return to you verbal repayment. But I assure you that the world shall see that the real expressions of my friendship to you shall be an infallible sign of my change of fortune. As for your desires, they are all so just, that I shall endeavour to have them all satisfied, not without hope to give you contentment in some of them . . .

Your most assured, real, faithful, constant friend,

CHARLES R

P.S. Defer your going beyond seas as long as you may without breaking your word.

For Montrose, there was to be no pardon. He must leave Scotland, perhaps for ever. He had been granted until September 1st to be gone, remaining thereafter on forfeit of his life. Loyal to the end, he respected Charles's mad postscript bidding him stay as long as he could. Somehow, there might still be some opportunity to do the King service. It was a dangerous liberty. On August 31st, when the ship appointed to carry him abroad arrived in Montrose harbour, its villainous captain demanded time to caulk and rig before he put to sea, and boasted in his cups that he had been instructed to which Covenanting port to deliver James Graham. Only on September 3rd, after three nerve-racking days searching for a vessel, did the little party of royalists at last find the means to escape. Sir John Hurry, Drummond of Balloch, Harry Graham, John Spottiswoode, George Wishart, a young German servant named Rudolph, and a Frenchman named Pardus Lasound whom Montrose had taken into his service on the death of his old master Lord Gordon, took passage from Stonehaven for Norway. That night of September 3rd, Montrose escaped in a small boat disguised as the servant of his private chaplain James Wood. Once at sea, he transferred to a larger ship anchored off the coast which granted him passage to Bergen in Norway.

He was thirty-four years old, and he had lost everything. His barony of Mugdock had passed into the greedy claws of Argyll. Kincardine was rubble, Old Montrose spoiled and desolate. His son James lay under the hand of the Covenant, whose ministers strove unceasingly to educate the boy in their own image. Lady Montrose was dead, and Napier, and Spottiswoode and Nat Gordon and Lord Gordon, and his servants shot at Kincardine and the Irishes slaughtered at Newark Castle and so many others. It had all been for nothing. His King was the prisoner of his deadliest enemies. The war was lost. Perhaps in those days when he heard of war from his fellow students at Angers, or listened to yarns of how the day was won at Breitenfeld from Leven and his officers around the camp fire in that first Bishops' War, it had seemed a fine thing to ride out in shining armour to tilt with the forces of evil. Montrose had learnt that he had a genius for battle, and by his behaviour he had shown himself to be one of the great knights of his age, who never suffered a man to be killed in cold blood if he could help it. But he had also learnt the terrible nature of defeat, which had stripped from him everything and everyone he most dearly loved and cast him adrift, an exile deprived of his cause. The gay days, the laughing days when life was a glorious gamble were ended. He had known the exultation of playing a game for the greatest stake imaginable: a kingdom. Now he knew the agony of having lost it.

# CHAPTER THIRTEEN

## *The King's Pawn*

---

THERE ARE MANY men who can play the hero at the head
of an army or facing odds of ten to one. There are far fewer
who could have maintained their courage, their honour and
loyalty under the circumstances in which the Lord Marquis of
Montrose found himself for the next three years.

He and his little party landed at Bergen in Norway early in
September 1646, to be kindly received by Thomas Gray, the
Scot who commanded the royal castle above the town.
Montrose set off almost immediately across the frozen mountains to reach a port from which he could sail for Denmark. He
hoped to seek the help of King Christian IV, who had always
been a loyal supporter of Charles I. When he discovered that
the King was away in Germany, he moved on to Hamburg.
There he found lodgings until he could take stock and make
some plans for the future.

From the day that Montrose became one of the principal
supporters of the Covenant, through the stormy months of his
conversion to the cause of Charles I, then later during his
service as the King's Lieutenant, his enemies accused him of
ambition and overbearing pride. It is probably true—and
nothing for him to be ashamed of—that for some time he
coveted high office under the crown. But by the time he reached
the safety of Europe at the end of his epic crusade, the last of
that young appetite for worldly prizes was gone. He was
dedicated passionately, single-mindedly, to the cause of Charles
Stuart in Scotland and England. He resigned himself to a life
of poverty, weary intrigue and frustration in the service of the
King rather than accept great rewards from the hand of any
other man.

Far away in the hills for the past two years, he had had no
inkling of his own rising fame at every Court in Europe. Now,
for the first time, he learnt how the great captains of the age in
Sweden and France, Germany and the Low Countries had

followed his battles with astonished admiration. He was famous. Men begged the honour of his company at their tables to hear of his brilliant dispositions at Auldearn, his lightning march back from Dundee, his great descent on Inverlochy. Princes clamoured for his services. Cardinal de Retz wrote wonderingly: "The Count of Montrose, a Scot, and head of the house of Graham, is the only man in the world who has ever conjured up for me the spirit of those heroes whom one has otherwise only seen in Plutarch's *Lives*, and has sustained the King of England's cause with a greatness of soul unparalleled this century."

Montrose was offered rich rewards to sell his services to European armies. He might without disgrace have become a Scottish general in the great tradition of those who served the French monarchy through the centuries. Yet he spurned every advance, turned down every offer that seemed to conflict with his duty to Charles I. From Hamburg, he began a three year struggle to revive the King's cause in Scotland.

He had lingered at Stonehaven until the eleventh hour, and then sailed only with the deepest reluctance. He knew that it was impossible for the King to make terms with the Covenanters, and he had prayed that he might be ready to take a hand when the last semblance of hope collapsed. That first winter on the continent, as every ship brought gloomy tidings of the Scots' negotiations with the English Independents for the person of the King, he yearned desperately for the arms and money to go back to Scotland and prepare for the imminent crisis. In a wistfully romantic gesture that was characteristic of him at this time, he sent to the King a sword which Charles somehow received. It was the Lord Marquis's way of showing that his own was still at the disposal of his royal master. Crawford had gone straight to Paris, to the Court of the exiled Henrietta Maria at the Louvre, when he had convoyed the remaining Irishes to their homes. He took with him details of Montrose's plans for raising an army of 20,000 men in Scotland. Now, Montrose lingered in Hamburg week after week waiting for word from the Queen, imagining that at any moment he would receive the order to equip his expedition and sail.

Charles himself wrote in January, unable to give him orders because he had no code book, but begging him to address himself to the Queen. Yet it was not until February 5th, 1647,

a week after the Covenanters had handed over their King
to the English for £400,000 in one of the most contemptible
bargains in history, that Henrietta Maria at last wrote to
Montrose about his proposals of the previous autumn.

COUSIN,
I am very happy to have this opportunity of writing to
you in the meantime, until I can furnish you with more
dispatches, regarding the proposition submitted to me by
my Lord Crawford on your part . . . of which I approve
extremely, and as I hold it to be of great importance to the
service of his Majesty, I shall do all that I can to further it,
and labour therein with all my power . . . I am truly your
very good and affectionate cousin and friend,
**HENRIETTA MARIA.**

But as Montrose and his anxious little following read the
Queen's gracious letter and another that followed it, they saw
nothing to suggest that there were any practical plans to assist
them. The Lord Marquis had by now probably heard enough
reports from Paris to know the nature of the pathetic, squab-
bling, intriguing, petty, wasteful society that surrounded
Henrietta in exile; so many of the finest and most loyal
cavalier soldiers were pushed aside by the crowd of courtiers
and place-seekers and sycophants. It was obvious that the
Queen would do nothing quickly for the Scottish project,
perhaps nothing at all until Montrose in person could argue
for it. The King had promised him an Ambassadorship to
enable him to call upon the Courts of Europe rallying support
for the royalist cause. Montrose and the other Scottish
royalists of his "Great Family", as he called them, must also
have been very hard up by now. Heaven knows what they
had all been using for money through the winter in Germany.
Finally, Charles himself in his last letter to his Captain-
General had ordered him to go to France. Early in March
1647, Montrose and his little following set off from Hamburg
to ride to Paris and lay their case before the Queen's throne.
Somewhere in Flanders as they were on the road, Montrose
had his first sour taste of the reception in store for him. He was
intercepted by John Ashburnham, one of the King's Gentlemen
of the Bedchamber. He had come to beg the Lord Marquis to

return immediately to Scotland and renew the struggle, rather than go on to the capital. With exquisite politeness, Montrose answered that he would perform this very service for his King at the first opportunity. But he had lost everything he possessed. He had neither money, nor arms, nor credit. Until they were forthcoming, there was nothing that he could do. Then Ashburnham revealed his real purpose in coming: If Montrose would not go back to Scotland, he begged, then would he not at least make peace with the Covenanters? Lord Jermyn, the Queen's Favourite, was the leader of the dominant Court faction whose fervent hopes rested on yet another incredible dream of alliance between the Irish and the Covenanters. Jermyn, Ashburnham and the others were now appalled by the prospect of the Lord Marquis striding into Paris with his maddening principles and implacable loyalties and hatreds, to wreck all their schemes. Ashburnham assured Montrose that there would be no difficulty in getting an order from the King to satisfy his Captain's conscience in anything that might be necessary.

"To this Montrose replied, that no man was readier to obey the King's instructions in all that was just and honourable, but not even the King should command his obedience in what was dishonourable, unjust, and destructive to his Majesty himself."[1] In a cold rage, he mounted his horse once more and rode on down the muddy road to Paris.

It was the beginning of three years of frustration and disappointment. Henrietta Maria's Court had no good will to spare for the man who crossed their plots and passions. When Montrose asked Jermyn for the Letters of Credence which the King had authorized him to receive as Ambassador Extraordinary, his lordship haughtily disowned any knowledge of them. When he begged the Queen for 6000 pistoles to take back to Scotland and raise an army of 10,000 men, she refused him although she thought nothing of giving two of her French servants a gift of 2000 to celebrate their wedding day. His presbyterian soul was affronted by the gay, loose-living life of the Court, while the King lay prisoner in the hands of his enemies. When it was suggested that his nineteen-year-old niece Lilias Napier might become a Maid of Honour, he recoiled at the notion: ". . . For there is neither Scots man nor woman welcome that way; neither would any woman of honour and virtue (chiefly a woman) suffer themselves to live in so lewd and worthless a place."

As for his own life, he told the Cardinal de Retz, Coadjutor of Paris: "He would conform himself to the conditions in which the King, his master, was: that he would set up no equipage for appearing at court; that he had a Great Family but had little left for maintaining it."

It was now almost as it had been in London in the years before the War: the Scots lived in their own tight little circle, despising the English and being despised by them. Montrose went everywhere with young Napier. Crawford, Hurry, Wishart, Harry Graham and a handful of others lived close to him, talking and planning incessantly. But they were removed from the mainstream of Court life. His enemies began to speak now, as they had so often in the past, of his intolerable pride. It is certainly true that all his life he was seen to better advantage by his subordinates than by his equals. His passionate devotion to his officers and to his men was not matched by his tact in dealing with the great nobles of Scotland and England. As his obsession with his huge task grew, so too did his difficulty in sharing the vision with lesser mortals. He was much admired by his contemporaries, but probably not much liked. He judged them by his own impossibly high standards, and they felt very uncomfortable with him as a result. He never attempted to practise flattery on courtiers and politicians whom he found contemptible. Not surprisingly, they returned his dislike in full measure.

It was left to the princes of Europe to honour the greatness of Montrose. Late in 1647 the first part of George Wishart's Latin memoirs of his campaign *Res Montisros* was published in Holland, becoming an instant bestseller and enraging the lords of the Covenant when they heard of James Graham's latest conceit. Cardinal De Retz was among the chief men of France who threw open their doors to the honoured *Compte de Montrose*. Mazarin himself offered Montrose the rank of Lieutenant-General in the French army and the post of Captain of the *Gens d'Armes*. He promised that he could quickly become a Marshal of France and captain of the King's Guard. The rich pay and perquisites from his posts would have made him one of the greatest men in Europe, fit to stand beside Condé himself. Chafing impatiently in Paris, spurned by

Henrietta Maria, he thought of accepting. But at last he decided that he could not think of service to the King of France. It would be incompatible with his first loyalty: to the King of England. He declined Mazarin's offer.

He was more attracted by the idea of a temporary commission with the Holy Roman Emperor. He accepted an invitation to visit Ferdinand III, and when he reached him at last in Prague after riding the breadth of Europe to find him, he was received with all the honour and stately ceremony due to one of the great captains of his day. He was presented with the crimson baton of a Marshal of the Empire, and was granted a commission to raise forces under the personal command of the Emperor himself. From Prague he travelled through Hungary and Poland, Prussia and Denmark (where he was welcomed by King Christian) before continuing to Brussels, where he was to meet the Emperor's brother Archduke Leopold of Austria, and arrange his future. But by one of those strokes of fate that recur throughout the career of Montrose, he reached the Archduke too late. One day before he arrived at his headquarters, on August 20th, 1648, he had suffered catastrophic defeat by Condé at Lens. There was now no prospect of service in Flanders for Montrose. He returned to the little brotherhood of Scottish royalists, to learn the latest news of the fate of Scotland and of King Charles.

In the months that followed the Scots' sale of their King to the English it had slowly become apparent to them what a wretched bargain they had made. Half the money they expected was never paid. They had lost their only bargaining tool in their fanatical struggle to enforce presbyterianism south of the Border. The Covenanters were always chronically fractious. Amidst the turmoil that followed the Civil War, with huge uncertainties about the future government of both Scotland and England, new and extraordinary alliances and enmities developed in which almost the only common factor was hatred of Montrose. Hamilton—the old, false, feeble Hamilton—had gained his freedom at the end of the war, and returned to Scotland with his character somewhat restored in the eyes of some Covenanters as a result of his confinement and of their own weariness of Argyll. Charles, now imprisoned at Carisbrook, hastened to take advantage of the existence of the new moderate party among the Covenanters. He agreed a secret treaty with Loudon, Lauderdale and Lanark, by which presbyterianism would be given a three-year trial in England. A new party was born in Scotland to restore Charles to the throne on the basis of this Engagement. It was led by Hamilton, and its members were henceforth known as the Engagers. They had a large majority in the Scots Parliament, although Argyll would have nothing to do with them, and the fanatics of the Kirk were bitterly hostile. They now embarked on their blundering attempt to save the King's crown.

Jermyn, Henrietta Maria and most of the Court in exile passionately supported the Engagers and hoped for great things from their army. Montrose, inevitably, opposed them to the uttermost. He argued that it was impossible to trust any of the Covenanters, and that the incompetence of the Engagers would anyway undo them. It was not his business to voice the other overwhelming arguments against the Engagement—that most English royalists abhorred a Restoration on such terms, and that most shrewd Scots understood that Charles I had no more intention of keeping his side of such a bargain than of flying to the moon. The Engagers' campaign was based on a grotesque fantasy. The men who supported it were seeking compromises and means of escape from their own excesses that were never realistic. They came to their inevitable undoing at Preston on August 17th, 1648, when Cromwell contemptuously smashed their invading army and captured Hamilton.

The prisoner was allowed to see his King once more. "My dear master," cried Hamilton, falling on his knees, deeply moved. "I have been so indeed to you," answered Charles, embracing him. Hamilton was doomed to go to the block, and in this his last fall, he had brought down his "dear master" with him. After Preston, Cromwell's remaining doubts about the King were swept aside. He became convinced that he must die. On January 30th, 1649, Charles I walked from the Banqueting Hall in Whitehall to his execution.

Montrose was in Brussels more than a week after the event when news reached him, probably from Hyde, of the murder of the King. In a manner that to a modern reader may seem extraordinary, for a terrible moment he lost control of himself: ". . . He fainted in the midst of his attendants, falling down like one dead," wrote Wishart.[2] "When at length he recovered, after many deep groans, he broke out into these words: 'We must die, die, with our gracious King. May the God of life and death be my witness, that henceforth life on earth will be bitterness and mourning!' Among those who stood around him, I, who write this history, happened to be present. . . ."

Fully to understand the violence of Montrose's reaction to the death of his King, one must look back far beyond the seventeenth century, to the chivalric passions of the great knights of the fourteenth and fifteenth amongst whom to swoon, far from being unmanly, was the mark of a soul that had succeeded in soaring to the summits of emotion. Montrose's famous love poem sometimes seems to echo the same period and the same emotions. It is generally considered to be political. Yet it also seems to reflect a concept of love that is wholly mediaeval and chivalric.

Montrose's devotion to the King had become an obsession, and Charles's death now struck into the innermost corners of his soul. It was his good fortune that he had never known the dead King well enough to perceive the enormity of his failings. Charles had not lived long enough for Montrose to be compelled to face the reality of his master's lifetime of broken promises and betrayals. Most of Charles's ablest servants were men of the world who had loved him despite his shortcomings. But Montrose had formed an immaculate vision of his King which was never shattered, which he carried with him to the grave.

For two days after he heard the news, he remained closeted alone in his bedroom, receiving no one. On the third day, when Wishart was allowed at last to enter his master's room and break his solitary mourning, he found on his table a piece of paper. On it, Montrose had written his private requiem for Charles Stuart.

> Great, Good, and Just, could I but rate
> My griefs and thy too rigid fate
> I'd weep the world to such a strain
> As it should deluge once again.
> But since thy loud-tongued blood demands supplies
> More from Briareus's hands than Argos' eyes,
> I'll sing thy Obsequies with trumpet sounds
> And write thine epitaph in blood and wounds.

L

And now at last, as Montrose yearned from the depths of his soul to ride sword in hand upon his King's murderers, his pleadings for a new expedition into Scotland began to receive serious attention. Before the news of the King's execution, he had already been corresponding with Prince Rupert, with the young Duke of York, and most important with the Prince of Wales, who had broken away from his mother and Jermyn to establish his own household at The Hague. The Prince had been arranging a secret rendezvous with Montrose to discuss the future of Scotland when the terrible news of his father's death temporarily overthrew everything. Now, as the new King Charles II, he assumed command of the struggle to bring about a Restoration. On February 28th, 1649, Hyde was writing to Prince Rupert: "Our Court is full of Scots. The Earls of Lauderdale and Lanerick [Lanark] are here, being as they say, driven out of their country by the power of Argyll who is in firm league with Cromwell. Here is likewise the Marquis of Montrose, who is in truth a gallant person and very impatient to be doing; and though the Presbyterians are as busy as ever, yet I believe the next news I shall send you will be, that his Majesty entirely trusts Montrose and puts the business of Scotland wholly into his conduct."

On March 4th, 1649, Charles appointed Montrose once more Captain-General and Commander-in-Chief in Scotland.

Ever since Naseby, most English royalists had looked to Scotland to save the monarchy in both kingdoms. Cromwell and his army now absolutely controlled England. There was no immediate prospect of raising and equipping an army within its borders to defeat them. But in Scotland there had always been a strong undercurrent of monarchist sentiment. Since the murder of the King by the English, even Argyll and his party had begun to display their own strange brand of royalism, proclaiming Charles II King at the Mercat Cross in Edinburgh—provided that he signed the Covenant. Through the spring of 1649, the King at The Hague was in no doubt that he wanted an expedition to Scotland. He only continued to dally between the attractions of staking all his hopes on Montrose, and those of attempting to reach some agreement with Argyll and his party.

At the end of March, commissioners from Scotland, among them Cassilis and Robert Baillie, arrived in The Hague to meet

the new King. Their principal terms for his restoration were
the establishment of presbyterianism in England, Ireland, and
Scotland; and Charles's blanket authority for the past, present
and future deeds of parliament and the General Assembly of
the Kirk. He was also to rid himself of "James Graham, the
late Earl of Montrose, being a man most justly if ever any,
cast out of the Church of God . . . the most bloody murderer
in our nation". For the next two months, the arguments
between the Scottish factions dominated the life of the Court
at The Hague. The young Prince of Orange, Charles's host
and brother-in-law, begged him to accept Argyll's terms.
Lauderdale, among the old Engagers, bitterly opposed anything that Montrose wanted. Hyde, Charles's Chancellor,
equally despised Covenanters and Engagers. Jermyn and his
crew in Paris were hot for the Covenanting agreement.
Through it all, sombrely assured, passionate in his conviction and transparent in his honesty, strode Montrose. On
May 21st, 1649, a document in which he pleaded for the
rejection of the Covenanters' terms was read before the King's
Council.

It was typical of Montrose in its moderation and reason. He
did not seek to deny the Covenant that he himself had signed,
and saw no objection to the King signing it, provided that it
was confined to Scotland. But he was overwhelmingly hostile
to the scheme to compel England and Ireland to adopt
presbyterianism. He begged that each nation be allowed to
choose its own religion under a constitutional monarchy. He
denounced the Solemn League and Covenant with withering
scorn: ". . . It is so full of violence, injustice and rebellion
that, in my humble opinion, it were Your Majesty's shame and
ruin ever to give ear to it; it being nothing but a condemning
of your father's memory, joining all your dominions by your
own consent against you. . . . They would also force Your
Majesty to quit the form of service and worship in your own
family. And yet they made it a ground of rebellion against
your royal father that they but imagined he intended to meddle
with them in like kind. . . ."

Montrose's eloquence helped Charles to reach his decision.
The Covenanters' terms were rejected. Early in June their
Commissioners left The Hague. Charles himself was obliged to
transfer his Court to Breda as a result of growing Dutch political

embarrassment about his presence in their capital, but on June 22nd he wrote to Montrose: "The more to encourage you to my service, and render you confident of my resolutions, both touching myself and you, I have thought fit by these to signify to you, that I will not determine anything touching the affairs of that kingdom without having your advice thereupon. As also I will not do anything that shall be prejudicial to your commission. . . ."

Montrose was now Viceroy of Scotland, Captain-General and Admiral of the Scottish Seas, Ambassador Extraordinary to foreign countries. He had only to begin to clothe his great titles with the stuff of reality. He was beginning again where he had begun at Carlisle in August 1644, five years earlier. Thus far, the new rising in Scotland was himself, and nothing more.

As Montrose began to plan for his Scottish campaign, he was troubled by two overwhelming problems: he lacked an army of loyal and able men to take with him, and he must somehow find shipping for a descent on a hostile shore. As far back as September 1648, he had begun a courteous correspondence with Prince Rupert, now Admiral of the creaky little royalist fleet which he was struggling to build into a fighting force with his usual energy and inspiration. The formality with which Montrose phrased his first letter indicates that the two men were not close: "Your Highness shall be pleased to know, that I was ever a silent admirer of you, and a passionate affecter of your person, and all your ways." It was as near to courtly flattery as Montrose ever came. Probably he sincerely admired Rupert, and certainly he badly needed his brilliance and his fleet to land on the coast of Scotland. Again and again Montrose sought to arrange a meeting between them " . . . at which time I hope to let your Highness see all is not yet gone, but that we may have a handsome pull for it; and a probable one; and either win it, or be sure to lose it fairly . . .".
But Rupert was preparing his ships for sea, quelling a serious mutiny among his sailors, and defeating the intrigues of Jermyn and his friends, who laid snares for his undoing with the same petty viciousness they directed against Montrose. In January 1649 the Prince sailed for Ireland and subsequently for the West Indies. Montrose's brightest prospect of aid vanished with him.

By a curious twist of fortune, it was Rupert's mother, Elizabeth of Bohemia, the Winter Queen, who proved the staunchest and most comforting friend to Montrose in that last summer of his life, 1649, as he prepared for what he himself called his "Passion". He stayed with her as he planned his campaign. She wrote him bold, charming, affectionate letters as he travelled the Low Countries organizing the hunt for arms, money, and men. It was for Elizabeth that he was painted at this time by Honthorst, in the most famous portrait of his life, cased in black armour and holding his baton as a Marshal of the Empire.

Perhaps Elizabeth gave to Montrose a little of the love and laughter that had been so lacking in his essentially serious life. She was in her fifties now, very hard up and doomed to perpetual exile, for her husband's throne had been one of the first casualties of the Thirty Years War. Now her audience chamber was draped in perpetual black to mourn his death. But Europe had always adored the "Queen of Hearts", first for her beauty, then for her gaiety and warmth and optimism and gallantry. Even after thirteen children, she was still handsome, her haired dyed black since its natural fairness had faded, her long, oval face still warm and kindly. The Lord Marquis of Montrose affected her just as he had Cardinal de Retz. She had not believed that the world still knew how to mould the "gentil parfit knight". Rupert, her own son, had always been a professional soldier rather than a romantic crusader. She, who had known her brother Charles I's massive failings with sisterly clarity, must have marvelled to see Montrose's undying devotion to his memory. For her part, she returned to Jamie Graham her utter loyalty and support: "By great chance," she wrote to him in a typical flurry of concern, "I have found that the Prince of Orange will again extremely press the King to grant the Commissioners' desires and so ruin him through your sides. . . . For God's sake leave not the King as long as he is at Breda, for without question there is nothing that will be omitted to ruin you and your friends and so the King at last. It is so late I can say no more only believe me ever your most constant, affectionate friend, ELIZABETH."

In August, she was writing to him from her country house at Rhenen:

MY LORD,

I return you your letters, with my thanks for them. I
pray God keep the King in his constancy to you and his
other true friends and servants. But till he be gone from
where he is, I shall be in pain. While you stay in this country,
it will be a great charity in you to let me know the news you
receive; for here is none to be had, the place being very
barren of all news. We have nothing to do but walk and
shoot. I am grown a good archer, to shoot with my Lord
Kinnoul. If your office will suffer it, I hope you will come
and help us to shoot. Howsoever, I conjure you have no
friend esteems you more than doth she that is your most
constant and affectionate friend,

ELIZABETH.

Princess Sophia, Elizabeth's daughter who later became
Electress of Hanover, wrote her Memoirs forty years later. She
mentioned Montrose: "Since he was a very brave soldier and a
man of high merit, he thought nothing impossible to his
management and courage. He was sure he could restore the
young King if his Majesty would make him Viceroy of Scotland,
and, if he did him so great a service, the King could not refuse
him the hand of my sister Louise."

It is the only evidence of a romance that may have been the
second, and last, of Montrose's life. Princess Louise painted
and studied under Honthorst. Certainly she knew Montrose
that summer, when he was so close to her family. It must be
left to Margaret Irwin and other novelists to weave great tales
around such a fragment as the sentence above. It merely
remains one of the enchanted mysteries of history, why
Louise[3] became a Catholic nun and ended her days as Abbess
of Maubuisson.

But Montrose's romance with Princess Louise, if it was a
romance, was the only secret that he managed to keep close
that summer. The goldfish bowl existence of the royalist exiles
in France and the Low Countries was never conducive to
discretion. In two reports to his masters in London in the first
week of September 1649, Strickland, the parliamentary envoy
in Amsterdam, was able to write with appalling accuracy:
"Montrose hopes to raise a thousand horse and three thousand
foot, and with them to visit his countrymen. My Lord Kinnoul

who is well known in England, I hear, is gone to take possession
of some island in Scotland. . . . There is in Amsterdam a ship
in which is much arms and ammunition bound for Scotland
for the use of Montrose as I am informed. If there be any in
Scotland who desire such an information, it were well they
knew it. It is to be sent to some of the Isles, some say the
Orkades. . . . Montrose is expected in Hamburg."

In August at Elizabeth's house at Rhenen, surrounded by
all her beloved horses and dogs and monkeys, Montrose had
made plans with the Earl of Kinnoul for a small expedition of
80 officers and 100 Danes to establish a royalist bridgehead in
the Orkneys. They were compelled to make do with a poor
ship, and they were deeply unhappy about the lack of security.
But Kinnoul at last sailed, slipped the Parliamentary blockade,
and made a safe landing at Kirkwall. He was received by the
royalist Lord Morton whose son had been Montrose's standard-
bearer. The castle of Birsay became their headquarters and
500 local levies were quickly raised. Kinnoul reported
ecstatically to Montrose that "Your Lordship is gaped after
with that expectation that the Jews had for their Messiah, and
certainly your presence will restore your groaning country to
its liberties and the King to his rights".

David Leslie was well aware of the royalist landing, but
made no move to cross from the mainland of Ross, first because
of high seas, later perhaps because he believed that it would be
more expedient to confront the royalists when they reached
the mainland, as eventually they must. Kinnoul's messengers
travelled among the northern clans, the Mackays and
Mackenzies, alerting them to the second coming of the Lord
Marquis. Then they waited for Montrose.

The King's Viceroy spent a miserable autumn dispatching
emissaries to every Court in Europe in search of cash and men,
endlessly delayed when he sought to be setting sail, constantly
disappointed and betrayed. Sir John Cochrane, according to
Wishart, absconded with every penny he raised. Colonel
Ogilvy, who had been sent to Amsterdam, drank away all the
local contributions. Harry Graham, Montrose's faithful half-
brother, came back empty-handed from the Court of Branden-
burg. In many capitals, Covenanting agents had anticipated
Montrose's men, and deterred rulers from giving him their aid.
Jermyn and his friends thwarted Montrose at every opportunity,

as did Lauderdale and his little clique. This was a game at
which the Lord Marquis had never excelled. He was not a
man to whom begging came easily, even in the King's service.

He must have been troubled and a little bemused to receive
a letter from the King, written in mid-September: "I entreat,"
wrote Charles, "to go on vigorously and with your wonted
courage and care in the preservation of those trusts I have
committed to you, and not to be startled by any reports you may
hear as if I have otherwise inclined to the Presbyterians than
when I left you. I assure you that I am upon the same principles
I was and depend as much as ever upon your undertakings and
endeavours for my service, being fully resolved to assist and
support you therein to the uttermost of my power."

Uneasy in the face of such a warning, Montrose nonetheless
continued with his struggles to organize his expedition. He
went to Denmark, where he was kindly entertained by the new
King, and allowed to raise a few hundred men. He also met a
nobleman who generously lent him £10,000, a debt Charles II
later declined to repay. In Sweden, Queen Christina gave
him 1500 stand of arms and tacit consent to muster his
expeditionary force within her frontiers. For political reasons
she declined to do more. She needed the good will of the English
navy. In the end, Montrose's most valuable ally in Sweden
turned out to be a rich Scottish merchant named John Maclear,
an ardent royalist whose headquarters were in the port of
Gothenburg. When Montrose arrived there in mid-November,
Maclear advanced him £25,000 and became his chief
purchasing agent and commissary-general for the collection of
arms, ammunition, artillery and supplies for the voyage to
Orkney.

The expedition assembled at Gothenburg in conditions of
curiously public privacy. Spies reported every move to London
and Edinburgh, and the Swedish Provincial Governor of the
town, who was disturbed by all the warlike preparations taking
place under his nose, complained of Montrose's circumspection: "If a Swedish official meets him in the street or anywhere,
he immediately turns about or aside." His superior officers
tartly ordered the Governor to mind his own business. Recruits
continued to arrive from Denmark and Holland, although
some were held up in Hamburg for want of the fare to
Gothenburg. Ammunition and stores were stockpiled, little

enough of them, many royalists feared. All Europe watched
with cold fascination as the Lord Marquis prepared for his
great confrontation with the Covenant. It was the gossip of
every Court. Count Henry of Nassau reached The Hague from
Denmark, where he had heard all about Montrose's pleadings,
prophesying disaster for his expedition. Others, on the other
hand, believed that this utterly dedicated soldier, the Count of
Montrose, who had already wrought miracles once for his
King, was now on the verge of yet another crowning triumph.
Some hardened professional soldiers were attracted by the
prospect of service under the banner of so great a Captain.
None other than Sir James Turner, who found himself
unemployed after a spell of imprisonment in England, was
eager to take a commission under Montrose. He was at
Hamburg in November 1649: "If I had been provided with
money, without which I could put myself in no equipage, I
had run the hazard of going to Scotland with the rest who
accompanied the Marquis. But I could be master of no money
till I came to Holland. . . ."[4]

Turner languished unhappily in Europe for a time, lamenting the ill-fortune that kept him from joining the Lord
Marquis. He became very friendly with Colonel William
Sibbald—the officer who had served Montrose until he
betrayed him after Fyvie. Sibbald had now changed sides
again, and was off to Scotland carrying letters from Montrose
to prominent royalists. He too was very short of cash, and
Turner gave him a note to his own wife in Edinburgh, begging
her to advance Sibbald money. He was much dismayed later to
learn that his friend had been taken at Musselburgh.

It was the mark of this expedition of Montrose that he had a
hard core of professionals behind him—foremost among them
Sir John Hurry—but none of his old officers like Airlie, men
on whom he could rely both for leadership and inspired
loyalty. He must have enjoyed a reasonably amicable working
relationship with Hurry—probably the two men respected
each other as soldiers—but it is impossible to believe that they
were ever close. When Montrose finally sailed from Gothenburg, Ogilvy of Powrie was almost the only one of his old
officers beside him. His closest friend Lord Napier was left
behind in Europe to gather more arms and men.

Montrose's ships bearing his men and supplies sailed for

Orkney in mid-December, suffering some loss from pack ice off the Swedish coasts, according to reports that reached Edinburgh. It was a meagre enough force, perhaps 400 men, that landed at Kirkwall. The Lord Marquis had learnt only a week earlier of a serious blow that had already struck the advance guard in Orkney. By amazing bad luck, Lord Morton and Kinnoul had fallen ill and died within days of each other, leaving their forces leaderless. To Montrose, still at Gothenburg, it must have seemed that ill-fortune was crowding in upon him from every side. A man who had always strongly believed in the workings of Divine Providence for good or ill, he now found himself unable to sail because of contrary winds. As the weeks went by, delay piled upon delay as he lingered for more men, better weather, and finally, for new instructions from the King. It was not until mid-March 1650, after he had travelled overland to Bergen in Norway, that he boarded his little ship. *Shepherdess* for the journey to Kirkwall. He was already in Orkney when the King's messenger reached him, from Jersey, with two letters.

"MY LORD OF MONTROSE," began the confidential one, for the eyes of the Lord Marquis alone, "My public letter having expressed all that I have of business to say to you, I shall only add a word by this, to assure you that I will never fail in the effects of that friendship I have promised, and which your zeal to my service hath so eminently deserved; and that nothing that can happen to me shall make me consent to anything to your prejudice. I conjure you therefore not to take alarm at any reports or messages for others; but to depend upon my kindness and to proceed in your business with your usual courage and alacrity; which I am sure will bring great advantage to my affairs and much honour to yourself. I wish you all good success in it, and shall ever remain, your affectionate friend, CHARLES R."

It was as near to an apology as kings are accustomed to make. Charles, of course, had betrayed him. The second letter officially informed Montrose that he had opened negotiations with the Covenanters once more. It had all been in the wind for months, and Charles had feared that Montrose had discovered it when he wrote in September cautioning him not to believe any ugly rumours that he might hear. Now, it was a reality. The Covenanters could inform the people of Scotland that they were once more being received by their King. Why should any royalist join with Montrose, when tomorrow he might discover that the Covenanting army was the army of the King? Charles doubled his treachery by his order to Montrose in his latest letter: "We require and authorize you therefore, to proceed vigorously and effectually in your undertaking. . . ." The King wished to negotiate with the Commissioners with both carrot and stick, mailed fist and velvet glove. Montrose's expedition was intended to goad them to make their peace with him before his Viceroy burnt Scotland around their ears. It was a classic, subtle, flawed act of Stuart duplicity. He was to be the King's pawn in a deadly opening gambit.

Montrose might well have smiled softly as he looked beyond the letters in his packet from the King, and discovered the George and Ribbon of the Garter that came with them. From Orkney, he wrote back to the King on March 26th: ". . . I received yours of 12 January with that mark of favour wherewith you have honoured me, and for which I can make no other acknowledgement but with the more alacrity to abandon my life for your interests. . . ."

Kaiser Wilhelm said of Csar Nicholas in a moment of piercing perception: "The Csar is not treacherous, but he is weak. Weakness is not treachery, but it fulfils all its functions."

Even if Charles II cherished illusions about the prospects of the expedition in Orkney, his Scottish Viceroy had none.

# CHAPTER FOURTEEN

## *The Bridegroom*

---

SCOTLAND WAS TEARING herself apart. Men were weary of war and of the ministers and of Argyll and marching armies. Yet they saw no means to rid themselves of any of these things. The Scots had attempted to interfere in the affairs of England and had paid a terrible price, as they were to do again and again in the next hundred years. They had begun to glimpse the nature of the thraldom in which they had bound themselves to England when their king rode southwards in 1603, and which was to end in their own total subjection. The hierarchy of their own society would wither as all power was shorn from it, as all its vital functions were transferred to England. Some of their troubles they had brought upon themselves. Others were the direct consequence of the link with England.

The bloodshed in Scotland had already been terrible, and was not yet ended. By the time the royalists had had their revenge after the Restoration in 1660, almost all the major actors in the drama of the Covenant and the Civil War were dead.

In the spring of 1650, as the Lord Marquis of Montrose came hurrying to meet his destiny, he found few old friends or old enemies to receive him. It was as if Bradman had suddenly called on Newbury cricket club and invited the members to get up a couple of scratch teams to give him a game. Scotland and her great soldiers were exhausted. Reluctantly, such warriors as were to hand clambered to their feet, took up their arms, and prepared to fight one more campaign. But they were an unworthy cast for so great a tragedy.

Montrose's officers included two old enemies, Hurry and Lord Frendraught who had led the Covenanting cavalry against him at Aberdeen. Then he had Ogilvy of Powrie, Harry Graham, Morton's brother Sir James Douglas, and the

new Lord Kinnoul—the same William Hay who had so
gallantly saved the cavalry ensign after Philiphaugh. It may
have pleased the Lord Marquis to pretend to himself that his
four or five hundred Danish soldiers were to be the Irishes of
this campaign, and indeed they were no more mercenaries
than Alasdair and his company had been. Yet there was a
huge difference: the Irishes had been Gaels, kindred spirits
who perfectly understood the Highlands and Highland war. In
Scotland the Danes were lost souls. Had there been 5000 of
them, Montrose might have led them up the Canongate of
Edinburgh. But 500 men were a poor beginning to conquer
Scotland, unless the clans did their part very nobly indeed.

Montrose had great hopes of the Mackays and Mackenzies,
but the spirit of the Mackenzies had been dampened by their
abortive rising in March 1649 under Seaforth's brother
Pluscardine. Seaforth himself, now an avowed royalist amongst
the Court in exile in Paris, promised everything to Montrose
except his own presence. It was the story of Huntly all over
again. Then there were the Gordons, and Huntly himself. He
had taken part in Pluscardine's rising but was now furious
that he had not been awarded the Garter, and was reported to
be wavering between support for Argyll and for Montrose.
Montrose knew his man only too well, for this Huntly was
none other than the old, mad Lord Lewis Gordon. His father,
the curse of Montrose's last campaign, had been betrayed,
captured, and executed by the Covenanters early in 1649.
Aboyne had died in exile in France, of an ague. Lord Lewis
inherited the wreckage of his family's fortunes.

But if the royalists had doubts of their friends, they were
cheered by the plight of their enemies. Since the tyranny of the
Kirk had been confirmed in every corner of Scottish life by the
notorious Act of Classes the previous year, resentment against
the ministers and a numb yearning for peace and quiet had
spread across the nation. Even Argyll and his party admitted
that a King might be desirable. Many Scots went much
further and argued that a Restoration was indispensable.

The great army of the Covenant had been smashed at
Preston. It was now but a shrunken rump, for the government
had pitifully little money left with which to pay for it. Of
Scotland's generals, Leven was senile, Middleton was a wavering royalist, Baillie had been an Engager. David Leslie was left

with 3000 foot and 1500 cavalry with which to guard all of northern Scotland. Among his colonels, Holbourn had been with the beaten Covenant army at Kilsyth, and Strachan was a religious fanatic. The Covenanters garrisoned the castles of Caithness and Sutherland, which were under the orders of the Earl of Sutherland. They then waited with extraordinary passivity for the coming of Montrose.

The Lord Marquis passed the early days of April in Orkney assembling his little army. He now had 1000 Orcadian levies, willing enough royalists, but quite ignorant of war. There were perhaps fifty mounted gentlemen in his cavalry squadron, and of course the Danes. His first move was to detail a flying column under Sir John Hurry to cross the Pentland Firth and dash thirty miles south to seize the Ord of Caithness, commanding the narrow pass which he feared might be held against him by the Covenanters. As soon as Hurry sent word that he had secured the road, Montrose convoyed the remainder of his army in fishing boats to the mainland.

They formed up at the seaside behind the banners Montrose had chosen with such sombre imagination to fly above his army. The infantry bore a black standard on which were depicted the bleeding head of the murdered King and the motto: "*Deo et victicibus armis.*" The cavalry banner was also black, and showed three pairs of clasped hands holding drawn swords above the words "*Quos pietas, virtus, et honor fecit amicos*". The Lord Marquis's personal standard was of white damask. It showed two pinnacles with a river between, and a lion poised to spring across the chasm. Characteristically, he had chosen a motto which brooked no compromise: "*Nil medium.*"

At Thurso they induced most of the local lairds grudgingly to take the oath of allegiance. A few gentlemen came forward to offer their services. They were sent to scour the countryside for recruits. Then, leaving Harry Graham with 200 men to secure this northern bridgehead and raise such local levies as he could muster, Montrose marched southwards across the hills until he struck the coast just above Dunbeath Castle, Sir John Sinclair's clifftop fortress which was garrisoned for the Covenant and commanded by his wife. Around April 17th, five days after crossing for Orkney, the royalist army set about besieging Dunbeath. Within a few days the castle capitulated. Montrose left 100 men to hold it and marched on down the coast to the Earl of Sutherland's principal stronghold, Dunrobin. The Earl himself was already in Ross, but 100 Covenanting soldiers who had been hastily withdrawn from garrison duty at Tongue were ready for the royalists when they came. Montrose lost several men taken prisoner before he abandoned his attempt on Dunrobin. His scouts reported strong Covenanting garrisons in the strongholds southwards, around Dornoch Firth. Montrose decided against confronting them. He turned inland, to find a suitable rendezvous at which to await the coming of the royalist clans before striking towards Inverness and David Leslie. Passing by Lairg where they probably met a small reinforcement column moving down from Tongue, the little army moved on south-westwards to ford the Oykell at Rosehall. Then they marched downriver to the Kyle of Sutherland, at the head of the Dornoch Firth. Around the hill at Carbisdale, probably late on April 25th, Montrose ordered his men to camp. Where the ground fell away to the south-east, they set about digging a strong entrenchment. There were to be no more Philiphaughs, no more half-hearted defensive measures. His left flank was protected by the Kyle, his right and rear by steep hills. His men could rest comfortably in the narrow pass by the waterside until the Monroes and Rosses and Mackenzies and the other clans of which Montrose had such high hopes could send news of their coming. The royalists settled down to wait.

It is hopeless to pretend that the conduct of Montrose in this last campaign can easily be explained or understood. Why, for example, did he drastically weaken his slender force by leaving behind 300 men around Thurso and Dunbeath; why for that matter did he trouble with attacking castles at all? It is unconvincing to argue that he needed to keep open a line of communication and retreat to Orkney: the old Montrose would have spurned any such recognition of possible defeat. If he was obliged to retreat to the islands again, then his campaign would have ended.

The far north of Scotland had nothing to offer him strategically. It would have been infinitely more promising for him to break through to Badenoch, to Aberdeenshire and the Gordon country and Perthshire where he knew every pass and burn, where he could call on veterans whom he could trust implicitly. Instead, he lingered at Carbisdale waiting on wavering clansmen of unproven worth. At Thurso he had already been disappointed to discover how reluctant were gentlemen of Caithness to come forward—he had been obliged to issue a tough proclamation to persuade them to do so. Those royalists who joined his standard, he had assured the people of Scotland in his Declaration, published in Edinburgh in December to the fury of the Kirk, "whatsomever shall behappen, they may at least be assured of Crastinus's recompense, that, dead or alive, the world will give them thanks". But gratitude and glory had lost much of their savour, even to the highland clans, by the spring of 1650. There had been too many stricken fields and smoking scaffolds.

It may well be that Montrose's hesitant movements through Caithness and Sutherland were caused by dissensions within his little army. The Orcadians probably grew restless as they marched further and further from their islands, which most of them had never left before in their lives. The Danes must have found the harsh hills of northern Scotland an unnerving campaigning ground—the emptiness, the wet, misty mornings and endless moonscapes. If Montrose himself was in a fey, mystic mood, careless of his own fate, not all of his officers shared it, and they might reasonably have been nervous and exasperated about the clumsy progress of the advance. The royalists who camped at Carbisdale were not a happy band.

Perhaps if Montrose himself had been in Scotland through the last few months, communicating personally with the clan chieftains and gauging for himself the mood of their followers, he might have been better able to judge his moment. If he had been able to mount a combined operation with Rupert to seize a port such as Inverness or Aberdeen, use it as a base for his campaign and then advance southwards supported from the sea, he would have had a better chance. As it was, like the Airborne Division at Arnhem, the royalists had now begun their attack hopelessly far from any of their vital objectives, and they had been obliged to waste precious time and dissipate their slender strength to no useful purpose.

Fundamentally, also, he was once again caught in the old, highland trap. Even if he was able to advance southwards, his campaign was still utterly dependent on the clans. Whatever disenchantment existed with the Kirk and with Argyll in the heart of Scotland, in the Lowlands it was wholly eclipsed by the people's hatred and fear of the highlanders. Some historians have argued that at the beginning of his 1650 campaign, Montrose was in with a chance because the mood of Scotland was increasingly sympathetic to a Restoration; that Pluscardine's Rising had shown that the spirit existed if only Montrose could harness it to his military genius. But the gulf between Highlander and Lowlander remained unbridgeable. The royalists would never regain Scotland until they had won over the lowlands. Lowland Scotland would have spurned the Second Coming had it been heralded by a Gordon or a Macdonald. Their hatred for Montrose was implacable. They desired his destruction above all things.

Considering that David Leslie had been well aware of the royalist muster on Orkney for months, his response to Montrose's advance was sluggish. He had to reach James Graham before the clans gathered to join him, before he slipped away into the hills beyond reach of any regular army. But it was not until April 25th—the day the royalists reached Carbisdale—that Leslie had concentrated his 4000 men and felt able to start forced marching for the north. He sent gallopers to the colonels of his cavalry detachments in Banff and Moray, Strachan and Hackett, ordering them to ride hard for Sutherland and harry Montrose until the army could reach them. Strachan may have been a religious fanatic, but he was also a crack cavalry leader. Gathering his own men and those of a Colonel Ker, he raced for Tain at the foot of the Dornoch Firth. There he met Hackett and his men, another Irish troop, and a platoon of musketeers from Lawers's regiment. Together, they made a column of only 256 men, but they were all veterans. Strachan despised Leslie and his "levy of knaves". Without lingering for reinforcements, he moved deliberately up the Firth to look for Montrose.

The fortune of war, which had so often favoured Montrose, now smiled grimly upon Strachan. The Earl of Sutherland had 300 men in the area, and the Covenanter dispatched them to block the road south to Harry Graham and his men, who were reported to be moving towards a rendezvous with the royalist army. Four hundred men of the Rosses and Monroes whom Strachan met at Tain also attached themselves to him. They had fought with the royalists in Pluscardine's Rising a year earlier and had now almost certainly been on their way to

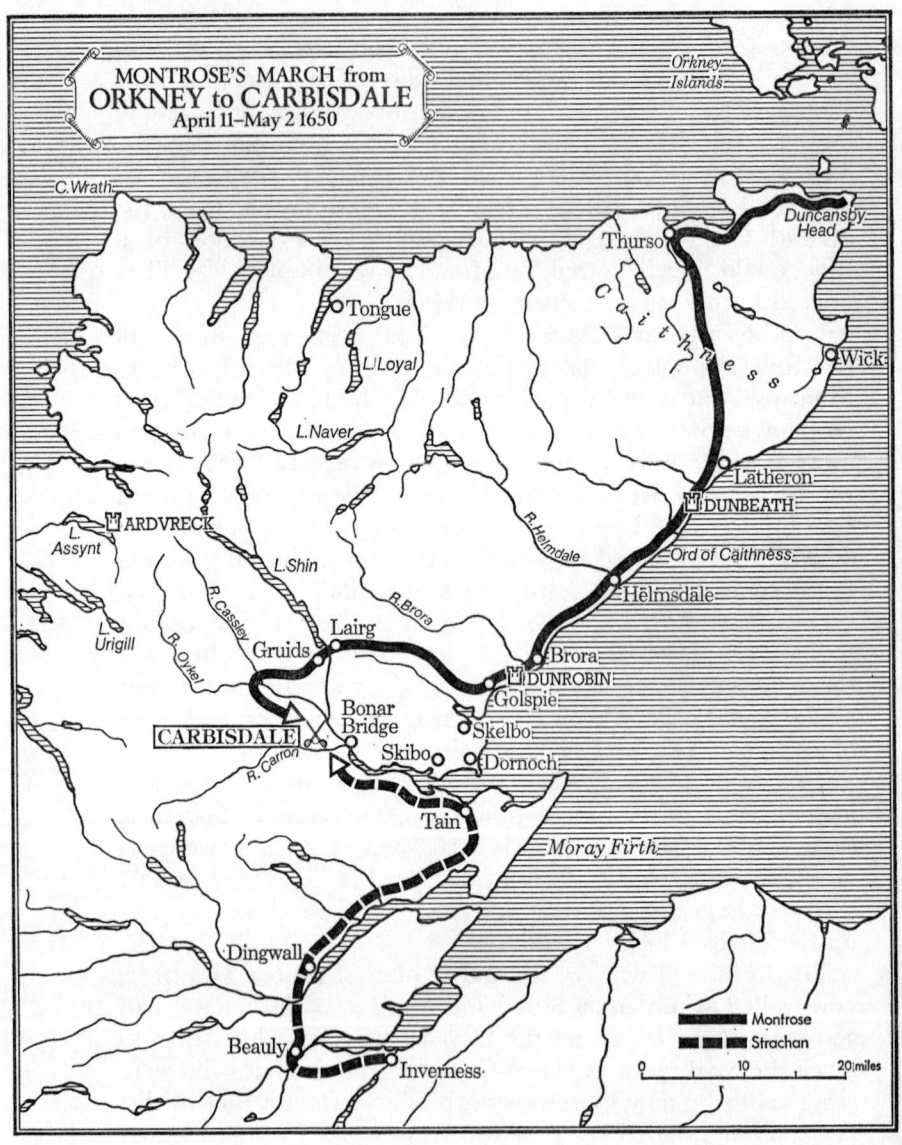

MONTROSE'S MARCH from
**ORKNEY to CARBISDALE**
April 11–May 2 1650

*Orkney
Islands*

C. Wrath

Thurso

*Duncansby
Head*

Tongue

*Caithness*

Wick

L./Loyal

L.Naver

Lâtheron

ARDVRECK

DUNBEATH

L.
Assynt

L.Shin

*R.Helmdale*

Ord of Caithness

R.Brora

Helmsdale

L.
Urigill

R.Cassley

Lairg

Gruids

Brora

DUNROBIN

Golspie

R.Oykel

R.Carron

Bonar
Bridge

Skelbo

**CARBISDALE**

Skibo

Dornoch

Tain

*Moray Firth*

Dingwall

Montrose

Strachan

Beauly

Inverness

0        10        20|miles

join Montrose. But seeing Strachan's formidable column of horse so near at hand, they cannily changed their plans. The Covenanter accepted their offer to reconnoitre Montrose's positions, probably as much as anything to prevent them from reporting to the royalists about his own. But he was shrewd enough to put little trust in their loyalty, and he cannot have been surprised to observe, as they approached Carbisdale, that the clansmen had moved cautiously away from his squadrons, and climbed a little way up the hill to the west to see what would happen next. It was about three in the afternoon of April 27th, 1650.

As soon as Strachan's scouts reported the strength of Montrose's position, he perceived that he could not attempt a frontal attack. He must lure the royalists onto lower ground. Halting his main body in the thick cover beside the Dornoch Firth, perhaps four miles short of the royalist camp, he sent forward one troop to expose themselves below Carbisdale.

Of all Montrose's battles, Carbisdale is the most unsatisfactory to reconstruct. The evidence is very slender, and some of the Lord Marquis's admirers have blurred harsh realities to soften the bitterness of defeat. Even some modern historians, notably Buchan, have coupled Carbisdale with Philiphaugh as a surprise and a skurry that somehow need not be classed among Montrose's real battles. It is difficult to accept this view. Strachan handled matters very well that tragic afternoon beside the Kyle of Sutherland, and Montrose on any interpretation handled them very badly. It is impossible to arrive at any reconstruction which is completely satisfactory, but it is at least possible to decide the broad outline of what took place.

Robert Monro of Achness and his three sons were Montrose's scoutmasters. They had informed him that there was only one troop of Covenanting cavalry within miles of Carbisdale. When Strachan's solitary troop appeared in front of the royalist entrenchments, they may have persuaded Montrose that they were alone. But if this was so, why did he muster his entire army? He sent Major Lisle, the English royalist who commanded his own fifty horsemen, to scout. Lisle allegedly returned to report that there was only the one troop of enemy cavalry. According to one modern historian Montrose then advanced *"with the main body of foot to reconnoitre"*.[1] No commander in his senses would have brought forward his whole army to "reconnoitre", nor have led them all down from an entrenched position to deal with a single troop of enemy horse. There seem to be only two conceivable explanations. Either Montrose was getting his army on the march, was setting off southwards and was caught by Strachan at a fantastically lucky moment. Or, much more probably, he was uneasily aware that there was a substantial enemy force in the offing, even if he was uncertain of its strength; and he was advancing to engage them. In either case, he allowed himself to be surprised. Just as at Philiphaugh, there had been a terrible failure of intelligence and scouting. It is impossible to exonerate Montrose from responsibility for serious errors. To argue that his army was only a scratch force of untrained levies is quite true, but misses the point. At Carbisdale, admittedly largely because he lacked capable subordinates, Montrose blundered headlong into Strachan's trap.

As soon as the Covenanter saw the royalists leaving their hilltop positions, he cantered forward at the head of his men along the waterside, crossing the Carron river and then halting once more in thick cover. Within a few minutes, he saw his forward troops retreating towards him, behind them Lisle and the royalist cavalry in hot pursuit. Strachan waited until Lisle was almost on his positions before spurring forward with the hundred men of his squadron knee to knee behind him. They crashed on Lisle's handful, who turned in shocked horror, fleeing back on the advancing companies of Montrose's foot. On came Strachan's men, Hackett's squadron behind his own, riding hard as they could go on the broken heath, the thunder of their hooves terrorizing the Orcadian levies as they watched the mass of horse and steel bearing down on them. Any man who has seen racehorses run shoulder to shoulder can imagine the terror flailing hooves and glinting breastplates inspire in men not trained to face them. The levies broke and fled before the first Covenanter had drawn blood. The Danes fired a volley or two as they retreated into the scrub, but they had been irretrievably shaken by the first Covenanting on-slaught. Montrose's officers and closest followers were left alone to fight for their lives.

Lisle and most of his horsemen were dead within a few moments. Ogilvy of Powrie went down, Menzies of Pittfoddells who carried the standard, Douglas and Gordon. Hurry, who

had commanded the van, was lying bleeding and helpless.
Montrose himself and Frendraught were wounded. The army
was breaking up. They could hear the screams of the terrified
Orcadian levies as they floundered in the Kyle attempting in
vain to swim to safety, drowning in their corselets and equipment. The Covenanters rode after them into the water, hewing
and hacking whenever a limb rose from the swell. The only
man Strachan lost in the day was a trooper drowned in that
mad pursuit, though he himself took a musket ball on his belt
buckle.

The Rosses and Monroes now swarmed shrieking down the
hill to seize upon the wounded and stake their claim to the
plunder. The battle had been decided in a few minutes, but
the killing continued for hours. Strachan's exultant, muddy
troopers brought to him one by one the royalist standards they
had picked up from the field. Hundreds of Orcadians were
dead. The Covenanters began to herd together the miserable
clusters of prisoners. "In the very field the victors gave thanks to
God for their happy success," wrote Gordon of Sallagh.[2]
". . . The countrymen of Ross and Sutherland continued the
killing of such as escaped from the battle many days thereafter." There were sixty-one captured officers including the
wounded Hurry, 386 men, including most of the Danes, and
two Orcadian ministers. To Strachan's chagrin, however,
James Graham himself was not to be numbered among either
the captives or the dead.

Montrose's horse had been killed under him. Bleeding and
exhausted, he stood gazing desperately at the mobs of plunging
horses and flying men, appallingly aware that he saw before
him the end of four years' struggle and all his great hopes.
Suddenly, beside him, he found Frendraught, also wounded
but pressing the reins of his own horse into his hand. As a
nephew of Sutherland, Frendraught could be sure of mercy,
but there could be none for the Lord Marquis of Montrose.
Clumsily, he pulled himself into the saddle. He saw Monro of
Achness frantically pointing the way to the Kyle. Past the
handfuls of fighting men, and the first looters already stripping
the corpses, they spurred madly for the Kyle and floundered in.
He saw Monro and his sons, Major Edward Sinclair and
Sinclair of Brims around him. As they swam, someone shouted
to him. Ah, yes, every Covenanting trooper in Sutherland

would be upon him as soon as they glimpsed the George and
Garter Ribbon on his breast. As they urged their horses up the
northern shore of the Kyle, he tore off his decorations and
tossed them to the ground. The little party galloped away up
the river.

It is easy to imagine that by now, Montrose himself with his
awful awareness of disaster, his exhaustion and his wounds was
no longer leading the party. Probably he rode blindly after
Monro and the others, deep in pain and unhappiness. He had
failed, and he must have seen that this time there could be little
hope of coming back. He had promised everyone so much—the
King, Elizabeth, Hyde, his own officers—and he had betrayed
them all. Men in the extremities of shock and excitement are
tipped over into the depths of depression, and Montrose must
now have nursed a terrible sense of destiny denied. Monro or
one of the others was talking about separating. He saluted the
Lord Marquis grimly and rode down into the bed of the Oykell
with his sons. He was for the south-west across the hills.
Montrose and his little party moved on up the Oykell, heading
northwards perhaps with thoughts of Strathnaver, that chilly
bower for so many highland fugitives.

Somewhere in Strath Oykell, Montrose and the others lost
their horses. It is difficult to believe that they willingly
abandoned them to make themselves less conspicuous, as some
commentators have suggested, for without mounts they became
doomed men. Perhaps the beasts foundered after being
ruthlessly ridden so far. The snows still lay on the hills that
April, and Strath Oykell is one of the most terrible wildernesses
in all Scotland. These were the uncompromising, cruel hills of
the west, rising sheer and falling steep against the grey skies,
promising nothing beyond each crest except an eternity of
crests to the horizon. One of Montrose's companions collapsed
of his wounds and of exhaustion. The others separated.
Montrose, at last, was alone. He was lost and starving, feverish
and aching from his wounds. He chewed his gauntlets in his
hunger as he staggered on, his mind wandering, his strength
slipping away.

Some time on April 29th, he reached a sheiling near Loch
Urigill. The cottager gave him bread and milk. As he lay
shivering and exhausted upon the straw on the floor of the dim
little hovel, to the family's horror they saw, advancing up the

valley, a Covenanting patrol. Every man Leslie could spare was in the saddle now, hunting with the promise of huge reward for James Graham, alive or dead. Montrose was hurried out into the yard. In the freezing mud under a sheep trough, he listened while the troopers asked their questions, searched, and at last rode away down the hill. Montrose crawled out of his hiding place to offer his gratitude to the family that had saved him. They must have looked with strange fascination on this gaunt, ragged, unshaven creature whose long hair was streaked with mud and blood, yet who spoke so softly and told them that he was the mighty Montrose. Deeply moved, he told them that he would never again expose anyone to such risk to save his own life. Then he stumbled away into the snow.

When at last he looked down the hill and saw below him the lonely tower of Ardvreck Castle, on its peninsula reaching out into Loch Assynt, encircled by mountains, he was at the end of his tether. It was the usual two-storey miniature fortress, primitive enough living quarters for a laird, but elevating him to mastery of the pass by the lochshore to the north-west. Montrose thanked God for his good fortune in coming upon it. Neil Macleod of Assynt was Seaforth's man, was the same gentleman, almost certainly, who had been with him during the abortive siege of Inverness in the spring of 1646.

Somehow, Montrose staggered the last mile to the castle walls. It is said that it was young Macleod's wife who received the Lord Marquis, weak and ill, at her door. Soon after his arrival Major Sinclair was also brought in, having been found wandering in the mountains. Today, Ardvreck Castle lies open to the skies on one side, where the wall is gone. But it is still possible to see the vaulted cellars, half-full of earth, in which Montrose and Sinclair were now conducted by their hosts. There they lay, encircled by the dank stone walls and stench of Macleods while one of the laird's men rode hard for Tain. Four days after their arrival, Macleod of Assynt joined the legion of the damned by selling his guests to the Covenant for the promise of £25,000 Scots.

Colonel Strachan had ridden south with the captured royalist colours to receive the congratulations of the Covenanters. It was Major-General Holbourn who arrived at Ardvreck on May 4th. Leslie, who was now at Tain, sent him with a troop of horse to fetch James Graham to meet his judges.

On May 1st, the King had signed the draft of the Treaty of Breda with Argyll's Commissioners. He agreed to sign the Covenant and enforce Presbyterianism in England. Sir William Fleming was about to leave for Scotland to order Montrose to halt his expedition, to explain that the King had had no choice but to make terms with the Covenanters once his great plans for an Irish rising had come to nothing. If Montrose was still in arms in Scotland, he might prove an embarrassment to his royal master. Much worse, however, the first rumours of Carbisdale had begun to reach the continent. Montrose defeated and in chains would be a most unfortunate burden upon the prospects of the King. While the Lord Marquis, at Ardvreck, languished in his misery for his failure to fulfil his great hopes for his King, to Charles in exile his Scottish Viceroy had ceased to be an asset, even a pawn, in the tortured game he was playing for his throne.

Holbourn led his prisoner back down Strath Oykell without kindness or chivalry, the rat-catcher of the Covenant going meanly about his business. Yet now, as Montrose began his long journey down the length of his country for the last time, his captors began to see to their dismay that the people of Scotland had entered into a great conspiracy: they sought to enable the Lord Marquis to defy all the humiliations and indignities thrust upon him by the Covenant, to bring his own destruction to naught.

The famous accounts of the Lord Marquis's stately progress towards his death have often been published, but this seems no reason to deny a reader the privilege of hearing again of the last glorious days of Montrose, as his own contemporaries saw them. His "Passion", his final struggle to overcome the Covenant by dignity and greatness of spirit, now began.

On the night of May 6th, his captors quartered themselves upon the Dowager Lady Gray at Skibo Castle, just north of the Dornoch Firth.

"On the arrival of the Marquis and his guards, she prepared a suitable entertainment for them. She presided at the dinner table, at the head of which, and immediately before her, was a leg of roasted mutton. When Montrose entered the room he was introduced to her by the officers who escorted him, and she requested him to be seated next to her; but Holbourn, still retaining the strict military order he observed in his march, placed the Marquis between himself and another officer, and thus he sat down at Lady Skibo's right hand and above his noble prisoner, before the Lady was aware of the alteration. She had no sooner observed this arrangement than she flew into a violent passion, seized the leg of roasted mutton by the shank and hit Holbourn such a notable blow on the head with the flank part of the hot juicy mutton as knocked him off his seat, and completely spoiled his uniform. The officers took alarm, dreading an attempt to rescue the prisoner; but the Lady, still in great wrath, and brandishing the leg of mutton, reminded them that she received them as guests; that as such, and as gentlemen, they must accommodate themselves to such an adjustment of place at her table as she considered to be correct; and that although the Marquis was a prisoner, she was more resolved to support his rank when unfortunate than if he had been victorious; and consequently, that no person of inferior rank, could, at her table, be permitted to take precedence over him. Order being restored, and the mutton replaced on the table, every possible civility was thereafter directed by all present towards the Marquis."[3]

On the morning of May 7th, Montrose was ferried across the Dornoch Firth to Tain, where David Leslie took personal command of the process of humiliation that the Covenanters had decreed for their stricken foe. At the centre of a sombre, sordid, brutal procession, Montrose was led down the east coast of Scotland on the long journey towards Edinburgh.

"Now I set down that which I myself was eye-witness of," wrote James Fraser, who at the age of sixteen followed the march with awed fascination. "The 9th of May, 1650, at Lovat, he sat upon a little shelty horse, without a saddle, but a quilt of rags and straw, and pieces of rope for stirrups; his felt fastened under the horse's belly with a tether; a bit halter for a bridle; a ragged old dark reddish plaid, a *montrer* cap, called *Magirky*, on his head; a musketeer on each side, and his fellow prisoners after him.

"Thus conducted through the country, near Inverness, under the road to Muirtown, where he desired to alight, he called for a draught of water, being then in the first crisis of a

high fever. And here the crowd from the town came forth to
gaze. The two ministers . . . wait here upon him to comfort
him; the latter of which Montrose was well acquainted with.
At the end of the bridge, stepping forward, an old woman,
Margaret MacGeorge, exclaimed and brauted saying—
'Montrose look above! View these ruinous houses of mine
which you occasioned to be burnt down when you besieged
Inverness!' Yet he never altered his countenance; but with a
majesty and state beseeming him, kept a countenance high.

"At the cross, a table covered. The Magistrates treat him
with wine which he would not taste but allayed with water.
The stately prisoners, his officers, stood under a forestair and
drank heartily. I remarked Colonel Hurry, a robust, tall
stately fellow with a long cut on his cheek. All the way through
the streets Montrose never lowered his aspect. The Provost,
Duncan Forbes, taking leave of him at the town's end, said—
'My Lord, I am sorry for your circumstances.' He replied—'I
am sorry for being the object of your pity.' The Marquis was
conveyed that night to Castle Stewart where he lodged.

"From Castle Stewart the Marquis is conveyed through
Moray. By the way some loyal gentlemen wait upon His
Excellency, most avowedly, and with grieved hearts; such as
the Laird of Culbin, Captain Thomas Mackenzie Pluscardine,
the Laird of Cookstoun, and old Mr Thomas Fullerton his
acquaintance at College. He was overjoyed to see these about
him; and they were his guard forward to Forres, where the
Marquis was treated; and thence afternoon, convoyed to
Elgin city, where all these loyal gentlemen waited on him, and
diverted him all the time, with allowance of the General.

"In the morning Mr Alexander Symons, parson of Duffus,
waited on him at Elgin, being college acquaintance with the
Marquis, four years his co-pupil at St Andrews. This cheered
him wonderfully as the parson often told me. Thence they
conveyed him all the way to the River Spey and a crowd of
royalists flocked about him unchallenged. Crossing the Spey,
they lodged all night at Keith; and next day, May 12th, being
the Sabbath, the Marquis heard sermon there. A tent was set
up in the fields for him in which he lay. The Minister, Master
William Kinanmond, altering his ordinary, chose for his theme
and text the words of the Prophet Samuel to Agag, King of the
Amalekites, coming before him delicately: 'And Samuel said,

As thy sword hath made women childless, so shall thy mother be childless among women etc. . . .' This unnatural merciless man so rated, reviled and reflected on the Marquis in such invective, virulent, and malicious manner, that some of his hearers, who were even of the swaying side, condemned him. Montrose patiently hearing him a long time, and he insisting still, said 'Rail on Rabshakeh' and so turned his back to him in the tent. But all honest men hated Kinanmond for this ever after. Montrose desired to stay in the fields all night, lying upon straw in the tent till the morning."

Thus they progressed past Montrose's great battlefields, along the roads he had ridden so often at the head of his highlanders, the royal standard flying above him. The Covenanting herald went before him now, crying according to his order, "Here comes James Graham, a traitor to his country!" Yet still the country people whose homes had been ravaged by the Irishes, who in many cases had lost all they possessed in the war, hesitated to stone and abuse the "viperous brood of Satan" as the ministers of the Kirk so earnestly desired.

On May 15th, at Kinnaird, he saw his father-in-law Southesk and his youngest children Robert and Jean. It was an awkward, halting meeting. Before his captors, he would admit no great display of emotion. He said goodbye to the family, pale and unshaven, his eyes glittering feverishly. Then he was led on to spend the night at the House of Grange, a few miles short of Dundee. It was now that the courageous chatelaine enabled him to make his one attempt at escape.

". . . So soon as their quarters were settled and that she had observed the way and manner of the placing of the guards and what officers commanded them, she not only ordered her butlers to let the soldiers want for no drink, but she herself, out of respect and kindness as she pretended, plied hard the officers and soldiers of the main guard (which was kept in her own hall) with the strongest ale and aquavite, that before midnight all of them (being for the most part highlanders of Lawers's regiment) became stark drunk. If her stewards and other servants had obeyed her directions in giving out what drink the outer guards should have called for, undoubtedly the business would have been effected, but unhappily when the Marquis had passed the first and second sentinels that were sleeping upon their muskets and likewise through the main guard that were lying in the hall like swine on a midden, he was challenged a little without the outmost guard by a wretched trooper of Strachan's troop that had been sent at his taking. This fellow was not one of the guard that night, but being quartered hard by, was come rammelling in for his bellyful of drink when he made this unlucky discovery, which being done, the Marquis was presently seized upon and with much rudeness (being in the Lady's clothes which he had put on as a disguise) turned back to his prison chamber. The Lady, her old husband, and all the servants of the house were made prisoners for that night the morrow after when they came to be challenged before those what had command of this party. . . ."4

Dundee, which had more cause than most cities of Scotland to hate Montrose, received him with kindness and sympathy the next day, May 16th. Then across the Firth of Tay he was led through Fife, so many of whose sons had died at Kilsyth and Tippermuir. Early on the afternoon of May 18th, he reached Leith. It was the day that Sir William Fleming arrived with orders from the King that he should disband his army. Perhaps Montrose still cherished vague prospects of a trial, of efforts to secure clemency by his friends and by the Princes of Europe. Probably he was too ill to care. The rulers of the Covenant had anyway already decided his fate. He was to be killed quickly, before any outside agencies could meddle with the course of justice, before any embarrassing pressure could be brought upon them to stay the Hand of the Lord. Montrose was to be hanged on a gibbet till he was dead with Wishart's *History* and his own Declaration tied around his neck, "and to hang three hours thereafter in the view of the people; and thereafter he should be beheaded and quartered, his head to be fixed at the prison house of Edinburgh, and his legs and arms to be fixed at the ports of the towns of Stirling, Glasgow, Perth, and Aberdeen; and if he repented that the bulk of his body should be buried . . . in Greyfriars, if not, to be buried in the Burgh-Moor".

At four o'clock on the afternoon of May 18th, the Magistrates met Montrose at the Water Gate of Edinburgh. They had prepared for his humiliation a cart with a high seat to which he was to be bound, so that when the mob stoned him he might not be able to raise his hands to protect himself. The hangman, in his black hood, mounted the cart to drive him through the city. Montrose paused before climbing up, and turned to the magistrates: "Without betraying the slightest emotion he inquired if their instructions were to compel him to do so. They answered in the affirmative and that such were the orders of Parliament. 'Oh,' he said immediately, 'if that is the way they mean to treat us, let us mount!'

"In all the way there appeared in him such majesty, courage, modesty and even somewhat more than natural, that these common women who had lost their husbands and children in his wars, and who were hired to stone him, were upon the sight of him so astonished and moved, that their intended curses turned to tears and prayers, so that the next day all the ministers preached against them for not stoning and reviling him. It is remarkable that, of the many thousand beholders, only the Lady Jean Gordon, Countess of Haddington, did publicly insult and laugh at him; which, being perceived by a gentleman in the street, he cried up to her that it became her better to sit upon the cart for her adulteries. The Lord Lorne and his new Lady were also sitting on a balcony joyful spectators; and the cart being stopped when it came before the lodging where the Chancellor, Argyll, and Warriston sat that they might have time to insult, he, suspecting the business, turned his face towards them, where upon they presently crept in at the windows; which being perceived by an Englishman, he cried up, that it was no wonder they started aside at his look, for they durst not look him in the face these seven years bygone."

It is still a deeply moving experience today to stand in the Canongate of Edinburgh, where Montrose drove by, and look up at the trusses and balcony of Moray House, where Argyll drank deep of his revenge upon James Graham. In Scotland it sometimes seems that the hand of the Covenant still conspires to deny the memory of Montrose. There is no plaque to tell the story of Moray House, just as the guide book to Blair Castle omits all mention of its greatest days as Montrose's head-quarters, just as Kincardine and Ardvreck are without their just memorials. Argyll did his work well.

Montrose was three hours on his long, hideous parade through the streets of Edinburgh that May afternoon. It was seven o'clock before he was delivered into the hands of the

terrible Major Weir, Captain of the Town guard, at the
Tollbooth. "Fellow, there is drink money for driving the cart,"
the Lord Marquis told the hangman, passing him a gold
piece with unshakable dignity. Perhaps he imagined that
now, at last, he would be left in peace in his dungeon. But it
was not to be so. Some of the members of Parliament and the
ministers came to torment and question him. He refused to
talk to them until he had rested: "The compliment they had
put upon him that day," he told them calmly, "had been
somewhat tedious."

On Sunday and again early on Monday morning, Montrose
was visited by deputations of ministers and members of
Parliament alleging their eagerness to bring him to repentance
for his horrible crimes, but more plausibly impatient to ogle
James Graham now that at last he had been "brought lower".
Contemptuously, the Lord Marquis informed them that if they
believed they had dismayed him by his journey in the cart they
were much mistaken, "for he had thought it the most honourable and joyful journey that he had ever made". His accusers
alleged, preposterously, that he was "given to women". They
charged him with using "Irish papist rebels and cut-throats to
kill his own people". He reminded them proudly that David in
the cave of Adullam had used a strange fighting force. Then
when they accused him of breaking the Covenant, he made his
great and famous reply: "The Covenant which I took I own it
and adhere to it. Bishops, I care not for them. I never intended
to advance their interests. But when the King had granted you
all your desires, and you were every one sitting under his vine
and his fig tree—that then you should have taken a party in
England by the hand, and entered into a League and Covenant
with them against the King, was the thing I judged my duty to
oppose to the yondmost."

The ministers urged him once more to repent of his sins. He
answered with quiet conviction: "I am very sorry that any
actions of mine have been offensive to the Church of Scotland,
and I would with all my heart be reconciled with the same.
But since I cannot obtain it on any other terms—unless I call
that my sin which I account to have been my duty—I cannot,
for all the reason and conscience in the world."

He had breakfast, bread dipped in ale, when the gloomy
procession had shuffled out. He was refused leave to shave

himself, or even to have a barber shave him, lest he seek to cheat the Covenant of its revenge: "I would not think but they would have allowed that to a dog." But he had been permitted to receive at least the new clothes that were sent in to him by his devoted niece, Lady Napier. "In a suit of black cloth and a scarlet coat to his knee trimmed with silver galouns and lined with crimson taffeta; on his hand a beaver hat and silver band", he was led forth to face the Parliament of Scotland.

A public letter from the King to Montrose, ordering him to disband his forces, was already before the Estates. It was a matter of urgency to dispose of James Graham before Charles once more set foot in his native land. A further letter, allegedly from the King, was now laid before Parliament in which he said "he was heartily sorry that James Graham had invaded the kingdom, and how he had discharged him from doing the same, and earnestly desired the Estates of Parliament to do him that justice as not to believe that he was accessory to the said invasion in the least degree".

Ronald Williams's argument that this letter was most unlikely to be the work of the King, that it was probably a forgery by Argyll or one of his colleagues, is convincing. Perhaps Charles may be spared the odium of at least this final act of betrayal. But the consequence of the letter's publication was the same as if it had indeed come under his seal. It swept away the last hints of misgiving among the members of the Estates about making a quick end of Montrose. Once the letter had been published, there was no time for Charles to disown it. It is also most unlikely that he would have chosen to do so even if he could, if he had believed that renunciation would have cost him his agreement with the Covenanters. Montrose had become expendable. Worse than that, it had become essential that he should die.

At ten o'clock that Monday morning, James Graham was brought before Parliament by the magistrates of Edinburgh.

"As I hear you are in some manner reconciled to the King," he said, "I regard this Assembly just, as if his royal Majesty were here in person. For this reason only do I appear before you bare-headed and plead my cause. . . .

"What my carriage was in this country, many of you may bear witness. Disorders in arms cannot be prevented; but they were no sooner known than punished. Never was any man's blood spilt but in battle; and even then, many thousand lives have I preserved. . . .

"And as for coming at this time, it was by his Majesty's just commands, in order to the accelerating the treaty betwixt him and you; his Majesty knowing, that, whenever he had ended with you, I was ready to retire upon his call. I may say, that never subject acted upon more honourable grounds, nor by so lawful a power, as I did in these services. . . .

"I did engage in the first Covenant, and was faithful to it. . . . For the League, I thank God I was never in it; and so could not break it. How far religion has been advanced by it, and what sad consequences followed on it, these poor distressed Kingdoms can witness. . . .

". . . Be not too rash; but let me by judged by the laws of God, the laws of nature and nations, and the laws of this land. . . ."

All this Montrose had said for posterity. His words were wasted on his accusers, who had brought him before them only to pronounce doom upon him.

"The Lord Chancellor replied, punctually proving him by his acts of hostility, to be a person most infamous, perjured, and treacherous, and of all that ever this land brought forth, the most cruel and inhuman butcher and murderer of his nation, a sworn enemy to the Covenant and peace of his country. . . .

"He made not reply; but was commanded to go down on his knees and receive his sentence, which he did: Archibald Johnston the Clerk Register, read it, and the Dempster gave the doom; and immediately arising from off his knees, without speaking one word, he was removed thence to the prison. He behaved himself all this time in the House with a great deal of courage and modesty, unmoved and undaunted, as it appeared, only he sighed two several times, and rolled his eyes amongst all the corners of the House. . . ."[5]

The ministers came to him once again in his cell in the Tollbooth later that day. He told them that he was indebted to Parliament for the dignity that they had heaped upon him "for I think it a greater honour to have my head standing on the ports of this town than to have my portrait in the King's bedchamber; I am beholden to you lest my loyalty be forgotten, ye have appointed four of the most eminent towns to bear witness of it to posterity".

He talked to Robert Baillie for a time in a corner of his cell—though that tireless chronicler left no word of what was said. Then he begged them all to leave him: "I pray you gentlemen, let me die in peace." He was left to the mercy of Major Weir.

"The barbarous villain treated the heroic Marquis of Montrose with all imaginable insolence and inhumanity when he lay in prison; keeping him in a room in which was no other light than that of a candle, and his lighted tobacco, which he continually smoked with him, though the Marquis had an aversion to the smell of it above anything in the world. Nay, he would even disturb him in his devotions, making his very calamities an argument that God as well as man had forsaken him; and calling him dog, atheist, traitor, apostate, excommunicated wretch, and many more such intolerable names."[6]

Thus through the last hours of his life Montrose was tortured by the minions of Argyll and of the Kirk.

Gazing around the cell in which he lay, he must have remembered Ogilvy, Crawford, Wishart and all his other friends who had lain there until his great victory released them. Now, there were only the cries and chatter and rude laughter of his fellow prisoners echoing through the dim passages. From time to time, doors slammed and guards changed. There were the distant sounds of the street cries of Edinburgh, of horses and carts passing by outside in the freedom.

Montrose must have been tormented by knowledge of the King's agreement with the Covenanters, the negation of everything that he had sought to achieve. But he had never been a skilful politician. All his life, his efforts to form alliances based on honesty and decency and optimistic moderation had foundered. He would always remember the clean air of the hills and the gay laughter of Alasdair's mad Irishes with more affection than the Courts and drawing rooms in which he had stifled. At least the march from Orkney had recaptured for a brief spell the magic of the old days in the hills with Ogilvy and Airlie and George Gordon. He had purged his soul of four years of misery in Europe, intriguing amongst and importuning men he cordially despised.

He was fundamentally a simple man, who chose to see men

M

and deeds in cloudless shades of good and evil, black and white.
Listening to the sounds of Edinburgh beyond the walls, he
remembered the days when he strode past the Tollbooth with
his bravoes behind him, one of the great lords of the Covenant.
That had been before he discovered his true path to fulfilment,
as the servant of Charles Stuart. Since then he might proudly
avow that like Butler's royalist, he had been unswervingly

> True as the dial to the sun,
> although it be not shone upon.

The days of his greatness had been incredibly short: he had
become the King's Lieutenant in August 1644, and had fought
Kilsyth the following July. Even today, he was only thirty-eight
years old. He had for so long been called an arrogant young
man stuffed with pride. His conceit was that of most men who
believe that they have a mission. He had been convinced that
a revelation had been vouchsafed to him of what was good for
the future of Scotland, and he spurned those who did not see
matters through the same glass. His redeeming grace was that
his conceit was for his cause, and not for himself.

Would Carbisdale and Philiphaugh overshadow the glory of
his great victories as a soldier? No, for much too much had
gone before them. He had tamed the unruly clans for long
enough to achieve his "Year of Miracles". Tippermuir was a
masterpiece of improvisation, Fyvie a classic defensive action.
The march on Inverlochy would always be remembered as one
of the most imaginative strokes in the annals of war. His
dispositions at Auldearn mark him among the great tacticians,
his skill in bringing Baillie to battle at Alford was a superb
piece of battle planning. At Kilsyth, he had finally faced all
that the lords of the Covenant could throw against him, and he
had defeated them. Montrose would rank as one of the greatest
captains of his age. Had he been granted the opportunity to
meet Cromwell on anything like equal terms, it is most unlikely
that he would have left the field defeated. For military imagination, for inspired leadership and tactical brilliance, he must
rank as Cromwell's peer.

Montrose had secured his place in history as a great general
and also, by no means the lesser achievement, as a great
gentleman. By the manner of his progress towards the gallows,

he had humbled the tyrants who ruled Scotland, as surely as ever he had crushed them upon the battlefield. He was ready for the last act.

With a diamond on the window of his cell,[7] he is said to have scratched his own valedictory:

> Let them Bestow on every airth a limb,
> Then open all my veins, that I may swim
> To thee, my Maker, in that crimson lake;
> Then place my par-boil'd head upon a stake,
> Scatter my ashes, strew them in the air;
> Lord! since thou knowest whence all these atoms are,
> I'm hopeful thou'lt recover once my dust,
> And confident thou'lt raise me with the just.

Early on the morning of May 21st, he heard the trumpets sounding, the harsh bellow of orders, the tramp of marching feet. A strong guard was mustering to prevent any possibility of last-minute rescue. "What, am I still a terror to them?" he asked with amused scorn. "Let them look to themselves, my ghost will haunt them."

Warriston, the Clerk Registrar, found his godly sensibilities affronted when he came to the prison and saw Montrose combing out his long locks in readiness for death. He launched into one of his torrents of religious rhetoric, checked only when Montrose interrupted him: "While my head is my own, I dress and arrange it. Tomorrow, when it is yours, you may treat it as you please."

At two o'clock in the afternoon, they came to tell him that it was time. "In his going down from the Tollbooth to the place of execution, he was richly clad in fine scarlet, laid over with rich silver lace, his hat in his hand, his golden hat band, his band and cuffs exceeding rich, his delicate white gloves on his hands, his stockings of incarnate silk, and his shoes with their ribbons on his feet. . . . All these were provided for him by his friends, and a pretty cassock put on upon him, upon the scaffold, wherein he was hanged. To be short, nothing was here deficient to honour his poor carcase, more beseeming a bridegroom than a criminal going to the gallows."[8]

The gibbet, thirty feet high, stood by the Mercat Cross; a

great crowd stood round, held back by soldiers. He had been forbidden the usual privilege of making a final speech, but a boy took notes of all that he said to those around him on the scaffold:

"I am sorry if this manner of my end be scandalous to any good Christian here. Does it not often happen to the righteous according to the way of the unrighteous? Doth not sometimes a just man perish in his righteousness, and a wicked man prosper in his wickedness and malice? . . . But I must not say but that all God's judgements are just, and this measure, for my private sins, I acknowledge to be just with God, and wholly submit myself to him. . . .

"I acknowledge nothing, but fear God and honour the King, according to the commandments of God and the just laws of Nature and nations. I have not sinned against man, but against God. . . .

"I am sorry they did excommunicate me; and in that which is according to God's laws, without wronging my conscience or allegiance, I desire to be relaxed. If they will not do it, I appeal to God, who is the righteous judge of the world, and will, I hope, be my judge and saviour.

"It is spoken of me that I should blame the King. God forbid! For the late King, he lived a saint and died a martyr. I pray God I may end as he did. If ever I would wish my soul in another man's stead it should be in his. For his Majesty now living, never any people, I believe, might be more happy in a king. His commandments to me were most just, and I obeyed them. . . .

"I shall pray for you all. I leave my soul to God, my service to my prince, my goodwill to my friends, my love and charity to you all. And thus briefly I have exonerated my conscience."

He gave some money to the hangman before they tied around his neck his Declaration and Wishart's *History* as his sentence had decreed. His last words were: "May Almighty God have mercy on this afflicted country." Then he mounted the ladder.

"It is absolutely believed that he hath overcome more now by his death in Scotland, than he could have done if he had lived," wrote an Englishman who stood wondering among the great crowd at the foot of the scaffold. "For I never saw more sweeter carriage in a man in all my life. I would write more largely if I had time, but he is just now a turning off from the ladder; but his countenance changes not. . . ."

"It being now late, I confess I am weary," wrote Archibald Campbell, Marquis of Argyll, to his niece's husband Lothian, that night. "For all last night my wife was crying, who, blessed be God, is safely brought to bed of a daughter, whose birthday is remarkable in the tragic end of James Graham at this cross.

". . . He got some resolution after he came here how to go out of this world, but nothing at all how to enter into another, not so much as once humbling himself to pray at all on the scaffold, nor saying anything on it that he had not repeated many times before when the ministers were with him. For what may concern the public, I leave it to the public papers. . . ."

"And in all their executions," wrote the Edinburgh diarist James Nicoll, "it is evident that the malignant persons died for the most part without repentance. . .

"In the end of this month of May a man was burnt in Edinburgh for lying with a cow. Both he and the cow burnt upon castle hill."

The work of the Lord ganged bonnily on.

# POSTSCRIPT

Two days after the death of Montrose, Elizabeth Lady Napier sent two men to search amidst the awful darkness of the Burgh Moor for the grave of Montrose. His excommunicate remains, shorn of the limbs sent to be stuck upon the gates of the principal cities of Scotland, had been buried among the rude pits dug for felons outside the city walls. Somehow they found what they sought and set about a ghastly piece of butchery, groping amidst earth and old bones to cut out the Lord Marquis's heart. He himself had wished Lady Napier to have it. Now, in deadly secrecy, it was embalmed and sealed in a small steel case. This, in turn, was set in a gold filigree box, and thence in a great silver urn which became one of the Napier family's most cherished possessions. Lady Napier had herself painted standing beside it. The urn was eventually lost, but her descendants honoured the filigree box and its contents among their heirlooms until after innumerable adventures around the world, it disappeared in France in 1792.

Young Lord Napier, who had fought beside Montrose, died in exile in Holland a few weeks before the Restoration in 1660.

James, second Marquis of Montrose, returned to Scotland during the turmoil of the 1650's and spent some time in prison. At the Restoration, he took his rightful place once more as head of one of the great families of Scotland. He lived until 1669.

Poor Frendraught, who gave Montrose his horse at Carbisdale, seems to have died in prison along with Kinnoul. The Orcadian prisoners were made slaves in the coal mines of Fife.

Sir John Hurry and Sir John Spottiswoode went to the Maiden on May 29th, 1650. On June 4th Hay of Dalgetty and Colonel Sibbald were executed, so Sir James Turner "lost both my friend and my money".

Most of the Irishes who marched north to Kintyre with Alasdair Macdonald before Philiphaugh had been slaughtered after surrendering on quarter to David Leslie in May 1647. Alasdair's father, old Coll Keitach, was hanged. He himself was killed six months later. The pretensions of the Antrim Macdonalds to Kintyre were thus brutally brought to nothing.

Colonel Strachan died—of religious mania, it is said—within a year of Carbisdale. David Leslie lived to become Lord Newark and die at a ripe old age in 1682.

Lanark, Hamilton's brother, died of his wounds after Worcester.

George Wishart became Bishop of Edinburgh.

Warriston, chief fanatic of the Covenant, was extradited from exile in France in 1663. His family was already ruined and he was found to be quite mad, but he went to the scaffold nonetheless.

Lord Airlie, who must have been tough as old boots, lived until 1666, when his son Ogilvy succeeded him, living until 1704.

Argyll, after sailing an extraordinary course between Cromwell and Charles II throughout the upheavals of the 1650's, had no friends left to save him by the coming of the Restoration. He had quarrelled even with the Kirk. In 1651, incredibly, he had set the crown on the head of Charles II at Scone. But there were far too many scores against him for this or his almost pathetic protestations of loyalty to the new King to save him. In July 1660, judgement fell upon the Campbell under the most dramatic circumstances. He was arrested by Garter King of Arms before the Court in London, and led away to the Tower. In December he was taken to Edinburgh for his trial. The young Marquis of Montrose declined to take any part in the grim proceedings. He said that "he had too much resentment to judge in that matter".

It was yet another extraordinary twist of fate that the new royalist Chancellor of Scotland was the Earl of Middleton—yes, that same Middleton who had fought the Bridge of Dee and ridden down on Montrose at Philiphaugh. There was never any doubt about Argyll's end. Middleton had orders to rid the King of his most astonishing, most over-mighty Scottish subject. On May 27th, 1661, Argyll was taken out to die at the Maiden escorted by a detachment of mounted Lifeguards, soldiers with colours lining the streets. He was allowed to meet his Maker with much more dignity than he had permitted to Montrose, eleven years earlier almost to the day. He spent the morning with his friends, had lunch, and then walked to the scaffold with his chaplain beside him. He surprised some and disappointed others by his complete self-possession. He was determined to give the lie to all the years of taunts of his cowardice, to lay the memory of his flights from Inverary and from Inverlochy and from Kilsyth. After his death his head was stuck up on the Tollbooth spike where that of Montrose had sat for so many years. It is Christian to feel forgiveness. But it is also deeply satisfying to know that Archibald Campbell did not die in his warm bed at Inverary.

On May 11th, 1661, while Argyll still lay in his dungeon, all Edinburgh lined the streets as the remains of the Lord Marquis of Montrose, solemnly gathered from the city gates of Scotland and from the grave on Burgh-Moor, were borne in procession up the Canongate from Holyrood Chapel for their State Funeral. By order of the King, the Lord High Commissioner, the peerage and Parliament of Scotland mourned behind the coffin. Twenty-six companies of foot marched before them, and soldiers lined the streets with swords drawn as the cortège passed. The bells of Edinburgh pealed slowly in salute, the guns of the Castle booming accompaniment.

Old enemies were there, and old friends: Marischal and Callendar; Thomas Saintserf and the Lord Marquis's half-brother, now Sir Harry Graham; Graham of Morphie, Black Pate and the young Frendraught; the new Lord Napier and, of course, the second Marquis. Many of the bearer party were the noble sons of the men who had known Montrose: Mar, Atholl, Seaforth, Hartfell, Sir John Colquhoun. A warhorse was led behind the coffin, saddled, with pistols holstered. The standard of the Grahams, the Lord Marquis's coronet and parliament robes, his spurs and corselet and purse and gauntlets were carried in procession past the huge, solemn crowds as the drums beat the funeral tattoo. The coffin was at last carried through the great doors of St Giles. Five volleys rang out from the muskets of the escort. The body of the Lord Marquis was laid in a grave beside his grandfather, the old Viceroy of Scotland.

The King's Champion was at last honoured, and at peace.

NOTES
SELECT BIBLIOGRAPHY
INDEX

# NOTES

## Chapter 1

1. See Read, *Mr Secretary Cecil*.
2. Paul Johnson, *Elizabeth*.
3. See Montrose household accounts for much domestic detail.
4. Ronald Cant, *The University of St Andrews*, p. 63.
5. The Scottish pound was only about a twelfth or thirteenth of the pound sterling, and thus the sums referred to throughout the text are much less enormous than they at first appear. Money was also sometimes reckoned in dollars and merks.
6. Saintserf, *True Funerals of the Great Lord Marquis of Montrose in the year 1661*.
7. See article on Bruneau De Tartifume in the *Revue de l'Anjou*, 1893, XXVI, pp. 5–22. Angers Municipal Library has much relevant material on the School of Arms.
8. Saintserf, *True Funerals, op. cit.*

## Chapter 2

1. See T. C. Smout's *History of the Scottish People* and C. V. Wedgwood's *The King's Peace* for much more detailed background.
2. Smout, *op. cit.*, p. 199.
3. Forbes-Leith, *Memoirs of Scottish Catholics During the Seventeenth Century*.
4. Robert Baillie, *Letters and Journals*.
5. Clarendon, *Great Rebellion*.
6. Wedgwood, *op. cit.*, p. 214.
7. *Letters and Journals, op. cit.*
8. *Ibid.*
9. Sir James Turner, *Memoirs of His Own Life and Times*.
10. Saintserf was sometimes rendered Sydserf. I have standardized as Saintserf throughout.

## Chapter 3

1. Spalding, *Memorials of the Troubles in Scotland and England*, p. 109.
2. *Ibid.*, p. 110.
3. Patrick Gordon of Ruthven, *A Short Abridgement of Britaynes Distemper*, p. 229.
4. Baillie, *Letters and Journals, op. cit.*, I, p. 213.
5. Spalding, *op. cit.*
6. *Ibid.*
7. Gordon of Rothiemay, *History of Scots Affairs*.
8. Clarendon, *op. cit.*
9. Gordon of Rothiemay, *History of Scots Affairs, op. cit.*
10. *Ibid.*
11. *Ibid.*
12. Gordon of Ruthven, *Britaynes Distemper, op. cit.*

*Chapter 4*

1. Clarendon, *op. cit.*
2. Baillie, *Letters and Journals, op. cit.*
3. See Willcock, *The Great Marquess.*
4. Maidment, *Scottish Pasquils*, II, p. 8.
5. Buchan, *Montrose*, p. 92.
6. Gordon of Ruthven, *Britaynes Distemper, op. cit.*, pp. 56–57.
7. Baillie, *Letters and Journals, op. cit.*
8. Quoted in Gardiner, *History of the Great Civil War*, IX, p. 27.
9. Baillie, *Letters and Journals, op. cit.*
10. *Ibid.*

*Chapter 5*

1. Baillie, *Letters and Journals, op. cit.*
2. Wishart, *Memoirs of James, Marquis of Montrose* (Murdoch and Simpson translation), p. 25.
3. *Ibid.*, p. 27.
4. *Ibid.*, p. 31.
5. Spalding, *op. cit.*
6. Clarendon, *op. cit.*
7. For a vivid description of the Siege of Gloucester and every other action in the Civil War, see C. V. Wedgwood's peerless *The King's War.*
8. For an excellent modern biography of the splendid Rupert, see George Malcolm Thomson, *Warrior Prince.*
9. Turner, *Memoirs, op. cit.*
10. The full text is quoted in Hill, *The Macdonnells of Antrim*, p. 267.
11. Turner, *Memoirs, op. cit.*
12. Wishart, *op. cit.*, p. 47.
13. *Ibid.*, p. 50.
14. Gordon of Ruthven, *Britaynes Distemper, op. cit.*, pp. 71–72.

*Chapter 6*

1. See Hill, *op. cit.*, footnote on p. 114, for an account of this curious alleged weapon and its later history. Also, *Dublin University Magazine*, XXXI, 221.
2. Father Macbreck, quoted in Forbes-Leith, *Memoirs of Scottish Catholics, op. cit.*, p. 287.
3. Gordon of Ruthven, *Britaynes Distemper, op. cit.*
4. Macbreck, *Memoirs of Scottish Catholics, op. cit.*, p. 230.
5. Gordon of Ruthven, *Britaynes Distemper, op. cit.*
6. *Ibid.*
7. Wishart, *op. cit.*, p. 57.
8. Rev. James Scott, *Perth Presbytery Records*, quoted in Napier.
9. Baillie, *Letters and Journals, op. cit.*, II, p. 226.
10. Macbreck, *Memoirs of Scottish Catholics, op. cit.*

*Chapter 7*

1. Wishart, *op. cit.*, p. 64.
2. Sir James Turner, *Pallas Armata.*

3. Gordon of Ruthven, *Britaynes Distemper, op. cit.*
4. *Ibid.*
5. Wishart, *op. cit.*, p. 69.
6. See Hubert Cole, *The Black Prince*, for a modern view.
7. Spalding, *op. cit.*
8. *Ibid.*
9. *Ibid.*
10. Macbreck, *Memoirs of Scottish Catholics, op. cit.*, p. 301.

*Chapter 8*
1. Macbreck, *Memoirs of Scottish Catholics, op. cit.*, p. 310.
2. *Ibid.*, p. 305.
3. Gordon of Ruthven, *Britaynes Distemper, op. cit.*
4. It would be absurd to pretend that it is possible to trace the last stages of Montrose's route with any certainty. I am still unsure which side of Ben Lui he marched. I chose the pass to the south-east when I retraced his route in December 1975. Like the reconstruction of Montrose's battles, a great deal must be intelligent guess-work. I have studied the maps drawn up by each of Montrose's biographers over the last century and more, together with those of Gardiner. It is impossible to arrive at a "correct" view. It is only possible to make a fresh assessment, correcting the most obvious errors.
5. Baillie, *Letters and Journals, op. cit.*
6. Wishart, *op. cit.*, p. 81.
7. Baillie, *Letters and Journals, op. cit.*
8. Turner, *Pallas Armata, op. cit.*

*Chapter 9*
1. Baillie, *Letters and Journals, op. cit.*, II, p. 263.
2. Gordon of Ruthven, *Britaynes Distemper, op. cit.*
3. *Ibid.*
4. Spalding, *op. cit.*
5. Gordon of Ruthven, *Britaynes Distemper, op. cit.*
6. Turner, *Pallas Armata, op. cit.*
7. Wishart, *op. cit.*, p. 95.
8. It is impossible to be sure of Montrose's route through the Trossachs, although the fact that he wrote to the King from Doune makes a nonsense of the map drawn by one recent biographer, which takes him nowhere near.
9. I have drawn heavily on the excellent map created by Brigadier Sym on the site of Auldearn for the National Trust. The Covenanters may in fact have advanced on a narrower front than that shown in my plan, but the essential facts of Montrose's dispositions are not seriously in dispute.

*Chapter 10*
1. It is interesting to notice how comprehensive was the system of issuing written orders even in such a wild army as that of Montrose. The Lord

Marquis even phrased his instructions in a style that would be readily recognized by any twentieth-century field officer.

2. Wishart, *op. cit.*, p. 106.
3. Previous biographers have placed Montrose's army forward of the crest of the hill, but in that event they would have been clearly visible to Baillie as he descended the Suie Road to the Don. Surely the Lord Marquis held them concealed beyond the crest until the Covenanters were committed, and then ordered the advance.
4. Wishart, *op. cit.*, p. 111.
5. Gordon of Ruthven, *Britaynes Distemper, op. cit.*

*Chapter 11*
1. Turner, *Pallas Armata, op. cit.*
2. I am indebted for some suggestions to Mr Michael Leslie-Melville, who lives above the site of Philiphaugh and has been studying the battle for years. He was kind enough to send me his comments at length, including his speculation that a Covenanting flanking force worked around the west side of the royalist camp from Linglie Hill while Leslie and Middleton drove down the river.
3. Scott, *Lay of the Last Minstrel.*

*Chapter 12*
1. *The Diplomatic Correspondence of Jean De Montreuil and the brothers de Bellievre 1645–48,* ed. Fotheringham, SHS, pp. 190, *et seq.*
2. Wishart, *op. cit.*

*Chapter 13*
1. Wishart, *op. cit.*, p. 192.
2. *Ibid.*, p. 228.
3. See Margaret Irwin's charming *The Bride* for a good romantic wallow on this theme. Regretfully, I must admit to scepticism about the real likelihood of a relationship.
4. Turner, *Memoirs, op. cit.*

*Chapter 14*
1. Williams, *Montrose*, p. 354.
2. Gordon of Sallagh, *Continuation of a History of the Earldom of Sutherland by Sir Robert Gordon of Gordonstoun.*
3. Dunrobin MS., quoted in Williams, *op. cit.*
4. Lord Somerville, *Memorie of the Somervilles.*
5. Sir James Balfour, *Balfour Annals.*
6. *Ravillac Redivivus*, quoted in Napier, p. 794.
7. Sadly the true provenance of this poem must remain in doubt. The evidence suggests that Montrose did not even have a window in his cell on which to scratch with a diamond. There are similar doubts about the equally charming parallel story of Raleigh and Elizabeth.
8. James Nicoll. See his *Diary* published by the Bannatyne Club.

# SELECT BIBLIOGRAPHY

Almost all the significant material on Montrose's life and times is in the National Library of Scotland, the British Museum, or the London Library, to all of which I am indebted for their courtesy and guidance. I have touched only lightly on the manuscript material in the Scottish Record Office, which has already been exhaustively studied and transcribed. The strain of reading seventeenth-century handwriting is considerable for a layman.

While they cannot properly be listed among the reference books, no bibliography of Montrose could omit Sir Walter Scott's *Legend of Montrose* and the two charming novels of Margaret Irwin, *The Proud Servant* and *The Bride*, which cause so many people to number the Lord Marquis among their heroes without troubling with his biographies.

Below I have listed the principal works which I have consulted for background and source material. I have left out several alleged biographies of Montrose which seem without merit; also innumerable contemporary pamphlets and chronicles of which I have read extracts but which it would be imprudent for me to suggest that I have studied at first hand.

BAILLIE, ROBERT, *Letters and Journals* (Bannatyne Club)

BUCHAN, JOHN, *Montrose* (Nelson: 1928)

BURNET, GILBERT, *History of My Own Times*

—— *Memoirs of the Dukes of Hamilton*

CANT, R. G., *The University of St Andrews* (Scottish Academic Press: 1970)

CLARENDON, EDWARD HYDE, EARL OF, *The History of the Rebellion and Civil Wars* (Oxford: 1826 edition)

FORBES-LEITH, W., *Memoirs of Scottish Catholics During the Seventeenth and Eighteenth Centuries*, vol. 1 (Longmans, Green: 1909)

GARDINER, S. R., *History of the Great Civil War* (Longmans, Green: 1889 edition)

GORDON, JAMES, OF ROTHIEMAY, *A History of Scots Affairs* (Spalding Club)

GORDON, PATRICK, OF RUTHVEN, *A Short Abridgement of Britaynes Distemper* (Spalding Club)

GRANT, I. F., *Highland Folk Ways* (Routledge & Kegan Paul: 1961)

GUTHRIE, HENRY, *Memoirs*

HILL, G., *The Macdonnells of Antrim* (Belfast: 1873)

JOHNSTON, ARCHIBALD, OF WARRISTON, *Diary 1634–39, 1650–54* (Scottish Historical Society: 1911 and 1919)

LANG, ANDREW, *History of Scotland* (Blackwood: 1906)

MACKENZIE, *Short History of the Scottish Highlands* (Gardner: 1908)

MACKINTOSH, JOHN, *History of Civilization in Scotland* (London: 1895)

MAHON, LORD, "Essay on Montrose", *Quarterly Review*, December, 1846

MATHEW, DAVID, *Scotland Under Charles I* (Eyre and Spottiswoode: 1955)

MALLET, *History of Oxford University*

MENZIES, G. (Ed.), *The Scottish Nation* (BBC: 1972)

NAPIER, MARK, *Memorials of Montrose* (Maitland Club: 1848)

—— *Memoirs of Montrose* (Stevenson: 1856)

SAINTSERF, THOMAS, *A Relation of the True Funerals of the Marquis of Montrose* (1661)

SCOT, SIR JOHN, OF SCOTSTARVET, *The Staggering State of Scotch Statesmen* (1754)

SMOUT, T. C., *A History of the Scottish People* (Collins: 1969)

SPALDING, JOHN, *Memorials of the Troubles in Scotland and England* (Spalding Club)

STEVENSON, DAVID, *The Scottish Revolution 1637–44* (David & Charles: 1973)

TURNER, SIR JAMES, *Memoirs of His Own Life and Times* (1829)

—— *Pallas Armata* (London: 1681)

WEDGWOOD, C. V., *Montrose* (Collins: 1952)

—— *The King's Peace* (Collins: 1955)

—— *The King's War* (Collins: 1958)

—— *The Thirty Years War* (Jonathan Cape: 1938)

WILLCOCK, J., *The Great Marquess* (Oliphant, Anderson & Ferrier: 1903)

WILLIAMS, RONALD, *Montrose* (Barrie & Jenkins: 1975)

WISHART, GEORGE, *Memoirs of James, Marquis of Montrose*, edited by Alexander Murdoch and H. F. Morland Simpson (1893)

YOUNG, BRIGADIER PETER, *The English Civil War: A Military History* (Eyre Methuen: 1974)

For anyone who proposes to visit the battlefields of Auldearn, Alford, or Kilsyth, William Seymour's *Battles in Britain 1642–1746* (Sidgwick & Jackson: 1976) includes admirable plans overlaid on aerial photographs of the countryside as it is today, together with useful background information about contemporary weapons and tactics.

# INDEX

## Compiled by H. E Crowe